NO BETTER HOME?

Jews, Canada, and the Sense of Belonging

Edited by David S. Koffman

This book begins with an audacious question: Has there ever been a better home for Jews than Canada? By certain measures, Canada might be the most socially welcoming, economically secure, and religiously tolerant country for Jews in the diaspora, past or present. *No Better Home?* takes this question seriously, while also exploring the many contested meanings of the idea of "home."

Contributors to the volume include leading scholars of Canadian Jewish life as well as eminent Jewish scholars writing about Canada for the first time. The essays compare Canadian Jewish life with the quality of life experienced by Jews in other countries, examine Jewish and non-Jewish interactions in Canada, analyse specific historical moments and literary texts, reflect deeply personal histories, and widen the conversation about the quality and timbre of the Canadian Jewish experience. *No Better Home?* foregrounds Canadian Jewish life and ponders all that the Canadian experience has to teach about Jewish modernity.

DAVID S. KOFFMAN is the J. Richard Shiff Chair for the Study of Canadian Jewry and an associate professor in the Department of History at York University.

No Better Home?

Jews, Canada, and the Sense of Belonging

EDITED BY
DAVID S. KOFFMAN

UNIVERSITY OF TORONTO PRESS
Toronto Buffalo London

© University of Toronto Press 2021
Toronto Buffalo London
utorontopress.com
Printed in the U.S.A.

ISBN 978-1-4875-0489-2 (cloth)   ISBN 978-1-4875-3111-9 (EPUB)
ISBN 978-1-4875-2357-2 (paper)   ISBN 978-1-4875-3110-2 (PDF)

Library and Archives Canada Cataloguing in Publication

Title: No better home? : Jews, Canada, and the sense of belonging /
    edited by David S. Koffman.
Names: Koffman, David S., editor.
Description: Includes bibliographical references.
Identifiers: Canadiana (print) 20200308459 | Canadiana (ebook) 20200308505 |
    ISBN 9781487504892 (hardcover) | ISBN 9781487523572 (softcover) |
    ISBN 9781487531119 (EPUB) | ISBN 9781487531102 (PDF)
Subjects: LCSH: Jews – Canada – Social conditions. | LCSH: Jews – Canada –
    Social life and customs. | LCSH: Jews – Canada – Identity. | LCSH: Jews –
    Canada – Intellectual life. | LCSH: Canada – Ethnic relations.
Classification: LCC FC106.J5 N6 2020 | DDC 971/.004924 – dc23

University of Toronto Press acknowledges the financial assistance to its
publishing program of the Canada Council for the Arts and the Ontario Arts
Council, an Ontario government agency.

This book has been published with the help of a grant from the Federation
for the Humanities and Social Sciences, through the Awards to Scholarly
Publications Program, using funds provided by the Social Sciences and
Humanities Research Council of Canada.

**Canada Council
for the Arts**

**Conseil des Arts
du Canada**

ONTARIO ARTS COUNCIL
CONSEIL DES ARTS DE L'ONTARIO
an Ontario government agency
un organisme du gouvernement de l'Ontario

Funded by the   Financé par le
Government   gouvernement
of Canada   du Canada

Canadä

Contents

NO BETTER HOME?

What Does It Mean to Ask the Question, "Has There Ever Been a Better Home for the Jews Than Canada?"

DAVID S. KOFFMAN

At this time of considerable worldwide anxiety about Jews' security – nationalism, populism, nativism, and racial tensions in the United States and parts of Europe, and ongoing if not deepening polarizations and anxiety about Israel across the Jewish diaspora – this book aims to contemplate Jewish life in Canada from a range of angles. It aims to widen the conversation about the quality and timbre of Canadian Jewry by bringing together eminent Jewish Studies scholars who do not usually think much about Canada, at least in print, with some of the best of those who have been scrutinizing it professionally for decades. The organizing question of this book – *Has there ever been a better home for the Jews than Canada?* – is an audacious one for scholars to pose, one whose answer risks degrading itself to apologetics or celebration, neither of which should be in the wheelhouse of scholarly writing.

But it is a question we ought to take seriously. First, the question is seldom asked. This is curious, because Canada may now very well be the safest, most socially welcoming, economically secure, and possibly most religiously tolerant home for the Jews than any other diaspora country, past or present. Jews in Canada today enjoy (1) high rates of voluntary religious participation at all denominational in-points; (2) relatively low rates of non-violent forms of antisemitism; (3) high degrees of Jewish literacy; (4) the capacity to exercise political power unfettered by antisemitism; (5) institutional completeness for Jewish communal needs; (6) thoroughgoing social acceptance; (7) significant cultural production; (8) public recognition; (9) comparatively low intermarriage rates; and (10) economic opportunities unrestricted by their Jewishness. These are powerful social markers of comfort and belonging for Canadian Jews. These yardsticks should be examined and appreciated. Canada is also home to the world's fourth-largest Jewish population, behind Israel, the United

States, and France, and may very well overtake France for third place within decades. Yet on the Jewish world stage, whatever attention Canada gets seems disproportionately quiet. Perhaps, to paraphrase Tolstoy, Jewries with tense histories are all different, while Jewries comfortably at home in their nations are all the same – and thus not considered worthy of attention. This bias, however, is patently myopic.

Though Jewish communities have continually lived in what we now call Canada since the mid-eighteenth century – long before Confederation in 1867 – Canadian Jews have been comparatively uninterested in the study of their own community, and have been relatively late to ponder their own national experience. German, British, and American Jewries began to study themselves in nineteenth century. The Verein für Kultur und Wissenschaft der Juden (Society for Jewish Culture and Science) was founded around 1819, and the American Jewish Historical Society and the Jewish Historical Society of England were established in 1892–93. Eastern European Jewish scholars founded YIVO to study their own communities in the interwar period, and Australian Jews began a society and began publishing the *Australian Jewish Historical Society, Journal and Proceedings* in 1938. In Canada, the Canadian Jewish Historical Society was not established until 1976. Canadian Jews began establishing community archives that same decade. The first robust national survey of Canadian Jewish life wasn't conducted by the community itself until 2018.[1] Given the size of its Jewish population, it is remarkable that Canada's Jews have not built a Canadian Jewish museum to tell the story of Jewish belonging in Canada.

"Has there ever been a better home for Jews than Canada?" is a question we ought to take seriously so that we can begin to unpack the wonderfully complex and ambiguous idea of home that is central to the essays that follow. What criteria ought to be used for evaluating the quality of home on this scale? Canada has provided solid legal and political security for the Jews, but perhaps a home with a bit of insecurity coursing through it, like the Jewries of the Golden Age of Spain, Weimar Germany, or mid-twentieth-century America, produces finer cultural and intellectual achievements. Does the good life spring from imperfect homes – the homes we reject and hope to improve when we establish new ones? In Jewish history, the experiences of leaving homes, of remembering left homes, of pining for a home away from home, or finding otherworldly homes or homes in text, have been woven deep into the fabric of Jewish culture.

Our question also happens to be a sesquicentennial one, since many of the essays in this volume grew out of a symposium held at York

University in the fall of 2017, during Canada's 150th birthday celebrations and cerebrations. This dimension to the question is not merely incidental though. It asks us to ponder the role of *appreciation* in critical assessment. In Jewish history, praise for the nation-state has most often been written in the apologetic mode, and there is no shortage of Jewish writing devoted to praising the national bodies of which they formed a part. Canadian Jews, French Jews, Algerian Jews, German Jews, and virtually every Jewish population has praised, celebrated, and made public spectacles about their loyalty to the nation that "hosts" them. Jewish communities across the globe have included prayers for their governments, militaries, and leaders in their *siddurim*, raised flags in their synagogues and organizations, sent their children to do battle in their armies, and facilitated meetings with elected officials to maintain and improve state–minority relations. This is perfectly natural. For historians however, these performances and writings are tinged with apologetics. How exactly should historians ask analytic questions of this nature without being patriotic or defensive? Where does sober appreciation end and political patriotism begin?

Making comparisons of the "better" homes for Jews is an exercise that might lead to another sort of problem: with whom should we compare? Our question therefore invites us to explore inadequately drawn comparisons too. Though comparing societies is tricky business, at least for historians, comparisons are invaluable. Canadian Jewry is often compared with that in the United States but can also fruitfully be compared with Jewish communities in many other countries – those emerged as colonies of European empires – say, the Jewries of Mexico, South Africa, Argentina, or Australia – and those in which Jews made homes for many centuries, such as Poland, Scotland, Uzbekistan, and Morocco. It is also helpful to compare the Jewish experience in Canada with that of other religious, ethnocultural, and immigrant communities. This nagging, decidedly non-academic word, "better," can also be the source for many fascinating puzzles. Comparing Jewish life in Canada with that of any of the other 107 diaspora countries would yield insightful parallels and divergences that scholars of Canadian Jewish life have not yet fully appreciated. Of course, comparisons between Canadian Jewish life and Jewish life in the United States has been a sort of structuring principle for all understandings of life in Canada, given the overwhelming size of our community neighbours and their influence. But comparing any diaspora Jewish experience with Israel poses a basic apples-and-oranges challenge. How might one actually compare the situation in which Jews have formed a small minority with the one in which Jews are the vast majority, and where, indeed, the state itself is based, at least in part, on its Jewish values, history, and destiny? Comparing Jewish life in Israel with that in Canada focuses our attention on the important question of Jewish power and its limits, in addition to the dramatically different demographic reality of Israel's Jewish majority. Some have argued about the virtues of diaspora living, about why it is good for the Jews to be relatively powerless, but they have argued this against an overwhelmingly strong conviction among world Jewry that it is better to have power and sometimes miscalibrate it than to suffer the insecurities of powerlessness. While we may be comparing apples and oranges, it would certainly be worth trying to compare Jewish life in Canada and Israel in a systematic manner, just as it would be worth drawing out the precise nature of the similarities and differences between Canada and the 106 other nations where Jews currently live.

Another way of approaching the question "Has there ever been a better home for the Jews than Canada?" puts the onus of examination on the vertical plane of Jewish history, rather than the horizontal landscape of global comparisons. It seems that by situating Jewish life in Canada in the *long durée* of historical homes for Jews, a similarly rosy picture would likely emerge. Modern, democratic nation-states, shaped over the course of the eighteenth and nineteenth centuries, were likely better for Jewish life than the kinds of pre-modern societies that came before. This is, of course, debatable, and we should not fall prey to a dolorous view of medieval and early modern Jewish life, as the great historian of the Jews, Salo Wittmayer Baron, cautioned. It goes without elaborating that twentieth-century non-democratic, totalitarian regimes were the worst homes Jews have had. But Jews certainly did suffer greater discrimination, were subject to more precarious fates in the hands of capricious leaders, weak tolerance systems, and populist revolts against whatever it was that Jews might have symbolized to them. Without the weight and security of legal rights for Jews in the pre-emancipation era, a certain insecurity governed Jews' ability to consider their host society as "home." Jews mostly defined at-homeness before emancipation with respect to other Jews than with their non-Jewish neighbours – in Torah as the portable homeland, a home distanced from the surrounding people and space. Perhaps Jewish life was "better" before the emancipation bargain, if "better" can measured by the sorts of tests that Jewish social scientists now, ironically, use – social cohesion, intermarriage rates, and religious and communal participation – to assess good home life. One person's rich Jewish life is another's ghetto. Surely living in a family home that can be locked from the inside is better than one that can be locked from the outside.

A distinct approach to answering our question shifts the focus onto Canada itself to assess its track record and current capacity to integrate and enfranchise ethnic and religious minorities in general, using Jews as a convenient case study, since Jews ambiguously straddle both the religious and the ethnic, though a problematic one, given that the vast majority of Jews in Canada are considered white. Does Canada offer the right mix of inclusion for religious and ethnic minorities without assimilative coercion? Might Canada do this better than any other state in the world today? If we consider the general preoccupations internal to Jewish civic and religious community leaders, Canadians chalk up many favourable social science measures of "success." Compared with US Jewry, or the Jews of France or England – as chapter 1 of this volume shows – Canadian Jews enjoy both low rates of intermarriage and high levels of Jewish institutional availability. For example, a wide range of their needs are met by Jewish associational life, from midwifery to end-of-life and post-mortem care; intellectual, cultural, and spiritual institutions; clubs, camps, and retirement centres; grocery stores and restaurants; and political and charitable opportunities. Furthermore, Canadian Jews have very high literacy rates, including early childhood education, day schools, after-school or adult education programs (a subject considered more fully in chapter 5), as well as an extremely learned body of Torah scholars. There are likely more yeshiva students in Canada, proportionally to the national Jewish population, than anywhere in the diaspora. Canadian Jews have relatively high synagogue memberships and denominational participation rates, and Canadian cities are the envy of UJA / Jewish Federation campaigns the continent over.

Jews are thoroughly enfranchised wherever power is wielded in this country, on Bay Street, on Parliament Hill, and in the nation's media centres. The Jewish vote has been taken seriously and courted by successive administrations at the federal and provincial levels. Although the topic has not yet been systematically studied, Jews seem to have had remarkably few barriers to municipal politics in small towns and big cities (chapter 9, on Toronto's first Jewish mayor, begins this important work). Violence against Jews is virtually unknown. Relative to other religious or ethnic minorities, Jews enjoy the advantages that come with relative affluence, though the notion that antisemitism has somehow disappeared from the Canadian landscape is folly. According to Statistics Canada, police report that hate crimes have increased since the sesquicentennial. While more of these crimes targeted Arab, Black, Muslim, and West Asian communities, reported hate crimes targeting Jews has grown by an alarming 63 per cent.[2]

The kinds of multicultural states that emerged after the Second World War, in which Jewishness is mostly voluntary, are likely better for Jews than were the classically liberal (or, all the more so, illiberal) centralized nation-states of Europe. The pressures of nationalism turned the questions about Jews' place in society into the "Jewish Question." In Canada, residency rights for Jews – the leading edge for the larger package of civil rights – were granted long before Canada gained its sovereignty, and legal and political emancipation for Jews was taken for granted at the time of Confederation, having already been extended by the British Crown for its colonies. Perhaps the toughest barrier for Jews was the Christian oath requirement for public office, but even that was rescinded fairly painlessly when the Jewish population was still minuscule. Just as Jews in Russia, Italy, Greece, or Hungary wanted to make homes among their non-Jewish neighbours, trading off degrees of group solidarity for strategic alignments with many sorts of non-Jews, Canadian Jews used some version of the Polish Bund's pragmatic notion of *Dokheit*, or "hereness," to make Canada home. So, if nineteenth- and twentieth-century nation-states struggled to deal with Jewish non-conformity, even as these societies transferred clerical power for secular law, twenty-first-century multicultural countries have no such problems. Post-national countries (as Prime Minister Justin Trudeau has referred to Canada) question Jews' place in them even less. In other words, Jews have worked very hard at making dozens of countries and regions home. The work in Canada was comparatively easy.

There are certainly flaws inherent in our question that should give us pause. What criteria ought to be used to determine a "better home," if one is concerned with rigour or accuracy? If social integration, equality, and religious freedom are the right measures of a good home, Canada seems to offer a pretty good one. If communities should be measured along Maslow's famous hierarchy of needs, making matters of physical safety, economic and political security the fundamental necessities upon which all else is built, then Canada certainly ranks high as well. But how exactly ought one rank a community's well-being on the higher Maslowian levels of "esteem" and "self-actualization"? Perhaps Canada's literary, cultural, and religious innovations and achievements are not as impressive as those of Germany, Poland, or America. Then again, perhaps only some measures of self-actualization emerge from good homes – things like religious innovation – while artistic ones emerge out of chaos, anxiety, and conflict – not the kinds of things we think of as elements of good homes. How should one measure this sort of cultural production anyway? Are elite or popular thresholds for at-homeness equally important to consider? In the realms of artistic production and religious innovation, does quantity trump quality?

The question invites us to consider still more assumptions in the way it sets up a seemingly natural comparison between Canada and other states, as if national borders centrally define the Jewish dimension of Jewish Canadians' lives. These boundaries may very well obfuscate the reality of Jewish connections and mobility, and distort how we construe our subject. The lived reality for most Jews in the nineteenth, twentieth, and twenty-first centuries, particularly if we look at the multi-generational experience, involves tremendous movement across national boundaries, and steady interaction between Jewish populations across borders. As Barry Stiefel and Hernan Tesler-Mabé rightly point out in the introduction to Neither in Dark Speeches nor in Similitudes, a book that highlights the porousness between Canadian and US Jewry, transnational perspectives simply elucidate Jewish history and heritage in Canada better than do nationalist ones.[3]

Finally, this book's central question may elicit the response, "Who's asking?" To make the question less of an armchair exercise, one would need to ask a wide variety of Jews from the past and present who have moved from another home to Canada (or vice versa) to compare homes and interpret "better." Such a study would likely yield a more robust and complex understanding of how Jews themselves have understood the advantages and challenges of Jewish life in Canada. But there is little doubt that countless Jews have made comparisons between their lives in Canada with their experiences in other countries. The fact that these sorts of evaluations have not become the focus of scholarly research or assessments does not mean that these sorts of comparisons are not already part of the historical record. The decision to immigrate from, say, Morocco, Ukraine, or Israel to Canada, involved a calculus about the "better home," just as the experience of newly arrived immigrants to Canada involved constant comparisons to the places they left behind.

This volume thus calls for a closer and more variegated exploration of unique segments of the Canadian Jewish population. Readers will notice that this book contains no essays devoted exclusively to the many communities of Jews whose experience parts in significant ways from the urban, non-Orthodox, Ashkenazi mainstream sense of belonging in Canada. Indeed, this book should be read as a call for scholars, community leaders, and observers to carefully examine the ways that these important and diverse sub-populations have negotiated and navigated their senses of belonging as both Canadians and Jews given its current Ashkenazi-centrism. A fuller answer to our question will critically require that we know more about how the experiences of haredim, Israeli-Canadians, Russian and former Soviet Jews, Sephardim, Mizrahim, LGBTQ Jews, and Latin American Jews complement and diverge from the insights the scholars in this book have been able to draw about this murky "sense" of belonging. The fullest answer would also demand that we know more about Jews from geographically marginal communities, requiring us to segment the population by age, political persuasion, and degree of religiosity. Alas, this book did not aim to write the definitive "answer" to the question of home or provide a total qualitative accounting of Canada's diverse Jewish population. Its design, rather, is to introduce a vital question that ought to be asked in as many ways as possible.

This book is divided into three sections, each branching off in its own direction from the question posed by the book's title. The first section, "Comparisons: Canadian Jewries and Other Jewries, Canadian Jews and Other Canadians," consists of chapters that compare Canadian Jewish life with Jewries in other places, or focus on Jewish / non-Jewish interactions in Canada. Sociologist Morton Weinfeld's essay, "A Privileged Diaspora: Canadian Jewry in Comparative Perspective," serves as the anchor of the volume. Weinfeld attempts to answer our question head on by comparing a series of social scientific data points, each of which reveals some aspect of Jewish self-possession or indicator of communal and religious freedom as shaped by state or society. His reading of the data suggests, rather forcefully, that the answer is yes.

The next chapter is by a leading historian of American Jews, Hasia Diner. Her essay, "Destination World Jewry: The United States versus the World," provides an immediate and dramatic counterpoint to Weinfeld's claims and a sober counterargument to readers eager to bask in overzealous Canadian pride. Diner argues that Canada was a pale second choice for would-be Jewish migrants, far behind the United States throughout the era of mass migration, suggesting that the United States stood as the great exception for world Jewry looking for a new home.

The following chapter by Jeffrey Veidlinger, "To Guarantee Their Own Self-Government in All Matters of Their National Life": Ukrainians, Jews, and the Origins of Canadian Multiculturalism," explores the interaction between Jews who migrated to Canada to escape "Ukrainian Cossacks" and Ukrainians who migrated to Canada to escape "Jewish Bolsheviks." Veidlinger explores the ways in which these minority groups' imported ideas about collective identities shaped the most important dimension of late twentieth-century Canadian social politics. His chapter brings original insight to the historical influences that shaped Canada into a state that aimed to encourage minorities to feel at home by remaining attached to their own unique cultures.

Kalman Weiser's chapter, "Vilna on the St Lawrence: Montreal as the Would-Be Haven for Yiddish Culture," describes how Jewish intellectuals in the first half of the twentieth century envisioned both Vilna and Montreal as the cities in which modern Jewish culture might thrive. Passionate community- and culture-oriented visiting observers of Montreal's unique Jewish culture, argues Weiser, helped raise expectations that the city might prove a fertile home for Yiddish language and culture, sheltered from some of the assimilationist forces that Jews faced in cities in the United States, a hope all the more poignant in the wake of Jewish Vilna's tragic decimation during the Second World War.

Chapter 5, "Jewish Education in Canada and the United Kingdom: A Comparative Perspective," by sociologist Randal F. Schnoor, examines data that reveal Canadian Jewry's relative strength in proffering rich Jewish educational opportunities for their own. Since rates and levels of Jewish education, in Schnoor's view, surpass other indexes of strong communal life and secure Jewish identities – things like synagogue attendance, ritual observance, or intermarriage – Jewish education might symbolize Jews' own sense of enfranchisement in Canada.

My own contribution to this volume, "The Unsettling of Canadian Jewish History: Toward a Tangled History of Jewish–Indigenous Encounters in Canada," argues for the need to re-examine Canadian Jewish history through the lens of Jewish–Indigenous encounters. It suggests that pluralism and diversity are inadequate analytic terms for understanding how and where Jewish life – and indeed all ethnic groups – fits into the settler-society enterprise known as Canada.

The second section of this book, "Case Studies: Historical Episodes, Literary Creations," consists of a series of essays by historians that focus on specific circumstances in time and essays by literary scholars who unpack texts that work as prisms through which to appreciate the subtle and complex ways in which Canadian Jews have grappled with ideas of home. In her essay "Crossing in/to Canada: Canada as Point of Arrival in Holocaust Survivor Memoirs," Mia Spiro examines what Holocaust survivors destined for Canada thought about it as a prospective home on arrival, and how they struggled with the forced and chosen transformations of their lives after migrating here. Spiro finds that these literary documents reveal existential negotiations of survivor-migrants that were subtle and profound, not simple experiences of relief on arrival. Survivors' senses of Canada show something of the core problematic that many of the survivors experienced – of simultaneous being and non-being.

Complementing the Spiro essay is Ruth Panofsky's "The 'Nu World' of Toronto in Bernice Eisenstein's *I Was a Child of Holocaust*

Survivors." Panofsky's chapter is a study of the first graphic memoir of a second-generation Holocaust survivor, a challenging work that brings to life the author's and her parents' efforts to cope with the Shoah in three distinctly local zones of Toronto. Panofsky's essay highlights the ongoing nature of the problem of how a sense of home can be created in the haunting wake of the Holocaust.

In his essay, "Nathan Phillips: The Election of Toronto's First Jewish Mayor," historian Harold Troper tells the story of Phillips's rise to power. Troper uses the 1954 municipal election as a symbol of the changes that Toronto was undergoing and the ways it had already begun its transformation into becoming a home for a diverse body of Canadian citizens. In the election, according to Troper, Phillips's ethno-religious heritage – his Jewishness – proved to be a key factor in this process.

Complementing Troper's focus on what elections reveal about communities' sense belonging, historian Ira Robinson writes of the 1976 provincial election of the Parti Québécois in "By the Rivers of the St Lawrence: The Montreal Jewish Community and Its Postmemory." His essay describes the demographic, institutional, linguistic, and political shifts that reshaped what being at home would mean for both Montreal Jews and Canadian Jewish life more broadly in the wake of the Quiet Revolution. Robinson's focus on a moment of contextual crisis for Montreal Jewry – its alarm at the prospect of losing its beloved city as a safe and stable home for Jewish life – offers a unique vantage point to contemplate the sense of communal belonging.

The section wraps up with historian Richard Menkis's essay, "In from the Margins: Museums and Narratives of the Canadian Jewish Experience." Menkis analyses the ways in which three museum exhibitions – one each in the 1970s, 1980s, and the 1990s – reveal changes in the ways that narratives of Canadian Jewish life have been represented and figured as part of the larger history of Canada. Menkis points to a significant transformation over these decades, from presentations that focus on the "contributions" of Jews to Canada, to a more nuanced portrait of Jewish life as one among many minority groups. Extending the historical trajectory into the future, Menkis's essay concludes with a call for Canadian Jewry to build its own national Jewish museum.

The final section, "Reflections: Personal Stories, Language," offers personal essays on Canadian Jewish identities moving in roughly chronological order. These essays speak to particular subsets of Canadian Jewish experiences; nearly all of them blend personal and scholarly voices in unique ways. Taken together, these writings bring thoughtful and intimate granularity to the book's grand theme, being at home as a Jew in Canada. This section of the book also contains essays that contemplate the notion of home based on language itself, and thus complicate and provoke the field of Canadian Jewish studies as a whole. Writer and scholar Norman Ravvin's "Pictures of New Canadians: An Immigration Story for Our Time," focuses on his grandfather's migration to the Canadian Prairies in the 1930s and his experiences with immigration officials and the ethnic-cultural folk festivals of the day (in which Jews did not have representation) and what they teach about how the meaning of home has changed over time.

Judith Baskin reflects on her Jewish childhood in Hamilton as the daughter of a Reform Rabbi and Rebbetzin in her personal essay "Under Gentile Eyes: My Jewish Childhood in Hamilton, 1950–1967." Her writing foregrounds the experience of being an outsider both as a Jew in a heavily Christian milieu and as the child of American immigrants in a small city with deep class tensions – another unique vantage point for reflections on belonging.

Lois Dubin's essay, "Montreal and Canada through a Wider Lens: Confessions of a Canadian-American European Jewish Historian," compares Montreal, the long-time epicentre of Canadian Jewish life, with port cities such as Trieste, Amsterdam, and Lisbon, where Jews made enduring and rich homes in the modern period. Her essay is a reflection on her career as a historian of early modern Jewish life, shaped by her Canadian orientation, and a blend of scholarly insight and memoirist reflection.

Yolande Cohen offers a similarly blended scholarly and personal identity history as a Sephardi woman. Her memoir, "Forgetting and Forging: My Canadian Experience as a Moroccan Jew," travels from Morocco to France, and from Israel to Canada, as it depicts some of the complex ways in which time and place shape our capacities for rootedness and transform the meanings of Jewish identity – in her case, the process of "becoming" a Sephardi Jew.

Anthropologist Jack Kugelmass revisits his Jewish youth during Canada's centennial programming in his essay, "Nothing Is Forever: Remembering the Centennial." His essay brings an anthropological sensibility and critical self-reflection to the questions of belonging as he crisscrossed the country, interacting with Canadian cultures and people far outside the parochial Jewish fold.

Rebecca Margolis offers one of two provocative arguments in this book that explore the intersection of language and Canadian Jewish life. Her essay, "*In der heym in Kanada*: A Survey on Yiddish Today," argues that Canada, more than any other nation, might be the best national home for Yiddish to flourish. Her essay draws from survey data she gathered about Yiddish in the wake of the Holocaust. Her essay contemplates Canadian Jewry's enduring bond with Yiddish, despite its transition from a vernacular a mode of cultural identification to link Jews to key aspects of Jewish life: family, lineage, heritage, and tradition.

The section finishes with a powerful essay by the great historian of Quebec Jewry – and importantly, the only non-Jewish contributor to the book – Pierre Anctil. His essay, "Which Canada Are We Talking About? An English-Language Polemic about French in Canadian Jewish History," challenges Canadian Jewish scholarship to better engage with French-language sources, calling out the field for its linguistic inadequacies.

The book's postscript has been written by the youngest contributor to the volume, historian David Weinfeld, who also happens to be the son of sociologist Morton Weinfeld, whose chapter opens the book. David's postscript, "Thin Canadian Culture, Thick Jewish Life," offers summary comments and closing reflections for the volume as a whole, and hints at some of the invariably new ways in which the question of Canada as home for Jews will be formulated as the future unfolds.

"What makes a good home?" is a good analytic question. North American Jews have long wrung their hands over the brilliant and oft-repeated observation that what seems to be good for individual Jews might be bad for the community's health. Since comparisons invite all sorts of problems for thinking about "better," asking them might require us to develop scholarship that reaches into new scholarly territory, widening our field beyond its traditional history, literature, and sociology, to social psychology, economics, and the emerging arena that examines well-being. The Canadian Jewish experience does make a difference to the unfolding of Jewish history writ large, and the questions we ask about it can lead us to good thinking about living good lives. Canada may also be a litmus test for the future if our children are to face an entirely new context of post-national, multicultural possibilities within which Jews must make their homes.

NOTES

This volume grew out of a symposium held at the Israel and Golda Koschitzky Centre for Jewish Studies at York University in autumn, 2017. I gratefully acknowledge the support of the York University President's Canada 150 Fund, its Robarts Centre for Canadian Studies, Harry S. Crowe Memorial Lecture Fund, and its Departments of History, Humanities, and Politics. My thanks as well to

Carl Ehrlich, Julie Feinberg, Irit Printz, and Debbie Lupton for their guidance and behind-the-scenes contributions.

1 "2018 Survey of Jews in Canada," Environics Institute, 11 March 2019, https://www.environicsinstitute.org/projects/project-details/survey -of-jews-in-canada.
2 "Police Reported Hate Crimes," Statistics Canada, accessed 24 September 2019, https://www150.statcan.gc.ca/t1/tbl1/en/tv.action?pid=3510019101.
3 Barry L.Stiefel and Hernan Tesler-Mabé, *Neither in Dark Speeches nor in Similitudes: Reflections and Refractions between Canadian and American Jews* (Waterloo, ON: Wilfrid Laurier University Press, 2016).

SECTION ONE

Comparisons: Canadian Jewries and Other Jewries, Canadian Jews and Other Canadians

1 A Privileged Diaspora: Canadian Jewry in Comparative Perspective

MORTON WEINFELD

How can we ever structure a reply to the question "Is Canada the best home for the Jews"? In this essay, my main frame of reference will be the Western liberal democracies of the past two hundred years. Anything outside that scope is beyond my area of expertise. My approach is resolutely comparative. One of my mentors was the prominent sociologist and political scientist Seymour Martin Lipset, a staunch comparativist. He used to say, and I am paraphrasing: *if you want to understand the Jews, study the Gentiles*. I have tried to follow in that vein. But the comparisons I offer here will be limited by time and space. I will not be discussing the Golden Age of Spain, Jews under Weimar, or the Jewish community of interwar Vilna or Warsaw. All were very positive locations for Jews, in different ways. Rather, I will compare the Canadian Jewish experience with that in the United States, France, and the United Kingdom. Those are the four largest diasporic communities we have today. And of course they are also Western liberal democracies.

I will be analysing Canada, and perhaps celebrating Canada and the Canadian Jewish experience. But Canadian Jewry has not yet made a significant and collective impact on the world's elite Jewish intellectual and cultural stage. In fact, the imprint so far has been a small one, in terms of Jewish thought and Jewish culture writ large. There have been well-known Canadian Jewish thinkers. One thinks of Emil Fackenheim, David Hartman, and Gunther Plaut. But these were scholars who were raised and nurtured outside Canada. As Canadians we can take great pride in someone like the multidimensional Leonard Cohen, who remained profoundly Jewish and Canadian while travelling the world. On a CBC radiopodcast his biographer recounted a Cohen comment about Judaism: "Asking me about being Jewish is like asking fish what they feel about water." So maybe his work, with its blend of Jewish and other traditions, is a kind of unique Jewish Canadian contribution with resonance in the broader Jewish cultural world.

In undertaking this comparison, it is important to note that Canada is a young country, younger than France and Britain, even younger than the United States. And therefore its Jewish communities, and Jewish scholars, are more recent. Rashi was writing his biblical commentaries a thousand years ago in Troyes, twenty-five miles outside Paris. There is not yet in Canada a large permanent museum dedicated to the Jewish experience in general and/or the Canadian Jewish experience. Maybe there will be one at some point. Such museums exist in the United States and in cities throughout Europe and even Australia. The Jewish museums in Australia celebrate with pride the Jewish representation among the first shiploads of petty thieves and criminals sent to found the colony.

In any case, this essay focuses not on individual achievement, but on the collective status of key diaspora communities today and in the recent past. First, I will focus on a range of general Canadian outcome measures for all immigrant minorities, looking at inequality/integration, and then cultural retention. Next, I will explore Jewish topics: antisemitism, and measures of cultural vitality and the quality of Canadian Jewish life. After analysing these two broad Jewish issues, I will make some general observations about Canadian Jewish life today and perhaps tomorrow.

The General Canadian Context for Minority Groups

How does Canada fare in terms of its general treatment of all minorities? If Canada does well by its other minorities in a comparative sense, then it is not surprising that Canada would also do well by the Jews. Are immigrant minorities well integrated? Are they able, if they wish, to retain their cultures and identities?[1]

By and large my field, sociology, suggests strongly that these two objectives for any person or community are a zero-sum operation. The more a person, the more a group, seeks to integrate fully into their host society, the less they will be able to maximize their cultural identity in any authentic way. For example, a member of the ultra-Orthodox Jewish community or, say, a Hutterite, will find it hard to become the president of the Royal Bank of Canada, or even a sociology professor at McGill – in the very unlikely event they would want that. One has to make a choice. There is a trade-off involved. As we shall see, for the Jews as a whole the trade-off seems relatively minimal.

So how does Canada fare in its treatment of minorities generally? The quick answer is: quite well. My students at McGill dislike that reply.

Most of them rightly focus on the very serious remaining flaws and inequities in Canadian society. But what follows emphasizes a broader and comparative picture.

Before analysing some comparative empirical evidence, let me share a revealing anecdote. In early 2017 I gave a talk at the University of Texas in Austin, about a similar sort of theme. The group in the audience consisted of academics interested in Canadian Jewish life and multiculturalism in Canada. I began my talk by showing a photograph that almost every Canadian has seen, of Justin Trudeau at the airport greeting families of Syrian survivors/refugees and hugging children. As I showed that picture you could have heard a pin drop. These were American scholars who had been living through the restrictive Trump experience, as it affected Syrian refugees and other immigrants generally. They were clearly struck by the different vibe that they got from this photo of Trudeau at the airport and Canada's admission of Syrian refugees. That photo, better than reams of data for some, conveys the current difference between Canada and the United States in terms of state attitudes to immigration and diversity.

Now for more objective measures comparing Canada, the United States, the United Kingdom, and France. A group of scholars at Queen's University has developed a Multicultural Policy Index, designed to measure the degree to which countries have crafted policies to promote multiculturalism and cultural retention.[2] What are such policies? They include:

1 Whether a society has affirmed in law multicultural principles
2 Whether school curricula promote multiculturalism
3 Whether the media are representative of and sensitized to cultural diversity
4 Whether there are exemptions – can rules be bent to accommodate minorities
5 Whether dual citizenship is permitted
6 Whether the state funds ethnic organizations
7 Whether the state supports bilingual education programs
8 Whether the state has affirmative action programs.

Countries can score 1 0.5, or 0 on each, reflecting full, partial, or no support for such policies. Canada's score is highest at 7.5, compared with 3 for the United States, 5.5 for the UK, and 2 for France. A large Canadian advantage. Next consider a Migrant Integration Policy Index (MIPEX). The index was developed by the Barcelona Centre for International Affairs, and the Migration Policy Group.[3] It measures the degree to which countries have policies that facilitate greater equality or integration of minorities across a variety of policy domains, including:

1 Labour market mobility: Can one move around in the labour market?
2 Family reunion: Is there an immigration policy that unites families?
3 Education: Is there full access to education?
4 Health: Is there full access to health care?
5 Political participation: Can one participate fully as a member of any kind of minority group?
6 Permanent residence: Can one get permanent residence?
7 Access to nationality: Can one become a citizen?
8 Anti-discrimination: Are there anti-discrimination laws?

Scores are tallied on these metrics, and here too Canada scores highest, with a 68, compared to 63 for the United States, 57 for the UK, and 54 for France.

Now consider another measure, actual political representation. We can compare the percentage of minority MPs with the minority percentage in the population. (A score of 1.0 would be full proportional representation.) Here again Canada does very well, with a score of 0.62, compared to 0.5, 0.625, 0.42, for the United States, UK, and France.[4] And what of visible minorities in the Cabinet? I use name recognition and biographies. Here too Canada does best with a comparable ratio of 0.95, compared to 0.49, 0.70, and 0.44 for the United States, UK, and France. Four of the six Canadian ministers are of Sikh background.[5]

Another indicator is the existence of openly anti-immigrant, xenophobic, or racist significant political parties with significant shares of the popular vote. Canada has none. (The new People's Party of Canada is seen as to the right of the Conservatives, and was polling at around 3 per cent throughout the summer of 2019 and received 1.6 per cent of the vote in the 2019 federal election). Some might claim that the Conservative Party is anti-immigrant. There are clearly elements in the party that are less open to diversity, certainly Islam, than the other major federal parties. But there is no comparison with the explicit pronouncements of the European ultra-nationalist parties. Both France and Britain have such parties, the Rassemblement National (formerly National Front) and UKIP, as indeed one can find today in most western and eastern European countries. Of course, the Republicans under Donald Trump could be seen in as being anti-immigrant and anti-minority, either directly or indirectly, though perhaps not as explicitly as some of the European far-right parties. Most of those European parties, to various degrees, carry antisemitic baggage as well.

And what of racist attitudes in the population? A variety of surveys have been done in these four countries, though they are not strictly comparable. Consider attitudes about Islam, which would be a minority group common to the four countries. In Canada 46 per cent hold unfavourable views of Islam, according to an Angus Reid poll in 2017.[6] In France and the UK about 40 per cent had negative impressions of Muslims, also similar to the United States.[7] No large gaps here. In all cases we have significant levels of Islamophobia.

Finally, as another measure, let us consider perceived discrimination on the part of a minority group. Once again, we will use Muslims as a common group. In Canada a poll in 2016 found 35 per cent of Muslims have "experienced" discrimination.[8] The level in the United States was 48 per cent, and in France, 69 per cent.[9] In the UK 46 per cent felt that "prejudice makes it hard to be a Muslim."[10] So by this measure Canada would also seem to be doing well.

If we assess all these data, then it does appear that Canadian immigrant minorities on balance compare well with those in the United States, Britain, and France. A positive image of Canadian multiculturalism, pervasive in Canada and around the world, seems to have some grounding in fact. Let us ask why that might be the case. It is unlikely that majority of Canadians, for some reason, have a kinder, more tolerant disposition. It's best to consider other explanations.

The first explanation might be that Canada had a much smaller slave population than in the United States. One factor among many here would be the absence in Canada of a significant plantation economy (even though most American slaves did not work on large plantations). So, this is simply an element of geographic luck. Canada's black population is mainly a postwar population, from the Caribbean, later from Africa, without the same multigenerational history of slavery and Jim Crow that has marked the United States. A second explanation for Canada's apparent advanced tolerance is that Canada's borders and geographic location sheltered the country from large-scale non-white legal and illegal migrations, from Latin America because of the United States buffer, and also from the Middle East and Africa due to the oceans. Again, simple geographic luck. A final possible explanation, perhaps most decisive, is Canada's history as a nation founded by two colonial powers. Though both subjugated the Indigenous population, the country's elites had to work out *a modus vivendi,* evident in the 1867 British North America Act, which recognized the foundational claims of both the English and the French. Once a country recognizes politically more than one ethno-national group, it can find space for many more, as reflected in the official adoption of multiculturalism in the 1980s.

It is not possible here to adjudicate among various possible explanations. But the evidence suggests strongly that Canada has been and remains a relatively welcoming country to its various non-charter immigrant groups. The earlier white immigrant groups are well integrated. And the more recent racialized minority groups, while still struggling against racism in various forms, would seem to face better prospects than in the other three comparable countries. So, this may augur well for Jews.

The Canadian Jewish Case in Comparative Perspective

Now let us compare the situations facing Jews in Canada and the other selected countries. Data sources are in the main social scientific surveys. These are: a 2018 national survey of Canadian Jews from Toronto, Montreal, Winnipeg, and Vancouver; Canadian 2011 census data; and recent surveys of the Toronto and Montreal Jewish communities.[11] For the United States, data are from the Pew survey of 2013.[12] For the UK, data are taken from work published by the Institute for Jewish Population Research or JPR.[13] The French data come from a study/survey of French Jewry.[14]

First some demographic data to set a basic context. The Canadian Jewish population of 390,000 has actually been growing over the past decades, a few per cent per decade. To be precise, from 1981–91 the population increased 14.4 per cent: from 1991 to 2001, up 4.2 per cent, and from 2001 to 2011, up 4.7 per cent. The US Jewish population of 6–7 million has been essentially static – any apparent modest recent increase is likely due mainly to wider definitions. In both Britain (270,000) and France (465,000), the Jewish population in past decades has declined. Jews comprise 2 per cent of the US population, compared to 1.2 per cent in Canada, 0.4 per cent in the UK, and 0.7 per cent in France. Population growth has often served as a variable reflecting the vitality of a community. Canada's Jewish population growth has been due mainly to less assimilation and lower rates of intermarriage, significant immigration levels, and higher fertility rates among the more numerous Orthodox and ultra-Orthodox segments. (The only European country that has seen an increase in its Jewish population has been Germany, a result mainly of large immigration flows from Israel and the former Soviet Union.)

What of antisemitism? The challenge of antisemitism has long been a major issue determining the degree of integration of Jews in the post-Emancipation West. Perhaps the best known measure of international antisemitic attitudes comes from the Anti-Defamation League. For years the ADL has been administering the same survey and computing the same index with the same eleven antisemitic items, asking random samples of five hundred in many countries whether they agree. Examples of such statements are: Jews are more loyal to Israel; they have too much power; they have too much control over global affairs;

they think they are better than other people; they have too much control over the media; Jews talk too much about what happened to them in the Holocaust. If a respondent agrees that six out of these eleven are certainly or probably true, they are counted as an antisemite. Using this index Canada in 2014 does reasonably well, with a score of 14 per cent of the population antisemitic. The United States at 9 per cent and the UK at 8 per cent do better; France is much higher at 37 per cent. (The nations of eastern Europe score higher still.)

What of antisemitism as perceived by Jews? One-third of Canadian Jews in 2018 said Jews "often" experience discrimination and 50 per cent said "sometimes." In terms of personal discrimination in the past five years, 21 per cent experienced discrimination due to religion and 18 per cent due to ethnicity/culture. The levels were similar in Toronto and Montreal. In the United States the Pew survey, with a different wording – "a lot of discrimination"– found 43 per cent. The United Kingdom found 11 per cent. France is much higher at 52 per cent. So here too there is a rough similarity between Canada and the UK, with France and the United States scoring much higher. While of interest to many social scientists, these attitudes are not always good indicators of the realities of Jewish life or predictors of future trends. Historical events do not always unfold based on popular attitudes. But in the Canadian case relatively moderate levels of antisemitic attitudes do match the absence of the extreme cases of antisemitism found in Europe.

One new British conception that has been suggested in the study of antisemitism is shifting from defining and counting antisemites to defining and measuring the scope and prevalence of antisemitic attitudes. Recall the ADL definition mentioned earlier, where someone who agreed with six of eleven antisemitic statements would thus be counted as an antisemite. What if many people in the country agree with only five? Or three? A new study has suggested counting the number of Britons who agreed with at least one antisemitic statement. Instead of low single digits as the number of British antisemites, in this study the answer was 30 per cent. That means that a British Jewish person interacting with non-Jews may hear one of those negative stereotypes expressed by 30 per cent of the British population. This is a different approach to measuring antisemitism than using a fixed binary to label individuals and would tend to explain why some Jews might perceive more antisemitism than clear antisemites. This approach can relate well to the current debate about anti-Israel or anti-Zionist statements. Many Canadian Jews may encounter such views, expressed either by individuals or on the media, and many will perceive these views, rightly or wrongly, as antisemitic.[15]

Let us now consider Jewish political representation, in Parliament, Congress, and other levels of government. After the 2015 election Canada was historically low at six (or 1.7 per cent) Jewish MPs, just above the population proportion of 1.2 per cent. This was up to 8 after the 2019 election.[16] Comparatively, around the same time, the United States rate was 5–6 per cent, the UK at 3–4%, per cent, and France at around 3 per cent, all many times higher than their population percentage.[17] I do not know why the Canadian parliamentary proportion is so low after the Justin Trudeau victory. But by this measure, at this time, Canada is lowest of the four.

Canada has also not done well at the very senior levels of national political leadership. Consider France, which seemingly has a weak record on Jewish issues of late yet still has had two Jewish premiers, Pierre Mendes-France and Leon Blum. Indeed, Blum was elected three times. And Britain has had two Jewish party leaders, Ed Miliband for Labour and Michael Howard for the Conservatives. (On the other hand, many British Jews saw the Labour Party under Jeremy Corbyn as tolerating open antisemitism.) In the United States, Joe Lieberman was the vice-presidential candidate in 2000. In Canada the closest case has been that of David Lewis, leader of the NDP, but with no realistic chance of being elected prime minister. It is not clear why this has been the case. Perhaps it reflects a kind of residual otherness at the top national political level, where the two founding European peoples dominate. At the provincial level, the news has been better. Consider Ontario. Though there has never been a Jewish premier of the province, three Jews have been elected as mayor of Toronto – Phil Givens, Nathan Phillips, and Mel Lastman – and three Jews have served as leaders of the three major Ontario provincial parties – Stuart Smith, Stephen Lewis, and Larry Grossman. Only BC has had a Jewish premier, Dave Barrett of the NDP. But at the federal level the record of representation has been weak. However, it is fair to say that individual Jewish Canadians have held prominent positions in governmental and political parties.[18]

Now consider measures of Jewish identity. In the sections below we will review a few variables that have emerged as "the usual suspects" in empirical analyses of modern Jewish identity. These are conventional measures, and some might suggest they reflect mainly past understandings of Jewishness. But they are still commonly used in all major social scientific work. Intermarriage rates have emerged, rightly or wrongly, as key measures of Jewish identity in Jewish communities. A 2018 rate for Canada was 25 per cent, for all ages. In an earlier Toronto survey we find a total intermarriage rate of 11.2 per cent, with 28.6 per cent for the children of the respondents. In the United States the 2013 Pew survey found a rate of 44 per cent in total, and 58 per cent was the rate for more recent marriages. In the UK and France, we find aggregate rates of 26 per cent and 30 per cent of Jewish respondents in mixed marriages. So, the Canadian/Toronto rate seems somewhat lower.

What of attendance at Jewish day schools? For adult survey respondents with some day school, we find 2018 rates of 43 per cent, with higher rates for Montreal over Toronto. This compares to the United States at 20 per cent, the UK at 51 per cent, and France at 23 per cent. In Quebec and in the UK the state contributes funding to Jewish day schools, which may explain higher rates in Montreal and the UK, and the lower rates for the United States, France, and Ontario. Were government funding available for Jewish day schools in Ontario, the rates would likely be far higher.

What of membership in a synagogue? We see 58 per cent in Canada, 31 per cent in the United States, and 56 per cent in UK; there is no comparable survey question for France. When asked if they had ever visited Israel, positive responses were 80 per cent for Canada, compared with 43 per cent in the United States, 95 per cent in the UK, and 75 per cent in France. Many of the Canadian advantages compared with the United States reflect higher proportions in Orthodox and fewer in Reform denominations.

Can data like these be aggregated in a meaningful way, given that the set of indicators above may not be perfect, and many others could have been added? (For example, on measures of education, occupation, and income, Canadian Jews rank as perhaps the most economically successful group in the country. But similar patterns can be found for Jews in the other three countries studied here.) They are "the usual suspects" used in measuring Jewish identity in conventional Jewish social science. My back-of-the-envelope interpretation of these Jewish data suggests there is an overall measurable Canadian advantage in terms of quality of Jewish life. This advantage, at least when compared with the United States, has led some observers to speak of Canadian Jewish exceptionalism.[19]

Are there other reasons why Jews do well in Canada? Canada's multicultural discourse and law, including Section 27 of the Charter of Rights and Freedoms and the creation of related funding sources, are of course music to Jewish survivalists' ears. But consider also immigration. Compared with the United States, one can argue that higher levels of Jewish identity are due to the percentage of Jewish foreign born: about 30 per cent in Canada compared with 14 per cent in the United States. This is a major gap. More foreign-born Jews in Canada can mean, in varying degrees, more religious or cultural tradition, more links to Israel, more experiences of persecution, more associations with major events of Jewish history. And this would be the case for all the waves of postwar Jewish immigrants to Canada.

Another, subtler, explanation could focus on the mass migration period and differential legacies. Compare Canada and the United States and consider the four decades from 1880 to 1920. Canadian Jewish mass immigration took place mostly in the years 1900 to 1920. The United States mass immigration period occurred earlier, 1880 to 1900. The later incidence of the Canadian Jewish immigration meant they had more time in Europe to experience Zionism (the first Zionist Congress took place in 1897), notably Labour Zionism, as an organized movement, as well as Yiddish culture and nationalism in its various forms. Thus, Yiddish culture, Jewish nationalism, and Zionism are stronger in Canada because of the later mass migration of eastern Europeans to the country.

There may be another possible explanation. Canadian history compared with that of Europe, the Middle East, and even the United States has been more tranquil in general in the postwar period and even before. It has been less contentious, less uncertain, less polarized. And this has had an effect on Jewish life in Canada, allowing a less constrained focus on group identity. The Jewish experience in Canada has been less "edgy" than it has been in the United States and certainly in Europe.

What does this mean? Jews living in Europe have likely experienced, directly or indirectly, their families' horrific struggles with war and repression, with fascism on the one hand and communism on the other. Recently Europe, notably France, has seen incidents of major anti-Jewish violence, as well as the rise of new xenophobic and ultra nationalist parties. On the left Jeremy Corbyn's leadership of the Labour Party in Britain was highly unsettling for many Jews, as was the Brexit debate. The United States has experienced a far more violent, more polarized and unsettled domestic history than Canada. The chronology would include the American Revolution, the Indian Wars, the Mexican wars, slavery, the Civil War, Jim Crow, McCarthyism and the Cold War, the Vietnam War, the civil rights movement, and 9/11 and its aftermath. The American lead role in the Middle East conflict adds to this stress. Under the Trump administration, diversity and immigration (of Latinos and Muslims) have become far more polarizing issues in the United States and Europe than in Canada. All these events and movements did not tear apart Canadian society as they have done in the United States and Europe. So, this trajectory makes for more tension for Jews in the United States and Europe. These communities seem to be more unsettled or more at the centre of contentious political discourse than in Canada.

The major example in Canada of the European/American tension over the past decades has been in Quebec. The emergence of the independence movement in Quebec and the rise of Quebec nationalism has been seen by Jews and others as dangerous and unsettling. Support for sovereignty has declined as of 2020, but new tensions have arisen since the 2008 debate on reasonable accommodation, the Bouchard-Taylor commission, the PQ's proposed Charter of Values, Bill 62 of the Quebec Liberal Party, and the recently passed Bill 21 of the CAQ provincial government. A Quebec consensus seems to support restricting religious expression in the public service, and thus may have an indirect and unsettling impact on Jews. But apart from this case, Jewish life in Canada has been spared the tensions experienced by other countries.

The Future

Despite current significant Canadian advantages, I tilt towards an increasing convergence hypothesis for the future of Canadian Jewish life. If or when the Canadian Jewish foreign-born levels decline to match those of the United States, there will be greater convergence between American and Canadian Jewish identities and behaviours. Canadian Jewish cultural life will still remain vital, but with a more hyphenated and hybrid orientation. There are many strong north-south tugs between Canada and United States, and between Canadian Jewish life and American Jewish life. The key rabbinical seminaries remain in the United States. Many Canadian Jews have children or other close relatives who study, live, and marry in the United States.

Apart from this convergence, there are two general trends that may also impact the Canadian Jewish future. The first is renewed antisemitism, and its link to anti-Zionism and condemnation of Israel. This issue is common to all diaspora communities. Of course, antisemitism has always been a major element of the Canadian Jewish experience. And indeed up to the 1960s one could argue that antisemitism was the single dominant feature of Canadian Jewish life, both objectively and in terms of subjective Jewish perceptions. Things began to change in the 1960s, when more space was created for Canadian Jews, and Jews created more space for themselves.[20] There was then a dip in Canadian antisemitism for some time. Yet in recent years there have been reports from the field, often from the university campuses, that there is a change in tone, discourse, and topic. In the eyes of many Canadian Jews, a new and potent stream of antisemitism has emerged, linked to the boycott, divestment, and sanctions (or "BDS") campaigns directed against Israel and to generalized anti-Zionist sentiments. This new discourse not only seems to focus on specific Israeli policies in matters like settlements but is perceived as seeking to undermine the very existence of Israel as a sovereign Jewish state. This issue of course is also found in the other countries discussed here, and it is not yet clear whether it will emerge in Canada to a greater or lesser degree than in other societies.

I have had Jewish students come to my office at McGill and say that they don't feel comfortable on campus. Similar feelings have been expressed at other universities in North America. Are they overstating the dangers? Will this new form of perceived antisemitism have a significant and lasting impact on Canadian Jewry, and if so, of what kind? The study of antisemitism, recently of less concern to social scientists studying modern Jewish life in Canada and the West, may be posed for a revival.

A final future challenge deals with Jewish identity itself. American data are illustrative. According to analysis of the 2013 Pew report data in United States, there is an increasing polarization in American Jewish life, between the Orthodox and the more liberal forms of Jewish expression. Orthodoxy and ultra-Orthodoxy are growing. At the other end of the spectrum, there is an increase in the number of Reform/mixed-marriage/new wave/new age/less affiliated kinds of Jews. What can be called the middle, often represented by Conservative Judaism, is shrinking. Indeed, fifty years ago Conservative Judaism was thought to be the future of American Jewish life. Sociologist Marshall Sklare and others have argued this forcefully.[21] It was a centrist alternative, a made-in-America religious option. But the opposite has occurred, and Conservative Judaism has been losing support. Canada has also witnessed a growth in the Orthodox and ultra-Orthodox population. At the same time there is growth in liberal and avant-garde Jewish options, catering to a growing mixed-marriage population. It is not yet clear if these trends in Canada will match the pace found in the United States.

So what might Canadian Jewish life look like in thirty or fifty years? The American projections based on Pew and the British projections from JPR are similar. Their future projections see relative growth among the Orthodox and ultra-Orthodox in both countries. Will we see the same patterns at work in Canada in the future? While predictions about the Jewish future are always risky, there is a good chance that we will.

To conclude, Canadian Jewry continues to enjoy a privileged position in the ranks of diasporic Jewish communities. There is a unique blend of relatively high participation in the host society combined with a relatively high degree of communal vitality. But there are challenges on the horizon. Stay tuned.

NOTES

1 Thanks to Sakeef Karim, doctoral student in sociology at McGill, for help in this section.
2 Keith Banting and Will Kymlicka, "Is There Really a Return for Multicultural Policies? New Evidence from the Multiculturalism Policy Index," *Comparative European Politics* 11, no. 5 (2013): 577–98

3 Migrant Integration Policy Index, "How Countries Are Promoting Integration of Immigrants" (Barcelona Centre for International Affairs and Migration Policy Group, 2015), https://MIPEX.eu/key-findings.

4 CPAC, "Electoral Reboot: Diversity and the Ballot," 7 October 2016, https://www.cpac.ca/en/electoral-reboot-diversity-and-the-ballot; Kristen Bialik and Jens Manuel Krogstad, "115th Congress Sets New High for Racial and Ethnic Diversity," Pew Research Center, 24 January 2017, https://www.pewresearch.org/fact-tank/2017/01/24/115th-congress-sets-new-high-for-racial-ethnic-diversity; Cherry Wilson , "Election Results 2017: The Most Diverse Parliament Yet," 11 June 2017, https://www.bbc.com/news/election-2017-40232272; "Diversity Gains Ground in France's New Look National Assembly after Vote," 21 June 2017, www.France24.com.

5 The White House, "The Cabinet," accessed June 2018, https://www.whitehouse.gov/the-trump-administration/the-cabinet; Parliament of Canada, "Ministry (Cabinet) as of January 29, 2018," https://www.ourcommons.ca/Members/en/ministries?ministry=29&precedenceReview=85&province=all&gender=all; Cherry Wilson, "Election Results 2017; BBC, "How Does Theresa May's Cabinet Compare to David Cameron's?," 14 July 2016, https://www.bbc.com/news/uk-politics-36788622; Government of France, "Composition of the Government," accessed June 2018, https://www.gouvernement.fr/en/composition-of-the-government.

6 Adam Frisk, "Nearly Half of Canadians View Islam Unfavourably, Survey Finds," *Global News*, 4 April 2017, https://globalnews.ca/news/3356103/canadians-islam-religion-trends-study/.

7 Will Dahlgreen, "Roma and Muslims Are the Least Tolerated Minorities in Europe," 5 June 2015, https://yougov.co.uk/topics/politics/articles-reports/2015/06/05/european-attitudes-minorities; Antonia Blumberg, "Americans Rate Jews Highest, Muslims Lowest, on Feeling Thermometer," *Huffington Post*, 15 February 2017, https://www.huffingtonpost.in/entry/americans-rate-jews-highest-muslims-lowest-on-feeling-thermometer_n_58a3579fe4b094a129ef90e9.

8 Environics, "Survey of Muslims in Canada 2016," April 2016, https://www.environicsinstitute.org/projects/project-details/survey-of-muslims-in-canada-2016#:~:text=Survey%20of%20Muslims%20in%20Canada, the%20respected%20Pew%20Research%20Center).

9 Pew Research Center, "U.S. Muslims Concerned about Their Place in Society," 26 July 2017, https://www.pewforum.org/2017/07/26/findings-from-pew-research-centers-2017-survey-of-us-muslims; Pew Research Center, "A Fragile Rebound for EU Image on Eve of European Parliament Elections," ch. 4, 12 May 2014.

10 Savanta ComRes, "BBC Radio 4 Today Muslim Poll," 25 February 2015, https://comresglobal.com/polls/bbc-radio-4-today-muslim-poll/.

11 Robert Brym, Keith Neuman, and Rhonda Lenton, *2018 Survey of Jews in Canada: Final Report* (Toronto: Environics Institute for Survey Research, University of Toronto, and York University, 2019); Charles Shahar and Tina Rosenblum, "Jewish Life in Greater Toronto: A Survey of the Attitudes and Behaviours of the Jewish Community of Greater Toronto" (Toronto: UJA Federation, 2005); Charles Shahar, "Jewish Life in Montreal: A Survey of the Attitudes, Beliefs and Behaviours of Montreal's Jewish Community" (Montreal: Fédération CJA, 2010).

12 Luis Lugo et al., "A Portrait of Jewish Americans," Religion and Public Life Project (Washington, DC: Pew Research Center, 2013).

13 David Graham, L.D. Staetsky, and Jonathan Boyd, "Jews in the United Kingdom in 2013" (London: Institute of Jewish Population Research, 2014).

14 Erik Cohen, *The Jews of France Today: Identity and Values* (Boston: Brill, 2011).

15 Daniel Staetsky, "Antisemitism in Contemporary Great Britain: Findings from the JPR Survey of Attitudes toward Jews and Israel" (London: Institute of Jewish Policy Research, September 2017).

16 Paul Lungen, "Six Jewish MPs Head to Ottawa," *Canadian Jewish News*, 10 November 2015, https://www.cjnews.com/news/canada/six-jewish-mps-head-to-ottawa; "List of Jewish Canadian Politicians, Wikipedia, accessed 24 May 2020, https://en.wikipedia.org/wiki/List_of_Jewish_Canadian_politicians.

17 Eric Bortelessa, "Almost 6% Percent of Congress Now Jewish," *Times of Israel*, 3 January 2017, https://www.timesofisrael.com/almost-6-of-congress-now-jewish-28-democrats-and-2-republicans; Jerry Lewis, "UK Parliament May Have Fewer Jewish MPs after Election," *Jerusalem Post*, 1 May 2015, https://www.jpost.com/diaspora/uk-parliament-may-have-fewer-jewish-mps-after-election-400773.

18 Morton Weinfeld, with Randal F. Schnoor and Michelle Shames, *Like Everyone Else but Different: The Paradoxical Success of Canadian Jews*. 2nd ed. (Montreal and Kingston: McGill-Queen's University Press, 2018), ch. 9.

19 Brym, Neuman, and Lenton, *2018 Survey of Jews in Canada: Final Report*, 5.

20 Harold Troper, *The Defining Decade: Identity, Polity, and the Canadian Jewish Community* (Toronto: University of Toronto Press, 2010).

21 Marshall Sklare, *Conservative Judaism: An American Religious Movement* (New York: Schocken, 1972).

2 Destination World Jewry: The United States versus the World

HASIA R. DINER

The theme posed by this volume can be thought of as both a question and a statement. As to the declaration of fact, Canada, for sure, provided a fine home for Jewish immigrants leaving to change the conditions of their lives in Europe during the great age of migration, which spanned the period from the mid-nineteenth century into the twentieth. It provided them with untrammelled freedom to find work, make a living, build families, and create the kinds of Jewish communities that they wanted. No one interfered with their practice of Judaism as a religious system, nor did Canadian authorities tell them that they could not form benevolent, educational, recreational, or cultural institutions that reflected the sensibilities of the Jews. They could, and did, publish newspapers, magazines, newsletters, broadsides, poetry, and novels in whatever language moved them. This culture of production reflected the will of the Jews only, and circulations depended upon what Jewish women and men wanted, and not on what some state official declared acceptable. This land, and its ten provinces, which eventually stretched from far out in the Atlantic to the Pacific, set up nearly no stumbling blocks to their participation in civil society, whether political, educational, or legal. Where the Jewish immigrants and, perhaps more importantly, their Canadian-born children, met limitations, those hurdles tended to flow from the actions of individuals who, for whatever reasons, resented or feared the influx of Jews into the social spaces that Christians defined as theirs. Those limitations rarely enjoyed the imprimatur of the state, and the Jews who chose Canada as their new home had little reason to see their migration decision as anything but positive.

As such, the more complex matter here involves the question of "no better home." Did Canada in fact offer the Jews of Europe, as they contemplated emigration, the best possible home? How can we historians measure the categories of "better" or "best"? Against what standards might we conceptualize this problem, given that "better" and "best" imply a comparison with something? What evidence can we marshal as a convincing yardstick to accept or reject the premise that no better home existed for modern Jews than Canada?

For one, "best" as a category of analysis needs to be considered around the matter of context and around the question, "best" for what? Any observer who considers the preservation of religious orthodoxy, whatever the faith tradition, to be most important, might conclude that a place where piety and strict observance of inherited practice flourish is best. The observer who believes that religions, like other cultural forms, should grow, shift, and change would not rank such a place very highly. "Best," as such, depends on the values of the one who measures, whether a professional historian or not.

Likewise, among Jewish historians, the question of "better" home raises the issue of Zionism and the comparison with the land that defines itself as a Jewish state. Did Canada provide a better home than Palestine in the early twentieth century as a possible place to which Jews could emigrate? What about after 1948 and the emergence of a sovereign Jewish state? For historians who write from a distinctly Zionist perspective, Canada could not be the Jews' better home. Contending that it was would stand as a rebuke to the Zionist idea of the "negation of the diaspora."

Jewish historians writing from Canada, as well as Canadian Jewish communal leaders, have waxed eloquently about Canada as a wonderful place. On one level, we cannot take the words of Canadian Jews – as individuals or as representatives of organized Canadian Jewish communal bodies – at their word that Canada constituted the best home possible. Not that they uttered words of gratitude to Canada, both before and after the Act of Confederation, insincerely. No doubt, the Jews who lived in Canada, who benefited from the opportunities involved in their transplantation from Europe – for the most part, a more fraught and limiting environment for the Jews – truly believed that Canada had been wonderful to them, even with moments here and there when they faced the hostility of some of their non-Jewish neighbours. Whether they lived in Montreal, Toronto, Calgary, Hamilton, Winnipeg, Vancouver, and even Moose Jaw, which provided a home for a small but vibrant Jewish community, they realized improvements in their lives, as compared to the experiences they had endured in Romania, Lithuania, Ukraine, Moldavia, Galicia, and the other regions and lands they left.

Yet words of gratitude and statements of no better home have coursed through Jewish history, as Jews understood themselves to be a minority living to varying degrees dependent on the goodwill of their non-Jewish host nations. Whether lauding Spain in the twelfth century or Germany in the early twentieth, Jews used the trope of gratitude as a survival strategy. Even when the Jews of these two places underwent their particular traumas of demonization, loss of status, brutality, or expulsion, they continued to look back to those places as the best possible home, until Spain or Germany changed radically for the worse. Gratitude for the disappeared golden age persisted in the Jewish imagination.

In modern Western democratic societies, of which Canada stands high, Jews endowed with full citizenship still offered words of gratitude. Never utterly convinced that the robust opportunity structure they enjoyed would really persist, the Jews of France, England, Australia, Canada, and the United States used moments in time, anniversaries, national holidays, and meetings with state officials, among others, to proclaim their gratitude and to thank the governments and the people for having provided them with the best possible home.

Understanding words of gratitude enunciated by a minority group for the country in which they live, and upon which they depend for rights and privileges, involves understanding the calculations determined by individuals and group leaders to serve as elements in a survival strategy. That rhetorical strategy, having been crafted in Sydney, London, Paris, New York, or Toronto, reflects both real fears and also sincere feelings of appreciation for the benefit of living in free, democratic societies.

Yet the matter of Canada's status as the Jews' best home, as the ideal spot in the world for Jews to live and make their homes, raises a host of analytic problems. Those problems do not, however, undermine the truth that the history of the Jews in Canada has been one of freedom, integration, access, and community and culture building. Canada must surely have been a much-desired spot on the world map that Jews in Europe contemplating emigration would have turned to it.

But, in fact, in the world of emigration communication – in the newspaper articles, the novels, the advice books published by immigration agencies, the broadsides, and other communiqués directing the attention of European Jews to "the new world" – Canada barely figured. Not that the place name never showed up, but in the vast compendium of words that circulated in the texts consumed by European Jews about possible new homes, Canada occupied a decidedly minor role. It loomed in only the most shadowy way in the Jewish imaginary in Europe.

Its minor status as a possible place to move to existed in the context of the reality that one place loomed large, larger than any place else. That place, the United States, captured the imagination of Jews since the late eighteenth century, as Yiddish and German fiction and nonfiction held up the word "America" as *the* place that would solve the

Jewish problem, for the Jews. Writers at the time, and historians since, have described how, as early as the 1820s, the Jews of Germany – and also non-Jews, importantly – succumbed to "America fever," a raging epidemic, as it were, that unmoored Europeans across the continent.

In the century of migration since the 1820s, more Europeans chose America than any place else. While we cannot dismiss the attractiveness of Argentina, Brazil, Australia, and Canada as magnets for immigrants, no place could compete with the United States, the world's largest receiver of newcomers. Its place at the top of the list involved not only numbers but also the duration of that migration flow and the diversity of the migration.

In this, Jews resembled all other Europeans. Over the course of the mass migration era, historians have estimated that one-third of all Jews left their homes and crossed some national border in order to find a new place to live. Of that one-third, over 80 per cent, possibly up to 90 per cent, chose the United States. The single-minded American focus actually makes Jewish immigration somewhat unique. Other people leaving their homes opted for a wider array of places, and while majorities still went to the United States, they did so less lopsidedly. Those men and women who left Italy, for example, chose South America, particularly Argentina, more often than the United States, while the largest number of Irish emigrants opted for the United Kingdom. In this context then, for Jews, Canada resembled France, England, and elsewhere in the British Isles, as well as Australia, South Africa, Argentina, Mexico, Cuba, and Palestine. Jewish emigrants who chose Canada over the United States, in other words, made an unusual migration choice. This fact, in turn, has numerous implications for thinking about Canada as the best home for the Jews.

Jews, again like all other immigrants, tended to migrate to places where they had family, friends, or other townspeople present, whether sons, fathers, husbands, daughters, or cousins who could provide information, links to employment, housing, and a community of kinship. Not having such a person in Canada essentially meant that the potential migrant would not choose it. Not only did chain migrations bring immigrants to a particular place, but the workings of this nearly universal system meant that they also kept immigrants away from that place.

Likewise, the more that Jews gravitated to the United States, the more the print culture and the flow of information went west to east, further exposing Jews in Europe to America – but almost nowhere else. Whether the Yiddish press or other kinds of texts, they focused on America, New York in particular, and that emerged as the lodestone for European Jews.

Additionally, as the United States took off in the mid-nineteenth century as the most dynamic economy in the world, American government agencies actively marketed the United States to white people in myriad places as a nation of immigrants, and an ideal destination. Directly and indirectly, the message beamed from America – a land always hungering for labour for the fields, mines, forests, workshops, and factories to produce the food, fuel, lumber, and finished products that people around the world consumed – that it wanted immigrants.

The economic take-off of the United States provided the foundation for its immigrant history. It, like Canada, had a vast land mass, but unlike its neighbour to the north, whose territory included massive amounts of uninhabitable and undevelopable land, every place in the United States could be settled and exploited for the purposes of making a profit. Both countries, we must remember, expanded and made use of the land to the tremendous detriment of native peoples, and both engaged in campaigns to push those people, the rightful possessors of the land, to the margins.

The fact that Canada did not take off economically until Great Britain essentially allowed it to, meant that the faraway colonial power controlled its destiny. It did so in ways that benefited the "mother country" first, and that meant that the United States, with its seemingly limitless resources, controlled its own economic destiny for much longer. Having liberated itself from England in the eighteenth century, for better or for worse, meant that no other country with its own economic agenda determined what could be done and by whom.

Economic possibilities mattered most, but imagery and rhetoric also played a role in shaping migration choices. No Canadian symbol or image could remotely compete with the power, for example, of the Statue of Liberty, which went up in New York's harbour in 1886. Despite its origins, which had nothing to do with immigration and the complicated and often hostile conversation in America about immigration, the words eventually emblazoned on its base, "send me your tired, your poor," did in fact electrify Europeans and others with knowledge that this place, the United States, offered them something incomparable, and something against which Canada could not compete. This held for Jews no less than for Italians, Greeks, Hungarians, Swedes, Norwegians, Lithuanians, and so on. The United States, not Canada, drew them.

Furthermore, although the figures are elusive, we know that many of the Jews who went to non-American destinations (Australia and South Africa excluded) chose those places so that they could leapfrog from there to the United States. The flow outward of Jewish immigrants from England, Germany, Ireland, Cuba, Mexico, Palestine, and Canada to the United States made those places "corridor" communities, places of transmigration. This corridor migration pattern persisted beyond the 1920s and the era of global immigration restriction. After the 1920s, a brisk dynamic of illegal Jewish immigration to the United States took off, and Jews entered Mexico, Cuba, and Canada in order to slip across the border, the northern one in particular not effectively controlled. Of the Jews seeking to leave Central Europe with the rise of Nazism as their motivation, most put the United States first on their list of desirable destinations, but went elsewhere, anywhere, when the doors to America remained shut to most. Likewise, after the Holocaust, Jewish aid organizations working in the displaced persons camps in Germany, Austria, and Italy reported that most of the survivors wanted the United States. As the Jews of the Soviet Union and other eastern bloc countries began to request permission to emigrate, they indicated that they hoped to go to the United States. They did not consider Canada a bad option, but they likely did not know much about it. The United States was the place they really wanted to go. The fact that the United States was a place where they had relatives and friends, that they knew much about through Jewish or general popular culture sources, and that they, rightly, believed to be a place of powerful economic possibilities for white people mattered as they made their choices. They could not always fulfil their wishes, but the wish had been there, to go to America.

Beyond America's economic lure for those Jews of Europe who sought out new homes in new lands, the power of the United States, the hegemon to the south, also shaped Canadian Jewish life. The power wielded by US Jewry as it dominated the Jewish scene may or may not have lessened the attractiveness of Canada. But the fact remains that on an institutional level, Canadian Jews lived in an American orbit.

Certainly that can be seen in the religious sphere. For the most part, Canadian rabbis, except for those trained in Europe, had studied and graduated from an institution in the United States. Particularly those who had attended the Hebrew Union College in Cincinnati (and then New York and Los Angeles) and the Jewish Theological Seminary of America received training at schools committed to a specifically American project. These rabbis then joined rabbinical bodies called, if Reform, the Central Conference of American Rabbis. If Conservative, their congregations belonged to the United Synagogue of America, its name even taking on the letters U.S.A., and as such boldly proclaiming its bond with the nation. Reform congregations, whether south or north of the border, affiliated with the Union of American Hebrew Congregations, and that body, like its Conservative counterpart, clearly felt no need to change the name to reflect the active membership of their Canadian peers. The Canadians, presumably, had to just live within bodies that did not put them on an equal footing and that existed deeply entwined in American life.

Likewise, Canadian Jews, particularly the eastern European immigrants who settled in Toronto and Montreal and worked in the garment trade as sewing machine operators, pressers, cutters, and finishers, participated in the labour movement, and, like their fellow and sister Jews in the United States, embraced unionization. But those who worked in the Canadian factories joined unions founded in the United States: the International Ladies' Garment Workers' Union and the Amalgamated Clothing Workers Unions. These unions welcomed Canadian members, but they maintained headquarters not in Ontario or Quebec but in New York. Union officials shuttled back and forth across the border when it came time for contract negotiations and during strikes, but the centre held in the United States.

This American-centredness of Canadian Jewish history cannot be brushed aside. The history of Canadian Jewry, for all its powerful tropes of freedom, acceptance, cultural creativity, and religious commitment, has to be analysed with an eye to the United States. But the reverse has not been the case.

American Jewish historians, those who have focused on the experience of Jews in the United States, whether writing about politics, culture, religion, labour, or any other aspect of the past, have had for the most part nearly nothing to say about Canada. Not to cast doubt on the excellence of their work, but they have focused only on the United States, recognizing their need to also contemplate Europe and the places Jews left. American Jewish historians have likewise looked to Europe and other places where Jews faced extreme difficulties. They have had to think about the distress of Jews in Romania, Russia, Poland, Germany, and the Ottoman Empire, among others, because American Jewish politics took some of its shape from the advocacy undertaken by American Jews for their co-religionists abroad. So in the period after 1948 it has been impossible to fully contemplate American Jewish history without figuring in events in the Middle East, in Israel, and in neighbouring lands. But, essentially, this history has had no place for Canada.

That the narratives constructed about American Jewish history have managed to ignore Canada does not take away from the reality that Canada did provide a comfortable locus for the creation of commodious homes for Jews, and offered them an environment in which they could work and make a living, acquire citizenship, and obtain access to political participation and educational opportunities. Canada certainly offered them a better home than the various ones they had left. That, however, does not mean that of the other places Jews went – the United States in particular – immigrants to Canada did better by choosing Canada.

3 "To Guarantee Their Own Self-Government in All Matters of Their National Life": Ukrainians, Jews, and the Origins of Canadian Multiculturalism

JEFFREY VEIDLINGER

My parents have a country home in Milton, about 60 kilometres west of Toronto. When we were kids we would spend the entire month of August up there, as well as occasional weekends throughout the year, and often the week of Passover. My brother, sister, and I spent much of our time hanging out with the neighbour kids, Mischa and Sasha Skoropad. I didn't know it at the time, but their last name hinted at a distinguished descent from Ukrainian nobility. Their father was the son of a Ukrainian immigrant who had fled the Bolshevik Revolution and took great pride in his heritage. He was a veterinarian who grew up with horses and raced his champion thoroughbreds at the Mohawk Racetrack not too far from our country home. By contrast, the only story I ever heard my parents tell about horses was when my father talked about how the Nazis turned his synagogue into a stable, back in Budapest.

Yet, here in Canada, my parents – the immigrant son of a Hungarian businessman and the daughter of a Polish shtetl rabbi – had managed to acquire a farm, whose wheat fields adjoined the grazing grounds of a scion of Cossack heritage. Over winter breaks at our country home, we celebrated Christmas with the Skoropads; in late February, we would all put on our skis and go into the woods to tap the maple trees; and in spring, during Passover, Mischa and Sasha would share our matzah, which tasted great dipped in fresh maple syrup. This personal story of inter-ethnic neighbourliness exemplifies to me Canada's modern identity of a multicultural mosaic – different ethnicities sharing their distinct cultures with each other while integrating new Canadian rituals into their lives. It is emblematic of the ways in which the ethos of multiculturalism has helped make Canada a welcoming place for many Jews.

Yet, as much as multiculturalism has contributed to forging a Canadian identity, it can also trace its origins in large part to the particular politics of Jewish life in early twentieth-century Ukraine. In this chapter, I argue that multiculturalism as a government policy emerged precisely in the interchange between Jewish and Ukrainian Canadians. It was a concept introduced to Canada in the 1960s by Ukrainian Canadians, who, in turn, adapted it from the notion of "national autonomy" that Jews had introduced to early twentieth-century Ukraine, where Jews were conscious of securing rights as a minority group within a largely binational (Russian and Ukrainian) state. Ironically, when multiculturalism made it to Canada in its new form, it was met with scepticism and even outright rejection by the organized Canadian Jewish community of the era.

On 8 October 1971, Canadian Prime Minister Pierre Elliott Trudeau announced that "a policy of multiculturalism within a bilingual framework commends itself to the government as the most suitable means of assuring cultural freedom of Canadians."[1] The promulgation of multiculturalism as an official policy of the Canadian government was the result of a nearly decade-long nationwide conversation about the nature of Canadian identity. It was a conversation that began as a response to nationalist unrest in Quebec and was stimulated by the Royal Commission on Bilingualism and Biculturalism, established by Prime Minister Lester B. Pearson in 1963. The conclusions of the Royal Commission led to the enactment of the 1969 Official Languages Act, the 1973 creation of a Ministry of Multiculturalism and a Canadian Consultative Council of Multiculturalism, and eventually to the 1988 Canadian Multiculturalism Act, which asserts that "multiculturalism is a fundamental characteristic of the Canadian heritage and identity" and "an invaluable resource in the shaping of Canada's future."[2]

Members of the Ukrainian Canadian community were the most vocal supporters of multiculturalism, offering it as an alternative to the notion of biculturalism, which they argued privileged English and French Canadians while marginalizing the "Third Element," the growing number of Canadians – constituting about a third of the population – whose roots were found neither in Anglo-Saxon nor French ethnicity.[3] Jean Chrétien, serving as Minister of Indian Affairs as the Royal Commission wrapped up its work, had similarly critiqued the commission for failing to sufficiently recognize the aboriginal peoples of Canada. His 1969 White Paper (Statement of the Government of Canada on Indian Policy) recommending the elimination of Indian Status and the granting of full and equal citizenship to the people of the First Nations was broadly rejected by the National Indian Brotherhood and other representatives of the First Nations on the grounds that it would require the First Nations to relinquish their distinct identity:

"Indians have aspirations, hopes and dreams, but becoming white men is not one of them," wrote the Cree lawyer and scholar Harold Cardinal in his influential *The Unjust Society*.[4] Canada's national minorities – its Third Element – rejected Chrétien's offer of full and equal citizenship as an invitation to complete assimilation.

However, it was, in fact, the objection of Ukrainian Canadians, who protested the notion of bilingualism for turning all but the French and the English into second-class citizens, that impelled a rethinking of the meaning of Canadian national identity and most directly challenged the Royal Commission on Bilingualism and Biculturalism.[5] Jarolsav B. Rudnyckyj, the Ukrainian linguist and Chair of the Department of Slavic Studies at the University of Manitoba whom Lester Pearson appointed to the Royal Commission, proposed an amendment to section 133 of the British North America Act, for instance, advocating that "regional languages" be given official recognition.[6] Ukrainian Canadian lobbying on the issue is one of the reasons Trudeau chose to launch his multicultural initiative at the Tenth Congress of the Ukrainian Canadian Committee in Winnipeg the day after his 8 October speech to Parliament. The Ukrainian vision of multiculturalism was further cemented with the appointment of the Canadian-born ethnic Ukrainian Norman Cafik as Minister of Multiculturalism in 1977.

The most important architect of Canadian "multiculturalism," though, was Paul Yuzyk, Professor of Russian and Soviet History at the University of Ottawa and later a Canadian senator. It was Yuzyk who first introduced the term "multiculturalism" to Parliament in his maiden speech on the Senate floor on 3 March 1964. In a speech rife with census data, Yuzyk criticized the recently created Royal Commission: "First of all," he declared, "the word 'bicultural,' which I do not find in any dictionary, is a misnomer. In reality Canada never was bicultural ... Canada has become multicultural." According to the 1961 Canada Census, just over half of the 18 million residents of Canada traced their ethnic roots to France (5.5 million) or the British Isles (4.2 million English, 1.9 million Scottish, and 1.8 million Irish). The remaining population, the "Third Element," consisted mostly of other Europeans, with 470,000 Ukrainians constituting the largest group after Germans. Canadian policy, Yuzyk argued, should reflect this demographic reality: "The Third Element ethnic or cultural groups should receive the status of co-partners who would be guaranteed the right to perpetuate their mother tongues and cultures, which should be offered as optional subjects in the public and high school systems and the separate schools of the provinces, and the universities."[7]

Yuzyk, who was born in Canada to Ukrainian parents, likely derived much of his thinking about multiculturalism from his studies of Ukrainian history, where these ideas of national autonomy were first implemented. Yuzyk would later outline a series of specific proposals for advancing multiculturalism, including the inauguration of multicultural grants in support of cultural exchanges, youth activities and multicultural centres, and requirements that federal cultural agencies such as the National Film Board, Public Archives, and the Canadian Broadcasting Corporation "enable all Canadians to gain an awareness of the cultural heritage of all of Canada's ethnic groups."[8] Most importantly, he advocated that minority languages be offered in regional schools as accredited courses and saw language as integral for the maintenance and continued production of national culture and for the preservation and practice of religion.

Although Yuzyk rarely spoke of multiculturalism as a by-product of the short-lived Ukrainian state that arose in the aftermath of the Russian Revolutions, he did note on the occasion of Ukrainian Independence Day in 1969 that "the Ukrainian National Republic was a modern state modelled upon those of the western world. It recognized the highest principles of democracy ... All minorities, including the Jews, were granted 'national personal' autonomy and representation in the government. The Ukrainian National Republic ... has much in common with Canada."[9] But Yuzyk's notion of multiculturalism remained exclusionary in important ways. He concluded his famous maiden speech on multiculturalism with the admonition: "Fundamentally, we are a Christian and democratic nation. Let us therefore not forget that all men are born in the image of God."[10]

It was in part in recognition that multiculturalism as envisioned by Yuzyk and others was premised on a common Christianity that led some Jews to reject the policy. "Multiculturalism corrupts our ethnic groups and certainly debases the political coinage of our nation," declared the prominent Jewish CBC commentator Larry Zolf. "I don't need a multiculturalism grant to be Jewish," he asserted in *Maclean's* magazine.[11] Although Zolf was not speaking on behalf of the Jewish community, he was one of the most prominent Jewish voices in the Canadian media. Organizations that did represent the Jewish community of Canada, though, were equally suspicious of the process. The Jewish Labour Committee, for instance, argued that French and English must continue to be Canada's only official languages, and rejected official multilingualism.[12] Saul Hayes, the executive director of the Canadian Jewish Congress, also opposed the policy. He hoped that the Royal

Commission would state "once and for all and no nonsense about it, that Canada is a partnership of two founding races."[13] The official Jewish community had learned how to navigate itself between these two "founding races" and Hayes was concerned that a splintering of power would diffuse the ability of Jews to intercede and lobby with the government. Hayes also recognized that Jews were accorded a respected status as a minority religious faith in the country and had secured a place for themselves behind Canada's Catholic and Protestant communities. If Canadian identity came to be regarded primarily in terms of ethnicity rather than religious faith, he feared, the Jews would become just one of dozens of ethnicities, behind Poles, Ukrainians, Scandinavians, and a growing number of other immigrant groups.[14] Hayes's position was supported by the same census data that Yuzyk drew upon. In 1961, 173,000 Canadians identified as Jews when asked their ethnicity, constituting 1 per cent of the total population of Canada. However, when asked to identify themselves by religion, 254,000 Canadians identified themselves as Jewish.[15] Eighty thousand Canadians – one-third of the Jewish population – identified themselves as members of the Jewish faith but not the Jewish ethnicity. Multiculturalism, then, by privileging ethnic identity over religious faith, threatened to diminish the portion of the overall population that would be counted as Jewish.

Indeed, for the most part Canadian Jews abstained from celebrating multiculturalism during its formative period. The *Canadian Jewish News*, for instance, largely ignored the debates on multiculturalism that so dominated other minority papers in the early 1970s, and instead focused its coverage on the politics of Jewish issues abroad – the Arab-Israeli conflict, Jewish life in Israel, and the campaign to save Soviet Jewry. Jewish Canadians tended to look outward towards Zionism for expressions of their national identity, or closed themselves inwardly, developing an insular society with low rates of intermarriage and a high level of institutional engagement with their own internal religious and cultural institutions. Before the advent of multiculturalism, Jews did not see themselves as an intricate part of the Canadian mosaic, but rather held themselves apart from it.[16]

In the 1960s, Canada was still structured along sectarian lines. Nowhere was this more evident than in the system of parochial schools in Ontario and Quebec. Education, religion, and culture were already woven into the fabric of institutional culture. In postwar Quebec, where a distinctly Jewish and Yiddish enclave emerged, national awareness, particularly around the twin roots of language and religion, was already heightened by Quebec separatism.[17] Unable to integrate into

Quebec society, which was contingent upon religion and language, the Jews of Montreal established a "third solitude." As historian Gerald Tulchinsky writes, the Jewish community of early twentieth-century Montreal "evolved a collective identity and a series of adaptive strategies for socio-cultural and economic survival" by becoming "in fact almost a separate community, one as distinct by its culture, institutions, legal status, self-perception, public image, and even in geographical location and economic activity, as either of the other two."[18] This phenomenon was perhaps most acute in Montreal, but also to a lesser degree characterized the Jewish communities of Toronto, Winnipeg, and Halifax. Jewish institutions – schools, theatres, libraries, musical societies, mutual aid societies, and advocacy groups – were well established and well supported throughout areas of Canada with significant Jewish populations. This institutional autonomy helped the community coalesce and retain a distinct identity.

In effect, Jewish Canadians were already effectively preserving their cultural, linguistic, and religious identities before the advent of multiculturalism. They had managed to establish a surrogate identity within their close-knit communities through autonomous institutions, a practice Jews had honed in East Central Europe. Ruth Wisse, a Canadian-born scholar of Yiddish and Jewish life, noted that in Europe, Jews "shaped literature in Yiddish, and to a lesser extent Hebrew, into an expression and instrument of national cohesion that would help to compensate the Jews for the absence of such staples of nationhood as political independence and territorial sovereignty."[19] Nowhere was this type of national cohesion achieved more completely than in Ukraine, during its brief period of independence.

Jews and Ukrainians have been living side by side for a thousand years.[20] Ukraine was the heartland of the Pale of Jewish Settlement, the area to which Jewish residence in the Russian Empire was restricted. It was the birthplace of the Hasidic movement and of Yiddish theatre, of Golda Meir and of Leon Trotsky. The Yiddish writer Sholem Aleichem was born there as were the Hebrew writer Haim Nahman Bialik and the Russian writer Isaac Babel. In other words, modern Jewish culture and politics – in Yiddish, Hebrew, and Russian – began, in large part, in Ukraine. But Jews and Ukrainians lived parallel lives in the homeland. They were truly, as Canadians would say, two solitudes.

Jews had been forcibly separated from Ukrainians, in part by the infamous May Laws of 1882, which forbade Jews from residing in rural areas where they could corrupt Ukrainian Christian peasants. Those laws, incidentally, were put into place by the antisemitic and fiercely xenophobic Russian minister of the interior, Nikolai Ignatiev. It is another irony of history that Ignatiev's great grandson, Michael, would become leader of the Liberal Party of Canada. The Ignatievs fled the Russian Revolution, landing in England in 1919, and in Canada a few years later. Today, Canada has the largest population of Ukrainians outside of Ukraine and Russia, with about 3 million people identifying themselves as having Ukrainian heritage, constituting almost 10 per cent of the Canadian population. They were fleeing from the same towns and villages that served as the birthplace of many Jewish immigrants to Canada.

Ukraine before the Russian Revolutions of 1917 was a multicultural society *avant la lettre*. Since the eighteenth-century partitions of the Polish-Lithuanian Commonwealth, the territory was divided into two parts: Western Ukraine, including Galicia and Bukovina, was under a moderately tolerant Austro-Hungarian state, and the rest of Ukraine was under Russian rule and subject to strict policies of russification, the promotion of Russian language and culture to the exclusion of other cultures. In both regions, Jews, ethnic Ukrainians, Poles, Germans, and Russians shared the territory, sometimes in peaceful coexistence, and sometimes – particularly in moments of war and revolutionary outbreak – in violent opposition to each other. It was in this climate, both in Austrian Galicia and Bukovina and in the Russian Pale of Jewish Settlement, that some of the most innovative ideas about living within a multinational state were formulated, theorized, and, after the collapse of the tsarist empire, enacted. Ukraine's Jewish population played an integral role in working out these ideas. They experimented with their implementation and lived with the consequences.

The pogroms of 1881 famously shocked the Jews of Ukraine into reassessing the role of Jews in national life. Writing in Odessa in 1882, in response to the pogroms and to Ignatiev's May Laws, the assimilated physician Leo Pinsker penned his "Autoemancipation," arguing that it is futile for the Jews of the world to wait for emancipation to be granted to them from the state. Jews needed to emancipate themselves by recognizing their own status as a nation: "Since the Jew is nowhere at home, nowhere regarded as a native, he remains an alien everywhere," Pinsker wrote. The problem with the process of emancipation as it was taking place in France and Western Europe, Pinsker continued, was that Jews were emancipated only as individuals not as a nation. The solution to antisemitism, he believed, was the recognition of Jews as a nation: "The proper, the only solution, is in the creation of a Jewish nationality," he wrote, "of a people living upon its own soil, the auto-emancipation of the Jews; their return to the ranks of the nations by the acquisition of a Jewish homeland."[21]

Pinsker's call for "autoemancipation" and the acquisition of a Jewish homeland became a rallying cry for the Hovevei Zion (Lovers of Zion) movement, the forerunners of the Zionist movement. These thinkers advocated that Jews were not just a religious sect, but rather were a nation of their own, and should be recognized as such. It was this assertion that Jews could best be identified as a nation rather than as a religion that formed the basis of the Zionist challenge to rabbinical Judaism. Pinsker's followers ascribed to the contemporary European understanding that every nation should have its own state. Some of his followers advocated the establishment of a Jewish national state in Palestine; others sought the establishment of Jewish territorial sovereignty in the diaspora.

In the large multinational Russian and Austro-Hungarian empires, though, some theorists began to challenge the notion that each nation should have its own state altogether, both on practical and theoretical grounds. These thinkers agreed with the Zionist definition of the Jews as a nation rather than a religion, but they rejected the maximalist Zionist call for territorial sovereignty in a nation-state where they would be protected by physical borders. Instead, they tried to envision a world in which different nationalities would live together, each expressing their own national ideas and cultures and each possessing their own autonomous institutions under the umbrella of a common multinational state structure. Those who believed such a society could be realized in the absence of territorial statehood became known as Autonomists.

The most prominent among Jewish Autonomists was the Belorussian-born historian and public intellectual Simon Dubnov, who in 1906 helped found the Jewish Socialist Labour Party (SERP), known for its endorsement of Jewish national-cultural autonomy as part of its political platform. In his "Letters on Old and New Judaism," published in the Russian-language Jewish journal Voskhod between 1897 and 1907, Dubnov set out a system for preserving national identity and autonomy within the Jewish diaspora. Drawing from historical precedent, he showed that minorities often functioned better in multinational empires, where a federal government managed external affairs and the overall economy, but allowed for broad cultural autonomy for minority groups. Dubnov believed that the civil rights granted to Jews by the French Revolution had forced the Jews to give up their distinct identity and their autonomous institutions, and had thereby led to the disintegration of the Jewish community. By giving up their own separate legal existence and cultural peculiarities, he maintained, Jewish communities of Western Europe had relinquished their communal identities and their very essence. They had been emancipated, but only as individuals, not as a nation. It was a dubious achievement they had reached by surrendering what it meant to be a Jew. By arguing that if Jews simply gave up their different dress, different language, different diet, and different legal system, they could become fully integrated as Jews into the French state, the French National Assembly and the Society of Jewish Notables had made a terrible mistake. It was these differences, Dubnov believed, that made Jews Jews. Judaism to Dubnov was not merely a confession, a creed, that one adheres to in private, but rather a public affirmation of community; it was an identity inseparable from the individual. To Dubnov, it was precisely a specific Jewish culture – language, cuisine, holiday observance, music, and dress – that constituted the essence of Judaism. To give up these identity markers and adopt French culture, or any other culture, would be to deny one's own identity. And it was this type of self-denial, Dubnov continued, this inability to fit in, that ultimately led to antisemitism.

Dubnov instead modelled his vision of national autonomy on an idealized version of the early modern Council of Four Lands in the Polish-Lithuanian Commonwealth, in which Jewish leaders held their own quasi-parliament to enact legislation and to adjudicate intercommunal disputes. Dubnov contended that the Council of Four Lands, which was often criticized as functioning as a state within a state, allowed the Jews of Poland to administer their own cultural, legal, educational, and religious affairs while acting as members of a multinational empire in the political sphere. Full political emancipation, Dubnov contended, could not exist without recognition of collective national rights.

Dubnov was certainly not the only thinker of his time and place to advocate for national rights within a larger collective. His celebration of national autonomy mirrored in many ways the national position of the Jewish Bund, which broke from the Russian Social Democratic parties in the belief that Marxism could best be communicated to the masses through their own languages. The Bund subscribed to the economic policies of the Russian Social Democrats, but championed Yiddish language and culture and refused to accept the argument that economic solidarity of the working classes cannot coexist with the recognition and celebration of the national distinctions and cultural differences among the members of the proletariat.

But Dubnov went one step further than the Bund, seeking genuine recognition of Jews as what Canadians today would call "a distinct society." "For the Bundists," he wrote, "the essence of Jewishness is only an ethnic or folk quality, not national-cultural ... They talk of the right to self-determination and even of national-cultural autonomy among the principles of universal freedom, but they do not care for the concrete development of national Jewish culture, for the organization of autonomous communities, or for national education, as a shield against assimilation."[22] Dubnov and his followers instead sought national rights on the basis of communal autonomy. They sought recognition, in his words, "of our national rights, such as communal self-government and cultural autonomy."[23] Practically, this ideal translated into a program that demanded public accommodation for Jewish religious observance, state-sponsored schools that would teach in the Yiddish language, but also teach a Jewish curriculum of Jewish history and Jewish culture (Dubnov even designed a textbook to be used in these parochial schools), and Jewish communal organizations with tax-collecting rights. Some in Dubnov's party imagined recognition of the Yiddish language as an official state language, which would give individuals the right not only to communicate with each other in Yiddish but also to petition the government in Yiddish, go to court in Yiddish, and draw up legally enforceable contracts in Yiddish.[24]

It may seem inconceivable that such a plan could have been put into place in early twentieth-century Ukraine. Yet it was. After the Revolution of 1917, a Ukrainian government, known as the Rada (the Council) came into being on the premise of the principle of national autonomy.[25] In its Third Universal, issued in November 1917, the Rada proclaimed: "Without separating from Russia, without breaking with the Russian state, let the Ukrainian people have the right to manage its own life on its own soil." Ukraine was seeking recognition of Ukraine as "a nation within a united Russia," prefiguring Stephen Harper's recognition of Quebec as a "nation within a united Canada." The new Ukrainian government also embraced the rights of national minorities within Ukraine. The Third Universal continued: "The Great Russian, Jewish, Polish and other peoples in Ukraine are granted national-personal autonomy to guarantee their own self-government in all matters of their national life." A Jewish Secretariat and later a Ministry of Jewish Affairs were established to regulate Jewish life and provide for equal access to education and government benefits for Jews. The government even printed its own currency with the denomination spelled out in Ukrainian, Polish, and Yiddish. It was a brief moment of multicultural collaboration.[26]

The type of national autonomy the Rada espoused did not translate well into the New World, where membership in the nation was predicated on civic participation rather than ethnic identity. In the United States, in particular, ethnic minorities were expected to meld into the "melting pot," a metaphor made famous by Israel Zangwill's 1908 play of that name. Zangwill, a British Jewish activist and strong advocate of Jewish national autonomy in Ukraine, had seen in America the possibility of complete assimilation and the effacement of all ethnic and national identities. This notion was accepted by some as an American ideal, but countered by others, including some within the American Jewish community. President of the American Jewish Committee Louis Marshall, for instance, argued that instead of eliminating cultural distinctness, Americans should seek to "preserve the best elements that constitute the civilization we are all seeking, the civilization of universal brotherhood."[27] In his influential 1924 essay "Culture and the Ku Klux Klan," the American Jewish educator Horace Kallen wrote of what he called "cultural pluralism" as an antidote to the "melting pot." In his 1915 article, "Democracy versus the Melting Pot: A Study of American Nationality," Kallen depicted an American Jewish community living an autonomous existence, possessing its own parochial schools, mutual aid societies, communal structures, and institutions.[28] Kallen and Marshall's vision was also embraced by Mordechai Kaplan, the founder of Reconstructionist Judaism, who argued that Judaism "is unthinkable apart from Jewish group life ... for Judaism to be at all possible, the Jews must live in aggregates that can exercise some form of autonomy."[29]

Within the Americas, the promise of cultural pluralism was more applicable to Canada, particularly in the post–Second World War era, after the country came to embrace John Murray Gibbon's 1938 vision of the "Canadian Mosaic" as an antidote to the melting pot. In postwar Canada, each nationality was encouraged to retain its own distinct identity while contributing to the nation as a whole.[30] Without the American pressure to assimilate, Jews in Canada were able to replicate the system of national autonomy that had characterized East-Central European modes of Jewish life.

Dubnov and like-minded Jewish and Ukrainian intellectuals had devised a version of what Canadian philosopher Charles Taylor would later call "a politics of difference."[31] They sought for Jews to be recognized as a distinct society within the larger polity while retaining their individual rights as citizens of the state. In Taylor's terms they believed that "political society is not neutral between those who value remaining true to the culture of our ancestors and those who might want to cut loose in the name of some individual goal of self-development."[32] Will Kymlicka, another Canadian scholar of multiculturalism, would summarize this idea by noting that "the demand for official recognition needn't take the form of a secessionist movement for a separate state."[33] Kymlicka famously argued that "a comprehensive theory of justice in a multinational state will include both universal rights, assigned to individuals regardless of group membership and group-differentiated rights or 'special status' for minority cultures."[34] This notion could just as easily have been spoken by Dubnov and the Jewish Autonomists.

The importance of distinct cultural values in the global age has been theorized by a variety of thinkers, many of whom – not coincidentally – are Canadian or Israeli-born. Columbia University Professor of Law Joseph Raz, who received his Magister Juris at the Hebrew University of Jerusalem in 1963, for instance, has written, "If culture, in its widest sense, is what holds a nation together and preserves it as separate from others, then the existence of a nation as a distinct social unit is contingent on the presence of a public sphere where the national culture is expressed, where an individual feels free to 'develop without repression those aspects of his personality which are bound up with his sense of identity as a member of his community."[35] Similarly, in her *Liberal Nationalism*, Israeli former Knesset member and Minister of Immigrant Absorption Yael (Yuli) Tamir notes that "this demand for a public sphere in which the cultural aspects of national life come to the fore constitutes the essence of the right to national self-determination. This right is to be distinguished from the right to self-rule, which is the right to take part in the political institutions that govern one's life."[36]

All these theorists echo, in many ways, the demands made by Dubnov's Autonomists and Cardinal's "'unjust society." They demand what Taylor terms a "space for recognition,"[37] a sphere in which individuals are recognized not only as individuals, but also as members of those groups with which they identify. "Understanding nationalism in terms of a 'call to difference' allows for a great variety of different responses," writes Taylor.[38]

The 1988 Canadian Multiculturalism Act, which recognizes the "cultural and racial diversity of Canadian society and acknowledges the freedom of all members of Canadian society to preserve, enhance and share their cultural heritage,"[39] could very well have come out of one of the Ukrainian Universals or the debates around national autonomy that raged in the Ukrainian Rada in 1918. In Ukraine, though, those declarations ultimately failed. The multicultural Rada collapsed and the Minister of Jewish Affairs quit in the face of pogroms that would ultimately kill about a hundred thousand Jews throughout Ukraine. Hundreds of thousands of survivors fled Ukraine to Munich, Berlin, Vienna, and Paris. Many ultimately ended up in America's melting pot. But those who made it to Canada probably felt more at home in the Canadian mosaic, where the wheat fields, politics of national recognition, and language laws, would come to echo their own experiences back home. Canadian multiculturalism in practice may not have lived up to its ideals, but its resilience as a national myth and its enduring popular support stand as a testament to the contributions of both Ukrainian and Jewish Canadians and demonstrate the ways in which the Jewish politics of early twentieth-century Ukraine are reflected in contemporary Canada.[40]

NOTES

1 Hugh Donal Forbes, "Trudeau as the First Theorist of Canadian Multiculturalism," in *Multiculturalism and the Canadian Constitution*, ed. Stephen J. Tierney (Vancouver: University of British Columbia Press, 2007), 27.
2 Canadian Multiculturalism Act R.S.C. 1985, c. 24 (4th Supp.).
3 Bohdan Bociurkiw, "The Federal Policy of Multiculturalism and the Ukrainian-Canadian Community," in *Ukrainian Canadian, Multiculturalism, and Separatism*, ed. Manoly Rupert Lupul (Edmonton: University of Alberta Press, 1978).
4 Harold Cardinal, *The Unjust Society: The Tragedy of Canada's Indians* (Edmonton: Hurtig, 1969).
5 Julia Lalande, "The Roots of Multiculturalism – Ukrainian-Canadian Involvement in the Multiculturalism Discussion of the 1960s as an Example of the Position of the 'Third Force,'" *Canadian Ethnic Studies* 38, no. 1 (2006): 47–64.
6 Michael Temilini, "Multicultural Rights, Multicultural Virtues: A History of Multiculturalism in Canada," in *Multiculturalism and the Canadian Constitution*, ed. Stephen J. Tierny (Vancouver: UBC Press, 2008), 53.
7 Paul Yuzyk, *For a Better Canada* (Toronto: Ukrainian National Association, 1973), 21–48.
8 Ibid., 105
9 Ibid., 212.
10 Ibid., 48.
11 Cited in Isydore Hlynka, *The Other Canadians: Selected Articles from the Column of "Ivan Harmata" Published in the "Ukrainian Voice"* (Winnipeg: Trident Press, 1981), 58.
12 Gerald Tulchinsky, *Canada's Jews: A People's Journey* (Toronto: University of Toronto Press, 2008), 448.
13 Cited in Harold Troper, *The Defining Decade: Identity, Politics, and the Canadian Jewish Community in the 1960s* (Toronto: University of Toronto Press, 2010), 71.
14 Ibid., 70–2.
15 1961 Census of Canada, accessed 25 June 2020, http://publications.gc.ca/collections/collection_2017/statcan/CS92-521-1961.pdf.

16   Michael Brown, "From Binationalism to Multiculturalism to the Open
     Society: The Impact on Canadian Jews," *Jerusalem Center for Public Affairs*, 16
     July 2006, http://jcpa.org/article/from-binationalism-to-multiculturalism-
     to-the-open-society-the-impact-on-canadian-jews/; Michael Brown, "A
     Case of Limited Vision: Jabotinsky on Canada and the United States,"
     Canadian Jewish Studies 1 (1993): 1–25.
17   See Rebecca Margolis, *Jewish Roots, Canadian Soil: Yiddish Cultural Life in
     Montreal, 1905–1945* (Montreal and Kingston: McGill-Queen's University
     Press, 2011).
18   Gerald Tulchinsky, "The Third Solitude: A.M. Klein's Jewish Montreal,
     1910–1950," *Journal of Canadian Studies* 19, no. 2 (Summer 1984): 96. For an-
     other use of the term, see Michael Greenstein, *Third Solitudes: Tradition and
     Discontinuity in Jewish-Canadian Literature* (Montreal and Kingston: McGill-
     Queen's University Press, 1989).
19   Ruth R. Wisse, *I. L. Peretz and the Making of Modern Jewish Culture* (Seattle
     and London: University of Washington Press, 1991), xiii.
20   For a recent reminder of the coexistence between Jews and Ukrainians see
     Paul Robert Magocsi and Yohanan Petrovsky-Shtern, *Jews and Ukrainians:
     A Millennium of Co-Existence* (Toronto: University of Toronto Press, 2016).
21   Leon Pinkser, "Auto-Emancipation," 1882, https://www.jewishvirtuallibrary
     .org/quot-auto-emancipation-quot-leon-pinsker.
22   Simon Dubnow, *Nationalism and History: Essays on Old and New Judaism*
     (Philadelphia: Jewish Publication Society of America, 1958), 208–9.
23   Ibid., 212.
24   For more on notions of Jewish diaspora nationality and cultural autonomy
     see Simon Rabinovitch, *Jewish Rights, National Rites: Nationalism and Auton-
     omy in Late Imperial and Revolutionary Russia* (Stanford, CA: Stanford Uni-
     versity Press, 2014); Joshua Shanes, *Diaspora Nationalism and Jewish Identity
     in Habsburg Galicia* (Cambridge: Cambridge University Press, 2012); Joshua
     M. Karlip, *The Tragedy of a Generation: The Rise and Fall of Jewish Nationals in
     Eastern Europe* (Cambridge, MA: Harvard University Press, 2013).
25   For more on national autonomy in Ukraine see Henry Abramson, *A Prayer
     for the Government: Ukrainians and Jews in Revolutionary Times, 1917–1920*
     (Cambridge, MA: Ukrainian Research Institute and Center for Judaic
     Studies, Harvard University, 1999).
26   Taras Hunczak, ed., *The Ukraine, 1917–1921: A Study in Revolution* (Cam-
     bridge, MA: Harvard University Press, 1977).
27   "Louis Marshall on Zangwill's 'Melting Pot Theory," *The Jewish Exponent*,
     12 April 1918, 8.
28   Horace M. Kallen, "Democracy versus the Melting Pot: A Study of
     American Nationality," in *Jews & Diaspora Nationalism: Writings on Jewish*

Peoplehood in Europe and the United States, ed. Simon Rabinovitch (Waltham, MA: Brandeis University Press, 2012), 155–68.

29 Mordechai Kaplan, "The Future of Judaism," in Rabinovitch, ed., *Jews & Diaspora Nationalism*, 178.

30 John Murray Gibbon, *Canadian Mosaic: The Making of a Northern Nation* (Toronto: McClelland & Stewart, 1938).

31 See Charles Taylor, "The Politics of Recognition" in *Multiculturalism: Examining the Politics of Recognition*, ed. Charles Taylor et al. (Princeton, NJ: Princeton University Press, 1994), 25–73.

32 Ibid., 58.

33 Will Kymlicka, "The Sources of Nationalism. Commentary on Taylor" in *The Morality of Nationalism*, ed. Robert McKim and Jeff Mc Mahan (New York: Oxford University Press, 1997), 56–65 at 59.

34 Will Kymlicka, *Multicultural Citizenship: A Liberal Theory of Minority Rights* (Oxford: Clarendon Press, 1995), 6.

35 Joseph Raz, *Morality of Freedom* (Oxford: Clarendon Press, 1986), 207.

36 Yael Tamir, *Liberal Nationalism* (Princeton, NJ: Princeton University Press, 1993), 8–9.

37 Charles Taylor, "Nationalism and Modernity," in McKim and McMahan, eds, *The Morality of Nationalism*, 31–55 at 46–7.

38 Ibid., 51.

39 Canadian Multiculturalism Act R.S.C., 1985, c. 24 (4th Supp).

40 For some thoughts on the continued resilience of multiculturalism in Canada see Michael Adams, *Could It Happen Here?: Canada in the Age of Trump and Brexit* (New York: Simon and Shuster, 2017).

4 Vilna on the St Lawrence: Montreal as the Would-Be Haven for Yiddish Culture

KALMAN WEISER

"Now we want to reveal a great secret," confided Yitshok Varshavski, the journalistic pen name of I.B. Singer, to readers of New York City's Yiddish daily *Forverts* on the eve of 1947: "Jewish Montreal is a reincarnation (*gilgul*) of Vilna." In the article that followed, however, there was nothing particularly supernatural in the flattering appraisal of a writer today renown for invocations of Jewish folklore and mysticism in his stories and novels. Beyond noting similarities in the northern climate, hilly topography, and the palpable Catholic presence between the fabled "Jerusalem of Lithuania" and Canada's most populous city, Singer drew attention to the pre-eminence of Yiddish language and culture among its Jews. With its roughly 75,000 Jews shortly after the Second World War, Montreal possessed only a tiny fraction of the mammoth Jewish population of New York City, where Singer had emigrated from Warsaw in 1935. But, unlike the Jewish metropolis on the Hudson, home to more than two million Jews,[1] many of them Yiddish-speakers, it was a "fortress of Yiddishism." "Here [in Montreal] the New York indifference, the New York pessimism" with regard to Yiddish culture, he announced, "is wholly lacking." Singer concluded optimistically that "Montreal is becoming the Jerusalem of North America."[2]

For Yiddish writers, performers, educators, intellectuals, and cultural activists, the Holocaust meant not only the trauma caused by the murder of the largest part of European Jewry. It also meant the near complete destruction of the European basis for the modern secular culture that had emerged in Yiddish since the nineteenth century. Like many of his colleagues, Singer continued to draw inspiration for his work from the disappeared world of his youth while yearning for the large and appreciative, multigenerational audiences that seemingly only pre-war Europe could offer.[3]

Nostalgia for the heyday of Yiddish was not limited, however, to writers in post–Second World War immigrant centres. Yiddishism, the movement to fashion a modern European culture in the Jewish vernacular, reached its apex around the time of the First World War. The promise of national cultural autonomy in new states arising from the wreckage of the Russian and Austro-Hungarian empires then loomed on the horizon. Cultural pessimism had, however, begun to gnaw at Yiddish writers by the mid-1920s as they could not fail to notice the accelerated decline of Yiddish in almost all countries where Jews had become citizens since the war. But as Singer recalled, "When a Warsaw writer succumbed to pessimism and began to think that Yiddish is becoming extinct, there was a cure for him: travel to Vilna. There he saw with his own eyes how Yiddish blooms." Likening the Canadian city's diverse Yiddish cultural institutions and leading personalities to those of pre-war Vilna, he concluded that "Montreal is following in Vilna's path. Let's just hope it has a better fate."[4]

Contemporary scholars have shed light on the development of the unique character of Montreal's Jewish community and its transformation from a minor centre subordinate to New York City into a major centre of Yiddish culture in its own right following the Second World War.[5] Relatively little attention, however, has thus far been given to external, contemporaneous perceptions of Montreal's importance for Yiddish culture in the first half of the twentieth century. A number of observers writing for both the New York and Polish Yiddish presses noted by the opening decades of the twentieth century the growing importance of Montreal as a Jewish demographic and cultural centre. Montreal, they noticed, was becoming home not only for eastern European Jewish immigrants and their children but for the Yiddish language itself. Their travelogues proposed a number of cultural, political, and sociological factors to account for the resilience of Yiddish language and culture there at a time when its decline beyond the immigrant generation was more keenly felt elsewhere in North America. "The Jew in Montreal," concluded one visitor in 1912, "represents a new type of Jew in America. More distinguished, more serious and prouder of his nationality."[6]

But Singer may very well have been the first journalist to consciously equate the two cities, conferring upon Montreal the cultural mystique surrounding Vilna. Building on his depictions and those of other Yiddish journalists visiting Montreal prior to the 1950s, even if impressionistic and to some extent tendentious, this chapter will explore the significance of Vilna and Montreal as symbols of hope for those invested in the creation of a modern Jewish culture primarily in

Yiddish. It begins by surveying the sociolinguistic landscape of each city separately before exploring the impression Montreal made upon eastern European Jewish writers visiting from Poland and the United States. Finally, it explores those factors identified as contributing to the strength of Yiddish language and culture in the two cities in order to deepen our understanding of linguistic responses to the breakdown of traditional Ashkenazic society and the pursuit of cultural autonomy by Jews in diasporic contexts.

Vilna

With the Third Partition of Poland in 1795, the final act of dismemberment of the once mighty Polish-Lithuanian Commonwealth by its neighbours, Vilna passed into the hands to the Russian Empire. According to an official count in 1909, its population of 205,250 inhabitants was divided between Poles (37.8 per cent), Jews (36.8 per cent), Russians (20.7 per cent), and Lithuanians (1.2 per cent).[7] The rural population of its environs consisted, however, mainly of speakers of Belarussian, a language, like Lithuanian, typically dismissed as a mere "peasant" tongue by Jews and non-Jews alike.[8]

Traditional Jewish society in the Russian Empire, as elsewhere in eastern Europe, was internally bilingual: Hebrew, the prestigious written but unspoken holy language associated with the rabbinic elite, existed in a complementary relationship (diglossia) with Yiddish, the lower-prestige vernacular shared by all Jews. Their knowledge of gentile languages was typically limited and depended on the degree of an individual's contact, which was primarily instrumental (such as commerce and providing services), with non-Jewish peasants, landowners, or officialdom.

Only in the mid-nineteenth century did non-Jewish languages begin to make significant, if still humble, inroads into Jewish society. When adopting a gentile language, Jews typically chose the language of local power or prestige: Polish in Congress Poland and Galicia despite being under Russian and Austrian rule, respectively; German in the Baltic region of the Russian Empire, where German had been the dominant language in cities such as Riga for centuries; and Russian in the Pale of Settlement, the western provinces of the Russian Empire where Jewish residence was permitted.

By the 1860s, a small class of modernizing Jews had begun to avail itself of educational, vocational, and residential incentives for russification offered by the Russian Empire to its Jews. At the turn of the twentieth century, Vilna Jewry remained overwhelmingly Yiddish-speaking.

But its upper bourgeoisie and intelligentsia were increasingly raising their children in the hegemonic language of the empire, which conferred prestige and opened the doors to new socio-economic opportunities. The adoption of Russian language and culture in private and public life did not imply identification, however, with Russian ethnicity or social integration for Jews, who remained subject to discriminatory laws in the absence of religious conversion. The result was a class of unemancipated Russian-speaking Jews, not Jewish Russians – a nuisance no less irritating to Polish nationalists, who condemned them as pernicious russifiers bent on undoing the historic Polish character of the country.

The trend towards russification was to an extent reversed during the First World War, when the German occupation of Poland-Lithuania made the public use of Russian suspect. The competition between rival Polish, Lithuanian, Russian, and Belarussian nationalist movements to determine the political future of the city further encouraged Jews to speak a language of their own in order to preserve neutrality. Naturally, this was a boon for the rival Yiddishist and Hebraist movements. Each sought to transform traditional diglossic Jewish society into a secularized, monolingual one (or in some cases, bilingual – Yiddish along with a vernacularized Hebrew, as was the desire of the left wing of Labour Zionist party Poale Zion) as part of a larger program for Jewish "national revival" that would impede linguistic assimilation.

Further, German authorities encouraged the development of mother-tongue education for the various local peoples of the region, opening the doors for the first time to legal networks of secular, co-educational schools functioning in Yiddish by more left-leaning Jewish political parties alongside ones operated in Hebrew (or Hebrew with Yiddish) by Zionists of various stripes. Jewish nationalists and socialists alike saw in these schools the foundation for future national cultural autonomy that would permit Jews and other peoples the fullest exercise of civil and politics rights while maintaining their collective distinctiveness within a larger multi-ethnic society.

Confronted with the apocalyptic convulsions of the First World War and its uncertain aftermath, many of Vilna's Jewish partisans and publicists endeavoured to create an image of the city as the expression of inextirpable Jewish rootedness in eastern Europe and the harmonious coexistence and productive cross-fertilization of tradition and modernity. The Vilna mystique was built upon the special place the city occupied in Jewish consciousness as a centre of traditional religious scholarship, a home to the secularizing influences of the Jewish Enlightenment (*Haskalah*), and as a leader in the creation and publication of modern Hebrew and Yiddish literatures. It was also the birthplace of the Jewish socialist party, the Bund, and played a precocious role in the development of Zionism among Jews in the Russian Empire towards the turn of the twentieth century. Vilna was thus well positioned to play a leading role, both practically and symbolically, in shaping Jewish modernity.

While many Jewish nationalists had hoped for Vilna to become the capital of an independent Lithuanian state promising them national cultural autonomy, the violently contested city changed hands multiple times. Ultimately, it was relegated to the periphery of a reconstituted Polish state whose political, economic, and cultural centre was Warsaw. Vilna was consequently separated from its Lithuanian hinterland as well as from important commercial and cultural connections with Russia following the First World War. Polish, a language with which few Vilna Jews had previously identified, replaced Russian as the prestigious language of state and society.

State support for schools in Jewish languages, the foundation of programs for national cultural autonomy embraced by virtually all Jewish political parties, was enshrined in the 1919 Minorities Treaty signed by a newly independent Poland. These promises were never fulfilled by Poland's central government, however. Only a minority of ideologically committed parents sent their children to the networks of private Yiddish and Hebrew schools that had emerged in the war years. Most Jewish youth in interwar Poland attended tuition-free state elementary schools, where they acquired the Polish language and enthusiastically imbibed Polish high culture. At higher levels of education, however, discrimination made it difficult for Jews to obtain admission to Polish state high schools, and graduates of high schools functioning in Jewish languages seldom obtained recognition of their diplomas for the purpose of university admission. Those who could afford it typically studied in private, Polish-language Jewish schools that offered the state curriculum in the hope of being accepted to universities despite unofficial quotas.

Prior to the First World War, Polonization had reached only a small part of the Jewish population in Russian Poland: the so-called Assimilationists, who saw themselves as Poles by nationality and Jews by religion. Now, in contrast, it affected ever larger segments of the Jewish population that were previously indifferent or hostile to it – so much so that the disappearance of Yiddish became a source of worry for secular Yiddishists and religious Jews alike. But the dominance of ethnically and religiously exclusivist currents in Polish society ensured that the interwar generation of Polish Jewish youth would undergo acculturation without integration: it increasingly spoke Polish and identified with the values of the Polish state but existed largely within its own multilingual (Yiddish, Hebrew, and increasingly Polish), social, political, and cultural spheres. The tendency towards linguistic Polonization coupled with a strong Jewish political and cultural orientation was even most pronounced in Galicia, where Polonization had been most advanced before the First World War thanks to Poles' political dominance in the province during the Habsburg era.

In Vilna, as elsewhere in interwar Poland's multi-ethnic eastern borderlands (*kresy*), where no nationality was culturally dominant, demonstrative support for Yiddish was greater than in Warsaw. The absence of significant populations of Hasidim, who rejected all forms of secular Jewish nationalism, and of ideological Assimilationists also made opposition to Yiddishism less strong. The social and physical distance between the various strata of Jewish society was also weaker, and even its professional class was not ashamed to display signs or to speak its mother tongue with clients. Despite widespread poverty, a larger proportion of Jewish children attended schools functioning in Yiddish and Hebrew in the Vilna region and the *kresy* than other parts of the country. Finally, Vilna dialect was widely acclaimed throughout Poland as the model for Yiddish speech, whereas that spoken in a Warsaw routinely described as tumultuous, overcrowded, and riven into mutually hostile factions was denigrated as ugly, ungrammatical, and riddled with Polonisms.

True, the number of Yiddish newspapers and journals, schools, theatre troupes, and the like of the larger, more internally diverse, and more cosmopolitan Warsaw dwarfed those of Vilna. Warsaw was indeed the European metropolis of the Yiddish press, theatre, and literature, as well as the city with the largest Jewish population (about 352,000 – 30 per cent of the city's population compared to Vilna's 55,000 or 28 per cent in 1931) on the continent.[9] But it was also the centre of a rapidly growing Polish-language Jewish culture while Vilna was not home to a single Polish-language Jewish daily. It was thus not the size of Vilna's Jewish community that set Vilna apart in the twentieth century. Rather, it was distinguished by the intensity of Vilna's cultural activity, its demonstrable commitment to a future for Yiddish alongside Hebrew, and its celebration as a site of Jewish authenticity and cultural continuity. Vilna was the unofficial "capital of Yiddishland," the extraterritorial republic of Yiddish language and culture whose heartland was in eastern Europe but which had "colonies" across the globe.

Nonetheless, here, too, there were signs that all was not well with Yiddish and that even Vilna could not insulate itself from broader trends towards language shift.

Montreal

Eastern European Jews who began to arrive en masse in the United States in the 1880s encountered a substantial Jewish "Establishment" of largely German origin that was prosperous and encouraged their acculturation to American norms. Moreover, under the sway of a Jewish immigrant intelligentsia espousing socialist cosmopolitanism, many immigrants saw little value in Yiddish beyond using it as a tool for the dissemination of information and ideology; others, particularly traditionally religious Jews, were likely little interested in politicized questions of identity. By contrast, as historians of Montreal Jewry note, the first mass wave of Yiddish-speaking Jews arrived in Canada towards the beginning of the twentieth century, when very few Jews lived in the country. They came particularly after a series of pogroms beginning in 1903 in the Russian Pale of Settlement and in the wake of the failed 1905 Russian Revolution and its violent aftermath. Such traumatic experiences, which undermined faith in emancipation and social integration, helped to galvanize sympathy among them for the pursuit of national rights, including cultural and linguistic self-preservation. As Rebecca Margolis, a contributor to this volume, explains, in Montreal, "the city's Jewish ideological nexus lay at the intersection of eastern European post-1905 socialism and Zionism, with the labour Zionist Poale Zion (Workers of Zion) organization instrumental in the creation of lasting Yiddish educational institutions in the city."[10]

These newcomers to Montreal quickly outnumbered the Jewish community of a few thousand "assimilated" – anglicized, partly Sephardic – Jews who had settled there since la Nouvelle-France had come under British rule in 1759. To the dismay of these established "Uptown" Jews, who identified with English culture and opposed efforts to entrench Yiddish as a form of self-imposed ghettoization, they developed a vibrant network of educational, cultural, political, and labour organizations functioning in Yiddish and, to a lesser extent, Hebrew in an already linguistically and nationally divided city. They thus created the framework to absorb a later wave of immigration of war refugees and Holocaust survivors that would further swell the city's now substantial Jewish population. Among them were a number of distinguished writers, intellectuals, and cultural activists who had already made names for themselves in Europe, helping to establish the city's prominence in the Yiddish-speaking world.[11]

Being of diverse origins in eastern Europe, Montreal's Jews lacked, of course, the sense of centuries-old rootedness and homogeneity possessed by Vilna Jewry, much of which had migrated to it from nearby *shtetls* in the late nineteenth century. Further, while similar in absolute size to that of Vilna, Montreal's Jewish community of about 60,000 made up only about 6 per cent of the city's much larger overall population in 1931 as compared with Vilna's 28.2 per cent.[12] Montreal Jewry was also residentially and occupationally more mixed with other groups who shared their socio-economic class, particularly other European immigrants and native francophones. It shared, however, with Vilna Jewry (and much of eastern European Jewry more broadly) a will to preserve its own distinctiveness and a sense of exclusion from gentile society. The third-largest group in Montreal, Jews tended to reside in tightly grouped neighbourhoods straddling the dividing line between the English and French parts of the city – out of communal cohesiveness and because they found themselves largely unwelcome in societies which had little or no desire to integrate foreigners.[13]

Upon arriving in Montreal, Yiddish writers homesick for Europe could not fail to remark positively upon the resemblance of its natural landscape and architecture to what they had known in eastern Europe. "Entire streets look as if in a *shtetl* in Poland or Galicia," observed one writer as Jewish life was being brutally uprooted by war on the eastern front in 1918. Its peacefulness compared favourably with the "boisterous" New York: "A lot of houses with courtyards, life is so calm and cozy. One's eye rests here from the accursed tenement buildings, a curse that is unknown here. Small buildings, small houses, small trees, small gardens, small porches – what a pleasure it is!"[14] To Singer's delight, winter brought "real" snow, furs, and sleds pulled by horses and dogs, as in the Old Country.[15]

Not all impressions, however, were welcome. Given the historic animosity of the Catholic Church to Jews and Judaism, the presence of so many black-clad "priests, monks, and nuns of various orders"[16] evoked fear and reminders of medieval intolerance among some observers.[17] Yet, this discomfort quickly faded and even expressions of antisemitism seemed less threatening here than in eastern Europe, where violence and boycott were increasingly the norm. Ironically, one of the few journalists to contrast Toronto and Montreal declared the former a far more Jewish city precisely because of its more pronounced antisemitism, which resulted in widespread residential and professional discrimination. In contrast with Toronto's English Protestants, he explained, Montreal's French Catholics hurled insults at Jews "from the mouth, not the heart."[18]

The prevalence of Yiddish in both Montreal and Toronto and its quality never failed to impress observers familiar with Jewish communities in the United States. The integrationist ethos that reduced Judaism to a religious rather than national category that seemed to reign in the United States meant a lack of enthusiasm for Yiddish, if not outright embarrassment by it in many Jewish circles. A pleasantly surprised visitor in 1916 remarked, "I never heard youth in New York streets speak Yiddish so fluently and readily as in Montreal."[19] Visiting Yiddishists throughout the first half of the twentieth century and beyond expressed satisfaction at the "pure" and "folksy" Yiddish, one notably free of anglicisms, in the mouths of even Canadian-born speakers.[20] Whereas status-conscious mothers were denigrated for speaking Polish, even if imperfectly, with their children in Warsaw and Łódź,[21] the American Yiddish press rejoiced in Canadian-born mothers competent in English speaking Yiddish with their progeny.[22]

Journalists unanimously identified the contest for hegemony between Canada's two "founding nations" as the chief reason for the vibrancy of Yiddish in Montreal in contrast with other North American cities, where the primacy of English went unchallenged. Montreal's anglophone Protestant minority dominated business and commerce but anglophones represented a minority vis-à-vis the city's francophone, largely working-class majority. They were vastly outnumbered in the rest of the province of Quebec by rural French Canadians, who, like their urban relatives, were known for their loyalty to the Catholic Church and large family size. As early as 1912, one journalist noted the beneficial effect on Jewish identity and language loyalty of a bitter struggle between English and French populations, which was reflected in the existence of separate school systems along linguistic and confessional lines.[23]

Yiddish writers typically considered language essential to the preservation of national particularity and were reluctant to consider any other language, with the possible exception of modern Hebrew, an appropriate medium for the intergenerational transmission of Jewish cultural values. They therefore paid special attention to the development of Jewish schools as a barometer of the well-being of Yiddish culture. In New York and elsewhere in the United States, Yiddish-language schools organized by left-leaning elements existed exclusively as afternoon supplementary schools offering instruction a few days a week or on weekends. In Montreal, by contrast, they functioned daily and not merely as supplementary schools. By 1942 the city's first full day school teaching in Yiddish began operations, to be followed soon afterwards by additional ones using Yiddish, Hebrew, or some combination thereof according to their ideology.[24] In marvelling at Montreal, writers praised the vibrancy of a Yiddishist intelligentsia not estranged from the mass of working-class Yiddish speakers, the existence of a multitude of cultural institutions (above all, the Jewish Public Library), and strong Orthodox, Hebraist, and Labour Zionist presences that were not hostile to Yiddish and, despite their differences, were able to collaborate in matters of common Jewish concern – all factors consistent with pre–Second World War descriptions of Vilna, but not of more polarized Warsaw or New York City.

But the lure of English also did not escape them; French, despite being the language of the majority and politics, was hardly the language of socio-economic mobility.[25] Observers noted that Yiddish-speaking immigrants could often communicate in French with their neighbours, co-workers, and clients but seldom chose to assimilate to French culture even when living among francophones.[26] Jewish parents enrolled their children exclusively in the schools of the English-language Protestant School Board rather than in French Catholic schools, from which all non-Catholics were excluded. For the purpose of education, Jews were considered "honorary Protestants."[27] Jewish taxpayers contributed to the upkeep of the Protestant School Board and Jewish children were officially exempt from Christian religious instruction without penalty but Jews could not be elected to sit on the School Board itself. Unofficially, Jewish pupils were denied access to schools outside of neighbourhoods with dense Jewish populations and Jewish teachers were granted employment only in these same schools. Yiddish reporters noted that dissatisfaction with this situation led to a number of attempts by Jews over the years – unsuccessful because of disagreements within Jewish society as well as external opposition – to create their own school board supported with tax monies.[28] At the post-secondary level, Jewish students found themselves subject to admissions quotas at elite McGill University. Jewish efforts to enter in significant numbers the sacred precincts of English high culture and prestige were thus rebuffed; at the same time, Jews' growing identification with the powerful language and cultural institutions of the English minority inspired resentment among the francophone majority.[29]

Concluding Thoughts

Yiddish writers visiting Canada from abroad seldom explicitly contrasted Montreal with Toronto, the city with the second-largest Jewish population in the country and the site of its own Yiddish cultural institutions. Instead, in much the same way that they compared Warsaw with Vilna, Yiddish cultural activists expressed their disappointments and anxieties about the fate of Yiddish culture, as well as their hopes and dreams for it, by comparing New York City with Montreal. In New York, Jews found that acculturation, especially via a non-denominational public school system, permitted them access to the majority society to an unprecedented, if not unlimited, degree; in Montreal, by contrast, they found that being caught between the two proverbial solitudes of English and French Canada, with neither the dominant nor the majority culture eager to embrace them and no all-encompassing Canadian identity to adopt, provided them with a not unfamiliar context for the cultivation of Jewish culture.

In both Vilna and Montreal, a mixture of external exclusion and internal motivation within a compact population contributed to the resilience and, in the eyes of foreign observers, greater cultural vibrancy of Yiddish than elsewhere. Montreal, and Canada more broadly, suggested an alternate model to the American experience of indifference to or distaste for immigrant languages and culture while still offering substantially the same economic opportunities, physical security, and political rights. In this way, it offered a glimpse at the fulfilment of the eastern European ideal of national cultural autonomy.

Ultimately, Yiddish did not withstand the inroads of the dominant language of the larger society any more than in Vilna or New York. If in 1931, 99 per cent of Montreal Jews reported Yiddish as their mother tongue, by 1951 this number had declined to 54.4 per cent.[30] Even still, despite language shifts and with growing affluence and the relocation of the community away from some of its primary cultural institutions, Singer maintained in 1963 that Montreal remained a "fortress of Yiddishism."[31] Ben Zion Goldberg was decidedly less sanguine in 1955:

Montreal was once renowned in Jewish America. It was a centre of Yiddishism or of Jewish culturalism, of the Jewish intelligentsia. The best Jewish school and the biggest one in North America was supposed to be there. The largest, if the not the first, Jewish library was created by Yiddishist elements there. And most importantly, in Montreal the Yiddishist intelligentsia was not an island in a sea of other elements as in cities in the United States but a sea unto itself ... if there were a place in Anglo-North America where Jewish cultural autonomy was a possibility, it was in Montreal, and if Jewish parents had only wanted, they could have had a complete Jewish school system in Hebrew and Yiddish.[32]

It is worth recalling that, in this respect, Montreal was hardly unique. Throughout eastern Europe in the interwar period, Jewish parents increasingly registered their children for schools of the dominant nationality, even when its language had been completely unknown to them prior to the First World War. This was true even in the Baltic states, where, unlike Vilna in Poland, state funding existed for Jewish schools and, as Ezra Mendelsohn notes, "where conditions were ideal for the flourishing of Jewish national education."[33]

Much has changed in the linguistic landscape of Jewish Montreal since the 1960s. Above all, Yiddish has radically receded as a native language outside of Hasidic circles while the gains of English have been halted by a combination of factors: the pro-French language policies launched since the Quiet Revolution, the departure of more than 30,000, primarily anglophone, Jews within two decades since,[34] and the sizeable influx of francophone, especially Sephardic, Jews.

Today, the province of Quebec pays for the vast majority of the tuition of the private schools where roughly half of Montreal Jewish children study in some combination of French, English, Hebrew, and Yiddish.[35] If schooling is the essential basis for the eastern European ideal of cultural autonomy in the diaspora, Montreal Jewry has come much closer to the realization of this ideal – changes in the nature of Jewish identity since the period of mass immigration notwithstanding – than Jewish communities in either Poland or the United States in the interwar period and perhaps in any other country in the contemporary world. How much closer is a question worthy of further investigation. It warrants comparison above all with other centres of immigration where Jewish nationalism was strengthened where Jews were caught between rival nationalities and languages, such as between English and Afrikaans in South Africa or Flemish and French in Belgium, or where the parochial nature of society impeded integration, as in Catholic Argentina.[36]

NOTES

1 Lloyd P. Gartner et al., "New York City, 1920–1970," in *The Encyclopedia Judaica*, ed. Michael Berenbaum and Fred Skolnik, vol. 15., 2nd ed. (Detroit: Macmillan Reference USA, 2007), 212
2 Yitskhok Varshavski, "Itstike montreol dermont on der amoliker vilne," *Forverts*, 31 December 1946.
3 On Singer's post-Holocaust career, see Jan Schwarz, *Survivors and Exiles. Yiddish Culture after the Holocaust* (Detroit: Wayne State University Press, 2015).

4 Varshavski, "Itstike montreol dermont on der amoliker vilne."
5 See, for example, David G. Roskies, "A Hebrew-Yiddish Utopia in
   Montreal," in *Hebrew in America. Perspectives and Prospects*, ed. Alan Mintz
   (Detroit: Wayne State University Press, 1993); Rebecca Margolis, *Jewish
   Roots, Canadian Soil. Yiddish Culture in Montreal, 1900–1945* (Montreal and
   Kingston: McGill-Queen's University Press, 2011); Pierre Anctil, *Histoire
   des Juifs du Québec* (Montreal: Éditions du Boréal, 2017).
6 Ben Moshe, "Der yidisher tsenter fun kenede," *Yidishes tageblat*,
   24 September 1912.
7 Timothy Snyder, *The Reconstruction of Nations: Poland, Lithuania, Ukraine,
   Belarus, 1569-1999* (New Haven, CT: Yale University Press, 2003), 309.
8 The Vilna section here is based largely on my book *Jewish People, Yiddish
   Nation. Noah Prylucki and the Folkists in Poland* (Toronto: University of Toronto Press, 2011) and my previously published essays: "The Jewel in the
   Yiddish Crown: Who Will Occupy the Chair in Yiddish at the University
   of Vilnius?" *Polin* 24 (2012): 223–55; "The Capital of 'Yiddishland'?" in
   *Warsaw. The Jewish Metropolis. Essays in Honor of the 75th Birthday of Profes-
   sor Antony Polonsky*, ed. Glenn Dynner and François Guesnet (Leiden: Brill,
   2015), 298–322.
9 Ezra Mendelsohn, *The Jews of East Central Europe between the Two World
   Wars* (Bloomington: Indiana University Press, 1983), 23.
10 Rebecca Margolis, "*Ale Brider*: Yiddish Culture in Montreal in New York,"
   European Journal of Jewish Studies 4, no. 1 (2010): 144.
11 Ibid., 142–8; Anctil, *Histoires des Juifs*, chapters 2–4.
12 Anctil, *Histoires des Juifs*, 86. Mendelsohn, *The Jews of East Central Europe*, 23.
13 Anne Read, "The Precarious History of Jewish Education in Quebec,"
   Religion & Education 45 (2017): 1, 2; Anctil, *Histoires des Juifs*, 160–1.
14 Eliash, "Dos hartsike Montreol," *Dos yidishes tageblat*, 26 July 1918.
15 Varshavski, "Itstike montreol dermont on der amoliker vilne."
16 Tsivyon, "A briv fun kenede," *Forverts*, 13 April 1920.
17 Eliash, "Dos hartsike Montreol."
18 Ben Finkel, "Toronto iz a mer yidishe shtot eyder montreol," *Forverts*,
   11 May 1928.
19 Y. Entin, "Dos yidishe lebn in montreol," *Der tog*, 21 February 1916.
20 Tsivyon, "A briv fun kenede."
21 Weiser, "The Capital of 'Yiddishland'?," 315.
22 Y.D. Goldman, "Montreol – di yidishste shtot in amerike," *Yidishes tageblat*,
   21 August 1918; Varshavski, "Itstike montreol dermont on der amol-iker
   vilne."
23 Ben Moshe, "Der yidisher tsenter fun kenede," *Yidishes tageblat*,
   24 September 1912.
24 Margolis, *Jewish Roots, Canadian Soil*, 132.

25 Tsivyon, "A briv fun kenede."

26 Eliash, "Dos hartsike montreol."

27 On this subject, see David Fraser's important study, *Honorary Protestants: The Jewish School Question in Montreal, 1867–1997* (Toronto: University of Toronto Press, 2015).

28 A. Vohliner, "Der opklang fun keneder shprakhn kamf in der yidisher gas," *Der tog*, 10 March 1916; "Fun yidishn lebn in kanade. A geshprekh mitn yidishn zhurnalist un klal-tuer h'yankev rasnovski fun montreol," *Haynt*, 23 August 1927.

29 Eliash, "Dos hartsike montreol."

30 Anctil, *Histoires des Juifs*, 288.

31 Yitskhok Varshavski, "Montreol – a festung fun yidishizm," *Forverts*, 5 March 1963.

32 B.Ts. Goldberg, "In gang fun tog. Ayndrukn – montreol," *Der tog morgn zhurnal*, 15 April 1955.

33 Mendelsohn, *The Jews of East Central Europe*, 235.

34 Read, "The Precarious History of Jewish Education in Quebec," 35–6.

35 Ibid., 30.

36 Commenting on the strength of Zionism in Canada, Belgium, and South Africa prior to the First World War, Michael Brown notes: "That all three were binational countries where two competing nationalities grew increasingly intolerant of each other and even more so of outsiders is hardly coincidental." See Michael Brown, "Divergent Paths: Early Zionism in Canada and the United States," *Jewish Social Studies* 44, no. 2 (1982): 164.

5 Jewish Education in Canada and the United Kingdom: A Comparative Perspective

RANDAL F. SCHNOOR

Whenever thinking about the relative strength of Canadian Jewry compared to other countries, I, like many of my colleagues, almost instinctively turn to the Unites States to begin this comparative exercise. As I have faithfully taught my students for more than a decade now, Canadian Jewry takes pride in the fact that, compared with American Jews, Canadian Jews demonstrate higher levels of Jewish commitment on many standard normative behaviours. Putting aside issues around Jewish education for the moment, compared with American Jews, Canadian Jews have lower rates of intermarriage, make proportionally more visits to Israel, donate proportionally more money to Jewish causes, observe religious rituals more strictly, and are more likely to speak Hebrew or Yiddish.[1]

Like other scholars, I have been somewhat preoccupied with uncovering possible reasons why Canadian Jews score higher than American Jews on these measures. My version of this explanation suggests that it is time to move beyond the conventional "time-lag" or "generation-lag" theory as the primary explanation for these differences. This is the well-known theory that Canadian Jews are one generation closer to the "old country" and therefore simply one step behind in the inevitable process of assimilation. Elsewhere I have suggested four other explanations that consider more carefully the historical, political, and geographical nuances of the North American Jewish context.[2] First, in contrast to the United States where by the middle of the nineteenth century the Jewish populations had spread out to cover several large metropolitan areas in the east coast, midwest, and gulf coast, Canada's Jews have been primarily concentrated in just two cities in the centre of the country (Montreal and Toronto). With this high level of geographical concentration, Canadian Jews were able to develop a more cohesive national community infrastructure that included a viable representative national body (Canadian Jewish Congress). Second, unlike the United States, Canada has simply never had a large and dominant presence of Reform Jewry. As a force for a more liberal and less traditional expression of Jewishness, Reform has been a less potent force in Canadian Jewish life and has had less impact on the country's Jewish psyche or worldview. Third, the impact of Holocaust survivors looms larger in Canada, where we see a much higher proportion of survivors in the population. The more Jewishly engaged tendencies of these survivor immigrants have left their imprint on the Canadian Jewish mindset.[3] Finally, I have suggested the very birth of Canada differs significantly from that of the United States. While the United States was born of a revolution against British rule, Canada's origins included a constitutional appreciation of two distinct cultural groups (English and French).[4] Starting in the 1960s Canada's policy of biculturalism evolved into multiculturalism, where comprehensive legal protection was enacted to protect the rights of minority groups to maintain their cultural heritages.[5]

The Strength of Jewish Education in Canada

With this mantra of Canadian–US Jewish differences established, I now turn back to take a closer look at this comparative question through the important lens of contemporary Jewish education, one of my areas of continued interest as a sociologist of Canadian Jewish life. Why is Jewish education so important to consider in examining the strength of a particular Jewish community? With declining levels of synagogue attendance and religious observance more broadly throughout much of the Jewish world, it is no secret that Jewish education has taken on much of the responsibility for creating and nurturing the Jewish identities of the younger generation to help ensure a strong Jewish future. This is accomplished through enriching Jewish literacy by way of specific religious and cultural content, as well as socializing young Jews within their own minority group with the goal of promoting Jewish friendships, social networks, and ultimately Jewish marriages. As my colleague Morton Weinfeld aptly puts it: for many Jewish leaders assimilation and intermarriage are considered the central disease of the community, and Jewish education has been deemed the most effective vaccination.

To connect this theme of Jewish education more explicitly with the overarching theme of this volume, and as stated in the introduction, in many ways Canada is one of the most socially welcoming and religiously tolerant home for the Jews as compared with other diaspora homes, past or present. Indeed, Canada has provided an environment that supports high levels of Jewish institutional completeness. This has allowed for the development of myriad Jewish schools, schools that, in turn, have helped produce proud levels of Jewish engagement and literacy. Beyond merely *permitting* the building of these parochial schools, however, one may ask to what extent does Canada actively *enfranchise* Jews as an ethnic/religious minority in the country? The case study of Jewish schools offers an important litmus test for the pertinent question asked by Koffman at the beginning of this volume: "Does Canada offer the right mix of *inclusion* for religious and ethnic minorities without *assimilative coercion*?" Clearly, with dozens of Jewish schools in Canada, Canadian Jews are not being coerced to assimilate; quite the opposite, as they are given ample opportunity to immerse their children in Jewish language, culture, and tradition. But what of inclusion? How does Canada compare in its *active* support of these Jewish schools? In order to examine whether Canada is the best home for the Jews, this is a central concern to explore.

Jewish education today takes on many diverse forms. "Formal" Jewish education refers to Jewish instruction found in the classrooms of Jewish day schools (full day program) and Jewish supplementary schools (afternoon or Sunday schools). The growing world of "informal" education refers to the worlds of summer camps, youth groups, and Jewish travel opportunities (Birthright Israel, March of the Living, among others). While recent studies on Jewish overnight camps[6] have demonstrated the effectiveness of this more experiential style of Jewish education, many years of research have clearly documented that Jewish day school is the gold standard for instilling strong Jewish identities. Based on a large sample of respondents from the 2001 American National Jewish Population Survey, Steven Cohen reported that day schools produce the most powerful effects on future adult Jewish identity, as compared with other forms of Jewish education, in terms of Jewish observance, affiliation, and belonging.[7] Similarly, research among Montreal Jews in 2010 reported that attending a Jewish high school is the second most predictive factor of ritual observance later in life, after current denomination.[8] It is the strength of the Jewish day school that will serve as the focus of this chapter.

How well does Canada fare in this domain? When it comes to Jewish education, "is there no better home for the Jews than Canada?" As a minority group deeply concerned with its future continuity, the Jewish community of Canada devotes substantial resources to Jewish education. In fact, no ethnic or religious minority group in Canada has an educational system for its youth as extensively developed as do the Jews. This certainly includes a large range of all-day parochial Jewish schools. To continue our trend above of comparisons with the United States, Canadian Jewry has indeed differentiated itself with its more rapid growth and popularity of the Jewish day school.

It is true that the predominant model in the first several decades of Jewish life in Canada was akin to the American one: that Jewish youth would attend public school to become acculturated into the dominant milieu, while attending parochial Jewish school for a few hours only in the late afternoons or on Sundays. By 1940 this trend began to change as Canada's first day schools were launched. In Toronto these were Orthodox in orientation and did not receive any financial support from the existing Jewish Federation of Toronto, which was made up of non-Orthodox Jews who considered these schools to be too narrow and parochial, and only for a small minority of children. These new schools were thus entirely funded by contributions from parents and private groups. Interestingly, it was not long before non-Orthodox Jews changed their tune and came to the same conclusion that private full-day Jewish schools were indeed essential institutions to ensure a Jewish future for their children, albeit designed with a less traditional curriculum and environment.[9] By the 1960s the non-Orthodox established the first such day schools of their own. By the mid-late 1970s Jewish day school enrolment gained substantial momentum. This is more than a decade before such momentum developed in the United States.

A more specific history of Toronto's Jewish school system will give a fuller sense of its rapid growth and proliferation. The first two all-day private Jewish schools, alluded to above, were established in 1942 with the opening of both Associated Hebrew School and Eitz Chaim School. As mentioned, these schools were Orthodox in orientation. It was not until two decades later that in 1961 that the United Synagogue Day School (now called Robbins Hebrew Academy) was established, a day school within the Conservative movement. Bialik, a secular Yiddishist school was established in the same year. The first day school under the umbrella of the Reform movement, Leo Baeck, was established in 1974.[10] In the 1990s and onwards non-denominational or community/pluralist schools flourished with the establishment of the Toronto Heschel School (1996), Paul Penna Downtown Jewish Day School (1998), and the Montessori Jewish Day School (2000).

One challenge facing the graduates of these early Orthodox elementary day schools in the 1940s and 1950s was the lack of Jewish high school in which to continue their parochial education. As a result, the early graduates enrolled in public school. By the 1960s the Orthodox community addressed this challenge. For the graduates of Associated Hebrew School, a modern Orthodox, co-educational, Zionist Jewish

High School was established in 1960 by the name of the Community Hebrew Academy of Toronto (CHAT). For the graduates of Eitz Chaim, a more traditionally Orthodox, gender-segregated high school was established (Ner Israel for boys in 1960; Bais Ya'acov for girls in 1961). For the graduates in the 1960s of the newer non-orthodox elementary schools the more liberal CHAT was the place of choice. Interestingly, as more and more non-Orthodox students enrolled in the school, some families became concerned about the less religious atmosphere at the school. Looking for a school somewhere in the middle ground between CHAT and Ner Israel/ Bais Ya'acov, these parents established a gender-segregated, religious Zionist school: Yeshivat Or Chaim for boys was founded in 1973 and Ulpanat Orot for girls was founded in 1975.[11] The irony should not be lost here. From criticizing private all-day parochial schools for being a dangerously insular option for a fringe minority, non-Orthodox Jews later became so attracted to these schools that they drove the Orthodox right out of their own schools.

This long history of internal jostling between different segments of the Jewish community notwithstanding, Toronto Jewry clearly takes pride in housing the largest variety of Jewish day schools in the country, with more than twenty-five from which to choose. As outlined, these schools cover the full range of Jewish denominations including Orthodox, Conservative, Reform, secular, non-denominational/community, among other designations.

By the numbers we can observe that while in 1970 less than three thousand students were enrolled in just a few Toronto Jewish day schools, by 1985 Toronto had more than twelve Jewish day schools with close to eight thousand students at the elementary and high school levels.[12] By 2002 there were twenty day schools with an elementary school population of close to nine thousand students (constituting about 34 per cent of the total Jewish school-age population) and a high school population of more than 2,600.[13] This total figure remained at approximately 11,000 in 2013.

What accounts for this dramatic rise of Jewish day schools in Toronto over the last several decades? Here are two factors to consider. First, Canada's new ethos of multiculturalism originating in the 1960s, brought about a new confidence and comfort for one of Canada's minority groups in developing a comprehensive parochial school system of its own. It had become much more acceptable for Jews to show interest in deepening their own culture and identity through the development of private Jewish education.[14] Fears of assimilation accelerated this process. Second, what we may call Jewish *embourgoisement* plays a role. Although Toronto is one of the few cities in the world where substantial Jewish immigration continues, the majority of Jewish children in the city are at least second-generation Canadians. Their parents are among the most socially integrated minority groups in the city. They have used their disposable income to build and finance many new schools, suburban synagogues, and other community institutions to demonstrate and celebrate their cultural distinctiveness.[15]

The Importance of the Comparative Perspective in Jewish Education

While Toronto thus shows tremendous strength in its day school achievement, especially as compared to overall American trends, it is time to look beyond our southern neighbours to gain a wider, more global perspective. Interestingly, when we examine the United Kingdom as a point of comparison things begin to look different. Toronto and London both serve the largest Jewish population centres of their respective countries. In addition, the Jewish population sizes of these cities are quite similar (Toronto at approximately 190,000 Jews; London at approximately 180,000 Jews), thus allowing for a useful comparison.

Staetsky and Boyd's 2016 research[16] on British Jewish education is very instructive for our purposes. Perhaps surprisingly, their research reveals that the growth of Jewish day enrolments in London (and the United Kingdom more generally) have been significantly more dramatic than what has occurred in Toronto. As we can see in figure 5.1, whereas Toronto had only approximately 3,000 students in Jewish day schools (elementary plus high school) in 1970, London already had over 8,000 students. While both cities show a similar increase throughout the 1970s and 1980s, it is the late 1990s where we see considerable divergence. From 1995 to 2015 day school enrolments almost doubled in size in London, reaching over 23,000. At the same time day school enrolments in Toronto rose only from approximately 9,000 to approximately 10,500 students, an increase of only 17 per cent. The 10,500 Jewish students in Toronto represent a total that is already in gradual decline from its peak of about 11,500 in 2005. What is more remarkable is that these dramatic increases over the last several decades in London have taken place against the backdrop of a slightly declining overall Jewish population. The opposite has been the case in Toronto, where the Jewish population has been growing slightly over the last few decades. In terms of proportions of Jewish school-age children who attend Jewish day schools, the differences are again significant. Currently in London around 60 per cent of Jewish school-age children attend Jewish schools, whereas the numbers in Toronto are approximately half at 30 per cent.

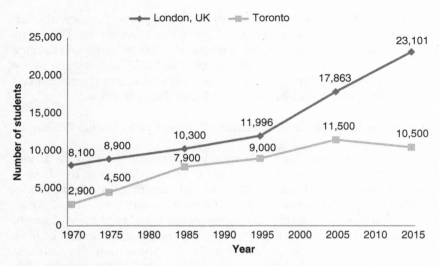

Figure 5.1   Jewish day school enrolment levels in London and Toronto. The UK data come from Staetsky and Boyd (2016). The Toronto data are based on estimations provided by the Koschitzky Centre for Jewish Education (Jewish Federation of Greater Toronto).

In keeping with the research that reports on the significant advantages of Jewish day school enrolments, we observe that London (more dramatically than Toronto) "increases opportunities for young people to learn about Judaism and their Jewishness, to develop a strong Jewish social circle, and be actively socialized into Jewish communal life," as Staetsky and Boyd write.[17]

What accounts for this dramatic increase in Jewish day school enrolments in London? Similar to the situation in Toronto, it is reasonable to suggest, as the British authors do, that this represents the parents' response to the perceived weakening of Jewish identity in the United Kingdom and thus an attempt to provide a strong grounding in Jewish life for their children, including, and perhaps especially for those parents who do not feel equipped to do so themselves. Social momentum plays a part as well. As parents become more comfortable with placing their children in the more segregated setting of a Jewish school, the type of school that most of them did not attend themselves, it becomes more socially acceptable to do so. In time, other Jewish families also become more comfortable with this option. Concerns about antisemitism and other discomforts of being a minority in the general school system play a role as well.

While all these reasons are valid, they ignore the increasingly significant factor of affordability. The fact remains that as "state-schools" mainstream Jewish schools in the United Kingdom are free.[18] The right for Jewish schools to be government-funded has been enshrined in law in England since the mid-nineteenth century.[19] For North Americans struggling with the escalating fees of Jewish day schools this fact often comes as a shock. The great irony here is that while difficult economic conditions for Jewish families in Toronto will make them less likely to choose Jewish day school for their children, the same conditions in London often encourage Jewish families to turn to Jewish schools (as an alternative to prestigious and expensive private schools).

Indeed, as tuition increases have far surpassed standard-of-living increases, affordability of Jewish day schools in Toronto has reached a near-crisis situation with several schools downsizing, merging, or closing completely in the last ten years.[20] While average household income in Toronto rose 11 per cent between 2001 and 2011, Jewish elementary school tuitions rose by an alarming 61 per cent.[21] As I have written elsewhere, Jews in Ontario who wish to enrol their children in Jewish day school are faced with serious financial challenges.[22] In 2016 Jewish day school tuitions in Toronto ranged from approximately $13,000 to $25,000 per year per child. This is a major financial commitment for most families, especially when there is more than one child attending these schools. For those who are quite affluent, these tuitions may not pose a particular problem. For those with particularly low incomes, the Jewish community provides substantial tuition subsidies.[23] The majority of families, however – the middle-class – are financially squeezed. They want their children to be exposed to Jewish life and culture and develop a strong Jewish identity through Jewish schools, but increasingly the high costs are not allowing it. When added to the onerous costs of home ownership in Toronto, especially in a Jewish neighbourhood, and maintaining a Jewish household and Jewish way of life, the cost of day school tuition is increasingly becoming out of reach for many families.

According to Grass Roots for Affordable Jewish Education, a Toronto organization formed in 2015 to address the affordability crisis, the proportion of families in Toronto who are willing to continue Jewish education after the elementary level has decreased significantly. In 2006, 79 per cent of students graduating from the Jewish elementary day schools went on to Tanenbaum Community Hebrew Academy of Toronto; in 2015, only 52 per cent of Jewish elementary students enrolled in TanenbaumCHAT. Directly related to this phenomenon is the dramatic overall decrease in enrolment in TanenbaumCHAT, which declined from a high of 1,530 in 2008–9 to 875 in 2017–18, a 42 per cent reduction.[24]

How has the Jewish community of Toronto responded to this challenge? In partnership with other faith-based communities (Muslim, Hindu, etc.), the Jewish community has lobbied the Ontario provincial government on this issue for many years, with little success. The United Nations High Commissioner for Refugees declared in 1999 that funding Ontario's Catholic schools to the exclusion of all others is discriminatory and violates the International Covenant on Civil and Political Rights. As a result, the Ontario Jewish Association for Equity in Education together with the Alliance of Christian Schools (a Protestant Christian school body) filed a lawsuit against the province. The suit was unsuccessful in the Supreme Court of Canada as the court ruled that while the province was indeed guilty of discriminatory behaviour, its policies were based on a constitutional provision and therefore the province was under no legal obligation to modify this policy.[25] As a result of this perceived injustice, many Jews in Ontario feel that their rights of equal citizenship are being violated.

In a positive development, in March 2017 a surprise announcement was made by TanenbaumCHAT and UJA Federation of Toronto that private donations of $15 million had been collected that would reduce the tuition of the high school from close to $28,000 per year to $18,500–$19,000 for the next five years. Supporting the theory that it is cost that is primarily keeping Toronto Jewish students from attending Jewish high school, this tuition reduction of approximately 30 per cent brought about 50 per cent more applications for the grade 9 class of 2018–19 compared with the year before: 300 applicants compared with 200. Despite this, the overall picture in the day school system has been one of continuing decline. It appears that without subsequent sizeable donations or other interventions the numbers of Jewish students in day schools, particularly after this current five-year period, will continue along a downward trajectory.

Taking a look across Canada more broadly, we observe that while other Canadian provinces do receive some provincial funding for their Jewish schools, the fees are still quite high and out of reach for many Jewish families. For example, average 2017 Jewish day school fees in Manitoba were $10,000, in Quebec 11,500, and in British Columbia $12,000.[26]

No better home for Jews than Canada? For those who are convinced that Jewish day schools are essential for perpetuating Jewish culture into future generations – and there are many who are so convinced – there are better homes for Jews than Canada. There are other countries that have structural conditions in place that make these schools much more affordable and thus allow for a more widespread immersion of

Jewish culture into the lives of young Jews. The United Kingdom is one example. Future research can also look at the interesting examples of Mexico and South Africa, where we see in both cases upwards of 75 per cent of Jewish children in Jewish day schools.

NOTES

1 Irving Abella, *Canadian Jewry: Past, Present and Future*. Inaugural Lecture, J. Richard Shiff Chair for the Study of Canadian Jewry (Toronto: Centre for Jewish Studies, York University, 1998).
2 Randal F. Schnoor, "The Contours of Canadian Jewish Life," *Contemporary Jewry* 31, no. 3 (2011): 194–6.
3 Abella, *Canadian Jewry*; Richard Menkis, "North of the Border," *AJS Perspectives: The Magazine of the Association for Jewish Studies* (Fall 2008): 27.
4 Of course, First Nation communities were, and continue to be, given lesser status than European settlers.
5 Abella, *Canadian Jewry*; Menkis, "North of the Border"; Gerald Tulchinsky, "The Canadian Jewish Experience: A Distinct Personality Emerges," in *From Immigration to Integration: The Canadian Jewish Experience*, ed. Ruth Klein and Frank Dimant (Toronto: Institute for International Affairs, B'nai Brith Canada, 2001), 20–3.
6 Celia A. Rothenberg, *Serious Fun at a Jewish Community Summer Camp: Family, Judaism, and Israel* (Lanham, MD: Lexington Books, 2016); Amy L. Sales and Leonard Saxe, *How Goodly Are Thy Tents: Summer Camps as Jewish Socializing Experiences* (Boston: Brandeis University Press, 2003).
7 Steven M. Cohen, "The Differential Impact of Jewish Education on Adult Jewish Identity," in *Family Matters: Jewish Education in the Age of Choice*, ed. Jack Wertheimer (Boston: Brandeis University Press, 2007), 34–56.
8 Charles Shahar, *Jewish Life in Montreal: A Survey of the Attitudes, Beliefs and Behaviours of Montreal's Jewish Community* (Montreal: Fédération CJA, 2010).
9 Etan Diamond, *And I will dwell in their midst: Orthodox Jews in Suburbia* (Chapel Hill: University of North Carolina Press, 2000).
10 Ibid.
11 Ibid.
12 Alex Pomson, "Jewish Day-School Growth in Toronto: Freeing Policy and Research from the Constraints of Conventional Sociological Wisdom," *Canadian Journal of Education/Revue canadienne de l'éducation* (2002): 379–98; B. Shoub, *Day School Enrollment* (Toronto: UJA Federation of Greater Toronto Board of Jewish Education, 1991).
13 Barry Shoub and Joyce Levine, *Population Survey* (Toronto: UJA Federation of Greater Toronto Board of Jewish Education, 2002).

14 Schnoor, "The Contours of Canadian Jewish Life," 191–2.

15 Pomson, "Jewish Day-School Growth in Toronto," 382–3.

16 Daniel L. Staetsky and Jonathan Boyd, *The Rise and Rise of Jewish Schools in the United Kingdom: Numbers, Trends and Policy Issues* (London: Institute for Jewish Policy Research, 2016).

17 Ibid., 29.

18 There is a modest voluntary monthly fee for the Jewish Studies portion of the school. Many families choose not to pay.

19 Helena Miller, "Beyond the Community: Jewish Day School Education in Britain," in *Jewish Day Schools, Jewish Communities,* ed. Alex Pomson and Howard Deitcher (Liverpool: Littman Library of Jewish Civilization, 2009), 193–206.

20 In 2017 the Thornhill campus of Leo Baeck Day School was forced to sell its building and move to rented quarters. In the same year the northern campus of TanenbaumCHAT closed down and merged with the Southern high school campus, a sudden move that was met with great frustration from the parent body. At the end of the 2018–19 school year Associated Hebrew Schools closed its Thornhill campus, merging with other school branches. At the same time Eitz Chaim Schools will also be closing down one of its campuses.

21 "Grassroots for Affordable Jewish Education," 2018, https://www.gaje.ca.

22 Randal F. Schnoor and Alex Pomson, "Le rôle des écoles juives à temps plein dans la vie des familles: le cas de l'Ontario (Jewish Day Schools in the Lives of Families: An Ontario Case Study)" in *Judaïsme et éducation: enjeux et défis pédagogiques,* ed. Sivane Hirsch, Marie McAndrew, and Geneviève Audet (Quebec City: Presses de l'Université Laval, 2016), 203–20.

23 The majority of these Toronto schools are affiliated with the UJA Federation of Toronto, which provides funding of approximately $12 million annually to support them. Of this, approximately $10 million is earmarked specifically for tuition subsidies. No other Jewish Federation in North America provides this level of tuition support. The level of support for tuition subsidies has remained frozen for the last several years, however, while need increases.

24 "Grassroots for Affordable Jewish Education," 2018, https://www.gaje.ca.

25 Michael Brown, "Canada: Jewish Education in Canada," in *International Handbook of Jewish Education,* ed. Helena Miller, Lisa D. Grant, and Alex Pomson (Dordrecht: Springer, 2011), 1141–53.

26 "Grassroots for Affordable Jewish Education," 2018, https://www.gaje.ca.

6 The Unsettling of Canadian Jewish History: Towards a Tangled History of Jewish–Indigenous Encounters

DAVID S. KOFFMAN

In her award-winning *Prairie Kaddish*, Isa Milman, a Victoria-based writer and the daughter of Holocaust survivors, hauntingly approaches the theme of loss in the middle of the twentieth century: loss of language, culture, and loved ones. It is an unconventional book, a mash-up of poetry and history that squeezes together graves and mourning rituals, the marked cemeteries of the Jewish agricultural colonies of the Canadian prairies with the unmarked cemeteries of the war-torn Russian Pale and European continent. Early in the book, Milman is heading towards the Lipton Hebrew Cemetery, 100 km north of Dysart, Saskatchewan, for the first time, pondering Jewish conceptions of death and dead bodies, when she observes the murals painted on Lipton's hotel facade: "I'd seen them on the way to the cemetery," she writes,

> The central panel showed a Jew in a black hat, wrapped in a blanket –
> or was it a *tallis*? – with a teepee in the background. Was there indeed a
> relationship between the Jewish settlers and the native people, already
> treatied onto reserves not far away? ... Such silence about the Cree and
> Métis people. Hardly mentioned in the Jewish memoirs I read, or in the
> recollections of the descendants of the settlers I sought out to interview.
> [...] Feeling my way back to the past, fingers groping for roots, roots be-
> coming fingers.[1]

Milman's book is about the connections between the living and the dead, about the sorted ways we humans make meaning out these connections, and it is a deeply Canadian book about homes lost. It is also, obliquely, about the surprising connection between Jews and Indigenous peoples in Canada – in her treatment, more of the poetic entanglements and absences on the theme of home, than the actual historical connections, of which she found few to none.[2]

This chapter aims to turn these connections from oblique to direct, and to spell out why connections between Jews and Indigenous peoples in Canada are important to the entire enterprise of Canadian Jewish history.[3] If one cannot – or ought not – ask about Canada *qua* home for the Jews without also asking about Canada *qua* home for other ethnic and religious minorities, one must pay particular attention to questioning how non-Indigenous Canadians speak about Canada as a home with respect to the past and present of Indigenous peoples. The original inhabitants of this land of incomplete conquests, to use Peter Russell's felicitous phrase, are being more frequently understood as founding people by non-Indigenous Canadians, though many Indigenous peoples have little interest in this kind of incorporation into Canadian national narratives. Seeing the particulars of Canadian minority histories through the lens of Indigenous–settler relations poses some serious challenges to those groups' historical narratives, just as paying attention to the place of Indigenous peoples in the constitutional arrangement that makes Canada a political entity and their places within the disputed sovereign territorial boundaries of the state, calls into question some of the assumptions about the extent and quality of belonging that other minority groups in Canada experience.[4] In this way, the immigrant–Indigenous encounter offers an important dimension to the home-making saga, to the story of particular minorities making a new home where others had been displaced from their homes. If settler society has an ongoing existence, we ought to disaggregate the immigrant/settler/guest populations and their respective encounters with Turtle Island's first peoples.[5] Examining how the religious, ethnic, and internal differences among the diverse sub-groups of immigrant/settler/guest populations shaped their respective encounters with Indigenous peoples may provide critical detail for the reconciliation process. For the purposes of this essay, we ask: What have Jewish–Indigenous peoples' interactions looked like? How might we think about Jews' home in Canada refracted through the prism of the interactions between the placed and the displaced?

We know very little at this point.[6] What we can say is that the idea of "aboriginality," as well as actual flesh-and-blood First Nations, Métis, and Inuit people have been present for the entire scope of Canadian Jewish history. There are hundreds if not thousands of sources from archives across Canada that, if taken together, would provide the basis for a thorough and complex inter-relational history of Jews and Indigenous peoples. A complex story of settling and unsettling certainly deserves a new body of scholarship based on research into primary sources.[7] For our purposes here, a wide-angle overview of this interactive history offers a kind of plea for thinking about Canadian Jewish life and the idea of "home" as seen through settler history.

First Cause: Business Opportunity and Settlement

The founding figures of the settled Canadian Jewish community were merchants who moved into Lower Canada in the wake of the British victories in New France in 1760. They travelled alongside soldiers and traders eager to expand enterprises in the fur- and pelt-rich lands south of James Bay, and subsequently, to territories west and north from there, or to supply British troops in their colonial ambitions against the French for the control of the fur trade with Indigenous peoples. Traders and sutlers (military provisions merchants) arrived with Amherst's troops and spread with the occupation of the St Lawrence Valley in the early 1760s with business networks that linked Saint-Denis-sur-Richelieu and Trois-Rivières to Montreal, New York, and beyond. Chapman Abraham, Gershon Levy, Benjamin Lyon, and Levy Solomons were among the fur traders, incorporated as the Northwest Company in 1779, a major operation in fur regions in the north, west, and interiors of Lower and Upper Canada. Their success rode on the financing and supply network of their ethnic and filial connections around the Atlantic colonial world.[8] Jewish merchant families entered into the historical drama of the Atlantic triangular trade world as part of a diasporic merchant minority community, helping circulate fur, gold, arms, seeds, tools, and slave bodies between Europe, its colonies, and Africa. Jews gained the foothold for permanent settlement in what would become Canada through Indigenous access to fur.[9]

These Jewish merchants became intimately involved in local economic changes and the political fall-out in and between nations that this lucrative business inevitably entailed.[10] Their interactions with First Nations involved a complex of economic, social, religious, political, and even sexual relations, about which we know quite little. The Berlin-born Ezekiel Solomons traded out of Montreal and Michilimackinac, and had several children with a Chippewa woman.[11] Abraham Jacob Frank married a Huron woman and then abandoned her when he left his fur region near Quebec City to rejoin his other wife in Montreal. Englishman Ferdinand Jacobs, perhaps the first Jew in western Canada, a man who served the Hudson's Bay Company between 1732 and 1775, married the half-Cree, half-English daughter of his former superior, Richard Norton.[12] Though these men married exogenously, they were not excluded from the budding Jewish community. On the contrary, they were among the founders of Shearith Israel in Montreal in 1768. We know far too little about these human engagements, though the fragments currently known hint at important questions about race, sexuality, language, and cultural exchange.

The pattern of business expansion and the social entanglement that accompanied it in Manitoba and the Pacific Northwest likely followed similar contours around the Great Lakes and Upper Canada. Jews started off as either peddlers or sutlers, bringing them into direct business contacts with Indigenous suppliers and producers. When they accumulated enough capital, they generally established larger general merchandizing businesses and consolidated larger zones of trade, typically moving to larger urban centres to participate in Jewish communal life. The genesis of Jewish business success in small towns throughout the country should be located in Indigenous business relations.

The Pacific northwest coast's network of Jewish entrepreneurs who built businesses around Indigenous trades offers a telling example. The Hudson's Bay Company, which had been granted exclusive rights for "Indian trading" by Great Britain, had dominated, sponsored, colonized, and policed the region. Their monopoly broke only after miners, speculators, and business-minded settlers rushed the Fraser River for gold in 1858, wherein dozens of Jewish entrepreneurs would be found trading with Indigenous peoples for furs, fish oils, sealskins, timber, and other goods, including heritage items.[13] Some Jews speculated in land.[14] By the 1860s, Jewish tobacconist and fur trader Meyer Malowanski, along with his non-Jewish Croatian partner Vincent Charles Baranovich, for instance, had developed one of the largest fur trading businesses on the coast by establishing a chain of posts from Bella Bella to southern Alaska.[15] Jews owned and operated all three of the "Cheap John" emporium stores that catered, in part, to the first generation of west coast tourists in Victoria. Entrepreneurs such as the brothers Levy, the brothers Shirpser, David Hart, and Mike Cohen helped grow the burgeoning industry.[16] Morris Moss, a man whose obituary celebrated him for "abandon[ing] the anxieties of Victoria life" soon after settling there from England, where he built a rewarding "life among the Indians at a trading post in Bella Coola." Moss proclaimed himself an "Indian Expert," and supplemented his trading post and seal fur business on Haida Gwaii (formerly known as the Queen Charlotte Islands) with work for the British Columbia Legislative Council, for which he handled a number of Indigenous murder trials and advised the government on Native customs in the 1860s. His successes bolstered his position in Victoria's Jewish community. Moss assumed the presidencies of a synagogue and a B'nai Brith lodge.[17]

The economic intermingling between Jews and Indigenous peoples continued into the early twentieth century, as the fur industry became industrialized. As historian George Colpitts has shown, in the 1920s and 1930s nimble Jewish, Lebanese, Armenian, and Roma "free traders" (so dubbed because of their independence from the Hudson's Bay Company) bought furs from Dene traders in northern Ontario and Manitoba, and moved them to cutters and stitchers on factory floors in Toronto, Montreal, and New York, and onto finishing houses and distribution networks in the United States and in continental Europe.[18] Jewish free traders brought in large hauls of furs and offered Dene traders more economic latitude, as well as credit, than did the HBC traders, who were under the command of a headquarters and therefore removed from the subtle fluctuations in timing and quality regarding shortages and spikes in demand.

These sorts of economic relationships presumably extended into all sorts of other interactions, about which we also know far too little. Jack Leve, whose business dealings with Cree peoples around James Bay and Sudbury facilitated his acquisition of Algonquian language skills, presumably had rich and complex interactions with the Nehi-yawak people his livelihood depended on in the 1920s and '30s. Leve's daughter, Judy Feld Carr, noted that "[w]hen I was born [in 1939], it took three months to track him down by dog-sled on Baffin Island to inform him of my birth."[19] Other intimate connections likely took place wherever Jews and Indigenous peoples fused their economic fates. George Simon grew up with an Indigenous nursemaid in Brant-ford, Ontario.[20] Harry Hirschfield of Hodgeson, Manitoba, celebrated as a "modern day trader, buying from Indian trappers, distributing to rural areas of West," developed a twenty-five-year-long friendship with Donald Muminawatum from Norway House while trading in furs, hides, senega root, bear gall, claws, and castorium in the 1940s, '50s and '60s.[21]

As a result of their involvement in markets for natural resources, Jews played a significant part in the development of one particularly important sub-market of Indigenous products: Indigenous heritage objects, also known as "curios." The buying and selling of things like wampum belts, totem poles, moccasins, and head-dresses, was an industry that linked rural outposts with national and trans-Atlantic markets for things "Indian," crossing national borders. The commodi-fication of these objects impacted the economics, politics, and cultures of the Indigenous sellers' communities and the white buyers' urban communities and cultures.[22] In Victoria, British Columbia, centre of the Pacific Northwest curio trade, the first generations of dealers included a significant number of Jews. Andrew Alfred Aaronson, Jacob Isaac, and Samuel Kirschenberg and his partner Fredrick Landsberg, owned and operated four of the five major companies active in the curio business on Johnson Street in Victoria.[23] At least seventeen Jews listed themselves as Indian traders in Victoria business registers.[24] (Jewish traders also dotted the west coast and the western territories in the United States, in Oklahoma and Nebraska, Utah and Nevada, Arizona and New Mexico.)[25] Pre-existing business relationships based on contacts, linguistic capacities, trading post locations, merchandising and distribution channels helped establish the commercial infrastructure for the curio industry.[26] John Jacob "Jack" Hart, an English Jew and former filibuster in Nicaragua, established himself as a merchant trader fifty yards from the Indian Reserve, selling liquor illegally to Haida and Tsimshian people for fur, silver, and gold work from skilled Native artisans.[27]

Through their business links with one another, turn of the century Jewish businessmen in Victoria, Omaha, and Santa Fe helped promote the Indigenous heritage industry across the continent. Jews sold Indigenous artefact collections to tourists and museums alike, creating new markets and creating value for heritage objects. Jews mediated the flow of these cultural objects, acquiring them from local homes and villages, and distributing them to fashionable city homes in Canada's and America's urban centres as decoration, tourist souvenirs, adventure memorabilia, and as objects suited for "playing Indian." They also moved these artefacts from trading posts to museums, where they formed collections as specimens of science displayed alongside exhibits of other so-called primitive peoples, or exhibitions of America's natural history, its geology, and flora and fauna. Victoria's J.J. Hart sold curios to middle-class tourists, to mail-order consumers, and to the World Columbian Exposition in Chicago in 1893, as well as a significant collection to the German Jewish immigrant anthropologist Franz Boas. Abraham and Rose Aaronson likewise sold hundreds of artefacts to tourists and museums including the American Museum of Natural History, the Ottawa Field Museum, and the Royal Ontario Museum in Toronto.[28] Other Jewish traders sold collections of Indigenous artefacts to the major natural history and ethnology museums, including ones in Chicago, Milwaukee, and Berlin.[29] The preservation, display, and sale of Indigenous heritage objects also served local tourist industries in the west. In British Columbia Jewish curio dealers worked with government officials like the Tourist Development Agency and the City of Victoria to help attract tourists eager to observe and experience the "exotic Natives."[30] Provincial and municipal agencies provided museum collectors with guides, Jews among them, and contacts with Indigenous sellers from whom such collections could be gathered.[31]

Understanding Jews' involvement with and appreciation of Indigenous heritage art and commerce is a fraught and complex development that had a range of outcomes and is subject to some interpretive dispute. We need to know more about the interactions between specific First Nations and settler Jews as the latter sought social integration and economic mobility among fellow whites on the frontier. Did Jews, as peddlers, military sutlers, and merchants, embrace or complicate colonial settlement and its politics of Aboriginal confinement? Was their Jewishness influential in shaping the social, religious, and economic realities of the frontier? Did First Nations make meaningful distinctions between Jewish and gentile settlers?

While commercial opportunity drew Jewish migration to Canada, its ultimate goal was stable resettlement and the establishment of Jewish communities. Settlement in Canada more broadly, west of the Great Lakes in particular, was premised on the myth that the land was free and empty of people, waiting for new colonists, supported and enabled by state and military policy that removed First Nations onto reserves and aimed to control key travel routes, sometimes by way of legal land ownership and the extinguishing of Indigenous rights to land by treaties, though in many cases (particularly in British Columbia) without the recognition of Aboriginal title. Capitalism colluded with colonialism in the making of Canada, and Jews were, willy-nilly, active agents in the colonial settlement process; Jewish peddlers were capitalism's cutting edge. They were often humble foot soldiers on the forefront of an expanding commercial frontier. Their small trading activities were linked to the large processes of transformations of people (including Jews and Indigenous peoples), land, and nation so that immigrant communities could resettle and create futures for themselves and their children.

Settler history and settler–Indigenous encounters are more clearly seen in rural settings and in small-town or county-level histories than in the larger cities where Canadian Jewish history is usually located (for sound demographic reasons). But the Canadian Jewish experience has not been exclusively urban, and settlement's impact on Indigenous peoples was as profound. As scholars of Indigenous history, activists, and government agencies have shown in great detail, fur trading like that of the Northwest Company as well as mining changed First Nations communities, disrupted traditional knowledge and practice, changed food, economics, culture, and language.[32] They also introduced new pathogens that were responsible for the deaths of an estimated quarter of a million First Nations people by the turn of the last century.[33] While First Nations communities tended to suffer geographic dislocation, political disorder, and cultural disruption in the west, Jews achieved stunning social mobility, religious latitude, relative economic security, and created scores of new communities.[34] In the words of William Toll, the historian of Pacific coast Jewry: "For Jewish men, the merchant role in the West enabled them and their families in a single generation to move from medieval artisanship and itinerant merchandising to the highest civil status."[35]

Most of the Jews who arrived on the rural margins of Canadian life in the late nineteenth and early twentieth centuries had been squeezed out of big cities for lack of employment opportunities. Some eastern European Jews became agriculturalists in the Canadian prairies as part of the Canadian government's efforts to place "desirable" European immigrants with farming experience onto the land that had recently been cleared of Aboriginal people by state authorities for this express purpose.[36]

First Nations displacement was necessarily connected to the Jewish experience, even though Jews did not craft the policies of Indigenous segregation and persecution, nor were these policies created for the particular benefit of the Jews. Yet the state permitted Jews to establish nearly 240 farms on one of the dozens of Jewish agricultural colonies built in Alberta, Saskatchewan, and Manitoba between 1882 and 1915, all of which were erected all on lands recently cleared of Aboriginal title by government authorities for the express purpose of making it "productive" for European immigrant builders of Canada. The Canadian state laid out the framework for establishing this European settlement in the Dominion Land Act of 1872, which subdivided townships, sections, and individual 160-acre plots, essentially given away for free. Some Jewish migrants, lacking agricultural training but sponsored and supported nonetheless by the Montefiore Agricultural Aid Society, Young Men's Hebrew Benevolent Society, Baron de Hirsch's Jewish Colonization Association, and/or the Jewish Immigrant Aid Society, took advantage.[37] As was the case with Jewish traders' encounters with Indigenous peoples, we just don't know enough about Jewish rural and agricultural settlers' impressions of or interactions with First Nations, but we can say that the impacts of this settlement process were felt unevenly by Indigenous peoples and Jews, and that home-making in the Prairies in the decades on both sides of this agricultural settlement in the early twentieth century involved displacing and "placing," settling and unsettling, and that these processes – like settlement process more broadly – were necessarily intertwined.

Jewish–Indigenous interactions that involved economic intercourse did not, of course, cease in the middle of the twentieth century. Future scholars interested in Jewish–Indigenous relations will likely find complex and ambiguous archival material with which they may develop histories of their interactions in three sectors, each sensitive in its own right: casinos, the energy industry, and in the liquor market. What were the historical conditions that led to Jewish involvement in the casino business, and what did their interactions with specific First Nations, under respective provincial gaming and gambling laws, look like? To what extent might questions about criminality, strategic inter-ethnic alliances, or exploitation be enriched by attention to places where Jews might have been involved in casinos?

Jews have not played a particularly large role in the energy sector, though someone like Michael Dan, the president of the Gemini Power Corporation and Regulus Investments Inc., a neuroscientist and philanthropist, has made a significant effort and donated large sums to advancing Indigenous health and economic outcomes (including a recent $10-million donation to establish the University of Toronto's Waakebiness-Bryce Institute for Indigenous Health) could offer an inroad to yet another important aspect of this history.[38]

An account of Jewish–Indigenous entanglements involving alcohol, an industry in which Jews have often played a significant role, before, during, and after prohibition, might also add yet another layer of complexity to the historical encounter. In addition to the Indigenous and Jewish sources that this history would have to consider, missionary sources, government and social service agencies and policies, legal regimes, and business records could shed light on a complex story.

"Canadian" Identity Formation

Connections between Canadian Jews and Indigenous peoples have not all been relegated to the realms of business and settlement alone. Other persistent and periodic linkages have been situated in the realm of the cultural imagination, rather than in actual face-to-face encounters. Anglo-Protestant ideas that brought Jews and Indigenous peoples together have taken a wide variety of forms, and each case ought to be considered within its own context for what each *imaginary* reveals about the non-Jewish and non-Indigenous peoples who crafted it. Canadians from a range of cultural locations have tied Jews and Indigenous peoples together, and have done so since before Canada became a state.

The oldest and most persistent of these imagined linkages between Jews and Indigenous peoples in Canadian history were derived from

biblical stories and were based on Christians' eagerness to make connections between their lives in the new world colonies and the history of ancient Israel. A diverse variety of Christian claimants made
a striking number of competing claims throughout the seventeenth,
eighteenth, and nineteenth centuries about the origins of the Native
inhabitants of the continent, and looked to the Hebrew Bible as concrete history. Some argued that "Indians" were part of the generation
of Babel, dispersed to North America at the earliest possible point in
the Bible's telling of human history, and could thus be derived from
pre-Hebrew "stock". While many argued that Indigenous peoples
had descended from one of the so-called lost tribes of Israel, others
claimed that they descended from or had made contact with ancient
Israelite, Canaanite, or Phoenician seafarers. All of these claims, evident in dozens of books, articles, lectures, and sermons produced and
reproduced for a range of scholarly and popular audiences, sought
to link Indigenous peoples with the Jews and the Hebrew Bible. Mar-
shalled by frontline missionaries, humble clergymen, and high-status
theologians alike, these claims all shared a stake in rooting the divine
biblical narrative onto Canadian soil, a version of history that would
make the lives of colonists central to God's plan on earth and to the
redemption at the end of time. Interestingly, these Indigenous–biblical
linkages were advanced by a range of other writers with no obvious
Christological ambitions, including scholars of geography, ethnogra-
phy, and philology, as well as the popular writers of "captivity" narratives. Though these claims were vigorously debated and discredited,
they were compelling enough to a range of writers and readers to have
kept a debate alive for nearly three centuries. Though these claims
were wildly inaccurate, and though their rhetoric stripped Indigenous peoples of their fundamental claims to indigeneity itself, these
ideas nevertheless brought Jews and Indigenous peoples together and
made them share some measure of identity that was central to Christian settlers' understandings of how and why Canada might be home.
The stories of Israelite Indians implied that the relocation of European
civilization onto the "new" landscape of natural beauty and bounty
was part of a necessary and perhaps even divinely inspired mission.
Christian colonists imaginatively made over Aboriginal places with
biblically inspired place names such as Beth El, Salem, Jaffa, Sharon, Bethany, Eden, Hebron, Goshen, and the Jordan River, as they
attempted to remake the Canadian landscape into a New Israel and
a place for Christian history to continue to unfold.[39] Jews and Indigenous peoples were both considered, in a curious way, *preliminary* to
Christian faith and settlement.[40]

The most regular exposure that Indigenous peoples had to Jewishness or Judaism surely came with their encounter with missionaries and the teachings these Christians brought concerning Israel and "the Jews."[41] The sheer number of missionary–Indigenous encounters, spanning a variety of Indigenous nations, coupled with changing historical and local circumstances and differences among evangelizing Christian denominations would likely yield further dimensions to the history of Indigenous–Jewish relations. What did missionaries try to teach Indigenous peoples about Jews? What were their aims in this preaching? To the extent that Christian teachings blended in some syncretistic way with cultural elements of each unique Indigenous culture, what shapes did Jews take on that made sense? How, or to what extent, did these figures of Jews or Jewishness impact the actual encounters that specific Indigenous groups may have had later with actual Jews?

Other nineteenth-century discussions central to the shaping of what it meant to feel or become Canadian also pivoted in part on imaginary connections between Indigenous peoples and Jews. Perhaps the most striking nineteenth-century example is Louis Riel's profound identification with Jewish mythology, and the key role it played in the development of Métis identity, and by extension the founding of the province of Manitoba and the very terms of Canadian confederacy. Riel was, quite possibly, the first Indigenous leader to make a place for the Jews in both his religious and political thought. In his letters, diary entries, and public speeches, Riel identified himself with biblical and messianic heroes. In one jail diary entry, a month before his execution for treason after the failed Northwest "rebellion" in 1855, he wrote, "The Indians of the northern part of this continent are of Jewish origin ... some Hebrew slaves on board, went astray around the time when the children of Jacob were wandering in the desert under the leadership of Moses." Addressing himself, Riel declared: "By the Indian blood that flows in your veins, you are Jewish. And through your paternal great-grandmother you belong to the Jewish nation as much as the first David belonged to the Gentiles, through his paternal great-grandmother."[42] Riel likened the Métis to the Israelites, "a persecuted race deprived of their heritage," wished to restore Judaic practices such as the Saturday Sabbath, and wanted to install the Jews in a New Judea on the shores of the Pacific, "to console their hearts for the mourning of 1800 years." Yet as a Catholic, he also saw Jewish conversion to Christianity as a necessary precursor to the ultimate redemption of world Jewry and unquestioningly accepted bigoted ideas about Jewish wealth. Riel's imaginary links to the Jews speaks to elemental issues of home-making and difference – Métis, outsiders, belonging, and Canadian identity.[43]

This realm of encounters between Jews and Indigenous peoples in the Canadian imagination found an echo in the ways that gentile writers used "the Jew" or "the Indian" in their discourses and how Jewish writers pondered their own relationships to Canadian place, identity, and destiny by imagining the Jewish relationship to "Indianness" as a way to work through Jewish questions about peoplehood in a Canadian context.[44] Riel's blended Indigenous-Jewish identity, for example, became a useful object in the writings of Adele Wiseman. In her play, *Testimonial Dinner*, which staged Louis Riel and John A. Macdonald in a trans-historical struggle for the spiritual fate of Canada, Wiseman used Riel to "express graphically [her own] feeling not only of how much the past influences the present, but of the fact that it is alive and functioning in the present, and active in determining the decisions which shape the future of the country and the individual destinies of our people."[45] In her play, three generations of immigrant Jews navigate their way through an imagined Riel–Macdonald structuring tension that forms an ongoing spiritual struggle for Canadianness, and the "living pre-history [that] has shaped three generations." Riel protests injustice, accusing Macdonald of being "proud of your nation of stolen land and respectable thieves" and laments that "we could have built a nation together had you recognized our right to exist, in our own way, as equals." As Riel and Macdonald exchange barbs and insults, the play's first act concludes with Riel declaring, "I am David Mordecai ... I am a Jew. A Jew! See, the blood of my Indian ancestors, Jewish blood in my veins."

Cultural reflections on elements of Indigeneity have provided a vehicle for Canadian Jews to think about home and the nature of their belonging. Though these sorts of imagined encounters are diverse and in no way straightforward or internally consistent, they lay bare some of the complex ways that Jews have utilized ideas of Indigeneity or aboriginality in order to work through questions of what it meant to belong in Canada or to have a Canadian identity. As Rebecca Margolis, a contributor to this volume, has shown elsewhere, two prominent Yiddish thinkers – H.M. Caiserman and B.G. Sack – shared an interest in the Mohawk English writer Tekahiowake (E. Pauline Johnson) in the 1920s and '30s.[46] In Tekahiowake these Jewish intellectuals found a shared history of persecution, a model of resistance to assimilation into Canadian dominant culture, and an exemplary minority intellectual who inspired pride in her difference and heritage.

Wiseman, Caiserman, and Sack were not alone in this interest. In fact, there is a steady stream of literary interest in Indigenous peoples and themes that runs through twentieth-century Canadian Jewish literature. Falk Zolf's 1954 autobiographical novel *Oif Fremder Erd* (On Foreign Soil) described a Jewish immigrant fantasy of an ancient Indian virgin sacrifice ceremony while visiting Niagara Falls.[47] Elhanan Hanson's frontier short stories *Trayder Ed* (Trader Ed) of 1957 made repeated use of Indigenous fantasies, characters, and themes.[48] Jewish Canadian literary figures writing in English also found Indigenous themes and characters useful in their novels, poetry, and short stories. Eli Mandel's *Out of Place*, Leonard Cohen's *Beautiful Losers*, and Mordecai Richler's *Incomparable Atuk* and *Solomon Gursky Was Here* all created Indigenous characters. Indigenous peoples and themes emerge from A.M. Klein's 1945 poem, "Indian Reservation: Caughnawaga," gave shape to the author's fantasy:

> Childhood, that wished me Indian, hoped that
> One afterschool I'd leave the classroom chalk,
> The varnish smell, the watered dust of the street.
> To join the clean outdoors and the Iroquois track.[49]

Klein's poem laments the disappearance of "braves, the faces like autumn fruit." He critiques, with some bitterness, the "bronze, like their nobility expunged" by the commercialization of Indian culture for tourists. Ultimately a reflection on his perception of the ghostly "disappearance" of Indigenous peoples and their homes, Klein describes how Indigenous grounds looked to him to be a "crypt," how their animals became "pale," and their own bodies lost the "shine of the fur," though, of course, the people of Kahnawá:ke never disappeared. Younger writers, like Norman Ravvin, another contributor to this volume, have written stories with Jewish protagonists who meet Indigenous characters (a Kwakiutl man in a delicatessen in New York in one story, and an amateur folklorist and ethnomusicologist named Red Thunder Cloud, the last speaker of his language, Catawba, in another).[50]

Canadian Jews have created Indigenous characters and used Indigenous themes in their fiction, poetry, and plays. In the absence of close readings of any of these works, suffice it to say that Canadian Jewish authors had some measure of identification and empathy with their Indigenous characters, or have looked to Indigenous themes in order to work through Canadian or Jewish issues. This sort of *sympathy by way of lament* is not unique to Jewish authors. Nor does the fact that Jewish authors have used ideas about Indigeneity in order to work through their own issues mean that they had any special affinity with Indigenous peoples; on the contrary, this literary activity may very well be better understood as one of the oft-cited forms of discursive colonialism, or what decolonization scholars Eve Tuck and Wayne Yang have called settler "moves to innocence."[51]

This Jewish capacity to engage with Indigenous themes in order to work through Canadian home-making questions was not limited to literature. The Canadian Jewish Congress bought the non-Indigenous Walter Redinger's four-cast fibreglass sculptures *Totems* in 1972 to greet its visitors at its national headquarters in Montreal. Aiming to "represent images of [the Canadian Jewish] past and present," the CJC looked to Indigenous symbolic forms to monumentalize its Canadian character and its connection to a long Canadian past. The Ottawa chapter of Hadassah WIZO arranged a display of Indigenous artefacts in 1979.[52] Important studies could be undertaken of Jewish involvement in the business side of First Nations and Inuit arts as dealers, entrepreneurs, and curators. The experiences and circumstances, decisions, and implications of the loose cadre of Canadian Jews who played significant roles in the Canadian Indigenous art world and market (particularly Inuit art) from the 1960s onward, including Stephen Lazarus, Avrom Isaacs, Harry and Marcia Klamer, Kiki and Si Gilman, Kate and Laurence Jacobs, Sheila Romalis, and Sandra Barz, await examination and contextualization.[53]

A similarly unexamined case study of Jewish-Indigenous "imagined relations" involves countless instances of Jews "playing Indian" at home and school, during holidays, parties, and pageants. It is worth asking about the Jewish dimension to this play, since Jews participated in this distinctly racial pastime *as Jews*, with their own set of racialized anxieties and investments, and their own communal and educational needs. It seems that Jewish "redface" performances took place among young Jews of the Porcupine Girls' League, Toronto's 59th Boy Scout troop, and the Kiwanis Clubs of the 1920s and '30s.[54] Indian play, imagined Aboriginality, and actual First Nations erasure were equally a part of working-, middle-, and owning-class Jewish recreational life in the summers of Algonquin, Muskoka, and Temagami for Toronto Jews, the Laurentians for Montrealers, and the north side of Lake Winnipeg for Winnipeggers.[55]

Playing Indian at Jewish summer camps – for example, Camp Northland (B'nai Brith), sponsored by Jewish organizations like the Hebrew Maternal Aid Society, the United Jewish Charities' Fresh Air Society, the Hebrew Maternity Aid Society, the Jewish Welfare Fund, and even the Canadian Jewish Congress; as well as private camps owned and operated by Jews for predominantly Jewish clientele like Camps Wahonowin, Winnebagoe, Wabikon, Tamarak, Tamakwa, and

Manitoubing – offer another example in which Canadian Jews wrestled with questions about their own Canadianness with recourse to Indigenous ideas, albeit imagined and invented ones in this case. As I have argued elsewhere, Indian play at Jewish summer camps offered overlapping lessons about character building, tribalism, and spirituality, race disappearance, colonialism, and more. By providing opportunities for campers to don so-called primitive Indian identities and then remove them once the summer was over, camps afforded Jews both a dose of anti-modernist respite from urban pressures, and reinforcement of urban, modern values. Even at Jewish camps that promoted specific ideologies, such as the Communist Workman's Circle Camp Yungvelt in Pickering or the Zionist Camp Balfour included some appeals to Indianness that are worth exploring further.[56]

Individual Activists in Law, Politics, and Social Science

Canadian Jewish empathy towards, sympathy for, identification with, appropriation of, and projection onto Indigenous lives expressed in the artistic works and community social programs they created have long been reflected and *operationalized* in the realms of social work, law, and politics by Jewish social activists and professionals. A significant number of individual Jewish liberals and progressives from the middle of the twentieth century onward devoted their energy to promoting the rights of First Nations and Inuit. Jewish doctors and nurses, lawyers and civil servants, educators, geographers, and policy makers all worked towards improving Indigenous peoples' lives, though no systematic study of individual advocates has yet to be undertaken.

The first Jewish activist for Indigenous empowerment in Canada was likely Franz Boas, father of modern anthropology. The complicated encounter between Boasian anthropologists, anthropology, and Indigenous peoples had a salient stream of Jewishness coursing through it. Though the discipline's ambivalent relationship with Indigenous history and politics has been commented upon extensively, the nature of the Jewish dimension of anthropologist/Indigenous history has been left under-interrogated.[57] Yet Boas's Jewishness most certainly influenced his scholarship and activism.[58] Boas's lifelong contribution to Indigenous life and cultural relativism began with his research expedition to and encounter with Baffin Island Inuit. Following his emigration from Germany, Boas continued with his career-shaping involvement with the Kwakiutl (Kwakwaka'wakw) on Vancouver Island and dozens of other Indigenous groups in Canada and the United States, serving as a supervisor and creative shaper of the entire first generation of professional anthropologists. Boas, of course, tirelessly promoted a vision for cultural pluralism and anti-racism as he reshaped the field of anthropology and sought influence in a range of policy circles.

Following in Boas's footsteps, many other Jewish anthropologists were committed to explaining Indigenous cultures and difference to whites, often not just in scholarly settings, but in activist ones as well. Edward Sapir produced a stunning scholarly output on North American Indian languages and cultures, and devoted a portion of his career to Indigenous civic uplift and policy redress. He also inspired dozens of influential linguists and anthropologists. Sapir worked as a field ethnologist at Geological Survey of Canada in the 1910s, studying Ojibwa in southwestern Ontario, and lobbied Canada's commissioner of Indian affairs, Duncan Campbell Scott, "as a first step in trying to do what I can to see justice done the West Coast Indians."[59] As the head of the Anthropology Division of the Geological Survey, he involved himself in details of Indigenous life in Canada where he hoped, according to his biographer, that "scientific expertise could aid Indian causes."[60] He placed the scientific skills of his division at the disposal of Indigenous communities as well as the federal government, worked to repeal an anti-potlach law in Canada, and negotiated to have eleven wampum treaty belts that were being exhibited at the University of Pennsylvania Museum repatriated to the Six Nations Iroquois Reserve in Ontario. Ruth Leah Bunzel studied the Káínawa (also known as the Kainai Nation or Blood Tribe) of Alberta, and worked on alcoholism as a barrier to economic and political advances.[61] David Goodman Mandelbaum, an anthropologist and trained rabbi, who began his career conducting fieldwork on the Sweetgrass Reserve with Cree Nation in Saskatchewan in 1940, devoted scholarly attention to Jewish and Native Americans throughout the 1930s.[62] Walter Goldschmidt worked in the field with Tlingit teachers to document occupation in their villages.[63] Each case deserves detailed research. Jews like Richard Slobodin, Harvey Feit, John Honigmann, Marty Weinstein, Hugh Brody, Pamela Stern, and Peter Usher undertook social scientific inquiry and fieldwork in the Canadian north between the 1930s and 1980s, and conducted most of their teaching and research careers in Canada. It is important to bear in mind, however, that despite most anthropologists' humanistic interests in their Indigenous subjects, anthropology has been, in many ways, a colonial project. The meaning or impact of some anthropologists' Jewishness, therefore, is both underdetermined and far from obvious.

These anthropologists shared something in common with the Canadian Jewish social workers, lawyers, nurses, and doctors who served Indigenous communities. We have no idea of the extent to which Jews took an interest in helping Indigenous peoples throughout the second half of the twentieth century, but there are many examples available to illustrate the point. Dr Fischel Coodin, for example, delivered an address to the Jewish Historical Society of Western Canada in 1968 entitled "Wandering Jew in the Artic" about his service and travels in the early 1960s as a paediatrician serving Inuit settlements around Churchill, Manitoba, and the Keewatin Region of the Northwest Territories, while the social worker and anti-racist activist Rodney Bobiwash worked at Toronto's Native Canadian Centre. Lea Roback, feminist, pacifist, bookseller, and trade unionist, spent part of her lifetime of advocacy work on Aboriginal women's rights in the 1960s.[64] The influence of these activists' Jewishness remains to be interrogated on a case-by-case basis, but it seems reasonable to assume that their sensibilities and activist agendas were influenced, at least in part, by the Jewish immigrant experience and by a shared vision of helping Canada become a more inclusive home.

Jewish lawyers worked on First Nations land claims, served as benefactors and jurists in the Canadian Civil Liberties Association, and have taken prominent roles in high-profile Indigenous cases, broadly concerned with social equality relevant to Jewish needs and anxieties. The lawyer Steven Aronson worked pro bono to earn an appeal and acquittal for Donald Marshall, a Mi'kmaq man who was wrongly convicted of murder and whose case raised a number of prescient questions about systemic anti-Indian biases in the Canadian justice system.[65] Alan B. Gold, a chief justice of the Quebec Superior Court, helped negotiate a settlement between the Mohawks of Kanesatake and the government of Quebec to help resolve the Oka crisis in 1990.[66] A cadre of lawyers and legal scholars have been active in legal and legal-scholarly discussions of Indigenous issues for the legal community and this country's judicial establishment, including Michael Asch, Norman Zlotkin, Jeremy Webber, and Harold Finkler.[67]

Little to no scholarship has yet been produced that examines the Jewish dimensions of the vocal and prominent Canadian Jewish researchers, journalists, or politicians Michael Posluns or Irwin Cotler and their respective engagements with First Nations advocacy issues. Posluns has helped raise the profile of Indigenous rights in Canada since the early 1970s with his radio documentaries and books, as an editor of *Akwesasne Notes*, as a court worker, as parliamentary adviser to the National Indian Brotherhood (the precursor of the Assembly of First Nations), and as an adviser to the Dene Nation and others on governance, land claims, mercury poisoning, and other issues.[68] The famed social justice advocate, MP, and cabinet minister Irwin Cotler devoted considerable energy to advocating for First Nations rights, inclusion, and redress. His 1995 lecture, "The New Human Rights Agenda," for example, outlined the milestones of the global and Canadian human rights legacy. In offering an agenda for the decade ahead, he highlighted "the plight of Indigenous peoples," along with combating racial incitement, the elemental right to food, and children and women as priority areas.[69] "If there is a case that is an historic and continuing assault on our human rights sensibilities as Canadians," Cotler argued, the plight of Aboriginal Peoples is "the single most important human rights issue confronting Canada today." His concluding reflection noted that "as history has taught us only too well ... while it may begin with Blacks, Aboriginals or Jews as victims of the violations of human rights, it doesn't end with them. The struggle against racism, antisemitism and the like must therefore not be seen simply as a Black issue or an Aboriginal issue or a Jewish issue, but as a profound justice issue of the first import."[70]

There have been many other tantalizing scraps of Jewish political discourse on the fate of Indigenous life in Canada, with commentary by Canadian Jewish social scientists and activists. Some of this commentary seems to reveal a measure of disjuncture between Jewish social thought and Indigenous perspectives, perhaps showing some of the limits of the liberalism that Jewish Canadians have adopted. In the 1967 NFB film "Encounter with Saul Alinsky," for example, shot on the Rama Indian Reserve, the famed American Jewish labour organizer tells Rama Indians: "I wouldn't live on a Jewish reserve!" As Alinsky advises young activists (possibly Duke Redbird, a member of the Saugeen First Nation) to seize the tools of power, to campaign to repeal the Indian Act, to bombard the media, and to assemble a legal team, they retort that the price they'd have to pay in identity terms by adopting this style of advocacy would be too high; they did not want to leave the reserve.[71] Morton Weinfeld, another contributor to this volume, once argued that Indigenous peoples might advance their community's long-term interests by developing both a "Zionist" commitment to their traditional territories on reserve, and a "Diaspora" set of community institutions off-reserve in cities across Canada that could support Indigenous culture, religion, and political rights from the places where Canadian power lay.[72] No study has yet to analyse or contextualize the ways in which the Canadian Museum of Human Rights, with its two galleries devoted to First Nations (originally inspired by and partly funded posthumously by Izzy Asper) wove together Jewish and Indigenous persecution for a national audience with public funding. Such a study could be the point of departure for a sober analysis of the thorny "comparative genocide" discussions in Canada that compare the Jewish and Indigenous experiences: their histories of suffering and the politics of recognition.[73]

Organized Advocacy and Solidarity

Advocacy work appealed not only to individual Jews who may or may not have understood their work to be connected to their Jewishness; the organized Jewish community also devoted its resources to Indigenous affairs as it sought to reshape the Canada it encountered as a pluralistic and fair nation. The Jewish Labour Committee began its work to organize Indigenous peoples in Ontario in the 1960s grounded in its desire to fight discrimination and defend minority interests.[74] Kalmen Kaplansky, and later Alan Borovoy, leaders at the JLC, engaged with a variety of Indigenous leaders and causes over the course of their careers. Borovoy, a lawyer who resolved dozens of Indigenous discrimination cases, also organized marches with hundreds of First Nations people from Kenora and from neighbouring reserves in the late 1960s to highlight bigotry and to demand services from the government including access to telephone infrastructure and an alcohol treatment centre.[75] Writing in his 2013 memoirs about the CJC's support for the JLC, which allowed it to leverage Jewish organizational power in addition to its unionist allies and supporters, Borovoy remarked that "unlike the CJC and most other Jewish anti-discrimination organizations, antisemitism was not necessarily the JLC's highest priority; it was equally immersed in combating discrimination against blacks, Asians and aboriginals."[76] No careful study of these sources – or other Jewish–Indigenous solidarity efforts – has yet to be undertaken, but we do know that when Borovoy left the JLC, he served as the general counsel of the Canadian Civil Liberties Association for forty years. A significant portion of its caseload dealt with Indigenous issues.[77] In the Maritimes, Cape Breton's Jewish community co-sponsored an Indian Non-Indian Relations seminar for residents in Sydney and on the Eskasoni and Membertou Reserves in 1972. Across the country and a decade later, the Winnipeg Jewish Social Services Mt Carmel Clinic began serving predominantly Métis and Native clientele after the Jewish community migrated out of the Jewish district around Selkirk Ave.

Communally sponsored Jewish social activism on behalf of Indigenous peoples increased after the 1970s, with Canada's new appreciation, valorization, and appropriation of Indigenous issues, in both urban and rural settings. This interest coincided with the emergence of multiculturalism and Canada's embrace of First Nations and occasionally Inuit themes and criticism of the erroneous idea that Canada can boast of a clean ethical posture vis-à-vis Indigenous peoples. As the pre-eminent voice that claimed to represent Canadian Jewish interests in the national public, legislative, and judicial spheres, the CJC took an active role in a divergent range of Indigenous matters. Interested in Jewish contributions to early Canadian life, the CJC kept records of Jewish merchants who were active during the wars of incomplete conquest, both French and Indian.[78] The CJC's interest in Indigenous issues and organizations, however, went far beyond that. Congress steadily kept track of Indigenous affairs, filtering "Indian issues" through the lens of Jewish issues, producing and circulating dozens of short articles devoted to Indigenous issues in their weekly and monthly *Inter Office Information* and *Information and Comment* circulars, each of which detailed some event or issue with which the CJC was involved. In the spring of 1950, one of the Congress's House of Commons observers reported to the CJC's Executive of the Joint Public Relations Committee that federal legislation was being passed for the provision of religious instruction to Indigenous students in schools. The circular noted that the proposed legislation in the "Act Respecting Indians" stipulated that "the Governor in Council may make regulations to provide for religious teaching in day schools" more broadly. If the federal government was prepared to pay for religious instruction for Indigenous students beyond provinces' respective mandates, these Jewish activists noted, a window might be open for the federal government to support Jewish education too.[79]

Indeed, throughout the late 1950s and 1960s, the CJC produced a series of reports on a range of issues that dovetailed with Indigenous issues, including fundamental rights and freedoms, the Criminal Code, freedom of religion, and anti-discrimination laws.[80] By the mid-1970s, Congress began to participate in and make its presence known at rallies for "Indian and Eskimo" land rights, suggesting that it was beginning to take an interest in public education and solidarity-building strategies that would take place in the public sphere and run parallel to Congress's continued behind-the-scenes *stadlanut* politics. By the late 1980s and early 1990s, Congress even turned some attention to social action work on residential schools.[81] It provided grants to Indigenous organizations like the Canadian Association for Support of Native Peoples, the Indian Eskimo Association of Canada, and the Aboriginal Healing Foundation from the 1960s through the 1990s,[82] and was attuned to governmental and constitutional issues like the Royal Commission on Aboriginal Peoples, and the government's Indian and Northern Affairs.[83]

Minority rights and the nature of Indigenous belonging versus Jewish belonging also concerned the CJC executive. CJC leaders responded to the Report of the Royal Commission on Bilingualism and Biculturalism of 1970 with briefs and inter-office circulars that included references to "Indians," particularly on matters that related to both Jewish and Indigenous issues such as ineffectiveness of anti-discrimination legislation, housing, employment, public office for immigrants, and language protections. Even the CJC's resistance to early multicultural policy made reference to Indigenous affairs. In more than one instance in the early 1970s Abe Arnold criticized federal policy for minimizing First Nations and Inuit grievances. "When PM Trudeau proclaimed [bilingualism and biculturalism] as government policy in 1971," he wrote, "it was interpreted in some quarters as the dawn of a new era of promise fulfilment for many of the tribes of people who have wandered into Canada, as the 'Land of Promise,' since Confederation."[84] Figuring all ethnic communities as "tribes," Arnold wrote that minorities like the Jews came to Canada "after the first two major tribes, the 'Francophones' and 'Anglophones,' who began the displacement of the original inhabitants of 'Canaan-ada' several centuries earlier. The native Indians and Eskimos have been trying to tell us that the 'promise' is really theirs, but now they are only one more voice in the babel created by the more vociferous elements of the newer tribes."[85] Arnold echoed this sentiment in an article on the Trudeau government's multicultural policy two years later, criticizing the new policy for relegating the cultural contributions of Indigenous peoples "to a footnote." Federal policy, he thought, did not live up to the promise of its virtues. Though this was but one prong in Arnold's critique of multicultural policy, the fact that it devalued Indigenous peoples made it, in his mind, a disservice to Canadian Jewry.[86]

Among Jewish policy advocates, social scientists, and others, the Jewish perspectives on Indigenous relations sat uneasily with the impacts of those engagements on actual Indigenous peoples. Among the most uncomfortable of these moments in the Jewish–Indigenous encounter is perhaps the Sixties Scoop, during which Jewish Family Services of Montreal was involved in adopting an unknown number of Indigenous children who had been forcibly removed from their homes by federal officials. In her account of growing up as an adopted Indigenous child in an urban Jewish family, the Cree-born Nakuset Shapiro wrote about her experience suffering bigotry, shame, and confusion.[87] It is one more fascinating and delicate piece of the puzzle that is needed to flesh out a fuller Jewish–Indigenous history.

The intensity of Canadian Jews' interest in thinking through Indigenous issues and establishing relationships with specific individuals and organizations increased after the turn of the millennium. In 2002

Jewish associations responded to the seemingly unprompted anti-semitic comments of a former Assembly of First Nations' (AFN) National Chief David Ahenakew after a lecture he had delivered to the Federation of Saskatchewan Indian Nations. Jewish intra-communal discussion about Indigenous issues as well as conversations between Jews and Indigenous leaders, residential school survivors, elders, and youth have intensified over the past decade and a half. Synagogue, day school, and JCC programs, film screenings, meetings, marches, and even Jewish-sponsored trips to Israel for Indigenous youth, women, and leaders have likewise expanded greatly.

I have attempted to map this recent Jewish interest in Indigenous issues elsewhere and to provide some analysis on how to understand and contextualize it.[88] In that survey essay, I found that the dozens of interactions and events that have taken place tend to cluster around themes of identity and mutual suffering, social justice, and questions of political and cultural sovereignty. These more recent engagements have come at a time when Canada has become absorbed with questions about Indigenous reconciliation on a national scale. They also emerged concurrently with the rise of Jewish anxiety over the debate about whether Zionism is best understood as a colonial, post-colonial, or anti-colonial state. Israel has been represented as a prime example of European settler colonialism, as a result of American imperialism, and – in sharp contrast – a model for Indigenous national rejuvenation, linguistic revival, and sovereignty successfully re-established. In these discussions, the idea of "indigeneity" has become a powerful rhetorical tool. But, as this chapter has shown, it is only the latest instalment in a long saga of interactions.

Conclusions – Home, Exile, Indigeneity

As this chapter has attempted to make clear, there have been a wide range of Indigenous–Jewish encounters since Jews first arrived in the place that would be Canada, each type centred on a distinct set of issues and deserving of deeper understanding. Indigenous matters have been a part of the Canadian Jewish experience in three realms: business and early settlement, Canadian identity formation, and liberal social politics of the organized Jewish community. While Indigenous matters have never been at the centre of Canadian Jewry's public focus, they have been far from obscure, as Isa Milman hinted they might. Attending to the connections between Canadian Jews and Indigenous peoples allows us to see that Canadian Jewish life has been about both the history of settler colonialism and the attempts to reverse its most deleterious effects on Indigenous peoples. Jews have contributed to Indigenous displacement as they have sought to make Canada their home, and have fought against Indigenous disenfranchisement while seeking to make Canada a better home. The diverse, competing, and even contradictory raw materials of Jewish–Indigenous relations suggest that home-making has its ambiguities.

The central insight that arises from this discussion of the Jewish–Indigenous relationship, I believe, is that the Jewish Canadian past is burdened because the history of the multinational mass migration that produced Canada *is* the history of colonialism, just as modernity consists of mass migration all around the globe, with all of its politics of inhabitation. Canadian Jewish history ought to be seen not just as a heroic story of immigrant ascent and accomplishment, but as part of the story of the juggernaut of modernity – colonialism. Insofar as professional scholars and popular opinion appreciate Canada as a good home for the Jews, it is because of the recognition that Canadian Jewish history is generally understood as a heroic immigrant ascent story. The political and social conditions of the liberal democratic societies of North America provided opportunities for persecuted or colonized Jews that weren't available in their former homes in European nation-states, or in the Russian, Ottoman, and Austro-Hungarian Empires.[89] Despite the distress of systemic and sometimes politically enshrined antisemitism, Canada (and other former colony societies) offered unprecedented economic opportunity for Jews, as well as social inclusion, political enfranchisement, citizen and human rights, and religious freedom. Canada has hosted an open and free market for religion, culture, and politics, of which Jews have taken full advantage to develop, free from coercion. These opportunities simply were not possible under the weight of European nationalism, its overtaxed land, and its often-incendiary debates about whether its Jewish populations should receive the full benefits of citizenship. They were even less available in those illiberal states and empires to the east of the liberal democracies. Opportunities like those enjoyed by Jews in Canada were not available in Europe, where Jews frequently suffered through the continent's violent upheavals.

Although this is a true story, it belongs inside a larger frame than the one immigrants and their descendants generally tell about Jewish ascendance, the story of how Jews fared under liberalism. The story of Jewish Canada more properly fits in the context of the massive wave of human migration that relocated tens of millions of people from Eurasia to in settler societies and colonial outposts. This migration transformation was as profound as any major change in the history of the Jews. The broader story includes immigrant ascent and enfranchisement, but it is freighted with political complexity and moral ambiguity since it also involved, *ipso facto*, Indigenous disempowerment.

It is into this context that Canadian Jewish history ought to be understood – as part of the history of conflict and contest, of the politics and the possibilities for groups and individuals that emerged from settler societies. Though we rarely ask *how*, the Jewish and Indigenous experiences have been entwined together in the history of colonialism, part of a process that implicates everyone on the globe. Though often poor, Jews arrived as, and remained among, the settlers, the more powerful in a complicated but astounding reversal of fortune. Yet Jews have also played a part in advancing a national vision of minority rights, Indigenous uplift, and perhaps even decolonization. These solidarity efforts were shaped by the complex history of Jewish persecution and began to be undertaken even without the full protection of Canadian law before the Second World War.

Canadian Jews' liberal commitment to advancing Indigenous rights issues has been both self-serving and other-serving, insofar as their vision for Canada as a "better home" has included advocacy work, based on their broad faith in state authority, rule of law, and public education. Their fight for Indigenous rights and social justice has thus been complicated by its insistence on conserving the liberal order in Canada. In this sense, Canadian Jewish advocacy has diverged from many contemporary Indigenous activists' less statist visions.

Widening the frame of Canadian Jewish history to include the uncomfortable fact of colonialism doesn't entirely undo the story that we know and tell about Canadian Jewish life: the immigrant success story. The fact that Jews were among the colonizers in a process that clearly harmed Indigenous peoples does not alter the need that Jews felt to immigrate from Europe and Russia. It doesn't ignore Jewish tribulations or accomplishments once they arrived in Canada. But it does contend with the politics of this mass migration, and asks us to consider and examine the social consequences for Jews, Indigenous peoples, and the idea of Canada as a place to call home. It calls for grappling with a more nuanced "settler-side" history.

NOTES

1 Isa Milman, *Prairie Kaddish* (Regina: Coteau Books, 2008).
2 Milman later reflected on this lacuna and unearthed a pair of stories about encounters between Métis and First Nations and the Jewish agricultural colonists (and anthropologists) of Lipton / Fort Qu'Appelle / Plains Cree around "Calling River." See Isa Milman, "Writing History in Poetry: The

Making of *Prairie Kaddish*," in *Kanade, di Goldene Medine? Perspectives on Canadian Jewish Literature / Perspectives sur la littérature et la culture juives canadiennes*, ed. Krzysztof Majer, Justyna Fruzińska, Józef Kwaterko, and Norman Ravvin (Leiden and Boston: Brill, 2018), 29–32.

3 My sincere thanks to Magdalene Klassen, Richard Menkis, and Harold Troper for their thoughtful feedback on earlier drafts of this essay. Outstanding flaws, omissions, and corruptions in my discussion remain squarely on my own shoulders.

4 Peter H. Russell, *Canada's Odyssey: A Country Based on Incomplete Conquests* (Toronto: University of Toronto Press, 2017).

5 Ruth Koleszar-Green, "What Is a Guest? What Is a Settler?," *Cultural and Pedagogical Inquiry* 10, no. 2 (Fall 2018): 166–77.

6 To my knowledge, there are only three articles that deal with Jewish–First Nations encounters in Canada: Rebecca Margolis, "Jewish Immigrant Encounters with Canada's Native People: Yiddish Writing on Tekahion- wake," *Journal of Canadian Studies* 43, no. 3 (Fall 2009): 169–93; George Colpitts, "Itinerant Jewish and Arabic Trading in the Dene's North, 1916– 1930," *Érudit: Journal of the Canadian Historical Association* 24, no. 1 (2013): 163–213; and David S. Koffman, "Suffering and Sovereignty: Recent Canadian Jewish Interest in Indigenous Peoples and Issues," *Canadian Jewish Studies / Études juives canadiennes* 25 (2017): 28–59.

7 See my history of the Jewish–Native American encounter in the nineteenth and twentieth centuries in the United States: *The Jews' Indian: Colonialism, Pluralism and Belonging in America* (New Brunswick, NJ: Rutgers University Press, 2019).

8 Adam Mendelsohn, "Tongue Ties: The Emergence of the Anglophone Jewish Diaspora in the Mid-Nineteenth Century," *American Jewish History* 93, no.2 (June 2007): 177–209.

9 These the families of Aaron Hart, Samuel Jacobs, Myer Michaels, Joseph Simon, Chapman Abraham, Levi Solonons, Benjamin Lyon, Ezekiel Solomons, Isaac Levy, Gershom Levy, Levy Andrew Levy, Jacob Berger, Joseph Rezner. See Denis Vaugeois, *The First Jews in North America: The Extraordinary Story of the Hart Family, 1760–1860*, trans. Käthe Roth (Montreal: Baraka Books, 2012), 30–77.

10 Alexander Henry, *Travels & Adventures in Canada and the Indian Territories between the Years 1760 and 1776*, edited with notes by James Bain (Toronto: George N. Morgang, 1901), 107–8.

11 Ibid.

12 Scott P. Stephen, "Wilderness Gentry: Jewish Fur Traders in the Eighteenth Century," in *Jewish Life and Times: A Collection of Essays*, ed. Daniel Stone and Annalee Greenberg, vol. 9 (Winnipeg: Jewish Heritage Centre of Western Canada, 2009), 8–17.

13 Helen Akrigg and G.P.V., *British Columbia Chronicle: Gold & Colonists* (Vancouver: Discovery Press, 1977).

14 Cyril Edel Leonoff, *Pioneers, Pedlars, and Prayer Shawls: The Jewish Communities in British Columbia and the Yukon* (Victoria: Sono Nis Press, 1978).

15 Christopher J.P. Hanna, "The Early Jewish Coastal Fur Traders," *The Scribe: The Journal of the Jewish Historical Society of B.C.* 19, no. 1 (February 1995), 9–14.

16 Christopher J.P. Hanna, "Mike Cohen: 'King John of the Red House,' *The Scribe. The Journal of the Jewish Historical Society of British Columbia* 19, no. 1 (1999): 29–34.

17 Harry Gutkin, *Journey into Our Heritage: The Story of the Jewish People in the Canadian West* (Toronto: Lester and Orpen Dennys, 1980), 35

18 George Colpitts, "Jewish Merchants and First Nation Trappers in Northern Canada's Industrializing Fur Trade, 1916–1939," unpublished conference paper, Canadian Historical Association, Victoria, BC, 3 June 2013.

19 Judy Feld Carr, "Now We Have a Home," as told to Eli Rubenstein, March of the Living, http://marchoftheliving.org/wp-content/uploads/2012/01/Now-We-Have-A-Home-CJN-Story-on-Judy-Feld-Carr-the-Birth-of-Israel.pdf; Jack Leve with Algonquin Women (Biscotasing, ON), Ontario Jewish Archives, c.1921, accession no. 1981-3-13.

20 George Simon with Aboriginal nursemaid (Brantford, ON), [189–], Ontario Jewish Archives, Blankenstein Family Heritage Centre, fonds 78, file 3, item 5.

21 William J. Sitwell, "Harry Hirschfield, Fur Trader." *Western People* 14 (1 November 1984).

22 David S. Koffman, "Jews, Indian Curios and the Westward Expansion of American Capitalism," in *Chosen Capital: The Jewish Encounter with American Capitalism*, ed. Rebecca Kobrin (New Brunswick, NJ: Rutgers University Press, 2011), 168–86. See also David S. Koffman, *The Jews' Indian*, chapter 3.

23 Roland W. Hawker, "The Johnson Street Gang: British Columbia's Early Indian Art Dealers," *B.C. Historical News* 22, no. 1 (Winter 1989): 10–14.

24 Lewis Levy, W. Cohn, Joseph Boscowitz, Morris Dobrin, Abraham Martin, and Abraham Israel of the firm "Martin and Israel – Indian Traders," Abraham Frankel, Hyman Copperman, Julius Seitz, Nathan Solomon, owner of "The Indian Store," Aaron Oldenburg, Leopold Blum, Lewis Goldstone, Samuel Myers, Henry Nathan, and Jules Friedman. Archives of Sarah H. Tobe, Cyril E. Leonoff, Christopher Hanna, and David Rome, "More Early Pioneers of British Columbia, 1858–1880s," http://www.jmaw.org/jewish-pioneers-british-columbia/.

25 See, for example, Eileen Hallett Stone, *A Homeland in the West: Utah Jews Remember* (Salt Lake City: University of Utah Press, 2001); Benjamin

Kelsen, "The Jews of Montana, Parts II–V," *Western States Jewish Historical Quarterly* 3, no. 4 (1971): 227–242; Benjamin Kelson, "The Jews of Montana, Part I," *Western States Jewish Historical Quarterly* 3, no. 2 (1971): 113–20.

26 Along with the market for southwest and Pacific northwest Native American goods, the third centre of the curio trade was in the Plains. Omaha, Nebraska's Julius Meyer was a significant player there. Earlier markets in upstate New York, Upper Canada, and the Great Lakes Region emerged with an earlier wave of colonizing settlement. Those markets included few or no Jews, though Jewish firms ran several important Indian fur trading operations.

27 Victoria Directory and *Victoria Times* advertisement, *The Scribe: The Journal of the Jewish Historical Society of B.C.* 19, no. 1 (1999): 9fn28.

28 Douglas Cole, *Captured Heritage: The Scramble for Northwest Coast Artifacts* (Seattle: University of Washington Press, 1985); Sarah H. Tobe, "Victoria's Curio Dealers," *The Scribe: The Journal of the Jewish Historical Society of B.C.* 19, no. 2 (1999): 15–18.

29 Hawker, "The Johnson Street Gang: British Columbia's Early Indian Art Dealers."

30 For a broader discussion, see Gerald R. McMaster, "Tenuous Lines of Descent: Indian Arts and Crafts of the Reservation Period," *Indian Arts and Crafts*, Canadian Museum of Civilization, 205–36.

31 Cole, *Captured Heritage*.

32 Carolyn Podruchny and Laura Peers, eds, *Gathering Places: Aboriginal and Fur Trade Histories* (Vancouver: UBC Press, 2010); Ginger Gibson and Jason Klinck, "Canada's Resilient North: The Impact of Mining on Aboriginal Communities," *Pimatisiwin: A Journal of Aboriginal and Indigenous Community Health* 3, no. 1 (2005): 115–139; Royal Commission on Aboriginal Peoples, *Report of the Royal Commission on Aboriginal Peoples* (Ottawa: Minister of Supply and Services, 1996); I. Sosa and K. Keenan, "Impact Benefit Agreements between Aboriginal Communities and Mining Companies: Their Use in Canada," Canadian Environmental Law Association, Environmental Mining Council of British Columbia, CooperAcción (2001), 1–2; Suzanne M. Barnes and Ruben J. Wallin, "After the Environmental Assessment: A Tale of Development on Attawapiskat Traditional Territory," *Journal of Aboriginal Economic Development* 6, no. 2 (Fall 2009): 20–4; Jen Jones and Ben Bradshaw, "Addressing Historical Impacts through Impact and Benefit Agreements and Health Impact Assessment: Why It Matters for Indigenous Well-Being," *Northern Review* 41, Resources and Sustainable Development in the Arctic (2015): 81–109; Colleen M. Davison and Penelope Hawe, "All That Glitters: Diamond Mining and Tłı̨chǫYouth in BehchokǫNorthwest Territories," *Arctic* 65, no. 2 (June 2012): 214–28.

33 James William Daschuk, *Clearing the Plains: Disease, Politics of Starvation, and the Loss of Aboriginal Life* (Regina: University of Regina Press, 2013).

34 Scholars of western Canadian Jewish settlement make almost no mention of treaties, removal policies, or even the Dominion Lands Act. S. Belkin, "Jewish Colonization in Canada," in *The Jew in Canada: A Complete Record of Canadian Jewry from the Days of the French Regime to the Present Time*, ed. Arthur Daniel Hart (Toronto and Montreal: Jewish Publications Limited, 1926), 483–8. See also several contributions to the *Canadian Jewish Reference Book and Directory*, ed. Eli Gottesman (1962), including Louis Rosenberg, "The Earliest Jewish Settlers in Canada: Facts vs. Myths," 139–55; Arthur A. Chiel, "Manitoba Established as Permanent Canadian Jewish Community in 1877," 217–23; A.J. Arnold, "Canadian Jewry on the Pacific Coast," 259–63; Mel Fenson, "A History of the Jews in Alberta," 281–285; Bruce Fergusson, "Jewish History in Nova Scotia Dates Back to 1752," 289–90; Harold A. Hyman, "The Jews of Saskatchewan," 293–94; Harold A. Hyman, "Jewish Farming Colonies," 294–6; I. Goldstick, "The Jews of London, Ontario: The First One Hundred Years," 323–332; and Benjamin B. Guss, "Canadian Jews in the Maritime Provinces," 335–40.

35 William Toll, "The Jewish Merchant and Civic Order in the Urban West," in *Jewish Life in the American West: Perspectives on Migration, Settlement and Community*, ed. Ava F. Kahn (Seattle: University of Washington Press, 2002), 83.

36 James William Daschuk, *Clearing the Plains: Disease, Politics of Starvation, and the Loss of Aboriginal Life* (Regina: University of Regina Press, 2013).

37 John C. Lehr, "'A Jewish Farmer Can't Be': Land Settlement Policies and Ethnic Settlement in Western Canada 1870–1919," *Jewish Life and Times* 9 (2009): 18–28; Abraham J. Arnold, "The Jewish Farm Settlements of Saskatchewan – From New Jerusalem to Edenbridge," *Canadian Jewish Historical Society Journal* 4 (1980); James Richtik and Danny Hutch, "When Jewish Settlers Farmed in Manitoba's Interlake Area," *Canadian Geographical Journal* 95 (1977): 32–5. Cyril Leonoff, *The Jewish Farmers of Western Canada* (Vancouver: The Jewish Historical Society of British Columbia and the Western States Jewish History Association, 1984); Louis Rosenberg, "Jewish Agriculture in Canada," *YIVO, Annual of Jewish Social Science* 5 (1950).

38 Geoffrey Vendeville, "Philanthropist and social entrepreneur Dr. Michael Dan receives honorary degree," 21 June 2018, https://www.utoronto.ca/news/philanthropist-and-social-entrepreneur-dr-michael-dan-receives-honorary-degree.

39 This writing-over event in Lost Tribes found an echo in a competing theory of ancient Israelite identity that claimed that Britons were derived from the ancient Israelites (rather than the new world's Indigenous peoples), similarly popular in colonial Canada.

40   Thanks to Magdalene Klassen for this further insight and wonderful expression.

41   Patricia Grimshaw and Andrew May, eds, *Missionaries, Indigenous Peoples and Cultural Exchange* (Sussex Academic Press, 2010).

42   Louis Riel to Ignace Bourget, 1 May 1876, Collected Writings 2-011, quoted and translated in Thomas Flanagan, *Louis David Riel: Prophet of the New World* (Toronto: University of Toronto Press, 1996), 84.

43   Riel's proposed New Judea was not the first colonization scheme linked to Jewish conversion. The American Society for Meliorating the Condition of the Jews established the New Paltz colony in Harrison, New York, in 1827, as a settlement for Jewish converts to Christianity who had emigrated to the United States. The society was founded by Joseph Frey, a German Jewish convert to Christianity who had immigrated to the United States in 1816. See "The American Society for Meliorating the Condition of the Jews, and Its Organ, the Jewish Chronicle," *The Occident and American Jewish Advocate* 1, no. 1 (April 1843). Thanks to Michael Rom for this insight.

44   How Indigenous writers and thinkers might have worked through ideas about their place in settler society with reference to the Hebrew bible, Jews, or Judaism is a subject taken up, in part, in Matthew W. Dougherty's *Land of the Jewish Indians: Religion, Emotion, and Early American Expansion* (University of Oklahoma Press, forthcoming). Given the tangled history of Christian missionizing and Indigenous life, one would expect to uncover much interesting material.

45   Adele Wiseman, *Testimonial Dinner: A Play* (Toronto: Prototype Press, 1978).

46   Margolis, "Jewish Immigrant Encounters with Canada's Native Peoples."

47   Falk Zolf, *Oif Fremder Erd* (Winnipeg: Israelite Press, 1945), 481. Thanks to Vardit Lightstone for the source.

48   Elhanan Hanson, *Ṭreyder Ed un andere dertseylungen fun Ḳanadas ṿayṭn tsofn un fun der alṭer heym* (Winnipeg: Dos Yidishe Vort, 1957).

49   A.M. Klein's The Rocking Chair, "Indian Reservation: Caughnawaga." *Poetry: A Magazine of Verse* (September 1945), 318–19.

50   Norman Ravvin, *Sex, Skyscrapers and Standard Yiddish* (Toronto: Paperplates Books, 1997).

51   Eve Tuck and Wayne K. Yang, "Decolonization Is Not a Metaphor," *Decolonization: Indigeneity, Education & Society* 1, no. 1 (2012); see also Corey Snelgrove, Rita Dhamoon, and Jeff Corntassel, "Unsettling Settler Colonialism: The Discourse and Politics of Settlers, and Solidarity with Indigenous Nations," *Decolonization: Indigeneity, Education & Society* 3, no. 2 (2014).

52   Showcase of North American Indian Artifacts at the Opening of Hadassah Wizo Month in Canada, September 1976, Ottawa Hadassah-Wizo fonds, Fond O0035; Ontario Jewish Archives, 4-484-010.

53 My thanks to Paula Draper for pointing me to these sources. Sandra Barz, ed., *The Inuit Artists Print Workbook*, 3rd ed. (New York: Arts & Culture of the North, 2004); Sandra Barz fonds. CA UMASC MSS 387 and others, University of Manitoba Archives and Special Collections; Avrom Isaacs fonds, Inventory #F0134. Clara Thomas Archives, York University; The Inuit Art Society, https://www.inuitartsociety.org/about/board/.

54 Sylvia Schwartz Fonds – Photographs, Fonds 80, Series 5-1, 3 images of girls playing Indian at cottage beach. Porcupine girls' league in native costumes (South Porcupine, ON), 1922. Ontario Jewish Archives, Blankenstein Family Heritage Centre, item 1603.

55 The fascinating literature on these recreational settings has not closely examined Jewish experience. See Patricia Jasen, *Wild Things: Nature, Culture, and Tourism in Ontario, 1790–1914* (Toronto: University of Toronto, 1995), 80–104; Sharon Wall, *The Nature of Nurture: Childhood, Antimodernism, and Ontario Summer Camps, 1920–1955* (Vancouver: UBC Press, 2009); and Peter Stevens, "Getting Away from It All: Family Cottaging in Postwar Ontario," PhD dissertation, Department of History, York University, 2010.

56 David S. Koffman, "Playing Indian at Jewish Summer Camp: Lessons on Tribalism, Assimilation, and Spirituality," *Journal of Jewish Education* 84, no. 4 (2018): 413–40.

57 For more of my thoughts on this subject, see Koffman, *The Jews' Indian*, chapter 6.

58 Boas's Jewishness is subject to growing scholarly discussion. See Douglass Cole, *Franz Boas: The Early Years, 1858–1906* (Seattle: University of Washington Press, 1999); Regna Darnell, *And Along Came Boas: Continuity and Revolution in Americanist Anthropology* (Amsterdam and Philadelphia: John Benjamins, 1998); Jeffrey David Feldman, "The Jewish Roots and Routes of Anthropology," *Anthropological Quarterly* 77, no. 1 (2004): 107–25; Gelya Frank, "Jews, Multiculturalism and Boasian Anthropology," *American Anthropologist* 99, no. 4 (1997): 731–45; Leonard Glick, "Types Distinct from Our Own: Franz Boas on Jewish Identity and Assimilation," *American Anthropologist* 84 (1982): 545–65.

59 Regna Darnell, *Edward Sapir: Linguist, Anthropologist, Humanist* (University of California Press, 1989), 109.

60 Ibid.

61 David M. Fawcett and Teri McLuhan, "Ruth Leah Bunzel," *Women Anthropologists: A Biographical Dictionary* (New York: Greenwood Press, 1988), 29; Regna Darnell, "Bunzel, Ruth Leah," in *Biographical Dictionary of Social and Cultural Anthropology*, ed. Amit Vered (London and New York: Routledge, 2004), 80. Esther Schiff Goldfrank, raised "in a Jewish household that was largely acculturated to American ways," according to one of her biographers, was also one of Boas's assistants; she contributed substantially to

the field of Pueblo and Zuni culture, pottery, mythology, and ritual poetry. On Esther Schiff Goldfrank, see Barbara A. Babcock and Nancy J. Parezo, "Esther Goldfrank, 1896–," in *Daughters of the Desert: Women Anthropologists and the Native American Southwest, 1880–1980: An Illustrated Catalogue* (1988); Margaret M. Caffrey, *Ruth Benedict: Stranger in This Land* (Austin: University of Texas Press,1989); Esther Goldfrank, taped interviews, Wenner-Gren Foundation, NYC; Melville J., Herskovits and Barbara Ames, "Goldfrank, Esther S.," *International Directory of Anthropologists*, 3rd ed. (1950); Charles H. Lange, "The Contributions of Esther S. Goldfrank," in *Hidden Scholars: Women Anthropologists and the Native American Southwest*, ed. Nancy J. Parezo (Albuquerque: University of New Mexico Press, 1993); Gloria Levitas, "Esther Schiff Goldfrank," in *Women Anthropologists: Selected Biographies*, ed. Ute Gacs et al. (Chicago and Urbana: University of Chicago Press,1988); Babcock and Parezo, eds, *Daughters of the Desert*, 38–9; Margaret Ann Hardin, "Zuni Potters and the Pueblo Potter: The Contributions of Ruth Bunzel," in *Hidden Scholars*, 259–69.

62 David Goodman Mandelbaum Papers, 1899–1991, BANC MSS 89/129 cz, Bancroft Library, University of California, Berkeley.

63 Ruth Landes Papers, National Anthropological Archive, Smithsonian. Linguistics giant Leonard Bloomfield on Cree and Ojibwe among many others, and Ruth Schlossberg Landes's the social organization of the Ojibwa in Manitou Rapids Ontario 1936.

64 Lea Roback Fonds, Fonds No. 1243 Jewish Public Library, Montreal; Michel Rioux and Maude Emmanuell Lambert, "Lea Roback," *Canadian Encyclopedia* (Toronto: Historica Canada, 2008).

65 Bill Swan, *Real Justice: Convicted for Being Mi'kmaq: The Story of Donald Marshall Jr* (Toronto: James Lorimer, 2013).

66 Geoffrey York and Loreen Pindera, *People of the Pines: The Warriors and the Legacy of Oka* (Boston: Little, Brown, 1999); John Ciaccia, *The Oka Crisis: A Mirror of the Soul* (Dorval: Maren Publications, 2000), 198–201, 198–201, 224, 290–3; Kathy L. Brock, "From Oka to Caledonia: Assessing the Learning Curve in Intergovernmental Cooperation," *Canadian Political Science Association Meetings*, Concordia University, Montreal Quebec, (1–3 June, 2010).

67 Michael Asch, ed., *Aboriginal and Treaty Rights in Canada: Essays on Law, Equality, and Respect for Difference* (Vancouver: UBC Press, 1997); Michael Asch and Norman Zlotkin, "Affirming Aboriginal Title: A New Basis for Comprehensive Claims Negotiations," in *Aboriginal and Treaty Rights in Canada*, ed. Michael Asch, 208–30; Michael Asch, "*Calder* and the Representation of Indigenous Society in Canadian Jurisprudence," in *Let Right Be Done: Aboriginal Title, the Calder Case, and the Future of Indigenous Rights*, ed. Hamar Foster, Heather Raven, and Jeremy Webber (Vancouver: UBC

Press, 2007); Harold Finkler and Alice Parizeau, *Deviance and Social Control: Manifestations, Tensions and Conflict in Frobisher Bay* (Montreal: Centre international de criminologie comparée, Université de Montréal, 1973); and Norman Zlotkin, "Judicial Recognition of Aboriginal Customary Law in Canada: Selected Marriage and Adoption Cases," *Canadian Native Law Reporter* 4 (1984): 1–12.

68 For example, see George Manuel and Michael Posluns, *The Fourth World: An Indian Reality* (New York: Free Press, 1974); *Michael* Posluns, *Speaking with Authority: The Emergence of the Vocabulary of First Nations' Self-Government* (New York: Routledge, 2007); David C. Nahwegahbow, Michael Posluns et al., *The First Nations and the Crown: A Study in Trust Relationships* (Ottawa: Arki and Nahwegahbow, 1983).

69 Larry Chartrand et al., "Reconciliation and Transformation in Practice: Aboriginal Judicial Appointments to the Supreme Court," *Canadian Public Administration* 51, no. 1 (2008): 143–53.

70 Irwin Cotler, "The New Human Rights Agenda: The First Sheldon Chumir Lecture," *Constitutional Forum* 6, no. 2 (Winter 1995): 39–43; see also Michael Posluns Fonds, York University Archives and Special Collections, York University, Fonds F0382.

71 Peter Pearson, *Encounter with Saul Alinsky. Part 2: Rama Indian Reserve*, National Film Board, 1967. 32 min.

72 Morton Weinfeld, "Canada's Native Peoples: A Jewish Perspective," *Viewpoints: The Canadian Jewish Quarterly* 3, no. 1 (Summer 1981): 16–24.

73 David MacDonald, "First Nations, Residential Schools, and the Americanization of the Holocaust: Rewriting Indigenous History in the United States and Canada," *Canadian Journal of Political Science / Revue canadienne de science politique* 40, no. 4 (2007): 995–1015.

74 Christopher John J. Chanco, "Diaspora Solidarities: Refugees, Human Rights, and the Jewish Labour Committee of Canada, 1936–1967" (MA thesis, Department of Geography, York University, June 2018).

75 "Jewish Labour Committee (1936–1980s)," Canada's Human Rights History, accessed 25 June 2020, https://historyofrights.ca/encyclopaedia/social-movements/rights-associations-second-generation/national-jewish-labour-committee-1936-1980s/.

76 Alan Borovoy, *At the Barricades: A Memoir* (Toronto: Irwin Law, 2013), 51, 81–9.

77 Alan Borovoy, *Uncivil Obedience: The Tactics and Tales of a Democratic Agitator* (Toronto: Lester, 1991); Alan Borovoy, *When Freedoms Collide: The Case for Our Civil Liberties* (Toronto: Lester and Orpen Dennys, 1988), 236–8.

78 Canadian Jewish Congress, Organizational Records, Fonds No. CJC0001; ZA 1761; ZA 1761-C20d, Canadian Jewish Archives.

79 CJC Archives, "Religious Teaching in Day Schools," FA 2101 PR 91 PR4.

80 Information and Comment Autumn 1961, FA 2-IAC-25, October 1951 FA 2-IAC-11, October 1958 FA 2-IAC-21, October 1959 FA 2-IAC-22.

81 Inter Office Information 03/19/1976 FA 2-IOI-S-769-S, 03/18-1976 FA 2-IOI-S-907-S, FA 1-IOI-3918.

82 CJC Archives Series EB, Box 02, File 03, DA 5-14-10.

83 CJC Departmental Files (Quebec Region) DB 23-08-17 1991-1992; National DA 19-25-05 1991–1993; and National DA 5-24-19 1980.

84 Abe Arnold, "A Commentary on the Recommendations of the B. & B. Report Vol. IV Dealing with 'Other Ethnic Groups,'" September 1970, Report of the Royal Commission on Bilingualism and Biculturalism, Abe Arnold Fonds, CJC Archives, Box 1, "Articles." Thanks to Amir Lavie for directing me to this source.

85 Ibid.

86 Abe J. Arnold, "Multiculturalism: Policy and Practice," October 1973, Winnipeg, Abe Arnold Fonds, CJC Archives, Box 1, "Articles."

87 "Sixties Scoop Adoptee Recounts Growing Up in Jewish Montreal Family," CBC News, 15 March 2016.

88 Koffman, "Suffering and Sovereignty."

89 Scholars debate whether the persecution and abuse that Jews suffered in Europe rendered them "colonized" subjects. See Ethan Katz, Lisa Leff, Maud Mandel, "Introduction: Engaging Colonial History and Jewish History" and Israel Bartal, "Jews in the Crosshairs of Empire: A Franco-Russian Comparison" in *Colonialism and the Jews*, ed. Ethan B. Katz, Lisa Moses Leff, and Maud S. Mandel (Bloomington: University of Indiana Press, 2017); Santiago Slabodsky, *Decolonial Judaism: Triumphal Failures of Barbaric Thinking* (New York: Palgrave Macmillan, 2014). The scholars of the Wissenschaft des Judentums movement among German Jewish intellectuals in the 1820s and 1830s articulated what they saw as the effects of Jewish–gentile relations in early modern and modern European history in remarkably similar terms to what post-colonial scholars, particularly in India, would later develop, e.g., Dipesh Chakrabarty, *Provincializing Europe: Postcolonial Thought and Historical Difference* (Princeton, NJ: Princeton University Press, 2000).

SECTION TWO

Case Studies: Historical Episodes, Literary Creations

7 Crossing in/to Canada: Canada as Point of Arrival in Holocaust Survivor Memoirs

MIA SPIRO

God damn them all! I was told
We'd cruise the seas for American gold
We'd fire no guns, shed no tears
But I'm a broken man on a Halifax pier ...
                        – Stan Rogers, "Barrett's Privateers" (1976)[1]

It was an unseasonably warm spring day in Scotland and I was driving from Glasgow to the Ayrshire Coast when I heard Stan Rogers's gravelly voice crooning "Barrett's Privateers" on the Celtic Radio station. The refrain of the famous Canadian folk song, "I'm a broken man on a Halifax Pier" struck me as poignant and yet disorienting, bringing me back to Canada and thoughts of "home." It was not 1778, we were certainly not Barrett's privateers, and I was headed for a very different pier – to go kite flying with my daughter on the beach. Yet, the song made me think of other journeys taken over the Atlantic: my paternal grandparents, who arrived on a Halifax pier from Poland with two young children and few belongings to settle in Atlantic Canada in the 1920s; my maternal grandparents who came to Montreal via Halifax in 1920; my in-laws who came through Pier 21 as postwar refugees. And my husband and I, who packed up our worldly goods in 2013 to settle in the United Kingdom and now had a Scottish-born daughter who said things like "wee ones" and sang folk songs unfamiliar to me.

Not only my personal history but recent scholarship in Jewish history and cultural studies have highlighted how migration as a topic raises profound issues about belonging and identity. At its core, crossing borders to settle in countries like Canada, the United States, Scotland, or other Western countries for that matter, has as its driving force a desire to improve one's situation. For many immigrants, it is a lonely process that severs ties from home, heritage, language, family, and friends; yet, it is also a life-affirming, creative, and ultimately optimistic pursuit. That is, when it is by choice. When it comes to Jewish migration, and especially post-Holocaust migration, the issues are far more complex. In diaries, memoirs, and oral narratives of Holocaust survivors, the journey to Canada in the years leading up to or following the Shoah is intensely emotional and difficult. These are migrations, after all, that may be positive and hopeful in purpose, but are nevertheless indelibly tied to persecution, isolation, trauma, and the parallel life in Europe that *might* have been. As Elie Wiesel famously noted, survivors face a different problem than Hamlet's simplistic question, "To be or not to be?" For survivors, their existence is framed by a more complex "To be *and* not to be."[2] It is a quote that psychologist and Holocaust scholar Henry Greenspan reflects on when he teaches about how the public constructs ideas of survivors: "What does it mean 'to be and not to be'?" Greenspan asks. "What can it mean for anyone?"[3]

The question of being and not being, of doubleness, is reflected in numerous Holocaust survivor testimonies and memoirs, especially at those specific points of transition between the "not to be" in Europe and the "being" at the moment of telling and writing the story. Prologues, epilogues, and endings can be key places where survivor memoirs reflect on that crossing and what the journey from Europe to places like Canada has meant. I became especially interested in border-crossing moments and the way place and time become articulated in Holocaust survivor narratives when I worked as an editor for the Azrieli Series of Holocaust Survivor Memoirs from 2009 to 2013. Established in 2005, the Azrieli Foundation's Holocaust Survivor Memoirs Program publishes a truly diverse set of stories (about eighty to date). In the printed preface of the Series the late David Azrieli, founder of the Azrieli Foundation and himself a survivor, relates: "In telling these stories, the writers have liberated themselves."[4] The implication seems to be both psychological and physical: in reliving their flight from persecution in Europe to Canada, the writers relate a story of finding a safe haven and freedom. More importantly, however, the message seems to be that they have undergone a journey towards the self, along with unburdening themselves of the past. Needless to say, a closer analysis reveals a much more complex set of negotiations between past and present – and an array of reasons for writing the memoirs. And yet, there is very little scholarship on the way authors of Holocaust survivor memoirs negotiate those physical and emotional transition points at the border between the past in Europe and life as a migrant in a place of safety. In this chapter, I examine a sample of ten memoirs from the Azrieli Series to highlight some of the ways individual writers articulate those negotiations and what those border-crossing moments might mean. As I will argue, a closer look at how the journey to Canada and arrival are expressed, and what happens to the text in terms of the narration of time, space, and emotions, can provide readers with ways to recognize and reflect on key episodes when questions of "to be and not to be" come to the fore for the survivor.

Oddly enough, for an event so significant, memories of the arrival to Canada seldom take up much space on the page in Holocaust survivor memoirs. Arrival often goes unmentioned in oral testimonies as well (this is true not only of arrival in Canada but of the United States too). This may be why the point of arrival has received very little attention from scholars in the field of Holocaust studies. Undoubtedly, this is linked to reader and listener expectations: the task of the Holocaust survivor memoirist is to relate his or her experience of the Holocaust. More recently, however, the focus in interviews and Holocaust education on relating "whole life" experience has done much to widen our understanding of those individuals whose childhood, family life, and present lives cannot be limited to a single classification such as "survival."[5] Widening the parameters of time and experience in memoirs and interviews has added depth to our conceptions of the past, of Jewish culture in modern Europe, and of post-Shoah migration and integration. It has also transformed how these encounters between past and present are represented and articulated within the limits of writing, a storytelling genre. Analysing what these modes of representation reveal about memory and the difficult nature of writing about the Shoah has become an important task for current Holocaust scholars.[6]

In my own literary analysis of the Azrieli Series memoirs, I will first begin with a few observations and questions about time, place, and space. Common to nearly all the memoirs in the series, the authors recount painful and confusing departures from homes, border crossings, trips on trains, on foot, and a final point of arrival in Canada. For the most part, it is from the relative comfort of "home" in Canada that the writer is sharing his or her story with the reader. I would emphasize *relative* since for many survivors the ordeal of writing and giving testimony is anything but comfortable – it would be an understatement to say that remembering loved ones murdered, homes destroyed, and lives ripped apart is heart-rending and distressing. What does it mean, then, to arrive at a final destination upon crossing an ocean of time and harrowing experiences? Are elements of those points of arrival (and points of writing) a "liberation," as the preface to the Azrieli Series

would imply? If so, which elements? Furthermore, what happens sty-
listically at these pivotal transitions in the narratives between the past
in Europe and the terminus, Canada? In other words, how do Holocaust survivor memoirs narrate those inarticulate moments when the
journey brings them to points that cross borders of place, time, and
understandings of the self? And what does the experience of "coming
to Canada" reveal about Canada as a home for Holocaust survivors?

Holocaust Memoirs: The Journey

If we think of Canada as a point of arrival, then we must also consider the journey that these narratives present to the reader. Indeed,
thinking of Holocaust memoirs as travel or journey narratives can offer
helpful tools for analysing the way time, place, and space function
in these works.[7] One only need think of the classic tales of Odysseus
and Marco Polo to appreciate the influence of travel writing in shaping readers' understanding of worlds unknown. In Jewish history, too,
journey narratives such as Benjamin of Tudela's vivid description of
twelfth-century Europe, Asia, and Africa is still the most reliable ethnographic source on the culture of Jewish communities. And while it may
seem incongruous, even absurd, to place personal and painful stories
of Holocaust survivors within a genre often linked with adventure or
exoticism, this type of literary analysis can reveal much about individual writers' attempts to relate their perceptions and make sense of their
experiences. Much like travel writing, the majority of survivor memoirs
begin from home and then unfold by narrating journeys by foot, train,
and ship, crossing borders into unknown worlds that are far from any
previous experience.

Traditionally, in travel literature the witness/writer is relating a
first-person, independent perspective that reveals truths about humanity.
This perspective and its attention to sensory and visual detail have always
lent these texts a particular type of authority. There was less of a chance
to refute those facts and truths about the world and humanity when the
writer could claim to "have seen with one's own eyes."[8] But it is not only
the unknown world observed that comes through to readers in journey
narratives. The narrator of the travelogue has the power to express who
they are and how they differ from others. How the individual authors
encountered life's challenges, both physical and psychological, reveals
as much about the exceptional personalities of the writers as about the
journeys they had taken. Likewise, the value placed on observation and
instinct has always meant that the travel writer could influence the reader
to reflect philosophically on approaches to life and its meaning.

Clearly, there are limits to how neatly one can fit Holocaust survivor memoirs and travelogues together. The voyage, after all, was arguably the most extreme experience in modern history. There are also important differences between memoirs and the classic travel text that become even more evident when reviewing unedited manuscripts rather than the published versions of Holocaust survivor memoirs. For one thing, most travel narratives follow a sequence of time and place. Because of the nature of traumatic memory and distance from the events, Holocaust survivor memoirs, much like testimonies, often jump around in time, repeat themselves, or otherwise reveal the difficulty in relating details of traumatic memory. Keeping the integrity of the memoirist's voice, while at the same time translating these journeys back into a chronology and language intelligible to the reader – and even clarifying opaque details of history – is often a thorny and ethically fraught task for editors. As scholars who analyse testimony importantly emphasize (for example, Christopher Browning, Shoshana Felman and Dori Laub, and Marianne Hirsch and Leo Spitzer), the *experience* of time and place is more fundamental to consider than the actual chronology and geography.[9] Time in a labour camp, concentration camp, or in hiding, for example, may have been experienced as an eternity. Home, cities, train journeys, or border crossings, on the other hand, while they may be brief, are laden with meaning and significance – the key to remembering a past that would otherwise be forgotten.

Aside from the experience of time, another theoretical tool that may further our understanding of the journey from Europe to Canada is an analysis of how place and space are experienced. What does the experience of "coming to Canada" tell us about Canada as a home for survivors of the Shoah? In the past few decades humanities scholarship has revisited the idea of place, looking at understandings of how memory, culture, and social and historical factors all affect our understandings of topography and location. Influential theorist Henri Lefebvre's *The Production of Space* was one of the first to insist on the distinction between "space" and "place." Space, according to Lefebvre, is socially and culturally constructed, but it is also a product of a specific historical "moment."[10] Although obviously related, place has different resonances than space for human geographers. Its significance is created more by individual imagination and is a product of individual and communal experience.[11] Canada as a space and destination at which the Holocaust survivor arrives distinguishes the Azrieli Series from other publishing projects (although this is not its only distinction). After all, the memoir writer will not return "home" at the end of the journey, as do the heroes of the classic epics. In the paradox that is Holocaust survival, neither have these individuals found themselves at the final terminus of Nazi genocide, the gas chamber. Instead, the narrators of the memoirs find themselves crossing oceans and borders to arrive in Canada as new immigrants. What does this change in destiny and destination mean in terms of the *topos* of travel?

In a close reading of the texts, the concept of Canada as a geographic place of arrival and as a metaphoric space in the migration journey is depicted in a number of ways: the strangeness, friendliness, loneliness, the unpleasant cold, the disappointment, the disorientation, the odd food, the hospitality of families who welcomed them. Always these moments are sensorily focused – on perception, taste, and feel. This is probably not surprising, as arrival is a point of the journey at the nexus of two entirely different epochs of life experiences. Perhaps for this reason, the arrival in Canada is so often brief, in some cases taking up only a few lines or a paragraph, even if the actual episode occurred over a few weeks or even months. It is an important moment, but fleeting, transitory, and contradictory. Possibly, then, rather than "space," the more accurate depiction of border crossing into Canada is as a "non-place (*non-lieu*)," a term coined by French anthropologist Marc Augé in his influential book of the same title, to refer to spaces of transience. Augé's examples of non-places would be a motorway, a hotel room, an airport, or a supermarket.[12] In other words, they do not hold enough significance in relational or historical terms to be regarded as "places." Their status is one of "in-between" where time and place are fluid and hybrid or seem to follow their own rules. The transit between Europe and Canada, past and future, creates another reality, and it is literally a short-lived jump over an abyss of encounters.

Canada as Non-Place: Memories of Arrival

The examples from the Azrieli Series that I outline below show how in those points of arrival to Canada memoirists are faced with recreating themselves in a new country while negotiating language, belonging, survival, and memory. The yearning to settle into their new environments and build a future home is palpable. Especially in the unedited versions of the texts, it is at these points that the narratives often depart from chronology and sequential order of events typical of the memoir and the travel genre. Separated from the fixity of time and place, these spaces of arrival thus reveal the idiosyncrasies of the individual, left to follow his or her intuition and feelings. These can be incredibly emotional episodes in the narratives, when writers realize that they have been wrenched from home and transported into the unknown. Equally, these can be inspired moments, when the perspective of the first-person "I" allows readers to glimpse the courage of the writer in facing yet another challenge. But always, these are points in the narrative where the unexpected creeps in, filled with contradictions and incongruities that disclose the inexplicable nature of the voyage.

While the wide range of depictions and reactions seem to defy categorization, if one thinks of arrival as a series of moments in a journey, then there are certain common threads that the reader can identify: the ship voyage, new tastes, trains to cities, first impressions of Canada, and the disarticulation and displacement of the migration experience. Within these moments, however, each author depicts the episodes distinctly, playing an active role in re-scripting his or her life and making distinct choices of how those dichotomies between past life in Europe and future in Canada are negotiated.

The Voyage: Digesting and Not Digesting

As an ultimate transition point in the voyage narrative, virtually all the memoirs mention the ship they took to Canada and the seasickness they experienced, a violent rite of passage to the new world. The passage overseas, which usually lasted between a week to ten days, easily takes on metaphoric resonances. Traditionally, the sea voyage in literature has been a symbol of chaos and deliverance from that chaos. It is the ultimate "non-place," suspended between two continents and two realities, with all the obscurity and symbolic implications of that crossing. Some of the survivors were still children when the ships set sail to Canada, their narration evoking the naive child's eye, with the bewilderment and confusion that such a new experience holds. Eva Felsenburg Marx, who turned twelve years old on the SS *Samaria*, arriving in Quebec City harbour in 1949, reflects, "All I remember about our ocean voyage across the stormy October Atlantic was that it was terrifying and terrible."[13] Judy Abrams, who also turned twelve during the trip overseas, characterizes the crossing as part of her ambivalent transition from child to woman—it was during the voyage that she had her first menstrual period: "'The joy and glory of becoming a woman' ... but there was only pain in my abdomen and nausea. 'Mother! I need some cotton wool!' was the only way I could find to share the embarrassing news."[14] The nausea and, in many cases, terror, experienced by many of the children are depicted even more vividly by those who came to Canada as adults. Interestingly, at this point many of the survivors turn from the first person "I" to "we," as if to emphasize the collective disempowerment and loss of agency of not only their families but the rest of the shipmates. Zsuzsanna Fischer Spiro (no relation) in her diary entry dated December 7th–31st, records the seasickness on the *Arosa Line* using powerful descriptors like "stricken" and "dread" to underscore the embodied nature of suffering the sea voyage: "we were awakened by strong waves and stricken by the dreaded seasickness ... it stayed with us for the whole of the sea voyage."[15] A similar sense of trepidation is faced by Willie Sterner. In almost epic terms, Sterner recalls the panic he felt on the ship voyage when the ship faced a storm: "The sky and ocean were black. Our ship seemed out of control – at times the mast was close to the water. We were all terrified, especially because this was our first ocean voyage. We were afraid that we wouldn't make it to Canada, but we pushed away our fears."[16] Sterner's feelings of lack of control and terror are conceived as a test of faith, a threat to his inner optimism and belief that he and his wife would have a chance to leave the terror of the Holocaust behind and make a new life for themselves.

Indeed, a number of the memoirs acknowledge that the sea voyage to Canada was an emotional as well as physical passage that was filled with paradoxes. It was, quite literally, an unsettling process; one cannot settle on a sea. The conditions on a closed ship are such that one is cut off from the rest of society, always "in-between" the launch point and its destination. Not only is it dangerous, but the ship or ocean liner is always and only a space that is transitory, the "non-place" of Augé's theory. At the same time, the imbalance that causes seasickness, as depicted by the memoirists, typically has within it a wide variety of other shifting emotions: hope, melancholy, excitement, fear, and anticipation. The apprehension connected to the storm mentioned above in Willie Sterner's sea voyage, for example, is starkly contrasted with the sense of hope that he underscores time and again: "We were all anxiously waiting to go to Canada, even though we didn't know anything about it. We were excited to be leaving the place that held so many bitter memories. We hoped for a better future for all of us in a new country."[17] The concern that the title of his memoir implies, *The Shadows behind Me*, is that no matter how far he sails from Europe, he is unable to leave behind those memories and people taken from him. Contradictory feelings of joy and melancholy are expressed even more bluntly in Nate Leipciger's memoir: "And our happiness at leaving could never be exuberant – the pain of losing our family was always just under the surface of our conscious minds. Leaving Europe meant leaving them behind, but we knew we would never forget them."[18] Certainly, as the very fact of writing the memoirs will attest, this expression of "never forget" and of bringing the past to Canada is true of each and every one of the books in the series.

If the sea voyage and seasickness endured by the authors cannot expel traces of the past, there is yet another embodied, sensory experience that many of the memoirs recall in detail: new types of food. As if integrating the new culture and hope for the future physically as well as emotionally, authors in those points of arrival to Canada recollect the exotic and paradise-like abundance linked with the new world – the first banana, orange, white bread, meals on trains, and Shabbat dinners hosted by welcoming committees and cousins. Eva Marx, for example, for her birthday present on the ship asks for "a dozen oranges, something we could neither obtain nor afford in post-war Czechoslovakia."[19] Another author, Molly Applebaum, who was eighteen when she crossed the Atlantic along with one thousand other Jewish orphans, summons up memories of food in great detail, linking the extravagance of regular meals (which she expects her reader would simply take for granted) and treats like chocolate with the equally unexpected foreign encounter with liberation. As if containing her entire history of deprivation in one line, Molly reminisces, "While on the ship, we were served food three times a day that was foreign to us – cornflakes, oatmeal, juices and generous portions of meat that we had no experience with in our memories."[20] Food as an emotional and cultural signifier is prominent when Molly and her friend Betty first leave the ship. Her very first encounter with Canada is experienced through this sensory shorthand that reflects on the scarcity of money, displacement, profound yearning, and resistance:

> Betty and I ventured out around the neighbourhood, and the grocery stores amazed us. We could not figure out why oranges and cabbages were displayed side by side. Also, the sight of so much food available for purchase was remarkable. We each had five dollars, given to us on leaving the ship, and we certainly were not ready to spend it at that time. (I also had twenty dollars sewn into the shoulder pad of my dress, which was to be used for emergencies only.) The chocolate bars were pretty enticing, but we resisted.[21]

The two girls, despite being tempted, are well practised at being on their guard, not knowing when the next emergency will arrive that will require Molly to unsew that twenty dollars carried among other resources weighing down her shoulders. And yet, these food encounters can be odd and humorous, as well – those times when culture and language clashes lead to misunderstandings. Michael Mason wryly observes his own strategy for ordering from a foreign menu when he first arrived in Canada: "I asked the waiter to bring us dinner because I wasn't familiar with the menu. He obliged and brought us a well-put-together, complete dinner. Some of our group at another table didn't speak English well and ordered three types of potatoes."[22] Mason's resourcefulness is undoubtedly a good lesson for anyone encountering a foreign menu, but it also very much characterizes his individual approach to life and survival throughout the book.

From a Train Window

Oddly, the actual border processes of arriving in Canada are hardly mentioned in the memoirs. Michael Mason is one of the few who describes disembarking from the ship where he and other war orphans were "placed into wire cages in a large reception hall. It made us feel like animals in a zoo. Thankfully, we didn't stay long in the cages ... with little questioning, we got our passports stamped and were admitted into Canada."[23] In most of the other memoirs in the series, the transition from ship to train and coach journey to major cities like Montreal and Toronto appears seamless, as it was for Amek Adler, who in the same sentence describes arrival in Quebec City: "after clearing customs, [we] got on the first-class train to Montreal."[24] The train journeys to those cities, significantly, provide some of the most compelling descriptions of the authors' first impressions of Canada and of the experience of migration.

Train journeys have generally functioned as a space where protagonists reflect on the past or open channels to memory and other aspects of character development.[25] Michel de Certeau, in *The Practice of Everyday Life*, notes that the train window "makes our memories speak or draws out of our shadows the dreams of our secrets" as the train's movement sets the rhythm for the speaker's memory process.[26] In Holocaust narratives, train journeys have other resonances, bringing to mind transports, cattle cars, and iconic images of the multiple tracks heading to Auschwitz-Birkenau. In contrast to other types of travel literature, where the rhythm and sway of the train car and sound of the engine open avenues for the narrator's musings into the past, the train journey in survivor memoirs most often highlights the unbridgeable void between then and now: the inarticulate and overwhelming aspects of survival that bring these authors to Canada. Henia Reinhartz's memoir provides a prime example of the silence that mirrors her family's sense of displacement and bewilderment on the train from port to city: "No towns, no people, just emptiness. Was this what Canada was all about? We did not know. No one seemed to know. People did not say much. We sat quietly in our places, faces glued to the windows."[27] This reaction of detached spectator to one's own life would seem apt for such a threshold moment. The tone is neutral, not sad or excited. Rather it consists of a suspended anticipation of what will come from that emptiness, a frozen moment in time and space between two realms.

The narration and commentary that accompany the movement between cities and spaces in the arrival process is very telling of the authors' own strategies of adaptation and integration. It is not so much the movement and train journey, but the observation that comes upon disembarking and encountering the landscape that is key to understanding these first encounters with Canada. As Augé emphasizes, "Space, as frequentation of *places* rather than a place, stems in effect from a double movement: the traveller's movement, of course, but also a parallel movement of the landscapes which he catches only in partial glimpses, a series of 'snapshots' piled hurriedly into his memory and, literally, recomposed in the account he gives of them."[28] In relation to the memoirs, that story of arrival in Canada is born within the encounter of landscape, train journey, and settlement.

Canada: True North White and Free

How does Canada itself fare as a place of arrival for Jewish Holocaust survivors? While many of the memoirs record their gratitude and excitement upon arriving in Canada, the Canadian government and foreign office were not necessarily hospitable to Jewish refugees in the 1930s and '40s, as Irving Abella and Harold Troper have pointed out in their influential work, *None Is Too Many*.[29] Successful integration often depended not on Canada itself but on the ease with which survivors found friends, family, or a community upon whom they could rely (and who knew what they had come from and the complicated nature of their pasts). As an imagined *space*, as opposed to a place, Canada nevertheless has symbolic meanings and expectations imposed on it by romantic, pastoral images of the "true white north." Andy Réti, whose chapter "The True North" relates his arrival in Canada in 1957 after surviving in the Budapest ghetto, confirms one image exalted in Canada's national anthem of a noble, free land. "I am very proud to be Canadian," insists Réti. "Canadians' tolerance, compassion and willingness to help others are universally known. [...] I did not know any of this on January 7, 1957 [...] I did not know about Canada's vast area, cold winter temperatures, incredible northern beauty and wonderful people or about the richness of the English language."[30]

Other memoirs reveal a more ambivalent encounter with Canada: the harsh reality of the Canadian climate and the economic realities of being refugees. Nate Leipciger, for instance, describes the "dilapidated" state of Quebec City in his stopover there, with its "cheap merchandise" in store windows. "Even in destroyed Germany, the buildings and stores with little to sell looked better. My father assured me that Toronto would be different."[31] Eva Felsenburg Marx likewise recalls her sense of antici- pation from the perspective of the window, "the flat, frozen landscape hurtling past" on her train journey from Quebec City to Montreal, as well as her dismay upon arrival in the city. "I fully expected the streets of Montreal to resemble Hollywood film sets. How disappointed I was upon our arrival in Montreal, the city that would be my home for the rest of my life! In the dead of winter, Montreal was freezing and inhos- pitable."[32] The view through the window of the train reveals little more about Canada than did the portholes of the ocean liner, images that re- call the fearful and expansive nature of indeterminacy, the protagonists frozen in time as the train hurtles its occupants from the known into a void of unknown feelings and observations. Like Eva Marx, when Michael Mason observes the cold landscape from the train window, he wonders how he can belong: "It looked so cold and there was so much snow that we were already talking about how we could get back to Europe!"[33] The exclamation point seems to underscore the absurdity of such a feeling. After journeys across the borders of Europe, long ocean passages, stopovers, and trains, an idea of "home" in Canada is still far from the imagination, shrouded in snow, in fog, and irreconcilable feelings of anticipation, excitement, disappointment, fear, and grief for hometowns destroyed.

No Words: Beyond the Border

While the physical landscape of Canada takes on the symbolic man- ifestation of the alienating and incongruous feelings of arrival, at the same time, the memoirs often reveal a lack of articulation about the migration experience that can seem at odds with other sections of the texts. There is a compact, even rushed quality about the migra- tion experience, a series of movements through years of acquiring language skills, finding jobs, moving from one apartment to another, and integrating into a new life. Especially for the survivors who were still children upon arrival, reflections on the inarticulate, almost stu- pefying quality of the migration experience are quite overt, such as Henia Reinhardtz's observation, cited above, that "People did not say much."[34] Gerta Solan similarly describes her family's arrival in Toronto's Chinatown with a mix of silent perplexity and bewilderment: "It was a world we had never seen before. Little vegetable stores, stores with windows where ducks hung on hooks, grease dripping down, and dirty sidewalks full of garbage. It was dismal. We didn't talk, didn't discuss our feelings. We knew that we were all having the same thoughts."[35]

There are a few obvious answers to why some of these sections are often brief, terse, and even paratactic in their style of prose. No doubt, disorientation and alienation play a large role in the memory of arrival. The fatigue and confusion of adapting to a new language and cultural context can, quite literally, render one "without words." The lack of focus in the descriptions often lies in sharp contrast to the specificity and chronology of the Holocaust years, which rely on historical context to pull the narrative forward and give the witnessing of events meaning. The historical timeline of the Holocaust is often a key focus of the editing process as well, with research and fact checking by editorial teams zoning in on Europe in the 1930s and '40s, a period that is well documented and thus often subject to more scrutiny by readers. While this is not true of all the memoirs, some of which go into rich depictions of life after the Second World War, the majority of memoirs do put more emphasis on the Shoah. Undoubtedly, reader expectation comes into play: not without reason, many authors assume readers are more interested in the Holocaust era than in how individuals lived and coped with their pasts after settling in Canada. Notwithstanding the psychological factors, the quality of descriptive detail can also simply come down to language. Not everyone who writes a witness account of their lives has the proficiency in their second language or ability to express the paradoxical and conflicting emotions involved in leaving Europe and making a new home in Canada.

What is clear, however, is that reunions and partings that take place at borders and train stations can be disorienting, exciting, bewildering – and also painful. Nate Leipciger's recollection of his father's wordless reunion with his uncle at the train station in Toronto upon arrival reminds us of this most poignantly: "I felt overwhelmed at being with family but I maintained my composure. I was a stranger ... I felt that any show of emotion would result in a breakdown and create a scene. My father was the only one who showed emotion; for the first time in my life, I saw him cry, his tears flowing uncontrollably and his body shaking as he hugged his brother."[36] It is a stark reminder that the long and arduous journey to freedom in Canada – over borders, in camps, in hiding, through landscapes of loss and pain, and over oceans – is never quite over.

Conclusions

Echoes of "Barrett's Privateers" may hark back to tears shed, hearts broken, oceans traversed before arrival at that Halifax pier. Yet, in those points of arrival to Canada in these Holocaust survivor memoirs, what we see is not one-way or even two-way journeys. Canada as the "non-place" of arrival, as a new home, and as a space where painful memories and hope collide is an incongruous site for these authors. What these memoirs reveal are journeys where the encounter between past and present is juxtaposed and at the same time remains coexistent and layered. These moments of border crossing contain important keys to the character that the writers are trying to project within the memoir, as well as a rare observation into strategies of how each individual copes with relating those painful memories. Yet, these points of arrival also reveal important and unresolved contradictions to that process. How is it possible "to be and not to be," as Henry Greenspan reflects on Elie Weisel's *Hamlet* quote? As Greenspan suggests, surviving is not living beyond and after, but is an ongoing life and an ongoing death: "A living and a dying after."[37] Nate Leipciger's memoir emphasizes this point when he notes how his relatives expected his family "not to think back on those times any more, as we were now in a new country." As he reminds the reader, "There was no way they could have understood that it was impossible for us to turn off our memories of the past, even though we may have wanted to."[38]

The spaces in these memoirs created by movement and border crossing into the future are also spaces where readers may reflect on life after the Holocaust more generally. After all, much like in any voyage, in the reading process we are in close proximity to strangers for extended periods of time. We get to know a small part of those strangers during our short trip through their lives to observe, perhaps learn something from their experiences. And yet it is a journey that we as readers can only glimpse at from a porthole, struggling to comprehend what that experience might mean. Greenspan's concluding thoughts perhaps sum it up best: "Despite all the efforts that have developed to make psychological sense of survivors' experience, the truth is that we are still struggling. Existing concepts simply do not well enough explain how the obvious strengths, creativity, and engagement so many survivors demonstrate really *can* coexist with a severity of injury that is also indisputable."[39] These memoirs are acts of creation that are future oriented, relating a cultural history to a future generation, influencing how we remember the Holocaust. And yet, how we encounter those texts, and what tools we use to understand them, is still a process very much in the middle of its journey.

NOTES

This research would not have been possible without the generous assistance of the Azrieli Foundation's Holocaust Survivor Memoirs Program, and especially its Managing Editor, Arielle Berger. I am grateful for her help in pointing me towards key examples outlined here and for her feedback. My thanks goes to Sam Tongue, whose assistance in collecting, compiling, and being a soundboard for the research was invaluable, and to Faye Hammill for her close reading and insightful comments.

1 "Barrett's Privateers," a modern folk song written by Stan Rogers, released on the album *Fogarty's Cove* in 1976, became the unofficial anthem of Atlantic Canada and the Royal Canadian Navy. It has been covered by a number of groups.

2 Elie Wiesel, *The Accident*, trans. Rosette Lamont (New York: Bantam Books, 1982), 54.

3 Henry Greenspan, "Imagining Survivors: Testimony and the Rise of Holocaust Consciousness," in *The Americanization of the Holocaust*, ed. Hilene Flanzbaum (Baltimore: Johns Hopkins University Press, 1999), 47.

4 The preface by David Azrieli first appeared in the *Azrieli Series of Holocaust Survivor Memoirs: Series 2* (Toronto: Azrieli Foundation, 2009). It has subsequently been published in all memoirs to date.

5 See Michael Gray, *Contemporary Debates in Holocaust Education* (Basingstoke and New York: Palgrave Macmillan, 2014), and Werner Dreier, Angelika Laumer, and Moritz Wein, eds, *Interactions: Explorations of Good Practice in Educational Work with Video Testimonies of Victims of National Socialism* (Berlin: EVZ Foundation, 2018) for more on this.

6 The excellent studies being done on the theme of Holocaust narratives, memory, and the limits of representation are far too numerous to name here, but some significant examples include: Sara R. Horowitz, *Voicing the Void: Muteness and Memory in Holocaust Fiction* (Albany: State University of New York Press, 1997); Lawrence L. Langer, *Holocaust Testimonies: The Ruins of Memory* (New Haven, CT: Yale University Press, 1993); Jakob Lothe, Susan Rubin Suleiman, and James Phelan, eds, *After Testimony: The Ethics and Aesthetics of Holocaust Narrative for the Future* (Columbus: Ohio State University Press, 2012); Michael Rothberg, *Traumatic Realism: The Demands of Holocaust Representation* (Minneapolis: University of Minnesota Press, 2000); Susan Rubin Suleiman, *Crises of Memory and the Second World War* (Cambridge, MA: Harvard University Press, 2006); James E. Young, *Writing and Rewriting the Holocaust: Narrative and the Consequences of Interpretation* (Indiana University Press, 1990).

7 I am not the first to consider Holocaust narratives within the travel genre. See, for example, Antonia Sousa Ribeiro's analysis of Jorge Semprun, Albert Drach, and H.G. Adler in "Cartographies of Non-Space: Journeys to the End of the World in Holocaust Literature," *Journal of Romance Studies* 11, no. 1 (Spring 2011): 79–89. The analysis there, however, focuses specifically on the journey to the concentration camp in literary works of the 1960s.

8 Peter Hulme and Tim Youngs, "Introduction," in *The Cambridge Companion to Travel Writing*, ed. Peter Hulme and Tim Youngs (Cambridge: Cambridge University Press, 2002). As Hulme and Youngs describe, in traditional forms of travel writing the claim to have been there and to have seen with one's own eyes could "defeat speculation" (4).

9 See for example, Christopher R. Browning, *Collected Memories: Holocaust History and Postwar Testimony* (Madison: University of Wisconsin Press, 2003); S. Felman and Dori Laub, eds, *Testimony: Crises of Witnessing in Literature, Psychoanalysis, and History* (New York: Routledge, 1991); and M. Hirsch and L. Spitzer, "The Witness in the Archive: Holocaust Studies/ Memory Studies," *Memory Studies* 2, no. 2 (2009): 151–70.

10 Henri Lefebvre, *The Production of Space*, trans. D. Nicholson-Smith (Oxford: Blackwell, 1991), 15.

11 See Phil Hubbard, Rob Kitchin, and Gill Valentine, eds, *Key Thinkers on Space and Place* (London: Sage, 2004), and David Cesarani, M. Shain and Tony Kushner, eds, *Zakor V' Makor: Place and Displacement in Jewish History and Memory* (London: Vallentine Mitchell, 2008).

12 Marc Augé, *Non-Places: Introduction to an Anthropology of Supermodernity* (London and New York: Verso, 1995).

13 Eva Felsenburg Marx was born in Brno, Czechoslovakia, in 1937. During the war, she survived by "passing" as a Christian child, separated from her parents for her own safety. Eventually reunited with her parents, she emigrated to Canada in 1949. Judy Abrams, born in Budapest in 1937, was hidden in an Ursuline convent from 1944 to 1945 and then placed with a family friend until the end of the war. In 1948, Judy and her parents made their way to Canada. See Judy Abrams and Eva Felsenburg Marx, *Tenuous Threads/One of the Lucky Ones*, Azrieli Series of Holocaust Survivor Memoirs, IV (Toronto: Azrieli Foundation, 2011), 131.

14 Ibid., 52.

15 Zsuzsanna Fischer Spiro was born in Tornyospálca, Hungary, in 1925. After surviving Auschwitz, Zsuzsanna married Joseph Spiro and had two sons. They left Hungary for Canada in 1957, following the Hungarian uprising. Zsuzsanna Fischer Spiro and Eva Shainblum, *In Fragile Moments/ The Last Time*, Azrieli Series of Holocaust Survivor Memoirs (Toronto: Azrieli Foundation, 2016), 42.

16 Wille Sterner arrived in Canada in 1948, after surviving the Krakow ghetto
    and multiple labour camps, including working at Oskar Schindler's
    Deutsche Emailwaren Fabrik. Most of his family were murdered at Tre-
    blinka. See Willie Sterner, *The Shadows behind Me*, Azrieli Series of Holo-
    caust Survivor Memoirs (Toronto: Azrieli Foundation, 2012), 131.

17 Ibid., 86.

18 Nate Leipciger, *Weight of Freedom* (Toronto: Azrieli Foundation, 2015), 178.
    Leipciger left Bremerhaven on the SS *Samaria* on 17 September 1948 and
    arrived in Quebec City on 28 September. He was reunited with family
    members in Toronto and settled there.

19 Abrams and Marx, *Tenuous Threads*, 118.

20 Molly Applebaum, *Buried Words: The Diary of Molly Applebaum*, Azrieli Se-
    ries of Holocaust Survivor Memoirs. (Toronto: Azrieli Foundation, 2016),
    93. Applebaum was born in Krakow in 1930 and lived in the Dąbrowa Tar-
    nowska ghetto. During the Nazi occupation, she spent two years hiding in
    a box buried under the dirt floor of a barn (1943–45). After pressure from
    the Canadian Jewish community, the Canadian government passed an
    Order-in-Council (1947) to allow one thousand Jewish orphans asylum, and
    in 1948, Applebaum (and Michael Mason, see note 22 below) emigrated to
    Canada. See Irving Abella and Harold Troper, *None Is Too Many: Canada and
    the Jews of Europe, 1933–1948* (Toronto: University of Toronto Press, 2012),
    269–74, for more detail on this Order and the underlying resistance to Jew-
    ish immigration in Canada.

21 Applebaum, *Buried Words*, 93.

22 Michael Mason, *A Name Unbroken* (Toronto: Azrieli Foundation, 2015), 62.

23 Ibid. Mason was one of one thousand Jewish orphans granted Canadian
    asylum in 1948. See note 19 above.

24 Amek Adler, *Six Lost Years* (Toronto: Azrieli Foundation, 2017), 53. Adler
    lived in Lodz with his grandmother, parents, and three brothers when
    the Second World War broke out. He survived Auschwitz-Birkenau and
    Dachau with support from his older brother, Ben. After working in Swe-
    den, he and his family made their way to Canada in 1954.

25 See Sabine Egger, "'The East' as a Transit Space in the New Europe? Trans-
    national Train Journeys in Prose Poems by Kurt Drawert, Lutz Seiler and
    Ilma Rakusa," *German Life and Letters* 68, no. 2 (April 2015): 245–67.

26 Michel de Certeau, *The Practice of Everyday Life*, trans. Steven Rendell
    (Berkeley: University of California Press, 1984), 112.

27 Henia Reinhartz, *Bits and Pieces* (Toronto: Azrieli Foundation, 2008), 76.

28 Augé, *Non-Places*, 86.

29 See Abella and Troper, *None Is Too Many*. Their work has also been devel-
    oped and critiqued in "None Is Too Many and Beyond: New Research on
    Canada and the Jews during the 1930–1940s," a special issue of *Canadian*

Jewish Studies / Études juives canadiennes 24 (2016). Thank you to David Koffman for highlighting this.

30 Ibolya Grossman and Andy Réti, *Stronger Together* (Toronto: Azrieli Foundation, 2016), 157.

31 Leipciger, *Weight of Freedom*, 179.

32 Marx, *Tenuous Threads*, 120.

33 Mason, *A Name Unbroken*, 62.

34 Reinhartz, *Bits and Pieces*, 76.

35 Gerta Solan, *My Heart Is at Ease* (Toronto: Azrieli Foundation, 2014), 72. Solan was born in Prague in 1929, surviving Theresienstadt and Auschwitz. After liberation she returned to Prague and her and her husband Paul lived there until the Soviet invasion of 1968. They then made their way to Toronto.

36 Nate Leipciger, *Weight of Freedom* (Toronto: Azrieli Foundation, 2015), 179–80.

37 Greenspan, "Imagining Survivors," 48.

38 Leipciger, *Weight of Freedom*, 180.

39 Greenspan, "Imagining Survivors," 49.

8 The "Nu World" of Toronto in Bernice Eisenstein's *I Was a Child of Holocaust Survivors*

RUTH PANOFSKY

In the aftermath of the Second World War, approximately 40,000 Jews who had survived the death camps of Europe made their way to Canada. The arrival of so many thousands signalled a radical shift in government policy that previously had denied entry to Jews seeking refuge from Hitler's scourge.[1] Among the survivors who reached Canada via the Bergen-Belsen displaced persons camp were Ben and Regina Eisenstein. The opportunity to begin life anew in Toronto's Kensington Market – at the time a predominantly Jewish enclave – was one of challenge and promise for the couple. It gave rise, many years later, to Bernice Eisenstein's *I Was a Child of Holocaust Survivors* (2006), the first graphic memoir by a Canadian to document the lived experience of the second generation.[2] Eisenstein's memoir combines prose and images to convey what it was like growing up in Toronto in the shadow of the Holocaust. A deeply personal account, it traces a daughter's fixation on the Holocaust as she struggles to fathom its lasting effects on her parents and their survivor friends.[3]

Eisenstein's work bears comparison with that of New York-based Miriam Katin. As the story of a daughter who yearns to understand her parents' experience of the Holocaust, *I Was a Child of Holocaust Survivors* specifically brings to mind Katin's graphic memoir *We Are on Our Own* (2006), an extraordinary tale of how a mother and her young daughter survived in wartime Hungary.[4] *I Was a Child of Holocaust Survivors* and *We Are on Our Own* are significant contributions that extend the repertoire of graphic works by second-generation writers beyond that of Art Spiegelman's *Maus* (1986; 1991), to cite the most famous example.[5]

Nu (Yiddish) is used to convey expectation. In the title of this chapter, "nu" is an obvious pun on the English "new."

More importantly, Eisenstein's and Katin's work indicate the need to attend to the lesser-known graphic narratives of second-generation women and to recognize their pioneering memoirs as central to Holocaust literature.

Eisenstein's project is animated by two core questions: how did her parents adapt to life in Toronto, and how did that experience of resettlement affect her as their daughter? Or, to ask as literary scholar Sara R. Horowitz does in reference to the novels of Canadian writers Anne Michaels and Nancy Richler, "Once lost, can home ever be recovered, or even approximated?"[6] Here, I interrogate Eisenstein's narrative representation of Toronto – first the vicinity of Kensington Market, then Wychwood, and later the suburbs – as a city where her parents first find shelter and eventually feel settled, but where they remain separate and apart from the wider community and are never truly at "home."

The Eisensteins arrive as "Greenies in the Nu World"[7] and gravitate to the familiar and protective atmosphere of Kensington Market, but daughter-cum-narrator Bernice[8] evokes her parents' feelings of distress that stem from past trauma, as well as a sense of alienation that takes hold on Canadian soil and is passed on to the second generation. Toronto is the locus of *I Was a Child of Holocaust Survivors*; as I show, however, the city grounds neither survivor parents nor their daughter who, jointly and individually, struggle to locate themselves in an environment that provides a tenuous sense of home, at best.

Before the second generation, which in addition to Eisenstein includes writers such as J.J. Steinfeld (1946–), Isa Milman (1949–), Merle Nudelman (1949–), and Judith Kalman (1954–), others wrote as survivors who had been transplanted to Canada. Poet Rokhl Korn (1898–1982) and novelist Chava Rosenfarb (1923–2011), for example, settled in Montreal in 1948 and 1950, respectively; each was a Holocaust survivor who became part of the city's Yiddish cultural scene, whose nucleus at the time was the Jewish Public Library. Yet, neither was ever at ease in Canada – a land far removed from the burial ground of Europe that held their loved ones and their memories of a past life – and more specifically Quebec, where they remained outsiders by virtue of their religion – neither Catholic nor Protestant – and their mother tongue – neither French nor English. As she herself admitted in 1971, Rosenfarb did "not feel at home in this country. Here, in Montreal, in the Province of Quebec, I have lived for two decades between the two solitudes – in my own solitude."[9]

Although Canada had given each writer the opportunity to pursue her career, neither Korn nor Rosenfarb felt called to limn the country where each lived out her life. As Rachel Seelig notes, "little mention is made of Montreal or Canada in the writing of Rokhl Korn produced there over three decades, a long and remarkably prolific period."[10] Similarly, Canada features only in a handful of short stories by Rosenfarb, an otherwise devoted novelist, known for her award-winning epic *The Tree of Life: A Trilogy of Life in the Lodz Ghetto*.[11] In fact, in the postwar imagination of Korn and Rosenfarb, Canada becomes either "ahistorical terrain" or a "neutral land of refuge"[12] – these descriptions originate with critic and translator Goldie Morgentaler – that gives rise to writing that is both informed by tragic events in Europe and characterized by a "profound sense of displacement and decline."[13]

In Toronto, where Ben and Regina Eisenstein arrive in 1948 – Bernice, their second daughter, is born one year later – divisions along religious and linguistic lines are less complex and more permeable than they are in Montreal. Nonetheless, the Eisensteins, like the literary Korn and Rosenfarb and so many other Holocaust survivors, are unable to root themselves in their new setting. Despite their willingness to adapt, the Eisensteins feel far less tied to Toronto than to their transplanted community of survivors. This is due, in large part, to the legacy of loss and the shared remembrance they bring with them from Europe, and which binds the survivors as a group. As Horowitz affirms, while "the memory of particular landscapes haunts people ... the memory of particular people also haunts landscapes."[14] For Bernice Eisenstein's traumatized parents, who "arrived in a new country draped in loss, with their memories deprived of the ability to offer comfort,"[15] Toronto thus becomes a city "animated, agitated, catastrophic, and haunted by absence and loss."[16]

I Was a Child of Holocaust Survivors was conceived as an extension of a lifelong quest: a daughter's propulsive search "for more in order to fill in the parts of my father that had gone missing."[17] In an attempt "to step into the presence of absence"[18] and uncover those missing "parts," Eisenstein set out to produce a graphic memoir. As she explains, the project "started with a painting of my father, begun a number of years after he had died. I missed him, and it seemed a way to bring him close ... While painting, I found myself engaged in a conversation with ... [him], about our relationship, about his past, of what I knew and what I didn't know. It was at that point that I realized I wanted to write as well, to see where that conversation would lead me."[19] *I Was a Child of Holocaust Survivors* is Eisenstein's metaphoric attempt to fully "see" her parents – "to find my father's and mother's eyes, looking out from behind barbed wire"[20] – and to situate them both, and particularly her more elusive father, on terra firma.

Upon arrival in Canada, Polish-born Ben and Regina Eisenstein rent a two-bedroom apartment on the second floor of a house on

Wales Avenue in Kensington Market. The first bedroom is used by the Eisensteins – father, mother, daughters Sharon and Bernice – and the second is rented out to an elderly boarder who shares both the kitchen and bathroom. In Kensington Market, the Eisensteins face a period of adjustment as they seek to establish themselves in an alien city. Although they lack the requisite experience, they soon open a kosher butcher shop on Kensington Avenue.

In less than two years, Ben Eisenstein and his one surviving brother Jacob (known as Jack), who reached Canada via Sweden in 1950, purchase a building on nearby Spadina Avenue. Brothers Ben and Jack now join forces: Ben attends to the Kensington Avenue butcher shop, while Jack oversees the street-level grocery store on Spadina Avenue. Immediately, their respective families – Jack Eisenstein is married to Regina's sister, Jenny – move into the two floors above the grocery store.

Despite his efforts to integrate, as well as his business and personal successes, all of Kensington Market can see that Ben Eisenstein is troubled. As "swift [to] anger"[21] as he is to express love, his behaviour is unpredictable. By day, he is outwardly a diligent husband and father whose inner self is impenetrable, even to his daughter: "What thoughts filled his mind during all those years as a kosher butcher, in his shop and when he drove a truck to make deliveries to neighbouring homes? Did he daydream himself into his youth, with his parents and siblings, in Miechow, [Poland,] before the war? Would he allow the silence of remembering what he could not voice to take him out of his routine?"[22] By night, he is either a devotee of Western movies on television or an inveterate gambler, a poker player whose penchant for cards causes constant conflict and a rift with his wife. Bernice speculates that the alternating need for the "release" offered by "the Wild West," where "rules were simple" – "Good beat Evil" and her father could imagine himself riding out "alongside his heroes"[23] – and the adrenalin rush of "excitement"[24] provided by gambling may have been adaptive responses to the lingering effects of Auschwitz, where Ben Eisenstein was stripped of all agency, daily life was at once highly regimented though arbitrarily governed and chaotic, and death was ever present.

Bernice's own experience of Kensington Market differs markedly from that of her parents. It is her first home, and its "maze of narrow alleys and densely packed-together houses"[25] become her communal "babysitter."[26] Its *shtetl*-like atmosphere – insular, warm, and familial – shields her, to some degree, from what she later identifies as her inherited "state of confusion."[27] In fact, Kensington Market is the site of Eisenstein's childhood innocence. There she lives for the first

Figure 8.1 "I Am Lost in Memory," from Bernice Eisenstein, *I Was a Child of Holocaust Survivors* (McClelland and Stewart, 2006). Reprinted with permission of the author.

four years of her life, absorbing a range of sensual experiences that she carries with her into adulthood: her toddler self immobilized by a tight "quilted snowsuit"; the sight of "giant wheels of cheese in the window" of the local cheese shop; the taste of sugar cookies from Lottmans' bakery on Baldwin Street; the airborne smells of fresh fish and pickles in brine; and the sounds of "klezmer music"[28] radiating from the Anshei Minsk Synagogue on nearby St Andrew Street.

The dominance of Yiddish, the language spoken by the eastern European Jewish immigrants who populated Kensington Market, adds to Eisenstein's sense of living in a world circumscribed as much by language as by geography. Yiddish is her mother tongue and her true "home";[29] as she admits, "Yiddish defines the world that I came from."[30] More importantly, the language also links her to the European past of her parents, since Yiddish filled "every step they had taken from one country to the next."[31] A shared language solidifies the relationship between daughter and parents; it also serves as an invaluable bridge between them, for Yiddish simultaneously reaches back in time and forward to the present. Thus, in Kensington Market Eisenstein learns "the way the past and a language are fastened together."[32] It is a valuable lesson taken literally, for eventually it leads her to explore her inheritance of Holocaust trauma by marrying the languages of memoir and painting.

When Bernice is aged four, the Eisensteins move out of the nurturing and safe environment of Kensington Market. Their new home on Braemore Gardens is located in the comfortable, mid-town neighbourhood of Wychwood. This house proves to be a transitional space, where they live for six years. Here, her parents travel to and from work in their butcher shop, her brother Michael is born, and Bernice and her older sister Sharon continue to thrive. To an observer, the Eisensteins might appear to be settling into life in Toronto and their family might seem to resemble the Canadian families in their district. But, in truth, harrowing wartime memories possess Ben and Regina Eisenstein. These recollections penetrate the facade of their lives on Braemore Gardens and transfer hauntingly to their daughter in the form of postmemory, to invoke Holocaust scholar Marianne Hirsch's defining term for "inherited memories" that are "shaped, however indirectly, by traumatic fragments of events that still defy narrative reconstruction and exceed comprehension."[33] Since the effects of these past events carry forward into the present, Hirsch warns, a child risks having her "own life stories displaced, even evacuated, by ... [her] ancestors."[34]

For the Eisensteins, day-to-day existence in Wychwood is less vivid than their remembrance of family and communal life in pre-war Poland.

In fact, by 1953, these memories, which elicit the dominant emotions of pain and grief, have become the truest signifier of home. For Bernice, however, the world begins to expand with the relocation to Braemore Gardens. She learns how to read and develops a love of books that is sustaining. As a child, she reads "to become all-feeling as the daughter of parents who have experienced unimaginable loss,"[35] and as an adolescent "to hear those whose voices have been silenced or lost, [and] to discover what I have not been told."[36] At the same time, she is "drawn outside by what was beyond our door"[37] and happens upon the Vaughan Theatre on nearby St Clair Avenue West. There her love of film is fostered; it is also where she first sees images of the Holocaust projected onto the large screen. Her cognition of the Holocaust, as well as her paired love of word and image, which she later brings together in her original artistic practice, is born of this neighbourhood as stimulus.

A final move to the suburbs, when Bernice is aged ten, takes the Eisensteins away from the centre to the north end of the city.[38] The parents no longer run a kosher butcher shop; they now work side by side in a recently purchased clothing store. Time has passed since their entry to Canada, and Ben and Regina Eisenstein have established a family and a business and have recently purchased a new home. Theirs is a typical 1950s suburban house, with a basement turned recreation room. Decorated in "reproduction Louis XIV" style, it is a home that suggests bourgeois comfort: it boasts luxurious living room "sofas covered in plastic"[39] and a dining room suite with a grand chandelier.

Notwithstanding several relocations, undertaken to improve the family's living conditions, their new suburban residence does not denote home for the Eisensteins. Rather, as Bernice intuits as a child, her parents are drawn most deeply to their close circle of friends, fellow survivors, referred to by their daughter as "the Group." It is only the Group, men and women who share a common past, that can provide her mother and father with a genuine sense of rootedness and connection – in essence, a feeling of home. Neither the city of Toronto, which accepted them after the war, nor their own children, who are of their present not their past lives, can offer the consolation they know with their friends. As she recalls with aching honesty, Bernice always felt that her mother and "father never made time for me ... Whatever age I go to, when I look for my parents, they're off somewhere with their group of friends."[40]

The members of the Group spend all their leisure time together, summer north of the city in Wasaga Beach, vacation in New York's Catskill Mountains, and attend one another's celebratory events, such as bar mitzvahs and weddings. Most, Eisenstein recalls, "were from my parents' hometowns or had grown up in the neighbouring area, but all were linked to the same past, sharing the same history, an unbroken chain of survivors ... They adhered one to the other with the kind of bond that would be hard to duplicate."[41] Since they can no longer lay claim to an actual home – home is in a Europe that now exists in memory alone – it is not surprising that the Group cleaves to the few living people who know the extent of their individual losses. They may reside in cities across Canada and the United States, but, as Eisenstein describes, they are "one another's [de facto] home, their own having been confiscated and destroyed."[42] Thus, the past inheres in each individual member of the Group, just as it serves to strengthen them as a unit.

Soon after this latest move, the relative ease of Toronto suburban life is disrupted by an unprecedented event: the 1961 trial of Adolph Eichmann, which is televised in Israel and seen around the world. The Eichmann trial results in heightened public awareness of the Holocaust and ongoing memorial efforts to "Never Forget" the Jewish genocide, but for eleven-year-old Bernice it is a shattering, personal experience. As a child, she had "absorbed the fact"[43] that her parents had survived the Holocaust, but all at once that knowledge becomes visceral: "I am standing at the back of the [recreation] room and it is dark except for the glow of the television. Pictures of skeletal bodies piled one on top of another are on the screen, and suddenly I am injected with the white heat rush of a new reality."[44]

The Eichmann trial is a catalytic event that ignites a mature apprehension – that her parents and their friends lived through an actual, historic event – and which ties Bernice to the Holocaust. She describes an "addiction" that takes her to the cinema and the library, "where I can see every movie and read every book that deals with the Holocaust" and score "the kind of [powerful] high H [i.e., the Holocaust] gives."[45] That she has inherited the contours, if not the details, of her parents' trauma becomes especially clear during adolescence.

It is also in late adolescence that Bernice comes to the sober realization that "growing up in the household of my parents was not tragic, but their past was. [And] My life was not cursed, theirs was."[46] She sees the magnitude of their torment; at the same time, she does not grasp its hold on her life. Unsettled and anxious "to discover my own way in the world,"[47] she leaves Toronto and lives and studies overseas in Israel and England for three years. A desire for intimacy and attachment leads her to make an early marriage that soon fails. In fact, as a young adult, Bernice is restless and searching, much like her survivor father. In the end, it is her private quest that returns her to the city of her birth, and which initiates the process of coming to terms with her parents' legacy

Figure 8.2 "The Kind of High H Gives," from Bernice Eisenstein, *I Was a Child of Holocaust Survivors* (McClelland and Stewart, 2006). Reprinted with permission of the author.

of trauma. Her memoir, conceived in childhood and produced after a painful and protracted gestation, is the result of her compassionate mind and original artistry.

Like her parents, who were forcibly uprooted and dispossessed and then unable to fully reorient themselves in the "Nu World"[48] of Toronto, Bernice finally concedes that she, too, knows the void that arises from alienation. This feeling of estrangement is linked inextricably to "the unbearable lightness of being a child of Holocaust survivors. Cursed and blessed. Black, white, and shadowed."[49] This is her bequest, transposed from the death camps of Europe to the city streets of Toronto. In the end, despite her empathic will, she cannot know "the full extent"[50] of her parents' loss and, by extension, her own foreshortened experience. Thus, as Hirsch could foresee, Bernice's "own life stor[y],"[51] which encompasses her sense of self and of home, is in the grip of postmemory.

For a more sanguine reading of such depletion, I return, by way of conclusion, to Horowitz's view that catastrophic "losses on multiple landscapes and in different histories converse and intertwine [in the Canadian landscape]. The result is ... a thickening of our understanding of the dimensions of both loss and, if not healing, then the capacity to move forward, to live afterward. The ability to experience love afterward and to create art out of haunted spaces does not erase past loss, but is textured by it."[52]

I Was a Child of Holocaust Survivors shows Ben and Regina Eisenstein moving "forward" after incomprehensible loss to make a life for themselves in a city that remains welcoming though alien. As a work of art, it is Bernice Eisenstein's "textured" response to the ineradicable suffering of Holocaust trauma, both lived and inherited. Finally, it is a daughter's expression of deepest gratitude to her anguished parents, who determine that to forge a new life in Canada, which only ever serves as their "approximate"[53] home, is nonetheless an act of will and of "love" that must counter the haunting pain of the Holocaust.

NOTES

1 Stuart Schoenfeld, "Jewish Canadians," *The Canadian Encyclopedia*, updated 18 March 2020, http://www.thecanadianencyclopedia.ca/en/article/jewish-canadians/.
2 Although there are a number of second-generation writers in Canada, Eisenstein is the first to produce a graphic memoir.
3 The author is indebted to Marina Tinkler for invaluable research assistance in preparing this chapter.

4 See Miriam Katin, *We Are on Our Own* (Montreal: Drawn and Quarterly, 2006). See also Miriam Katin, *Letting It Go* (Montreal: Drawn and Quarterly, 2013).

5 See Art Spiegelman, *Maus I: A Survivor's Tale. My Father Bleeds History* (New York: Pantheon, 1986) and *Maus II: A Survivor's Tale. And Here My Troubles Began* (New York: Pantheon, 1991).

6 Sara R. Horowitz, "The Geography of Memory: Haunting and Haunted Landscapes in Contemporary Canadian Jewish Writing," *Studies in American Jewish Literature* 35, no. 2 (2016): 216–23, at 222.

7 Bernice Eisenstein, *I Was a Child of Holocaust Survivors* (Toronto: McClelland and Stewart, 2006), 40.

8 For the sake of clarity, I use "Bernice" or "Eisenstein" to refer to the first-person narrator of *I Was a Child of Holocaust Survivors*, but I recognize her as an artistic construct of the writer/artist Bernice Eisenstein.

9 Chava Rosenfarb, introduction to *Exile at Last: Selected Poems* (Toronto: Guernica Editions, 2013), 11–16, at 12.

10 Rachel Seelig, "Like a Barren Sheet of Paper: Rokhl Korn from Galician Orchards to Postwar Montreal," *Prooftexts* 34, no. 3 (Fall 2014): 349–77, at 365.

11 See *Der boym fun lebn: trilogye*, 3 vols (Tel-Aviv: ha-Menorah, 1972); later translated from Yiddish into English by Chava Rosenfarb in collaboration with Goldie Morgentaler and published in three volumes by the University of Wisconsin Press as *The Tree of Life: A Trilogy of Life in the Lodz Ghetto. Book One: On the Brink of the Precipice, 1929* (2004); *The Tree of Life: A Trilogy of Life in the Lodz Ghetto. Book Two: From the Depths I Call You, 1940–1942* (2005); and *The Tree of Life: A Trilogy of Life in the Lodz Ghetto. Book Three: The Cattle Cars Are Waiting, 1942–1944* (2006).

12 Goldie Morgentaler, "Land of the Postscript: Canada and the Post-Holocaust Fiction of Chava Rosenfarb," *Judaism* 49, no. 2 (Spring 2000): 168–80, at 172.

13 Seelig, "Like a Barren Sheet of Paper," 360.

14 Horowitz, "The Geography of Memory," 218.

15 Eisenstein, *I Was a Child of Holocaust Survivors*, 27.

16 Ibid., 218.

17 Ibid., 16.

18 Ibid., 167.

19 Eisenstein quoted in Ruth Panofsky, "'Memories Seeded in Longings': An Interview with Bernice Eisenstein," *Studies in Canadian Literature* 43, no. 1 (2018): 272–85, at 276.

20 Eisenstein, *I Was a Child of Holocaust Survivors*, 24.

21 Ibid., 35.

22 Ibid., 41–2.

23 Ibid., 49.

24 Ibid., 43.
25 Ibid., 56.
26 Ibid., 57.
27 Ibid.
28 Ibid., 58.
29 Ibid., 62.
30 Ibid., 65.
31 Ibid.
32 Ibid.
33 Marianne Hirsch, "Postmemory," accessed 25 June 2020, http://www
    .postmemory.net.
34 Ibid.
35 Eisenstein, *I Was a Child of Holocaust Survivors*, 97.
36 Ibid., 96.
37 Ibid., 90.
38 Though unnamed, Eisenstein's suburbs evoke the neighbourhood of Bathurst
    Manor located in Toronto's North York district. By 1960, many survivors were
    living in "The Manor," as the neighbourhood was commonly known.
39 Eisenstein, *I Was a Child of Holocaust Survivors*, 119.
40 Ibid., 174–5.
41 Ibid., 158.
42 Ibid., 166.
43 Ibid., 20.
44 Ibid.
45 Ibid.
46 Ibid., 53.
47 Ibid., 24.
48 Ibid., 40.
49 Ibid., 167.
50 Ibid., 178.
51 Hirsch, "Postmemory."
52 Horowitz, "The Geography of Memory," 218.
53 Ibid., 222.

9 Nathan Phillips: The Election of Toronto's First Jewish Mayor

HAROLD TROPER

Ben Keyfetz, Toronto-based National Director of Community Relations for the Canadian Jewish Congress, remembered 1954 as an *annus mirabilis*,[1] and, miraculous or not, it was certainly a newsworthy year for Torontonians. Late in the summer of 1954, Marilyn Bell dominated the headlines when she became the first person to swim across Lake Ontario. Just after 11 p.m. on 8 September, the sixteen-year-old waded into Lake Ontario at Youngstown, New York, one of three long-distance swimmers hoping to cross the thirty-two miles to Toronto. One after another, the two other and more experienced swimmers gave up the effort and were pulled from the water. In the early evening Toronto's Marilyn Bell, defying expert predictions, was the only swimmer left. Bell swam on. Through the day and into the night excitement built as local newspapers published special editions on the young swimmer's progress and radio stations broadcast hourly updates on her progress. Could Marilyn Bell conquer the lake that defeated the other competitors? When an exhausted Marilyn Bell finally emerged from the lake at the Toronto breakwater just minutes shy of twenty-one hours after she began her swim, a crowd of more than a quarter-million packed the Sunnyside Beach area to celebrate the hometown girl's achievement. Toronto had a new hero.[2]

But Marilyn Bell's swim was just one noteworthy 1954 Toronto event. Earlier that year the province of Ontario restructured Toronto's political and organizational life. Recognizing that a rapidly growing Toronto and its suburbs required greater coordination of planning and services, the province conjoined the City of Toronto and its inner suburbs to form a new level of government officially called Metropolitan Toronto, or Metro for short. Metro was assigned responsibility for oversight of the region's arterial roads, major sewage and water facilities, planning, administration of justice, metropolitan parks, housing policy, public transportation, including the TTC, and, before long, the police service. To pay for it all, Metro was also granted power to tax property.[3] And, as if to underscore the new Metro's important role in management of public transportation, on 30 March 1954, Ontario Premier Leslie Frost and Toronto Mayor Alan Lamport, standing side by side, together pushed a lever that switched a nearby block signal from amber to green, initiating the inaugural trip of Toronto's and Canada's first subway northward along Yonge Street from Union Station to Eglinton Avenue.[4]

Six months after the Yonge subway line opened and a little more than a month after Marilyn Bell's swim, on 15 October Hurricane Hazel slammed into Toronto. Torrential rain and punishing wind swept over an unprepared Toronto and the surrounding region. In just a few hours the hurricane washed out major roads and highways, damaged or destroyed some fifty bridges, disrupted the cities electrical grid, swept low-lying homes out into Lake Ontario, and forced thousands to take temporary shelter in schools, armories, and other public facilities. More than eighty people lost their lives. As the city surveyed the damage, politicians and planners pledged to ensure the city would be better prepared should it face any future hurricanes. In the aftermath of the storm, a Toronto and Region Conservation Authority was created and assigned responsibility for protecting the region's floodplains and rivers systems. And, in order to prevent similar flood-related events in the future, Toronto's flood-prone low-lying areas, river estuaries, and ravine systems were permanently secured from housing and commercial development.[5]

While any one of these 1954 Toronto events was newsworthy in its own right, when Ben Keyfetz declared 1954 an *annus mirabilis,* he had yet another event in mind. In the first week of December 1954 Toronto voters went to the polls to elect a mayor and city council. For the first time in Toronto's history, voters elected a Jew, Nathan Phillips, mayor. And Nathan Phillips was not just *a* Jew. He was *the* Jew who ended a more than century-long history of Protestant mayors in Toronto, every one of them a member of the powerful Orange Order. For more than a century the Orange Order, a powerful Anglo-Protestant fraternal organization, wheeled extensive influence at City Hall, ensuring that municipal patronage in Toronto privileged the Orange Order and its friends. The Orange Order's fingerprints could be found on virtually every aspect of municipal activity – the issuing of licences, negotiating service contracts, and municipal hiring. If City Hall controlled it, the Orange Order had a hand in it.[6] The Orange Order, in league with the Lord's Day Alliance, also pushed back against any weakening of Sunday blue laws. Indeed, well into the postwar years, it is hard to exaggerate the influence of the Orange Order in ensuring that the public face of Toronto remained that of a stolid North American outpost of Protestantism that supported the imperial connection and adherence to lace-curtain values.

What of those of non-Anglo-Protestant heritage? As leaders of the Orange Order would have it, "outsiders" were expected to understand they were in Toronto not by right but by sufferance and to behave accordingly. That was certainly true of the political arena. Yes, there were Catholics and Jews elected to City Council from the more Catholic- and Jewish-populated corners of the city. But, well into the twentieth century, a prerequisite for being accepted as a serious political player in Toronto was membership in good standing with the Orange Order.[7] Nor was the Orange Order shy about displaying its power at the street level. For decades, every July 12th, the Glorious Twelfth, thousands of local Orangemen, dressing in the Order's distinctive sash and regalia, took to the streets for the Toronto Orange Day Parade in celebration of King Billy's victory over the Catholics at the 1690 Battle of the Boyne, a parade that rivalled Toronto's annual Eaton's Santa Claus Parade both in length and number of spectators. The 1954 Orange Day Parade took an hour to pass any one point along its route.[8]

But by mid-century there were significant signs of change, signs that Orange Order power in Toronto was on the wane. Most important was a post–Second World War shift in Toronto population following the reopening of Canada's doors to large-scale European immigration. This intake of immigrants was precipitated by a severe shortfall in domestic labour necessary to sustain a both unexpected and unprecedented postwar economic boom in Canada. As labour-intensive industry clamoured for workers, the federal government gradually reopened Canada's doors to Europeans, including many out of displaced persons camps in Germany, Austria, and Italy. Unlike pre-war immigration to Canada that was largely composed of agricultural labour and workers streaming into the Canadian resource sector, postwar immigration proved more urban and industrial. Toronto was soon Canada's single largest immigrant receiving centre and most of those immigrants were non-Protestant southern and eastern Europeans.[9] Much as Orange Order stalwarts might decry the arrival of so many "foreigners" – papists and Jews – there was no denying the old order and the narrow parochialism it harboured would have to give way. As the new arrivals and their Canadian-born children set down roots in Toronto, that city in turn gradually shifted away from being a staid backwash of empire – an empire increasingly more of ritual and memory than of reality – to being an ingathering immigrant city. As Jakob, a character in

Anne Michaels's novel *Fugitive Pieces* notes, in the decade following the Second World War Toronto was being reborn as "a city where almost everyone has come from elsewhere, a market, a caravansary, bringing with them their different ways of dying and marrying, their kitchens and songs."[10]

Much as some resented the intake of so many "foreigners," the non-Protestant population of Toronto continued to grow, including an increasing number of Jews. Part of the increase in Jewish numbers was a result of natural increase as the existing Jewish community participated in the postwar baby boom. But Jewish numbers also grew as a result of renewed immigration. In the decade that followed the Second World War, Canada took in approximately forty thousand Jewish immigrants – most of them Holocaust survivors and their children – the first major Jewish immigration into Canada since the mid-1920s.[11] The Jewish population of Metropolitan Toronto jumped from approximately 67,000 in 1951 to 89,000 in 1961, a one-third increase.[12]

With the growth of Toronto's Jewish population came growing determination on the part of the organized Jewish community to push back against an entrenched and often legally sanctioned racism and antisemitism that had for too long been a fact of Toronto Jewish life. Jim Walker, Camella Patrios, and Ruth Frager have documented the role of the organized Jewish community in energizing a public campaign to reduce if not eliminate antisemitism and racial discrimination.[13] In particular, the organized Toronto Jewish community worked to bring together others of goodwill – liberal churches, labour unions, progressive political groups, the mainstream press, and academics – to form an active and engaged human rights coalition. And the times were propitious. Following Canada's signing of the United Nations Universal Declaration of Human Rights in 1948 and buoyed by a slowly shifting human rights landscape in the United States, including an uptick in the struggle against racial segregation, there was a growing recognition within government and among the larger public of a need to strengthen human rights protection. Through the 1950s the cause of human rights would boast major breakthroughs on a number of different fronts. At the federal level, a new Immigration Act in 1952 effectively lifted long-standing regulations that previously restricted immigration from Europe and virtually barred immigration of Jews into Canada for most of the previous three decades.[14] What is more, a 1950s Supreme Court of Canada ruling declared *ultra vires* land titles containing restrictive covenants that barred Jews or other named religious, racial, or ethnic groups from purchasing property.[15] It should not be supposed that this Supreme Court's decision was universally welcomed. It wasn't. During an Ontario legislature debate on a bill to bring provincial legislation into line with the Supreme Court ruling, the Ontario premier received a letter from a friend, Ontario County Court Judge J.A. McGibbon. In his oft-quoted letter, McGibbon protested, "surely we have not arrived at the stage of life where the Government is going to take it upon itself to dictate to whom I must sell property, and whom I must have as my next door neighbour. I do not want a coon or any Jew squatting beside me and I know deep down in my heart you do not." The premier would have none of it. He replied that the judge was on the wrong side of history.[16] The legislation was enacted. A year later Ontario followed up with a Fair Employment Practices Act that curtailed employers' ability to demand job applicants divulge religious affiliation as a condition of employment.

Shortly thereafter, in 1953, Princess Elizabeth on a Canadian royal tour cut the ribbon to officially open Toronto's New Mount Sinai Hospital on University Avenue, twelve years after a provincial government–negotiated land swap saw the Hospital for Sick Children assume property for its new campus immediately south of Toronto General and allowed Mount Sinai Hospital to build a new facility directly across University Avenue from the Hospital for Sick Children. But the agreement did not stop there. Much to the displeasure of the boards of both Toronto General Hospital and the Hospital for Sick Children, the agreement also provided that both hospitals lift barriers to Jewish interns and residents and, equally important, promised that the New Mount Sinai Hospital, once it established a track record of service, would be considered for inclusion as a teaching hospital of the University of Toronto – a pledge that, once acted upon, meant the end to any and all religious, ethnic, and racial barriers to admission to the University of Toronto medical school.[17]

To many in Toronto, including Ben Keyfetz, the 1954 election of a Jewish mayor represented yet another sure sign that change was trumping continuity – that staid old Toronto the Good, a Toronto that in 1954 still prohibited store openings, movies, and sale of alcohol in restaurants on Sundays and, many joked, frowned on pleasure of any kind the other six days of the week, was finally emerging a modern and cosmopolitan city. Holy Blossom Rabbi Abraham Feinberg went even further. According to Feinberg, a true measure of a modern city is the degree of public acceptance of pluralism including religious tolerance. And the election of a Jew as mayor of Toronto demonstrated acceptance was fast becoming the Toronto reality. According to the rabbi, Phillip's being Jewish had proven of no electoral consequence. As Feinberg explained to a *Globe and Mail* reporter the day following Phillips's electoral victory,

what is most "noteworthy [about Phillips's victory] is the fact that religion was not permitted to be an issue in the contest." As far as Rabbi
Feinberg was concerned, the 1954 election of Phillips, one of Feinberg's
congregants, proved that "the assumption that a Jewish or Catholic or
Protestant vote exists in Toronto would be fatal to the political judgment and maturity of its citizens ...Toronto has grown up. The day of
political-religious venom has vanished, I hope forever, from our city."[18]

Rabbi Feinberg may have been impassioned but he was only partly
right. He was right that the election of a Jew was unprecedented. Where
Feinberg was wrong was in stating that the 1954 election saw the end of
appeals to "political-religious venom" and that Phillips's "religion was
not a factor in the election." Just the opposite. The issue of Phillips's
ethno-religious heritage was a key factor during the 1954 election as it
had been during all of Phillips's previous political career. The fact that
Phillips was elected mayor in 1954 did not make it less so and Phillips
know it. Recalling his 1954 electoral victory, Phillips noted, "one would
have to have been blind to not see that it [his being Jewish] was really
an issue."[19]

However, while Phillips was Jewish and never hid that fact, he
was hardly what one would call a *folks mench*, a man of the people.
Canadian-born Phillips was a lawyer by training and a member of the
Conservative Party. His first foray into Toronto politics was in 1923
when he made a run for City Council, not in a heavily Jewish area of
the city but in west-end Toronto's Ward 5 where the local Conservative
Party machine denied Phillips its electoral support, a denial that Phillips put down to antisemitism. Unwelcome in Ward 5, Phillips shifted
his political centre of gravity eastward to Ward 4, a heavily Jewish in-
ner-city ward that included Kensington Market, the garment district,
and surrounding residential areas. In 1924, he ran and was first elected
to City Council for Ward 4. Election after election, he was returned to
City Council for Ward 4. But while Phillips was a long-serving Jewish
member of City Council elected in a largely Jewish ward, he was regarded by many of the Yiddish-speaking and working-class Jews who
voted for him as something of a "white Jew" or "a non-Jewish Jew" who
represented the Jews of his ward but was not really one of them. While
municipal politicians did not openly campaign under party banners,
Phillips was known to be a member of the Conservative Party, which
by the mid-1920s was seen by many Jews as increasingly unfriendly to
Jewish immigration and the cause of organized labour – both important
to Ward 4. In addition to being a member of the Conservative Party,
Phillips's list of organizational affiliations included the Lion's Club, Kiwanis, the Island Yacht Club, and the Empire Club, hardly home turf

for most of his Ward 4 constituents. Nor was he likely to rub shoulders with many of his downtown Jewish voters at the more acculturated B'nai Brith and Holy Blossom Temple, where Phillips was also a member.[20] Why then did Jews vote for Phillips? Could it be precisely because many saw him as a "white Jew"? In sending Phillips to City Hall, his Jewish constituents might well have been less concerned about sending one of their own as they were sending a *shtatlan* – Jewish yes, but, unlike most of them, an intercessor comfortable dealing in the corridors of power, someone who could serve as a go-between themselves and the authorities.

If Phillips might be regarded as something of an outsider by the downtown Yiddish-speaking and working-class Jews he counted on for support, when it came to running for mayor, he also felt himself an outsider to the city's entrenched social and political power elite. Phillips's 1954 mayoralty campaign was his third run for the ribbon. He failed in both previous tries. In his 1967 autobiography, Phillips blamed these twin defeats on a gentlemen's agreement among Toronto's social and political movers and shakers that "a mayor of the Jewish faith was unpalatable."[21]

But why would a Jewish mayor, "unpalatable" only a few years earlier, suddenly become palatable in 1954? The backstory to the 1954 election is revealing. According to Phillips, after two electoral defeats, he was less than anxious to take another kick at the mayoral can, especially when the 1954 contest was shaping up as an easy win for the popular incumbent mayor, Allan Lamport.[22] But as the 1954 municipal election drew near, the mayoralty race suddenly took an unexpected turn. Shortly after the establishment of Metro Toronto, Allan Lamport resigned the mayor's position to become vice-chairman then chairman of the Toronto Transit Commission. The mayor's position suddenly empty, it fell to Toronto City Council to pick a replacement from within its ranks. With little more than four months remaining before the next election, Leslie Saunders, who had received the most votes of any candidate in the previous municipal election, was appointed mayor. Like Alan Lamport whom he replaced, Saunders was a member of the Orange Order. But Saunders was far more than a simple member. He was a stalwart of the organization, a bulwark in defence of Protestant hegemony, outspoken advocate of Sunday blue laws, and publisher of a rabidly anti-immigrant and anti-Catholic tabloid, *Protestant Action*.[23] He was also soon to become Grand Master of the Orange in Canada and the Order's Imperial Grand President.

It was not long before the newly appointed mayor's stridently anti-immigrant and anti-Catholic views became an issue for press and public debate. And perhaps nothing heated up that debate like the uproar created by the mayor's role in the 1954 annual Orange Day Parade. Saunders, the 1954 parade's grand marshal, used the occasion to deliver a statement celebrating the Orange Order. Not unexpectedly, the statement trumpeted the contribution of the Orange Order and Anglo-Protestant heritage, but, in an outburst even too much for some of his fellow Orange members of City Council, Saunders equated the 1690 Protestant victory over Catholics at the Battle of the Boyne and the partisan policies of the Orange Order to the 1945 Allied victory against "the Hun, the Nazi and the Fascist." What is more, Saunders did not issue his statement on Orange Order stationary or sign his statement as parade grand marshal. He signed his statement as mayor of Toronto and did so on official city stationery.[24]

What might have passed as just more of the usual Orange Order's British and Protestant triumphalism was by 1954 judged an unacceptably inflammatory affront to thousands of Catholics in Toronto, many of them immigrants who had arrived in Toronto in the years following the Second World War, many now voting citizens who might remember Saunders's anti-Catholic bias come election day. Toronto's daily newspapers attacked Saunders's statement as provocatively divisive, mean-spirited, and unwelcoming of the new pluralism of origins that was now becoming the Toronto reality. An editorial in the *Telegram* cautioned Saunders: "he should be doing no more than is expected of the Mayor if, in the future, he should wisely take precautions to avoid offending the religious sensitivities of any particular group of citizens ... There is danger the next election may be marred by religious controversy."[25] Rather than temper let alone rescind his statement, Saunders dug a deeper hole for himself by publicly insisting that he was pleased "to be able to make a statement of this kind to the people of Toronto on this great day in Orange history."[26]

Nathan Phillips, after stepping out of the political arena following his mayoral defeat at the hands of Lamport, watched the Saunders uproar from the sidelines. Phillips may have been shocked at the crudeness of Saunders's statement, but it was doubtful he was surprised by its sentiment. As a member of City Council from 1926 to 1952 Phillips came to know Saunders to be an equal-opportunity bigot, not just anti-Catholic but antisemitic as well. Historian Gerald Tulchinsky notes that in 1942, even as Saunders and Phillips served together on City Council, Saunders stirred the antisemitic pot by pointedly denouncing Canadian Jews as wartime slackers, disproportionately underrepresented in Canada's military, and "not doing their duty in the war." While the Canadian Jewish Congress lashed back that Saunders's bigotry blinded him to the truth, Saunders did not recant.[27] And, as the 1954 Orange Day parade incident demonstrates, the passage of time did little to soften Saunders's views on Catholics or Jews. But it was also true that, in spite of the changing character of Toronto – or perhaps because of it – as the 1954 municipal election drew near Saunders could still count on a hard-core of loyal supporters, especially in his east-end constituency, voters resentful that the Anglo-Protestant Toronto they cherished, the Toronto they felt was rightfully theirs, was being eroded by a growing population of Catholics and Jews, many of them recent immigrants.

But if some felt themselves displaced in the new Toronto, others welcomed a more diverse and cosmopolitan Toronto. And with Alan Lamport no longer in the mayoral race, those who regarded Saunders a divisive force out of step with a quickly changing city hoped for a champion to take on Saunders in the upcoming mayoral election. Could Nathan Phillips be that man? When approached by former supporters about whether he would challenge Saunders for mayor, Phillips, already a two-time loser, hesitated. He was tempted but unconvinced Saunders could be beaten and beaten by a Jew. As he weighed his chances, Phillips was approached by the *Toronto Daily Star*, Canada's largest daily newspaper and usually a backer of Liberal Party candidates, with the promise that the *Star* would endorse Phillips should he toss his hat into the ring. Encouraged but not yet convinced that Saunders was vulnerable, Phillips reached out to John Bassett, who less than two years earlier had become part owner and publisher of Toronto's other major afternoon newspaper, the Conservative Party–leaning *Toronto Telegram*. Bassett, perhaps thinking ahead to the day when he would expand the *Telegram* to include a Sunday addition and knowing Phillips to be no friend of Sunday blue laws and a pro-development politician who never saw a wrecking ball he didn't like, enthusiastically endorsed Phillips. Bassett not only offered to support Phillips but also backed up his endorsement by organizing a political fundraising dinner for Phillips at the Royal York Hotel.[28]

With the backing of both Toronto major afternoon dailies, Phillips, who enjoyed campaigning, poured his energy into the effort. Support from the *Star* and *Telegram* was important in the campaign, but two other factors also served Phillips well. First, although Phillips could claim a long record of service to the voters of Toronto, in 1954 he was not in municipal office. This proved an asset. While the press portrayed Saunders as inept, stumbling from one mayoral misstep to the next and turning City Hall into a three-ring circus, Phillips could claim both a wealth of municipal experience and no responsibility for the current state of affairs at City Hall. Instead, Phillips simply promised that, if elected, he would lead an administration fiscally prudent and free of both rancour and embarrassing controversy. Second, what had originally looked to be a two-way race, Saunders versus Phillips, or as Saunders would have it, Protestant against Jew, suddenly turned into a three-way race. Former Toronto Board of Education chairman Arthur Brown, who came second to Lamport in the previous election and was no friend of Saunders, decided that he too would take another run at the mayor's chair. Brown, endorsed by the *Globe and Mail* as he was in the previous election, proved a thorn in Saunders' side and quickly entered into a mud-slinging match with Saunders. Saunders, in turn, was convinced that the only reason Brown entered the race was to "split the Church and Gentile vote."[29] And Brown was not above suggestive innuendo. He condemned Saunders for reportedly maintaining a suite in the Royal York Hotel for out-of-the-way meetings of City Council executives and extravagant entertaining. The rumours, later proven false, of strange goings on in the suite were pounced on by the press, who were happy to condemn the alleged backroom shenanigans and waste of taxpayers' money. Phillips was not above adding a little fuel to the hotel controversy. Two days before the election, the *Star* published a front-page picture of Phillips pounding on the door of the hotel suite under a headline reading, "Who Pays for Suite? Let Saunders Answer $64 Question."[30]

But what of Phillips's Jewishness? How did that play with the voters? Rather than sidestep Phillips's Jewishness, the press offered it up as an asset, contrasting Phillips's pride of heritage with what they claimed was Saunders's Orange Parade–like record of sowing seeds of religious strife in the community. As the *Globe and Mail* put it, Phillips was campaigning on a "platform of tolerance."[31] And tolerance was Phillips's campaign promise. A Phillips's electoral advertisement in the *Star* and *Telegram* boldly proclaimed in capital letters that, if elected, he would "REPRESENT ALL THE PEOPLE."[32] In contrast, Saunders lent weight to the accusation that he was narrowly sectarian and out of step with a changing Toronto by citing himself as "Leslie Saunders, Protestant" in a listing of civic candidates published in his *Protestant Action*. This again opened the door to press claims that, unlike Phillips, Saunders was neither fit nor ready to serve the people of Toronto.[33]

As voters went to the polls on 6 December, the Phillips camp claimed to be guardedly optimistic, although Phillips privately believed Saunders maintained a slight edge. The turnout was small – only 33 per cent of eligible voters bothered to go to the polls. As results came in that evening, Phillips jumped into a wafer-thin lead. In spite of the three-way race, support from Toronto's two largest newspapers, a squeaky-clean record, and Saunders and Brown's public feud, Phillips ended up with only the narrowest of victories. He won with little more than 34 per cent of votes cast.[34]

Saunders was stunned at coming second. To the very end he was convinced he could not and would not lose – certainly not to a Jew. While Saunders did not challenge the vote count, he refused to concede until the next day after every last vote was accounted for. And in defeat Saunders proved less upset with Phillips than with Brown, whom Saunders accused of deliberately sabotaging the election by splitting the Christian vote and thereby permitting a Jew to sneak up the middle. For his part, Brown, who came third in the race, graciously conceded to Phillips when it was clear victory would not be his.[35]

In his victory speech, Phillips took the high ground and pledged to be the "mayor of all the people." But, in a brief aside, Phillips pointedly acknowledged Saunders's attempt to turn Phillips's Jewishness into an election issue. Without naming Saunders, Phillips left no doubt who he was talking about. "I cannot help but mention the sour note tossed into the election by one of my opponents that I am of the Jewish faith with the clear object of defeating me."[36] But if Saunders failed to defeat Phillips, this does not mean that Saunders was unsuccessful in his attempt to turn voters against Phillips because he was a Jew. While Phillips was widely acknowledged to be Saunders's main electoral rival and a vote for Phillips was said to be the best hope of unseating the unpopular Saunders, almost half of those who voted against Saunders cast their ballot not for Phillips but for Brown, the acknowledged third candidate in the race. One can only wonder if some of those might be voters who did not want to vote for Saunders but also did not want to vote for a Jew. In the end, more than 65 per cent of those who voted cast their vote against Phillips. As the *Globe and Mail*, which backed Brown, editorialized, the election was not so much a Phillips victory as a Saunders defeat: "It must be admitted ... that Phillips victory was due less to his own popular leadership than to the surprisingly emphatic rejection of Mr. Leslie Saunders' claim to re-election."[37]

Rabbi Fienberg proclaimed that the election of Phillips was proof that "the assumption that a Jewish or Catholic or Protestant vote exists in Toronto would be fatal to the political judgment and maturity of its citizens ... Toronto has grown up." But perhaps Toronto was not as grown up as Fienberg claimed. In 1954 Phillips's Jewishness still counted and, given his slim margin of victory, may have counted against him. And in an ironic twist, Phillips's slim margin of victory was likely delivered by Jewish voters who made up less than 5 per cent of the city's electorate.

While many recent Jewish arrivals were not yet citizens, and were therefore ineligible to vote, in so tight a race that Jewish voters were enough to put Phillips over the top. In conceding to Phillips, Brown took note of Phillips's source of greatest voter support: "Nate is getting his downtown [Jewish] vote where he always polls heavily."[38]

In the final analysis, was Ben Keyfetz right? Was 1954 an *annus mirabilis*? Phillips's 1954 electoral victory was more of a fluke than a miracle, let alone a resounding vote for ethnic and religious tolerance. But it also cannot be denied that Phillips's election, close as it was, represented a change in Toronto's political and social culture. After more than one hundred years, Toronto's mayor was not an Orangeman. And he was not a Protestant. The day after the vote, the *Star* noted, "Time and again 'Nate' Phillips has heard the 'wise guys' would never elect a candidate of the Jewish faith as mayor. But here he was in the number one position."[39] Saunders and those who attempted to frame the election as a struggle to defend Protestantism against outsiders might decry the end of the Orange Order's century's long grip on City Hall, but they would prove to be more and more in the minority. Even if many in 1954 may have cast their ballot against Phillips because he was a Jew, this would not be the case again. Phillips went on the win the next election with more than 70 per cent of the votes cast and the election after that with more than 80 per cent.[40]

NOTES

1 Benjamin Kayfetz and Stephen A. Speisman, *Only Yesterday: Collected Pieces on the Jews of Toronto* (Toronto: Now And Then Books, 2013), 118.
2 David McDonald and Lauren Drewery, *For the Record: Canada's Greatest Women Athletes* (Toronto: Wiley, 1981).
3 Alan Levine, *Toronto: Biography of a City* (Madeira Park, BC: Douglas and McIntyre, 2014), 203–4.
4 *Toronto Daily Star*, 30 March 1954, 3; *Toronto Telegram*, 30 March 1954, 1.
5 Jim Gifford, *Hurricane Hazel: Canada's Storm of the Century* (Toronto: Dundurn, 2004).
6 Hugh Garner, "How Canada's 'Blue-Law' Busybodies Boss You on Sundays," *Liberty Magazine*, November 1956, 1, 56–7.
7 For a well-researched study of the place and impact of the Orange Order on Toronto politics see William J. Smyth, *Toronto, the Belfast of Canada: The Orange Order and the Shaping of Municipal Culture* (Toronto: University of Toronto Press, 2015).
8 *Toronto Daily Star*, 10 July 1954, 1–2.

9   Harold Troper, "Becoming an Immigrant City: A History of Immigration into Toronto since the Second World War," in *The World in a City*, ed. Paul Anisef and Michael Lanphier (Toronto: University of Toronto Press, 2003), 19–62.

10 Anne Michaels, *Fugitive Pieces* (Toronto: Penguin, 1996), 89.

11 Adara Goldberg, *Holocaust Survivors in Canada: Exclusion, Inclusion, Transformation 1947–1955* (Winnipeg: University of Manitoba Press, 2015).

12 *Canadian Jewish Reference Book and Directory* (Ottawa: Jewish Institute for Higher Research, 1963), 173.

13 James Walker, "The 'Jewish Phase' in the Movement for Racial Equality in Canada," *Canadian Ethnic Studies* 34 (2002): 1–29; Alan Borovoy, Carmela Patrios, and Ruth Frager, "'This Is Our Country. These Are Our Rights': Minorities and the Origins of Ontario's Human Rights Campaigns," *Canadian Historical Review* 82 (2001): 1–35.

14 Ninette Kelley and Michael Trebilcock, *The Making of the Mosaic: A History of Canadian Immigration Policy* (Toronto: University of Toronto Press, 1998), 324–7.

15 James Walker, "Canadian Anti-Semitism and Jewish Community Response: The Case of Nobel and Wolf," in *Multiculturalism, Jews and Identities in Canada*, ed. Howard Adelman and John H. Simpson (Jerusalem: Magnes Press, 1996), 37–68.

16 Philip Girard, *Bora Laskin: Bringing Law to Life* (Toronto: University of Toronto Press, 2005), 259; Gerald Tulchinsky, *Canada's Jews: A People's Journey* (Toronto: University of Toronto Press, 2008), 414; Allan Levine, *Toronto: Biography of a City* (Madeira Park, BC: Douglas and MacIntyre, 2014), 208.

17 Leslie Marrus Barsky, *From Generation to Generation: A History of Toronto's Mount Sinai Hospital* (Toronto: McClelland and Stewart, 1998), 49–53.

18 *Globe and Mail*, 8 December 1954, 4.

19 Nathan Phillips, *Mayor of All the People* (Toronto: McClelland and Stewart, 1967), 98.

20 *Who's Who in Canadian Jewry* (Montreal: Jewish Institute for Higher Research, 1967), 313.

21 Phillips, *Mayor of All the People*, 91.

22 Ibid., 95.

23 Saunders was also an active member of the Salvation Army in which he held the rank of Sergeant Major. According to the *Globe and Mail*, from the age of ten Saunders played clarinet in Salvation Army bands until 1952 when his clarinet was stolen. *Globe and Mail*, 4 December 1954, 3.

24 Smyth, *Toronto, the Belfast of Canada*, 248–9.

25 *Telegram*, 13 July 1954, 6.

26 Jamie Bradburn, "Historicist: The Loyal Orangeman versus the Mayor of All the People," *Torontoist*, 18 September 2010, https://torontoist.com/

2010/09/historicist_the_loyal_orangeman_versus_the_mayor_of_all_the_people/.

27 Tulchinsky, *Canada's Jews*, 379–80.

28 *Telegram*, 3 December 1954, 5; *Telegram*, 4 December 1954, 1; *Globe and Mail*, 8 December 1954, 5; Phillips, *Mayor of All the People*, 95–6.

29 Leslie Howard Saunders, *An Orangeman in Public Life: The Memoirs of Leslie Howard Saunders* (Toronto: n.p., 1980), 128.

30 *Toronto Daily Star*, 4 December 1954, 1.

31 *Globe and Mail*, 7 December 1954, 1.

32 *Toronto Daily Star*, 5 December 1954, 37; *Telegram*, 4 December 1954, 11.

33 *Toronto Daily Star*, 6 December 1954, 6.

34 *Telegram*, 7 December 1954, 1.

35 Levine, *Toronto: Biography of a City*, 208

36 *Globe and Mail*, 7 December 1954, 6.

37 Ibid.

38 *Canadian Jewish Reference Book and Directory*, 173.

39 *Toronto Daily Star*, 7 December 1954, 7.

40 Phillips, *Mayor of All the People*, 115, 117.

10 By the Rivers of the St Lawrence: The Montreal Jewish Community and Its Postmemory

IRA ROBINSON

The [Montreal] Jewish community will not rewrite Psalm 137 to read: By the rivers of the St. Lawrence, there we sat down, yea we wept.

– Saul Hayes, 1977[1]

Introduction

The Montreal Jewish community has to be included in any book dealing with the subject "No Better Home for the Jews ... Than Canada?" For most of its history, the Montreal Jewish community was the largest and most culturally creative in Canada. Even to the present, decades after Toronto surpassed Montreal in terms of the size of its Jewish community, Montreal remains a major centre of Canadian Jewish life and creativity, widely celebrated, in the words of Ruth Wisse and Irwin Cotler, for "the virtues of [its] Jewish communal and cultural life."[2]

This chapter, therefore, concerns the Montreal Jewish community. I will examine this community, however, at the moment of the Parti Québécois (PQ) victory in the Quebec provincial election of 15 November 1976, an event that marked a turning point in Canadian, Quebec, and Montreal Jewish history.[3] At that moment, it must have seemed to many surprised and worried Montreal Jews[4] that their community, which had been characterized as "large, cohesive ... perhaps the strongest in North America,"[5] was not going to be "no better home for the Jews" much longer. I am therefore examining a Jewish community at a time of crisis, facing major political, social, structural, and potentially existential changes. I was initially inspired to approach this subject by an article written by Ruth Wisse and Irwin Cotler and published in

Commentary in 1977 entitled "Quebec's Jews: Caught in the Middle," which demonstrated a highly interesting anticipatory nostalgia for a Jewish community "of ripe promise that now may remain forever unrealized."[6]

Given the magnitude of what happened to the Jewish community of Montreal in the 1970s and the following decades, there is relatively little published analysis other than a few brief articles written in the five-year period after the election, all but one of which were written by Montreal Jews.[7] One possible reason for this lacuna is that a mere forty years has gone by since the event, and it may be that the perspective necessary for proper historical analysis is only now emerging. It may also be, as Robin Philpot remarks, that "Quebec separatism and everything related to it are issues English Canadians prefer not to discuss."[8]

Context

Before we begin to discuss these issues, we need to contextualize the Montreal Jewish community's reaction to the PQ victory in 1976. What happened to the Montreal Jewish community in those years closely paralleled what was happening to anglophone Quebec in general, and what happened to anglophone Quebec was directly connected with one of the most important mega-trends in Canada in the mid-twentieth century: the decline of Montreal as the main economic centre of Canada and its replacement by Toronto between the 1930s and the 1960s. Thus on the eve of the Quiet Revolution, Montreal was effectively no longer the economic centre of Canada that it had been since the mid-eighteenth century. That title was now definitively Toronto's.[9]

This long-term mega-trend was certainly familiar to knowledgeable observers of the Canadian scene like Canadian Jewish Congress (CJC) official Saul Hayes, who stated: "Some non-French Canadian businesses have shifted their plants to Ontario or New York State, but it is difficult to assess how much of this is due to the rise of the Parti Québécois since it has been going on long before the autumn of 1976."[10] It is almost precisely at the point of culmination of this process of Montreal's relative economic decline that the English economic and linguistic dominance of Montreal was challenged by the Quiet Revolution. Urbanist Jane Jacobs remarked: "Until the late 1960s, Montreal still seemed to be what it had been for almost two centuries: an English city containing many French-speaking workers and inhabitants. But in fact, by 1960 Montreal had become a French city with many English-speaking inhabitants. By the time people in Montreal, let alone the rest of Canada, recognized what was happening, it had already happened."[11] Demographically the results of this mega-trend were of prime importance. In the 1951 Dominion census, 86 per cent of Montreal Island residents reported either French or British origins. Jews in that census counted for about 5 per cent of the total population. By 1986, however, the British ethnic component on the Island of Montreal had declined to under 10 per cent and more than 30 per cent were members of a new category, "cultural communities." That term included Montreal's Jewish community, whose estimated numbers in the 1970s ranged from 110,000 to as high as 150,000,[12] among numerous other ethnicities.[13] In the decade after the PQ victory (1976–86), the anglophone population of Greater Montreal declined by one-sixth (99,000).[14] For the three decades after 1976, Statistics Canada notes that "from 1976 to 2006, 307,000 more anglophones left Quebec than anglophones migrated from other provinces to Quebec."[15]

As for the Jews, Stanley M. Cohen noted that a Montreal Jewish population decline most likely began in the years prior to the Part Québécois victory.[16] How many Jews left Montreal in those years is highly speculative. Mordecai Richler, writing in 1977, reported that "it is now estimated that between 10 and 25 per cent of Montreal's 115,000 Jews, most of them young, will have quit the city by year's end."[17] Kanigel, writing in 1980, stated that "nobody seems to know for sure" how many Jews had left Montreal for elsewhere and he mentioned that the numbers he had heard ranged from 5,000 to 25,000.[18] Others have estimated that in the four decades since 1976 nearly 500,000 Quebecers[19] and among them 30,000–40,000 Jews[20] have left the province.

Reactions within the Jewish Community

As early as the late 1960s and early 1970s the major changes in Quebec social and political life known as the "Quiet Revolution" began registering in earnest on the radar of Canadian Jewry. Thus Toronto rabbi Stuart E. Rosenberg was commissioned by the prestigious *American Jewish Year Book* (AJYB) to write an article on "French Separatism: Its Implications for Canadian Jewry" for its volume published in 1973.[21] At that early date, informed by the events of the "October Crisis," but well before the separatist PQ constituted a threat to become the ruling party in the province, Rosenberg speculated that Jews might "filter out of the province as French Canadian nationalism becomes stronger and possibly tainted with anti-Semitism."[22] Even at that early point, Rosenberg observed a "deep malaise" within the Montreal Jewish community despite the optimistic rhetoric of communal leaders.[23] Melvin Fenson in the AJYB further noted that from 1971 the Montreal Jewish community was characterized by "a spirit of introspection and self-analysis in which Jewish writers and the community's internal leaders sought to reassure themselves that they ... were trying to accommodate to the French fact."[24] It was nonetheless clear to observers like Saul Hayes, writing in 1973, that "the good old days are gone forever as far as the linguistic pattern of Quebec is concerned."[25]

In 1977, Wisse and Cotler began their sketch of post-1976 Montreal Jewish reality by stating that "ever a barometer of change, the Jewish community has entered upon a state of almost continuous caucus that reflects uncertainty about the present and anxiety about the future."[26] Morton Weinfeld, a contributor to this volume, expressed the community's existential situation in this way: "While the ... anglophone minority ... has been understandably worried ... by the recent turn in events ... the Jewish community ... has been particularly shaken."[27] Stories are told by Montreal Jews that illustrate this anxiety. According to one, Montreal Jewish parents spoke by telephone to their son who was in college in the United States just after the PQ victory. The son asked them why they were speaking to him in Yiddish, and the answer was: "who knows who is listening." Another story is told about a secret list of ethnic minority members held by the PQ.

Cohen notes that the Jewish community leadership was actively involved in the 1976 election, more than in any other Canadian election to that time.[28] The most noteworthy public involvement of a prominent leader of the Jewish community was that of businessman and philanthropist Charles Bronfman, to whom Mordecai Richler attributes the following public statement: "Make no mistake, those bastards are out to kill us."[29] This statement was a widely publicized segment of a speech Bronfman delivered to an audience of several hundred just prior to the November election. Elsewhere in that speech he threatened that he would move his Seagram holdings and the Montreal Expos Major League Baseball franchise out of Quebec in the event of a Parti Québécois victory. Such an event would "mean the end of the country and the destruction of the Jewish community."[30]

After the election, Bronfman was forced to issue a retraction of his statement, though in his retraction he reiterated that "I felt then as I do now, most passionately, that Canada is one of the great and blessed nations of the world. And to face the spectre of separatism which could tear our country apart was a prospect so shattering that what I said truly reflected my mood and my feelings of the moment." Montreal's prominent Jewish communal organization, Allied Jewish Community Services (AJCS), also found it necessary to publish a denial of any connection whatsoever with Bronfman's highly partisan pre-election speech allegedly delivered on its premises.[31] Bronfman's highly charged rhetoric certainly was far from being a unique anglophone reaction to the events of the Quiet Revolution, which revealed much ambivalence and many unresolved tensions between French Canadians and Quebec's anglophone population in general, and with Jews in particular. Bronfman's speech is in fact of a piece with the actions of the Royal Trust Company, which, in 1970, expressed itself during a provincial election campaign by ostentatiously assembling a convoy of nine Brinks trucks, allegedly carrying securities from its Montreal headquarters to its offices in Toronto.[32]

According to Weinfeld: "Perhaps more significant than Bronfman's remarks, however, is the fact that for many Montreal Jews, perhaps the majority, [Bronfman's] remarks rang true, reflecting fears long latent within segments of the community."[33] Observers of the Montreal Jewish community at that time uniformly reported widespread panic and shock. In the opinion of CJC official Jack Kantrowitz, this sentiment prevailed not because there had been no previous evidence available to the community that the times in Montreal were changing. Rather, in his opinion, despite continuing signals emanating from francophone Quebec from 1960 to 1975, Jews, much like other Anglo-Canadians, preferred to rely upon "routinized and structured patterns of thought and comportment."[34]

As members of the Jewish community began assimilating what was actually happening, Kantrovitz commented that many of them began feeling uncomfortable in Quebec and ill at ease with the direction which Quebec society was taking. For Kantrovitz, the linguistic difficulties that appeared front and centre constituted merely an "external vision" of a much deeper problem.[35]

Wisse and Cotler emphasized the fragile emotional state of Montreal Jews in the post-election period: "Already a trickling exodus ... has begun ... all the more painful in a community whose sedentary nature expressed a desire for genuine rootedness, not merely an unimaginative attraction to security (for which it was often derided)."[36] Their notion of Montreal Jews' strong attachment to Montreal is seconded by the observations of Shlomo Perel in his article.[37] In his analysis, Harold Waller reinforces Wisse and Cotler's comment by emphasizing the emotional panic many Montreal Jews felt at the time:

> Montreal's Jews are not very mobile in an emotional sense ... [they] have strong ties to their city. Most would never think of moving simply for reasons of professional advancement or similar conventional reasons. What would cause people to move in large numbers would be a feeling that they were being forced out because of political circumstances ... The very thought of it provokes severe psychological pressure in many. The very existence of a PQ government has left many in a depressed state.[38]

The fraught emotional state within the Jewish community was diag-
nosed by Michael Yarosky as stemming from the Montreal Jewish community's "traditional insularity and isolation."[39] One measure of this
isolation is that in 1970 Montreal Jewish leader Philip Vineberg could
dismiss French Canadian economic prospects by stating that the French
Canadian "is not trained to look to the solution of economic problems
with economic methods."[40] Perel commented that the communal isolation in which Montreal Jews lived with significant social distance
between them and the French Canadians who made up a majority of
Quebec's population, heightened the uncertainty Montreal Jews felt.[41]
Weinfeld also expressed this idea and spoke of "feelings of confusion
and dismay" among Montreal Jews, attributed by him to the large proportion of Montreal Jews (according to the 1971 census 26 per cent) who
were post–Second World War immigrants and had suffered under Nazism and Communism, as well as the legacy of historical expressions
of antisemitism in Quebec that had entered Quebec Jews' historical
memory.[42] These highly emotional feelings likely came to the fore also
because Montreal Jews, like Canadian Jewry as a whole, whether directly connected with victims of the Holocaust or not, had assimilated
the Holocaust and the early twentieth-century French Canadian antisemitism into their collective memory and were thus exemplars of the
phenomenon Marianne Hirsch has termed "postmemory," a personal
connection with the events of the Holocaust despite generational distance.[43] Perel reflected this sense of postmemory when he stated: "[T]he
Jews do have a vivid memory of the widespread antisemitism and
pro-fascism in the Quebec of the 1930s and 1940s ... This memory combines with a fear of living in a new country, dominated by strong nationalists of the once antagonistic nation, to prompt the Jews to put up
their historical antennae and to be very careful."[44] This Montreal Jewish
anxiety was thought by observers to be exaggerated beyond objective
circumstances.[45] Thus Cohen observed, "though their reasoning does
not stand up under objective scrutiny, they have not hesitated to draw
an analogy between Quebec and pre-Second World War Germany."[46]
This analysis was reiterated by Côte-St-Luc rabbi Sidney Shoham, who
stated, "The problem is fear of anti-Semitism, not the reality."[47]
   In his analysis, Waller also emphasized the Jews' fear of being cut
off from the rest of the anglophone Jewish world of North America,[48]
a fear that did not reflect the real situation according to Kantrowitz,
who expressed the opinion that closing off Quebec's borders was just
not in the cards for the Parti Québécois, which was, in his words, "a
democratic party operating in a democratic environment."[49] Waller also
mentioned the Jewish fear that an independent Quebec would cut the

social benefits they had enjoyed as Canadians and might also pursue a pro-Arab foreign policy.[50]

Saul Hayes understood the panic and shock of Montreal Jews in terms of their historical memory: "The Jewish community of Montreal, a very nonhomogeneous group, has one thing in common: anticipation of disaster. History has been unkind to them and the memory of abuse, degradation, pogroms lingers on."[51] Hayes supplemented his statement in this way: "Jews have long memories and a very extensive education remembering Amalek by whatever name he bears.[52] But, in the short run, the memory fails to acknowledge that practically all of Quebec's ills, as they affect the total population and are troublesome particularly to Jews, predate the November 15 election by ten years and some by two or three."[53] Hayes was attempting to tell the Jewish community of Montreal to "take a deep breath" while recognizing that the average Montreal Jew did not share his perspective. He stated:

> Even now, at this juncture in Quebec's history where anti-Semitism is at a very low level, where the Jewish issue never appeared in pre-election slogans, in election rallies. etc., the community is not solaced. It fears the unknown to a greater degree than perhaps do other ethnic elements of the population. While the initial excitement has somewhat abated, the mood can still be described as highly emotional, at times one of panic and, among groups whose provenance was Nazi-dominated Europe, of fear and apprehension that it can happen here.[54]

The Shift in Jewish Organizational Life to Toronto

It was clear to many contemporary Canadian Jewish observers by the early 1970s, particularly those in Toronto, that it was high time for Toronto to replace Montreal as the organizational capital of Jewish Canada.[55] Waller noted in his analysis that even though the Montreal Jewish community was still growing in the early 1970s, its growth rate had already slackened compared with that of Toronto.[56] This factor, accompanied by the growing realization that Toronto had overtaken and surpassed Montreal economically, engendered a movement within Toronto Jewry to establish the headquarters of the Canadian Jewish community there. Stuart E. Rosenberg, writing in the early 1970s, thus stated: "For many years, Montreal's Jewish leaders had been brought up on the belief that what was good for Montreal was good for the rest of the country ... The capital of Jewish Canada is still Montreal, but only because of historical precedent ... how long can it retain influence and authority based on seniority?"[57] In the post-1976 atmosphere,

Rosenberg's idea took the form of a more public challenge to the Montreal leadership. Thus in December 1976, at a Negev Dinner in Toronto, a suggestion was made by Phil Granovsky, president of the Canadian United Israel Appeal, that all national Jewish organizations move to Toronto. There was an immediate and hard pushback on the part of Montreal Jewish leaders. Thus Alan Rose, national executive director of the CJC, stated that his organization, then the premier Canadian Jewish organization, had no intention of moving. He added: "From a public relations point of view the whole suggestion would be blown up by the French Canadian press."[58]

Though the CJC never moved its corporate headquarters to Toronto, it lost much of its power in the decades after 1976 to the Toronto-based Jewish Federations of Canada–UIA, which in 2011 decided to effectively end the ninety-year career of CJC and replace it with the Toronto-based Centre for Israel and Jewish Affairs.[59]

Institutional Adjustments in the Montreal Jewish Community

As was already noted, the social and political events of the Quiet Revolution had made their mark on the Montreal Jewish community. One of the great events of the Quiet Revolution in Quebec was the retreat of the Roman Catholic Church from its previous institutional control of educational, health, and social services institutions. For its part, the Jewish community in Montreal had built up its complex institutional structure in the early to mid-twentieth century, reacting to a faith-based Roman Catholic and Protestant institutionalization of health, education, and social services in Quebec. All observers agreed that the Jewish community of Montreal was highly organized and networked.[60] As Weinfeld noted, the health, education, and social services institutional structure of the Montreal Jewish community was maintained long after the original discriminatory attitudes and faith-based institutionalization had abated,[61] and Cohen noted that Jewish community leaders in the 1970s were greatly concerned about the possibility of the loss of Jewish community control over its institutions.[62]

But what to do? Wisse and Cotler asked the following rhetorical question: "Does the uniqueness of the Montreal Jewish community justify a special effort at adaptation to the new situation in order to protect and nurture the community's many institutions and cultural achievements?"[63] Kantrowitz characterized the Jewish community as inward-looking, one that "concerned itself with its own affairs and practised a policy of mutual toleration and (largely speaking) indifference with the political process in Quebec."[64] Harold Waller reiterated this opinion, arguing, however, that the community's inward orientation beneficially affected the "intensity, vitality, and commitment of [Jewish] communal life."[65] Waller answered Wisse and Cotler's question with a definite affirmative,[66] even though it was clear that for the Montreal Jewish community, as Cotler subsequently stated, "the days of self-segregated solitude are over."[67]

As previously mentioned, the Jewish community leadership of Montreal had to scramble in order to deal with the new linguistic context in which it found itself. Most importantly, the empowerment of the French language in Quebec, through Bills 22 and 101, challenged both the community's educational system, one of its major priorities, and its long-established way of doing business in English. In 1969 Allied Jewish Communal Services of Montreal created a special committee in order to deal with the French fact in Quebec "positively and constructively as a Jewish community." This committee recommended hiring bilingual staff and putting francophone Jews on communal boards. The organization's 1970 annual meeting was largely devoted to the theme "Jews in the Quebec of the Future – Realité 1970."[68] Montreal Federation/CJA's 1974 *Annual Report* stated that the provincial laws that gave French legal priority in Quebec set the Jewish community "back on its linguistic heels" as it struggled to begin presenting itself publicly in French.

In the post-1976 atmosphere, the Jewish community leadership went beyond mere rhetoric concerning the community's changed situation to where it really counted – the budgetary process. It is noteworthy that in the ACJS's 1978–9 budget, half a million dollars less than in the previous year was allocated to the United Israel Appeal. AJCS executive vice-president, Manny Batshaw, tried putting the best face on things, and explained the budgetary move by stating: "There is a shift to a greater recognition of local needs ... It is interesting to note that at the board of trustees meeting, not a single question was raised about the fact that more money is going into local needs. This is because there is a desire to maintain a strong, viable Jewish community here."[69]

Montreal Jewish "Cultural Communities"

The Montreal Jewish community that existed at the time of the Quiet Revolution was strongly dominated by people with eastern European Ashkenazic ties. As Teboul observed, the Ashkenazic character of the Montreal Jewish community was an intrinsic part of its identity.[70] By the 1970s, however, there were two "cultural communities" of Jews in Montreal that did not completely identify with the ethos of the Montreal

Jewish community leadership. One of these communities, though itself Ashkenazic in origin, was ultra-Orthodox (*Haredi*) and thus did not fit in the communal ethos in which Orthodox Judaism was generally respected so long as it did not impinge on the personal lifestyle choices of community members.

In the 1960s the report of the Royal Commission on Bilingualism and Biculturalism noted the somewhat disruptive arrival of a distinctly ultra-Orthodox Jewish community in Montreal, which began, for most intents and purposes in the 1940s.[71] In this report, the commission stated that the arrival of Orthodox and Hasidic Jews in Montreal constituted something of a threat to some members of the older established Jewish community.[72] The tension between these two Jewish communities was expressed by the commission's researcher for Jewish topics, Ruth Wisse, in the following way:

> The orthodox and Hassidic Jews make up a small percentage of the total Jewish community in Canada and have little connection with other Jewish groups. Even so, their presence has tended to reverse the normal pattern of integration: Canadian Jews were most highly acculturated in the very earliest period of settlement; between 1840 and about 1940 they were differentiated by ethnic characteristics ... from the surrounding population, but there was much interaction between Jews and non-Jews, and a willingness to assimilate values of the new culture. Only now, in the latest phase of Jewish life in Canada do we have what usually comes at the beginning – enclavic groups, intent upon maintaining in unadulterated form their traditional mode of living![73]

The other major Jewish group present in Montreal in the 1970s that did not fit the pattern of the established Ashkenazic community were the Sephardim, North African Jews who had begun coming to Quebec in significant numbers in the late 1950s and who constituted a major portion of Montreal's Jewish population by the 1970s.[74] From the perspective of the Jewish communal leadership of the early 1970s, the Sephardic Jews seemed to pose an assimilatory problem. As Stuart Rosenberg put it, francophone Sephardic Jews in Montreal almost all went to English schools and faced "a choice of identifying either with the existing Anglophone Jewish community and probably losing his language and his unique French-Sephardic cultural heritage or with a non-Jewish francophone community and thus probably losing his Jewish religious connections."[75] Sephardic efforts to create their own parallel communal institutions were not always well received by the Ashkenazic communal leadership.[76] In particular, the founding of the first francophone Jewish school in Montreal, l'École Maïmonide in 1969, did not occur without a certain "grincement de dents" on the part of anglophone Jews.[77]

Ruth Wisse, in the Royal Commission Report mentioned above, spoke of the Sephardim as somewhat dependent on the more established Jewish community:

> North African Jews from French and Spanish Morocco, who came to Montreal and Toronto in the late 1950's and early 1960's, also added variety to the Jewish religious community. Their Sephardic form of Judaism set them apart in ritual and custom from most of their coreligionists in Canada. They quickly began to hold services according to the Sephardic rite, and sought aid from the Jewish community in setting up their own synagogues.[78]

It is no secret that the Ashkenazi Jewish communal leadership in Montreal maintained a somewhat patronizing attitude towards the Sephardim, and Michael Solomon, writing in the AJYB, posed the question whether these new francophone Jewish immigrants would be treated by the established Jewish community as equals. This attitude is further illustrated by Solomon's description of their religious situation in the early 1970s published in the AJYB: "12,000 North African Jews felt very much at home ... [their] services conducted according to *oriental ritual* [my emphasis]."[79] This is surely a case in which the Sephardic Jews in Montreal were "orientalized" by the Ashkenazic majority.[80]

Despite all the patronizing attitudes towards the Sephardim on the part of the communal establishment, it was no coincidence that the year after 1976 the Communauté Sépharade du Québec concluded an affiliation agreement with AJCS.[81] This began a process that, lasting several decades, has created the possibility for Sephardim to enter the leadership circles of the Montreal Jewish community.

Towards a Conclusion

As mentioned at the beginning of this chapter, soon after the November 1976 Quebec election, Montreal Jewish intellectuals Ruth Wisse and Irwin Cotler published their article "Quebec's Jews: Caught in the Middle," expressing their uncertainties about the future of the Montreal Jewish community. In the forty five years since they wrote their piece, a somewhat diminished and demographically different Montreal Jewish community maintains its place as the second-largest Jewish community in Canada. At the same time, the anticipatory nostalgia Wisse and Cotler expressed for Jewish Montreal as it was in 1976 and as it might have been has spread across the globe. Montreal Jews in their travels frequently encounter members of a Montreal Jewish diaspora in major cities from Toronto to Tel-Aviv. Stores selling "Montreal bagels" are located in cities as diverse (and far away from Montreal) as Boulder, Colorado,[82] Edinburgh, Scotland,[83] and Santiago, Chile.[84] Revolutions – even "Quiet" ones – have their repercussions.

NOTES

1 Saul Hayes, "The Jews of Quebec: Endangered Species?" *Congress Monthly*, June 1977, 12.
2 Ruth Wisse and Irwin Cotler, "Quebec's Jews: Caught in the Middle," *Commentary*, September 1977, 56.
3 Stanley M. Cohen, "Jewish Concerns in Quebec" *Canadian Zionist*, January-February 1977, 15.
4 Cohen asserts that "very few Jews" foresaw a PQ victory in 1976; ibid., 10.
5 Wisse and Cotler, "Quebec's Jews," 55.
6 Ibid.
7 In chronological order of publication, the articles devoted to the subject attempting a relatively instant analysis are:
   • Stanley M. Cohen, "Jewish Concerns in Quebec," *Canadian Zionist*, January-February 1977, 10–12, 15
   • Shlomo Perel, "Quebec's Nationalist Movement and the Future of Its Jews," *Israel Horizons* 25, no. 4 (April 1977): 23–7
   • Saul Hayes, "The Jews of Quebec: Endangered Species?" *Congress Monthly*, June 1977, 11–13
   • Ruth Wisse and Irwin Cotler, "Quebec's Jews: Caught in the Middle," *Commentary*, September 1977, 55–9
   • Morton Weinfeld, "La question juive au Québec," *Midstream*, October 1977, 20–9
   • Harold Waller, "Montreal Jews Face the Challenge of Quebec Nationalism," *Analysis* 65 (September 1978)
   • Jack Kantrowitz, "Jews in the New Québec: Where Do We Go from Here?" *Viewpoints* 10, no. 1 (1979): 5–10
   • Morton Weinfeld, "The Jews of Quebec: Perceived Anti-Semitism, Segregation, and Emigration," *Jewish Journal of Sociology* 22 (June 1980): 5–19
   • Robert Kanigel, Les juifs du Québec" *Moment* 6, no. 1 (December 1980): 38–48.

- Harold Waller, "Kehillat Montreal be-Mezuka Politit," *Gesher* 26, nos. 1–2 (1980): 88–112
- Harold Waller, "Canada," in *Zionism in Transition*, ed. Moshe Davis (New York: Herzl Press, 1980), 118.

Mordecai Richler's article "Oh! Canada!: Lament for a Divided Country," *Atlantic Monthly*, December 1977, 41–55, is not primarily about the reaction of the Montreal Jewish community, but does contain some material relevant to this analysis (pp. 50–1). Gerald Tulchinsky, in his 630-page treatment of the history of Canada's Jews, devotes approximately 1 per cent of the book (pp. 443–9) to the crisis brought about by the 1976 election. *Canada's Jews: A People's Journey* (Toronto: University of Toronto Press, 2008). Morton Weinfeld, in his survey *Like Everyone Else ... But Different* (Toronto: McClelland and Stewart, 2001) devotes less than 1 per cent of a 446-page book (pp. 268–71) to the issue.

8 Robin Philpot, preface to *The Question of Separatism: Quebec and the Struggle over Sovereignty*, by Jane Jacobs (Montreal: Baraka Books, 2011), x.
9 Marc V. Levine, *The Reconquest of Montreal: Language Policy and Social Change in a Bilingual City* (Philadelphia: Temple University Press, 1990), 41–2.
10 Hayes, "Jews of Quebec," 11.
11 Jacobs, *The Question of Separatism*, 14.
12 Michael Solomon, "Canada" *AJYB* 71 (1970): 357. On p. 355 of that volume, he gives the number of the Jews in Quebec as 122,000. In *AJYB* 72 (1971), 275, Solomon gives the figure of 130,000. Marvin Fenson in *AJYB* 75, 321, estimated the Jewish population of Quebec as "some 150,000." The Jewish population of Canada in 1977 was estimated by AJYB at 305,000. Leading Jewish centres were Toronto (115,000), Montreal (115,000), Winnipeg (20,000), Vancouver (12,000), and Ottawa (7,500). *AJYB* 1979, 192. Weinfeld notes that in the 1971 Census the number of Jews by religion in Montreal was 109,480. "Jews of Quebec," 6.
13 Levine, *The Reconquest of Montreal*, 216–17.
14 Ibid., 120.
15 "Portrait of Official Language Minorities in Canada – Anglophones in Quebec," http://www.statcan.gc.ca/pub/89-642-x/2010002/article/conclusion-eng.htm (accessed 11 October 2017).
16 Cohen, "Jewish Concerns," 12.
17 Mordecai Richler, "Oh! Canada!: Lament for a Divided Country" *Atlantic Monthly*, December 1977, 50–1.
18 Kanigel, "Les juifs," 47. Cf. Waller, "Canada," in Davis, ed., *Zionism in Transition*, 119, who mentions "a few thousand Jews."

174 Ira Robinson

19   Martin Knelman, "Director Revisits Exodus from Quebec in Documentary," *Toronto Star*, 29 April 2016.

20   Ron Csillag, "Will Rising Nationalism Renew Montreal Jewish Exodus?," Jewish Telegraphic Agency, 8 October 2013, http://www.jta.org/2013/10/08/news-opinion/world/rising-nationalism-bleeds-montreals-jewish-community?utm_source=Newsletter+subscribers&utm_campaign=9717900c2b-JTA_Daily_Briefing_6_18_2013&utm_medium=email&utm_term=0_2dce5bc6f8-9717900c2b-25348069.

21   Stuart E. Rosenberg, "French Separatism: Its Implications for Canadian Jewry," *AJYB* 73 (1972); 407–27.

22   Ibid., 409; cf. 417–18.

23   Rosenberg, "French Separatism," 422.

24   Melvin Fenson, "Canada," *AJYB* 75 (1974–5): 319–20.

25   Cited in ibid., 325.

26   Wisse and Cotler, "Quebec's Jews," 55.

27   Morton Weinfeld, "La question juive au Québec" *Midstream*, October 1977, 20–1.

28   Cohen, "Jewish Concerns," 10.

29   Richler, "Oh! Canada!: Lament for a Divided Country, 50. Cited in Levine, *The Reconquest of Montreal*, 111. Weinfeld's version reads: [The Parti Québécois] are a bunch of bastards trying to kill us," "La question juive," 22.

30   *AJYB* (1978): 277.

31   "Strong Reactions Continue Despite Bronfman's Retraction of Statement on Meaning of Separatist Victory," 1 December 1976, Jewish Telegraphic Agency, https://www.jta.org/1976/12/01/archive/strong-reactions-continue-despite-bronfmans-retraction-of-statement-on-meaning-of-separatist-victor.

32   Levine, *The Reconquest of Montreal*, 88. This publicity stunt turned into an indelible memory that was resurrected after the PQ win when Rabbi Sidney Shoham remembered that the day after the election saw "a regular parade of Brink's trucks to Toronto." Kanigel, "Les juifs du Québec," 47.

33   Weinfeld, "La question juive," 22.

34   Kantrowitz, "Jews in the New Quebec," 6.

35   Ibid., 10.

36   Wisse and Cotler, "Quebec's Jews," 57.

37   Perel, "Quebec's Nationalist Movement," 26.

38   Waller, "Montreal Jews," 5.

39   Cited in Kanigel, "Les juifs," 48.

40   Cited in Rosenberg, "French Separatism," 426.

41   Perel, "Quebec's Nationalist Movement," 26.

42   Weinfeld, "La question juive," 22, 24.

43   Marianne Hirsch, *Family Frames: Photography, Narrative, and Postmemory* (Cambridge: Harvard University Press, 1997); idem., *The Generation of Post-memory: Writing and Visual Culture after the Holocaust* (New York: Columbia University Press, 2012). Cf. Lizy Mostowski, "Postmemory in Canadian Jewish Memoirs: The Holocaust and Notions of a Jewish Homeland," *Israelis* 8 (2017): 155–6.

44   Perel, "Quebec's Nationalist Movement," 27.

45   For the most optimistic reading of this history, see Victor Teboul, *René Lévesque et la communauté juive: entretiens* (Montreal: Éditions des Intouchables, 2001), 21.

46   Cohen, "Jewish Concerns," 10, 15.

47   Kanigel, "Les juifs," 43.

48   Waller, "Montreal Jews," 8. Cf. Wisse and Cotler, "Quebec's Jews," 57; Cohen, "Jewish Concerns," 11; Teboul, *René Lévesque*, 22.

49   Kanigel, "Les juifs," 44; cf. Rosenberg, "French Separatism," 427.

50   Harold Waller, "Montreal Jews," 1; idem., "Canada" in Davis, ed., *Zionism in Transition*, 118.

51   Saul Hayes, "The Jews of Quebec: Endangered Species?," *Congress Monthly*, June 1977, 11.

52   On contemporary identification of enemies of the Jews as "Amalek," see Elliot Horowitz, *Reckless Rites: Purim and the Legacy of Jewish Violence* (Princeton, NJ: Princeton University Press, 2006), 107–46.

53   Hayes, "The Jews of Quebec," 12.

54   Ibid., 11.

55   Franklin Bialystok, "Postwar Canadian Jewry," in *Canada's Jews: In Time, Space, and Spirit*, ed. Ira Robinson (Boston: Academic Studies Press, 2013), 94.

56   Waller, "Montreal Jews," 1.

57   Stuart E. Rosenberg, *The Jewish Community in Canada*, vol. 1: *A History* (Toronto and Montreal: McClelland and Stewart, 1972), 142–3.

58   Bernard Baskin, "Canada," *AJYB* 77 (1977): 324.

59   Ron Csillag, "Canada's Restructured Jewish Advocacy Agency Gets Name," 23 August 2011, https://www.jta.org/2011/08/23/news-opinion/world/canadas-restructured-jewish-advocacy-agency-gets-name.

60   Waller, "Montreal Jews," 2.

61   Weinfeld, "Jews," 7.

62   Cohen, "Jewish Concerns," 11.

63   Wisse and Cotler, "Quebec's Jews," 55–6.

64   Katrowitz, "Jews in the New Quebec," 9. On the political indifference of Montreal Jews, cf. Rosenberg, "French Separatism," 425.

65   Harold Waller, "Montreal Jews Face the Challenge of Quebec Nationalism," 4.

66　Ibid., 9.

67　"Jewish Community Must Adapt to Change, Spokesman Insists," *The Suburban* (Montreal), 10 May 1978.

68　Michael Solomon, "Canada," *AJYB* 72 (1971): 276.

69　Bernard Baskin, "Canada," *AJYB* 80 (1980): 175.

70　Teboul, *René Lévesque et la communauté juive*, 22.

71　Steven Lapidus, "The Forgotten Hasidim: Rabbis and Rebbes in Prewar Canada," *Canadian Jewish Studies*, accessed 21 December 2017, https://cjs.journals.yorku.ca/index.php/cjs/article/viewFile/22624/21095.

72　Solomon, "Canada," 278.

73　R.R. Wisse, "Jewish Participation in Canadian Culture," an essay prepared for the Report of the Royal Commission on Bilingualism and Biculturalism (1967), Book IV, 98, accessed 21 December 2017, http://epe.lac-bac.gc.ca/100/200/301/pco-bcp/commissions-ef/dunton1967-1970-ef/dunton1967-70-vol4-eng/dunton1967-70-vol4-part1-eng.pdf.

74　Yolande Cohen, ed., *Les Sépharades du Québec: parcours d'éxils nord-africains* (Montreal: Del Busso Éditeur, 2017).

75　Rosenberg, "French Separatism," 420.

76　Teboul, *René Lévesque*, 61.

77　Ibid., 63. Cf. http://www.ecolemaimonide.org/histoire (accessed 3 December 2017).

78　Wisse, "Jewish Participation in Canadian Culture," 98.

79　Solomon, "Canada," 358.

80　Cf. Edward Said, *Orientalism* (New York: Pantheon Books, 1978).

81　Teboul, *René Lévesque*, 62.

82　Allyson Reedy, "New Bagel Shop in Boulder Is Serving Up Montreal-Style Bagels, Whatever That Is," *Denver Post*, 21 April 2017, http://theknow.denverpost.com/2017/04/21/woodgrain-bagels-boulder-montreal-style/142077/.

83　Mike Cohen, "Native Montrealer Makes It Big with Bagels in Scotland," *The Suburban* (Montreal), 13 December 2017, A4.

84　Montreal Bagel, accessed 3 December 2017, http://santiagobagel.cl/. On the Montreal bagel phenomenon, see Michael Kaminer, "In Bagel World, Montreal Goes Global," *Forward*, August 2018, 78–9.

11 In from the Margins: Museums and Narratives of the Canadian Jewish Experience

RICHARD MENKIS

In 1945, the amateur Jewish historian and cultural activist J.L. Livinson applied to the Historic Sites and Monuments Board of Canada for recognition of Canada's first synagogue. The Board rejected the application, with one member proclaiming that "he was not particularly interested in the commemoration of Jewish activities." He was catholic in his hostilities. When it was also suggested that there be a commemorative marker for four hundred African Canadians who lived on Vancouver Island before 1858, he was again not interested. He could not see how "the immigration of Negroes is a fact to rejoice upon."[1]

Rarely do we hear so clearly the voice of an agent of marginalization. And with decades of research after the publication of Benedict Anderson's seminal work on nationalism, we know that the nation is an imagined community forged, in part, from the narratives of memorials and museums. Sometimes I have wondered about the impact of memorials and museums. And then we get the reminders – the recent events in Charlottesville over Confederate symbols, or the protests over the statue of Edward Cornwallis in Halifax. Moreover, representations in museums should be understood synergistically with other forms of cultural representations. The Haitian historiographer Michel-Rolph Trouillot identifies four moments in the production of narratives when power can produce silences in historical representations. One of these moments is what he calls the "moment of retrospective significance," when a narrative is publicized for a broad audience as in a festival or a museum exhibition. We should understand these moments in tandem, for example, with the creation of archives, or in Trouillot's phrase the moment of "fact assembly."[2]

But here I am teasing out just one subject: museums. This study in cultural history parses and raises questions about the organizing question of this volume: Could there be a better home for Jews than

Canada? What kind of home would it be if the narratives of the Jewish community were not considered "Canadian" and not included in the national experiences depicted in state-sponsored exhibitions? And the corollary question is: How comfortable are Jews, in this home, telling their stories, including the stories of the marginalized (the poor) and the ostracized (the criminals)?

The silencing of the sort described at the 1945 meeting demonstrates the lack of acceptance of the Jews socially and culturally, and an attempt to perpetuate that marginalization. In order to show how Jews and the narrative of Jews in Canada have moved from the margins, this chapter examines three exhibitions that achieved national prominence in the past five decades. Moreover, an examination of these three exhibitions allows us to raise questions about Jewish cultural and civic engagement with a Canada striving for pluralism. The exhibitions are *Journey into Our Heritage* from the 1970s; *A Coat of Many Colours*, which was developed in the late 1980s and on display in the 1990s; and the narrative at the Canadian Museum of Immigration at Pier 21. These exhibitions were often complemented by a book or a movie that shared many of the features of the exhibition.

The Jewish Historical Society of Western Canada (JHSWC) produced the exhibition *Journey into Our Heritage*, which focused on Jewish life from Manitoba to British Columbia. In its earliest iteration, a group of community leaders in Winnipeg pulled together an exhibition in time for Canada's centennial in 1967. The Society displayed this modest exhibition in a community building, the local Young Men Hebrew's Association (YMHA).[3] In early 1968, the Manitoba Museum of Man and Nature wrote to the Jewish community and asked for help in collecting Jewish artefacts and documents for its exhibition when it opened in 1970. The museum also planned on a permanent collection for an ethnic archive section.[4] With the success of the YMHA exhibition and this interest from the province's flagship museum, local organizers were ready to take on a more ambitious endeavour. The result was *Journey into Our Heritage*.

In this, as in other cultural ventures, Manitoba's Jews were prepared for the new discourse and policies of pluralism coming out of Ottawa in the 1960s and 1970s.[5] When Lester Pearson called for a Royal Commission on Bilingualism and Biculturalism in 1963, he also called on the commission to explore "the cultural contributions of the other ethnic groups." Volume four of the report of that commission, which came out in 1969, dealt with issues relating to minority groups in Canada. In 1971, Pierre Trudeau announced his multiculturalism policy, which included plans to "multiculturalize" national agencies such as the Public

Archives of Canada and the National Museum of Man. The policy also promised to provide funding for projects coming out of the groups themselves.

The federal government announced its first grants for community-based projects in January 1972 with a deadline of 15 February. The JHSWC applied and received a grant for its museum project in mid-April. By the end of the year, under the co-sponsorship of the JHSWC and the Manitoba Museum of Man and Nature, *Journey into Our Heritage* opened in the major exhibit area, Alloway Hall. The out-reach to the Historical Society was part of a broader initiative. In the previous two years, the museum had presented other exhibitions in the hall, including a display on Ukrainian life.[6]

Spearheaded by designer Harry Gutkin, *Journey* was the first seri-ous museum exhibition on any aspect of Jewish life in Canada. After its successful run at the Manitoba Museum of Man and Nature, it was invited by the National Museums of Canada to submit a plan for a trav-elling exhibition. Upon receiving that funding, *Journey* travelled to six western Canadian cities and was viewed in three locations in Toronto, in London, Ontario, and in Ottawa before voyaging across the ocean to the Museum of the Diaspora in Tel Aviv. At least one reason for its national stature was its newness: there had never been an exhibition of Jewish life in Canada like this. In Toronto, the Canadian Jewish Con-gress Central Region Archives set up a special committee to promote the exhibition in Ontario. It used the occasion to call for local Jewish ar-tefacts and documents for the archive. It also arranged tours of Jewish sites in Toronto in conjunction with the exhibition "in order to demon-strate examples of our Ontario Heritage."[7]

The exhibition *A Coat of Many Colours* was more ambitious in scope, as it attempted to present the story of the Jewish experience across Canada.[8] The prime mover in this case was Andrea ("Andy") Bronfman. She was the English-born second wife of Charles Bronfman, one of the heirs of the famous Sam Bronfman and the Seagram's liquor empire that Sam built. She said the inspiration came during visits to the Museum of the Diaspora, when she left bewildered that there was so little representa-tion of Canadian Jews.[9] After some early missteps, the project became a joint venture between the Canadian Friends of the Museum of the Dias-pora, chaired by Bronfman, and the Canadian Museum of Civilization, which also coordinated the research. By then, institutions such as the museum had ample time to "multiculturalize." The country's commit-ment to multiculturalism became more formalized and deeper with the incorporation of multiculturalism in the patriated Canadian Constitu-tion, and with the 1988 Multiculturalism Act. The exhibition opened in

Ottawa in early 1990 at the Canadian Museum of Civilization. It then moved to other high-profile venues in Winnipeg, Saskatoon, Vancouver, Edmonton, Halifax, and Montreal, and to the Museum of the Diaspora in Tel Aviv.

To their credit, the producers of both *Journey into Our Heritage* and *A Coat of Many Colours* broke new ground. They raised the public profile of the history of Canadian Jewry, and to non-Jewish audiences they told the story of a minority group. The press gave good coverage to the exhibitions as they passed through their cities. Through a combination of their personal accomplishments and the reimagined relationship of the state with its minorities, Jews had "made it." As a result, they could present their story to both Jews and non-Jews. And that story would be not only in some unvisited corner of a Jewish communal building, but in leading cultural institutions. Each exhibition also helped nudge Canadian Jewish historical consciousness from an emphasis on written texts to visual and material cultures.

Not everybody was enthusiastic about what they saw, or didn't see, in the exhibitions and related publications and videos. In both exhibitions, business leaders had far more profile than labour leaders. Jewish radicals like the communists Joe Zuken, a longtime alderman in Winnipeg, and Fred Rose, elected by Montreal voters to Parliament, were not to be found. The exhibitions tamed Jewish participation in sports, limiting it Jewish teams in the community or individual stars. Where was the Jewish involvement in the rough-and-tumble worlds of boxing and horse-racing?[10] Jewish criminals, petty and not-so-petty, were also part of the Canadian Jewish experience. In reviewing Gutkin's book on Jews in the west – which replicated the emphases of the exhibition – the professional gadfly Larry Zolf looked at the cast of respectable characters in Gutkin's book. He wondered what happened to some of the less-than-savoury characters he knew in Winnipeg, such as "Duck" Levson, "Boozy" Rusen, "Coke" Lander, "Merve the Curve," and "Shecter the Connector."[11] Nor did one find in *A Coat of Many Colours* the story of Harry Davis, who died in a hail of bullets outside one of his Montreal gaming houses. Although the five thousand attendees at his funeral stopped traffic on one of the central streets of Jewish Montreal, the organizers of *Coat* apparently agreed with the Yiddish press. The *Keneder Adler* editorialized that Jews would be better off without the spectacle of gangland hits and that Davis's funeral did not deserve the attention it received.[12] Perhaps most surprisingly, both exhibitions minimized the history of antisemitism, and downplayed immigration restrictions. The latter should have been relevant to the narrative, in *Coat*, of the national experience of Jews.

How can we explain what was included, and what was not? Although two decades separated the two exhibitions, they shared a framing discourse. The promoters of *Journey* claimed they had two major purposes. First, they wanted to provide evidence of "the contributions of the Jews of Western Canada to the progress of Canada particularly in the fields of Arts, Sciences and Letters." They also wanted to demonstrate how the organized Jewish community, and individual Jews, contributed to the public life of Canada. In summarizing the purpose of *A Coat of Many Colours*, Andrea Bronfman said that they wanted to show "what Canada gave to its Jewish immigrants and what Canadian Jews were able to give back to the Canadian community."[13]

The repeated term is "contribution." It had a long history in Jewish apologetics and can certainly be found in the integrationist apologetics of Jewish museums in other national settings.[14] But this apologetic stance in other countries does not make it irrelevant for understanding the Jewish experience in Canada. For whatever reasons, insecurity not being the least of them, the Jewish creators of the exhibition decided, in Canada, that Jews had to prove their worth. The early language of multiculturalism – focusing on the "contributions" of the groups not included in Canada's two "founding" groups – reinforced this tendency. This discourse, as many critics pointed out, placed the minorities a rung below the two so-called founding "races." It also seemed to show no interest in how the group defined itself. Its tone was celebratory and did not invite reflection on inequalities, such as racism.

Moreover, who defined what constituted a "contribution"? In the case of *A Coat of Many Colours*, the outlook was elitist. The high profile of Andrea Bronfman and the Board meant that they had access to funding, and they could use their clout to get groups to lend their artefacts. There was, however, a downside. According to the curator of the exhibit, although it seemed that there was community engagement, "one might ask if it really was the community or simply a small segment of the community." She answered the question herself. The Board was, she admitted, "too involved in the curatorial process." She claimed that the staff heard concerns from historians and historical societies but "[i]n some cases we felt pressure from our sponsors and other interested people to consider various concerns at a rather late stage in the development process."[15]

Between the pressure to find "contributions," and the social outlook of the backers, there were blind spots. One reviewer of the exhibition pointed out that the creators of the exhibition had largely excised the story of Jewish workers and radical politics. Many Jews, especially in the garment industries, suffered from brutal exploitation and many offered resistance in union activities and radical politics. He also wondered about the limited emphasis on antisemitism and the restrictions on Jewish refugees when they were trying to escape Nazi persecution. The book that complemented the exhibition, by Irving Abella, did refer to this period. That is hardly surprising, given his co-authorship, with Harold Troper, of *None Is Too Many*. But it was not to be found in the exhibition: "The general public is not given enough information to come to a critical understanding of the deep anti-Semitism and racism that were so prevalent in all levels of Canadian society and government in the 1940s."[16]

Ironically, the strategy of selective representation can backfire. Could another minority group, poor and struggling, identify with the Jews who are presented in the exhibition? Moreover, the creators of the exhibition may have misread what engages museum goers. The popular Lower East Side Museum of the Tenement, founded in 1988, with exhibitions opening several years later, emphasized the hardships of immigrant life.[17] Historian Michael Berkowitz has described how the Jewish Museum in London was reluctant to put on an exhibition called *Ghetto Warrior: Minority Boxers in Britain*. The theme seemed too far removed from middle-class respectability, especially with boxing's association with gambling. But it became a popular exhibition, and the catalogue became the best-selling publication in the history of the museum.[18]

The earliest iteration of the museum and exhibitions at Pier 21, and specifically the representation of the Jewish experiences, shared characteristics with *Journey* and *Coat*. It was a retired immigration officer, J.P. LeBlanc, who advocated that the federal government should recognize the historical significance of this major port of entry for many Canadians. In 1988 he founded, and served as first president, of the Pier 21 Society. Over the next decade, the Society pressed to develop the site. On Canada Day, 1999, a new museum with a permanent exhibition opened its doors to the public.

Ruth Goldbloom, née Schwartz, was the second president of the Pier 21 Society. She was born in the small Jewish community of New Waterford on Cape Breton Island, attended Mount Allison and then McGill. She married into the well-known medical family, the Goldblooms, and in 1967 she and her husband moved to Halifax. Haligonians appreciated her intelligence and energy as she took on significant volunteer positions in local non-profit organizations. She was the first woman to chair the United Way campaign in Halifax and was the first Jew to chair the Catholic Mount Saint Vincent University. It was Pier 21, however, that became her passion in the 1990s and her best-known contribution to the city (and Canada). When she first walked onto the site of Pier

21 it was, in her words, "a derelict building, dilapidated building of the Halifax waterfront. Rat infested, pigeon infested, and I was terrified to walk around."[19] But with her seemingly boundless energy and her connections, she is generally credited with a major role in the 1999 opening. She also was a major figure behind the funds and profile necessary to establish Pier 21, in 2011, as one of Canada's six national museums. Pier 21 also joins the Canadian Museum for Human Rights as the only two national museums outside the National Capital Region of Ottawa-Gatineau.

The opening of the museum in 1999 was a fitting way to enter the new century. For much of the twentieth century, the promoters of heritage and tourism in Nova Scotia had invented a simplistic, largely Celtic, folk culture for the province. They thereby minimalized the ethnic diversity, such as the African Canadians who came in waves from the United States after 1776, or the fifteen ethnic groups who had settled in the steel-mill area of Whitney Pier on Cape Breton Island.[20] Pier 21 highlighted diversity rather than eradicated it, and Ruth Goldbloom both represented the change in the province's culture and promoted it. Appropriately enough, the exhibition also pointed out the role of Pier 21 during the Second World War – the troops who embarked and the lesser number who returned. But the emphasis was on the immigrants. The galleries were designed to lead the visitor through the stages of immigration. The visitor moved in the order of the experience. There was departure from the home country, the arrival by ship, the encounter with immigration officials and aid societies, and the train ride from Halifax.

The permanent exhibition, however, was criticized for its celebratory nature. A reviewer in the *Canadian Historical Review* appreciated how the museum stressed the central role of immigration in creating Canada. But she pointed out that "there is little discussion of those migrants who never made it onto ships because they were of the 'wrong' ethnicity or religion," nor was there treatment of those whom the government deported, or immigrants who voluntarily decided to leave Canada.[21] The author of an MA thesis that was defended shortly after the opening of the museum also stressed how the upbeat nature of the immigrant story ignored the presence of First Nations and the legacy of settler colonialism. She also noted that many – perhaps most – immigrants found the experience traumatic, and that was not presented in the exhibition. The overall effect led to a representation of contented immigrants and of a narrowly construed nationalism, a multiculturalism without blemish.[22] Perhaps most relevant to the Jewish community was the minimization of government restrictions when Jews were trying to escape the prejudices and persecutions in Europe once Hitler came to power.

When Pier 21 became a national museum on 3 February 2011, the inadequate celebratory quality of the old exhibition was even more blatant. Now the museum had to represent the story of immigration for all Canadians, whether they passed through Pier 21 or not. And now the national museum needed to acknowledge the role of government, especially Ottawa, in framing immigration policies that welcomed some and rejected others. The immigration restrictions on Jews received some attention when, two weeks before the opening of Pier 21 as a national museum, the movable sculpture *Wheel of Conscience* was unveiled. Architect Daniel Liebeskind designed *Wheel* to memorialize the ill-fated *St Louis* that could find no safe harbour – including Halifax – where it could disembark its Jewish refugees.[23] Still, the sculpture was not part of the exhibition and the creators of the exhibition did not integrate the narrative of government restrictions into the history of government policies. This was part of the larger problem with the exhibition, and scholars working at the museum identified many overlapping issues. Historian Steve Schwinghamer, for example, warned against glamorizing even the site of Pier 21, as its history, from its origins, was mired in conflict.[24]

After major renovations to the building, the Canadian Immigration Museum at Pier 21 reopened in 2015, with the important addition of the Canadian Immigration Hall. Using historians and professional curators who were well aware of the criticisms of the old museum, and who knew both the primary and secondary sources relevant to their topic, the museum has a narrative that avoids many of the previous pitfalls. An immigration timeline includes details on the racial hierarchies in immigration history.[25] While one might not always agree with certain specific elements of the narrative, it presents both the attitudes towards minorities and the inner history of the immigrant communities. In the case of the Jews, the narrative points to the Christie Pits Riots, although the genteel antisemitism of the boardroom may have had more impact. There are representations of synagogues with other sacred spaces and there is a reproduced front page of Montreal's Yiddish newspaper, the *Keneder Adler* in a section on ethnic cultures. The Canadian Immigration Hall has presented an unblinkered story of government policies, and in an exhibition dealing with multiple immigrants groups, Jewish life has been presented with some nuance.

When Pier 21 opened in 1999, the Historic Sites and Monument Board acknowledged the national significance of the site. They dedicated a plaque that stated: "The site witnessed the arrival of approximately one million immigrants, who have enriched the cultural mosaic." The language is certainly a far cry from the comments from the same Board, presented at the start of this chapter, that marginalized Jews and other minorities. This chapter has described how the narrative has moved from the margins. Beginning in the late 1960s, Jews organized exhibitions of Canadian Jewry. The shift in Canadian self-definitions and the adoption of the discourse of multiculturalism meant that Jews could receive government funding for their exhibitions. They could also present their narratives in high-profile museum settings. The central role of socially prominent supporters both signalled a new openness to minorities and a desire to influence how Jews are perceived. However, the celebration of Canadian diversity by these two Jewish exhibitions led to a suppression of the diversity within the Jewish community. Was a brittle self-consciousness not an admission that Jews were not comfortably "at home" in Canada?

There should be a museum of Canadian Jewish experiences. It should, however, proceed with caution and self-reflexivity. *Journey* and *Coat* deserve credit for offering innovative narratives of Canadian Jewry, based on images and objects, to new audiences. However, apologetic elements were in evidence, and could dull Jewish and Canadian self-understanding. Although the Canadian Immigration Hall at Pier 21 treats Jews as one minority among others, it has managed to present a critical and textured history of the Jews of Canada.

NOTES

1 As quoted in Cecilia Morgan, *Commemorating Canada: History, Heritage and Memory, 1850s–1990s* (Toronto: University of Toronto Press, 2016), 119.

2 Michel-Rolph Trouillot, *Silencing the Past: Power and the Production of History* (Boston: Beacon Press, 1995), 26–7. For the story of Canadian Jewish archives, synergistic with that of museums, see Richard Menkis, "Identities, Communities and the Infrastructures of History: Creating Canadian Jewish Archives in the 1930s and 1970s," in *History, Memory and Jewish Identity*, ed. Ira Robinson et al. (Boston: Academic Press, 2016), 233–56; and see the more recent and developed study by Amir Lavie, "The Past Is Not a Foreign Country: Archival Mentalities and the Development of the Canadian-Jewish Community's Archival Landscape during the Nineteen Seventies" (PhD thesis, University of Toronto, 2019).

3 Allan Levine, *Coming of Age: A History of the Jewish People of Manitoba* (Winnipeg: Heartland Associates, 2009), 351.

4 "Minutes of the Meeting of the History and Archives Committee of Canadian Jewish Congress, Western Region, Sunday March 17, 1968," Irma and

Marvin Penn Archives of the Jewish Historical Centre of Western Canada (Winnipeg) (hereafter, JHSWC), MG 6 D4 No. 27.

5 I have drawn attention to this in several articles: "A Threefold Transformation: Jewish Studies, Canadian Universities and the Canadian Jewish Community" in *A Guide to the Study of Jewish Civilization in Canadian*, ed. Michael Brown (Jerusalem and Toronto: International Center for University Teaching of Jewish Civilization and the Centre for Jewish Studies at York University, 1998), 43–69; "Negotiating Ethnicity, Regionalism and Historiography: Arthur A. Chiel and *The Jews in Manitoba: A Social History*," *Canadian Jewish Studies/Études juives canadiennes* 10 (2002): 1–31; and the aforementioned "Identities, Communities and the Infrastructures of History."

6 For this history, see "Brief to Be Used in Discussion of Future Relationship of Jewish Historical Society of Western Canada and the Canadian Jewish Congress and the Winnipeg Jewish Community Council," JHSWC, MG 6 D4, no. 27. Undated but from late 1972 or early 1973. See also the brief exhibition guide, *The Jewish Museum of Western Canada Presents Journey into Our Heritage / Sponsored by the Manitoba Museum of Man and Nature and the Jewish Historical Society of Western Canada in Alloway Hall from October 1972 to March 1973* ([Winnipeg]: Jewish Museum of Western Canada [1972]).

7 Ontario Jewish Archives (Toronto; hereafter, OJA), Fonds 4, Box 74-7-1, press release, undated but on basis of internal evidence, from mid-1978; OJA, CJC Archives, Jewish Historical Society, "Project Report – Journey into Our Heritage," undated but on the basis of internal evidence, from late 1979.

8 For background on the exhibition, see Sandra Morton Weizman, introduction to *Artifacts from "A Coat of Many Colours": Two Centuries of Jewish Life in Canada* (Hull, QC: Canadian Museum of Civilization, [1990]), 13–16.

9 "Coat of Many Colours: A Conversation with Andrea Bronfman," *Viewpoints* 18, no. 1 (1990), supplement to *Canadian Jewish News*, 12 April 1990.

10 The exception in *Coat* is Sammy Luftspring, but the emphasis there is on his decision to boycott the Olympics in Berlin in 1936. Luftspring agonized over the decision, which could have been used as a way to show how important sports was for Jews who had limited avenues out of the grinding poverty in the immigrant Jewish neighbourhood.

11 Larry Zolf, "Jewish Tales Untold: Gutkin's Pictures Don't Reveal the Entire Story," *Winnipeg Free Press*, 12 July 1980. This criticism of the book certainly applies to the exhibition. Other comments made by Zolf in that review were challenged.

12 Suzanne Morton, *At Odds: Gambling and Canadians, 1919–1969* (Toronto: University of Toronto Press, 2003), 119.

13 "Coat of Many Colours: A Conversation with Andrea Bronfman."

14 To see how this theme has coursed through post-emancipation Jewish communities, see the admirable summary by Richard I. Cohen, "The Visual Revolution in Jewish Life – An Overview," *Studies in Contemporary Jewry* 26 (2012): 3–24.

15 Sandra Morton Weizman, "Multiculturalism in Museums: *A Coat of Many Colours*: A Case Study" *MUSE* 10, no. 1 (Spring, 1992): 60–2.

16 Edward Tomkins, "Review: *A Coat of Many Colours*," *MUSE* 9, no. 1 (Spring, 1991): 94–5. An article in *Maclean's*, 16 April 1990, also noted that the exhibition did include some references to prejudice, but the issue was not "formally addressed."

17 If it did run afoul of immigrant groups, it was not because of the representations, but rather because, riding on its success, the museum's plans for expansion threatened the displacement of groups who still lived in the area. For an evaluation of the museum, in the context of other museums dealing with Jewish immigration, see Robin Ostow, "From Wandering Jew to Immigrant Ethnic: Musealizing Jewish Immigration," *Studies in Contemporary Jewry* 26 (2012): 137–9.

18 Michael Berkowitz, "Jewish Fighters in Britain in Historical Context: Repugnance, Requiem, Reconsideration," *Sport in History* 31, no. 4 (December 2011): 423–41.

19 Quote from "Oral history interview of Ruth Goldbloom by Steven Schwinghamer, 24 June 2011," Canadian Museum of Immigration at Pier 21 (Halifax), 11.06.24 RG; biographical information from obituaries in *Globe and Mail*, 30 August 2012, and *Canadian Jewish News*, 4 September 2012.

20 Ian McKay and Robin Bates, *In the Province of History: The Making of the Public Past in Twentieth-Century Nova Scotia* (Montreal: McGill-Queen's University Press, 2010). See also Ian McKay, *The Quest of the Folk: Antimodernism and Cultural Selection in Twentieth Century Nova Scotia* (Montreal: McGill-Queen's University Press, 1994).

21 Renée Lafferty, "Pier 21, Halifax Nova Scotia," *Canadian Historical Review* 82, no. 1 (March 2001): 172–4.

22 Tamara Vukov, "Imagining Canada, Imagining the Desirable Immigrant: Immigration Spectacle as Settler Postcolonialism" (MA thesis, Concordia University, 2000), especially 109–15.

23 Ostow, "From Wandering Jew to Immigrant Ethnic," 140–1.

24 Steve Schwinghamer, "'Altogether Unsatisfactory': Revisiting the Opening of the Immigration Facility at Pier 21," *Journal of the Royal Nova Scotia Historical Society* 15 (2012): 61–74. Framed in part by the work of Schwinghamer on the physical space, and highlighting the evidence necessary for a nuanced representation of immigration, see also Jay Dolmage, "Grounds for Exclusion: Canada's Pier 21 and its Shadow

Archive," in *Diverse Spaces: Identity, Heritage and Community in Canadian Public Culture*, ed. Susan L.T. Ashley (Newcastle: Cambridge Scholars Publishing, 2013), 100–21.

25 The website of the museum also has an article effectively contextualizing the story of the *St Louis*, thus strengthening the immigration timeline and contextualizing the Liebeskind sculpture. See Steve Schwinghamer, "Canada and the MS *St. Louis*," accessed 30 December 2017, https://www.pier21.ca/research/immigration-history/canada-and-ms-St-Louis.

SECTION THREE

Reflections: Personal Stories, Language

12 Pictures of New Canadians: An Immigration Story for Our Time

NORMAN RAVVIN

Ours is a time of immigration fever, not unlike periods of crisis that came before. The disasters that set off refugee crises take place far from Canadian ports and airports, but they reverberate here, forcing a review of immigration policies and ideals. Just as with past immigrants, present-day new Canadians face the grave challenge of becoming known by the mainstream. Being known – both understood and heard as a diverse community – is arguably a key part of being "at home." A version of this challenge showed itself in the embarrassing snafu over the plaque unveiled in September 2017 at Ottawa's new Holocaust monument, with its bureaucratically inspired language that neglected to mention Jews. To the casual viewer, even to a fair share of Canadian Jews, this gaffe must have seemed inexplicable. The monument's governmental minders – the Heritage Minister among them – had a deer-caught-in-the-headlights look of embarrassed shock. But I recognized in this little drama something characteristically Canadian in its interplay between the country's mainstream and its Jews, which takes us back to the early decades of the past century, when Jews were a large minority in the country but not an influential one. William Faulkner's darkly funny mid-twentieth-century quip points to that period's link with our own: "The past is never dead. It's not even past."[1]

My recent research and writing circle around my maternal grand-father's immigration from Poland in 1930, alone; his arrival on the Saskatchewan prairies; his four years as a de facto rabbi, teacher, and *shoichet* for Jewish farm communities; as well as his struggle to bring his wife and two young children from Poland in a period of ever-narrowing immigration possibilities. Although this narrative suggests motifs made familiar by Hesh Troper and Irving Abella's *None is Too Many: Canada and the Jews of Europe 1933–1948*, a glance at the book's subtitle places me at remove from their time frame.[2] Throughout my narrative the federal government was Conservative, led by an Atlantic Canadian transplanted to Calgary; the biases of Quebec parliamentarians had little influence; and though the Department of Immigration under the Conservatives had made it increasingly difficult for Jews to enter the country, the grim overseer of this project under the liberals, F.C. Blair, had not yet risen to full power.

What distinguishes the first half of the thirties – my grandfather's first Canadian years – and what have those years to do with our Heritage Minister's deer-in-the-headlights moment in Parliament? To convey this, I must tell two short stories associated with my grandfather's arrival in this country.

He arrived in late 1930, when a set of categories – Preferred, Non-preferred, Special Permit – guided immigration agents, commissioners, and Members of Parliament. Although Jews were likely to emigrate from countries dubbed "Non-preferred," which included Poland and Roumania, immigration agents were told not to place them there. Rather, they were placed in the "Special Permit" category where each application could be overseen by the department on a case-by-case basis. In the late 1930s, demographer and community worker Louis Rosenberg described this bureaucratic strategy as follows: "the Canadian government did not extend to all bearers of a passport issued by the Polish, Roumanian, Lithuanian, Austrian or other Government the same treatment and regulations, but made a distinction between the Jewish and non-Jewish subject of those countries."[3]

The correctness of Rosenberg's claim is supported by my grandfather's landing document, the "Canadian Government Return" form that listed him and his shipmates as they sailed from Southampton to Quebec in November 1930. He is listed among compatriots whose "Race or People" is inscribed variously as Russian, Ukrainian, and Polish. My grandfather carried a Polish passport, which did not designate religious background. On the landing document, in the column marked "Race or People," it is clear that a clerk, having looked at my grandfather's passport from *Rzeczpospolita Polska* – the new Republic of Poland – had begun to type P – . But this is struck out by hand and replaced with the pencilled sobriquet "Hebrew." Based on information in his visa file my grandfather's nationality had been replaced by a made-up, half-hearted category favoured by the federal bureaucracy, its immigration department, census takers, and transport clerks. He'd been branded on his way out to the wheat-lands with a scarlet "H."

This is a story of arrival. Did my grandfather care, or even notice that his nationality, acted on in his youth by two years as adjutant to a Polish Army officer in Warsaw, had been reformulated by an immigration clerk, backed up by Orders-in-Council and census data on the "Hebrews" of the Dominion of Canada? Most likely not. Off he went by CNR train across the country towards Vancouver, where his brother awaited him on the city's east side. There my grandfather upped his game – before leaving his Polish home he'd trained to *shecht* chickens. While in Vancouver a local *shoichet* trained him in the more onerous work of cattle slaughter, with the agreement that my grandfather would not become a competitor in Vancouver but would seek his first job elsewhere.

My second short story is one of music and folk culture in the late twenties and early thirties. These were years of subtle change in the discussion and events associated with Canadian cultural identity. The word mosaic showed up, as bureaucrats and academics mused about the impact of "Continental Europeans" on Canadian national identity and the settling of the "Last Best West." The CPR mounted a set of remarkable Folksong and Handicraft Festivals in the late twenties, which were held at their railroad hotels in Quebec City, Regina, Winnipeg, and Calgary. In 1930 the "Great West Canadian Folk Dance Folk Song and Handicraft Festival" took place at the Palliser Hotel, a short walk from the downtown Calgary streets where Jewish families lived and owned small businesses. The festival's main stage presented "Folksong" concerts, sometimes with dance programs, representing the cultures of Poland, Iceland, Denmark, Norway, Czecho-Slovakia, Holland, Hungary, Roumania, Jugo-Slavia, Ukraine, the Schwarzwald, and Finland. Among the Swedish folk dancers were thirty child performers. The Don "Kossaks" mounted a "Musical Quartette with Balalajka, Mandolina and Guitarre."[4]

While the Quebec festivals of 1927 and 1928 highlighted the province's folk heritage in craft and song, festivals in prairie cities had a multi-ethnic flavour and exhibited a kind of proto-multiculturalism that celebrated the "Canadian Mosaic." The pamphlet advertising the 1930 Calgary events could almost be mistaken for an album of ethnographic photography: Highlander dancers in quilts; Welsh in stovepipe hats; Danish folk dancers in lace caps and aprons; "Kossak" dancers in peaked Persian lamb hats, their sabres raised; a "Hungarian Cowboy" alongside a "Jugo-Slav Bagpipe player."[5] The pamphlet's preface highlighted song and craft with an eye to nation-building. The "main idea" of the festival, its writer tells us, was "to help Canadians to realize the priceless heritage which they possess in the traditional melodies which have been brought to this country by immigrants, and in some cases have been composed in this country by early settlers."[6]

The Calgary festival took place in the spring of 1930. My grandfather's train west brought him through town in November. The CNR depot stood a few blocks south of the Palliser on Seventeenth Avenue. If my grandfather had time to step onto the wooden boardwalk or to walk around the front of the depot, he would have seen Tin Lizzies parked at an angle. November in Calgary is grey. The Festival's folk-dancing and folk-singing ethnics were long gone. But someone might well have been waiting on the platform for another Jewish traveller from out east. My grandfather and he might have had a laugh regarding "Kossak" dancers passing through a town so far from the Russian borderlands. Just a decade before, decidedly non-musical Cossacks had rolled through his Polish village with the Soviet Red Army. In Calgary they danced.

This is fun to think about, but the activities at the Great West Festival highlight something peculiar. Among the early, important groups immigrating to the Canadian prairies who were invited to the Folksong festivals, there is a notable absence: Jews. Robert England, an early expert on the subject in his 1936 London-published study *The Colonization of Western Canada: A Study of Contemporary Land Settlement (1896–1934)* reminds us: "It is not commonly recognized that Jewish settlers were amongst the early settlers of Western Canada and that their settlement predates the German, Ukrainian, Doukhobor, Russian and Hungarian settlements."[7]

What do we learn from the Jewish absence at the Calgary festival and its counterparts? One cannot argue that all the invited groups represented their native country, since two – the Don "Kossaks" and the Schwarzwalders – are representatives of ethnic regional culture rather than national culture. We might hope that the Poles brought with them just a hint of Jewish music, since the two traditions enlivened each other. But if one listens to contemporary versions of the songs chosen by the 1930 Polish contingent (bearing names such as *"Pod Bialem Orlem,"* or "Under the White Eagle") there is no hint of klezmer or even gypsy influence on the Polish *kapela*. The Don "Kossaks" with their "Mandolina Quartette" are another group ripe for investigation on this front. Mandolin orchestras proliferated in Jewish groups on the Canadian prairies in the early part of the twentieth century.

Calgary's Glenbow Museum archive holds a remarkable photograph, which is not directly related to the 1930 Folk Song Festival but overlaps with it in uncanny ways. Dated 1929, the photo's title is "Peretz School Orchestra, Calgary, Alberta." Its black background is punctuated by thirteen figures, standing and seated, holding stringed instruments. Among them is a teacher – Mrs Smith – while the rest are young people aged ten to fourteen or fifteen. They hold mandolins of various shapes and sizes, a guitar, and, in the case of one young female performer, a tiny banjo. The female performers wear silk dresses and shawls with

long fringes, their dark hair glossy. In one, a youthful forehead is dec-
orated by a neatly curled lock of hair, Josephine Baker–style. The ma-
jority of the orchestra players look seriously at the photographer. The
Glenbow lists the names of those pictured. They include Ida Robinsky,
Anne Levine (she of the banjo and carefully placed lock of hair), Max
Eisenstadt, Morris Estrin, among others. The photograph would not
look out of place among those collected in the pamphlet for the 1930
Calgary Folk Dance and Folk Song Festival, with its "Czecho-Slovak
Dancers from Saskatchewan" and its "Irish Jig Dancers (Pupils of Alice
Murdoch, Calgary)."[8] The mandolin was a ubiquitous folk instrument
in eastern Europe, unique to no cultural locale. In the part of Poland my
grandfather came from, it was played by Poles and Jews. Immigrant
Jews brought mandolin music with them to western Canada, and it was
associated with secular Yiddish schools where folk culture was promoted, as it was at the Calgary Peretz School. The mandolin orchestra
was a rare venue available to young women who yearned to perform.
Anne Levine and her pals all lived a few short blocks from the Palliser,
almost in its shadow. Based on their photo, they were rarin' to go.

Their absence at the Palliser provides a fine example of what we can
learn, in the historical record, from absences. Throughout the teens and
twenties of the twentieth century, the Canadian self-image was increasingly troubled by what came to be known as "Continental Europeans,"
a group that arrived from central and eastern Europe and was, especially by the Depression era, under increasing scrutiny from official and
popular opinion. In the twenty years prior to my grandfather's arrival
the "problems" associated with these immigrants circulated in popular
and political discussion like bad weather. Immigration itself proved a
defining phenomenon. My grandfather was swept up in his own peculiar Polish Jewish version of these larger trends. His story helps us
consider how Canada defined itself anew in the early decades of the
twentieth century.

The country's railroads often present themselves as touchstones
in early immigration narratives. The CPR and the CNR – the latter a
government-owned outfit at this stage – made their bread by selling
tickets to newcomers as well as to local travellers, and understood
that the rail system would be more profitable if settlement grew west
of Winnipeg. In 1925 the federal Liberal government cut a deal with
the railways dubbed the "Railways Agreement," which gave the CNR
and CPR the responsibility to "select, transport and settle agriculturalists, agricultural workers and domestic servants from 'non-preferred
countries.'"[9] The agreement offloaded to the railways the provocative
project of attracting immigrants, as Canadians and their government

Figure 12.1 Peretz School orchestra, Calgary, AB, 1929 (Glenbow Archives NA-3300–1)

increasingly worried about the impact of "Continental Europeans" on national life. The epithet "Continental European" shows up in these years as a euphemistic term, at times as a seemingly neutral way of referring to people from countries that Canadian immigration regulations characterized as "non-preferred."

The CNR, as an arm of the federal government, busied itself documenting the progress of these newcomers in order to prove the success and profitability of settlement efforts. One remarkable outcome of this documentation was the creation of a photographic dossier by the railway that was meant to record immigrants' arrival and settlement, while attracting newcomers. Photos were taken at the Quebec City and Halifax immigration reception centres and on homesteads. Prints were collected in volumes for bureaucratic perusal, organized by province of settlement. Settler families were represented by a picture or two, which were affixed in the CNR's dossier in the old photo album fashion using adhesive corners. Beneath these appeared an account of

each settling "Head of Family," their "European Address," "Nationality," date of arrival in Canada, "Present Address," and sections farmed.
A summary of the settling family's progress and homesteading efforts
followed. The settlers were often categorized by settlement "scheme" –
how much money a family brought with them; their direct investment
in newly bought farmland; the number of children they brought from
Europe; and the locale they were obliged to farm.[10] Photos drawn from
this dossier found their way into newspapers and magazines as part of
ongoing public discussion about the daily life of immigrants.

CNR office correspondence about the photos is revealing. In 1929
the railroad's Superintendent of Land Settlement wrote to a colleague:
"The photographs are generally excellent. We would suggest, however, that in the future it would be a good idea to have the women
remove the head shawls before taking the photographs. Mode of dress
is responsible for much of the criticism of newcomers as 'foreigners'
and in our photographs it is well to have them look as 'Canadian' as
possible."[11] This proposal, put so plainly by one bureaucrat to his district subordinate, provides a fundamental proviso regarding the reception of immigrants in Canada over the course of a century. The same
proviso reverberates in Quebec today, with efforts by governments to
ban varieties of religious or cultural dress that are said to clash with
"Quebec values" or with the society's expressed "secular" character.
A commonly invoked canard suggests that because Quebeckers –
traumatized by their colonialist Catholic heritage – threw off their links
with an inherited religious culture, they resist such religious expression in newcomers to the province. This bears no relationship to logical
argument. One's own cultural and religious baggage and its character
in a secular era inflicts no imperative on others, who have entirely different cultural or religious heritage. The opinion of the CNR's superintendent seems to be, nearly a hundred years after it was set down,
a perfectly contemporary expression of an aggressive form of social
engineering: "it would be a good idea to have the women remove the
head shawls ... Mode of dress is responsible for much of the criticism of
newcomers as 'foreigners.'"[12]

I wonder how my grandfather was dressed when he met with Canadian immigration officers, first at the port of Gdynia in Poland and then
at Quebec City. I have few pictures of him in the period of his travel to
Canada. In a photo taken around the time of his marriage in 1928 he is
the picture of cosmopolitan suaveness in a tailored suit, dark striped
tie, high white collar with a collar pin, a white pocket square, his face
smoothly shaved. By the time he was active as a *shoichet* and religious
teacher and rabbi on the Canadian prairie, he wore his beard neatly

trimmed. But what of the rest of his comportment? To complement whatever decisions he made regarding clothing, there was the distinctively cosmopolitan German name, by way of introduction: Eisenstein.

Germans. They play an interesting role in the background of what I have set down here. Whether one were to read the minutes of meetings in the Parliamentary Privy Council chambers, or overhear the chatter in a smoking car full of CNR settlement agents, the German would be touted as the immigrant *non plus ultra*, that is, if one could not get the desired number of newcomers from the United Kingdom or the United States. Evidence of this appears in a photograph taken in 1908 by one of the CNR's hard-working photographers, John Woodruff. Three men stand with their back to some sort of wooden building, possibly an outbuilding at the Quebec port. For its use in the CNR dossier its descriptive title was "Pure Russian, Jew, German," which aims to "name" the three figures pictured.[13] What can we say about these three? They are males of roughly the same height, each with their particular headgear and heeled boots. They all have facial hair, though the "Jew" has the most, a dark beard that is trimmed but covers the bottom part of his face. The cap of the "Pure Russian" is a bit smarter than the one worn by the "Jew," and he has a stolid stance, whereas the "Jew" presents himself diffidently, standing a bit behind the other two. He alone has his back up against the wooden outbuilding. The German demands detailed comment. His hat is a gentleman's bowler. The white of his shirt is most prominent. He stands with his feet apart, jacket over his arm, a cigarette in one hand, the picture of casual confidence. He is the one among the three who might be described as an up-and-comer. If we were casting agents calling for a Canadian of his time he would be our man. Remarkably, too, the "Jew," like my grandfather with his landing document, has been stripped of his nationality. He is some vague nobody from Nowheresville, a figure of lore, a wandering Jew. Or, in his Canadian census-taker's guise, a "Hebrew." One wonders if the CNR knew the code behind the photograph's message, but maybe these ideas were simply in the air that people breathed in the early decades of the Canadian century, and Woodruff was not aware of his camera's editorial gaze.

There is a second context in which this photograph was used. In a 1910 article that appeared in *The Canadian Courier*, a "national weekly" magazine published in Toronto, the three figures appear as cut-outs in a group of twelve "Types" of "New-Comers" chosen from "Photographs Taken at Quebec and Halifax."[14] These exemplars are presented in two lines of six. The top row is headed by the "English" type, who is the trimmest, and, we must assume, the best-suited to Canadian life. The "Russian" from the original Quebec trio is dubbed an "honest plodder"

Figure 12.2 CNR photo of Immigrants at Quebec, "Pure Russian, Jew, German" (National Archives of Canada C-009798)

by the magazine's editors. The German receives a vote of confidence: "In Ontario, Thousands; in the West, Tens of Thousands." The "Jew," looking lost without his wooden wall to stand against, is fleshed out a bit and called a "Russian Jew." He is last in line in the bottom row, tagged with an insult, a kind of classroom bully epithet: "Not anxious to farm – a dweller in cities." At this point the railroad superintendents, the photographer-for-hire, and the magazine editor all shift into focus as an unwitting team of identity makers who present faux categories as meaningful commentary – as if the CNR photos were meant as templates rather than as pictures of real people. Jew. Russian Jew. Russian. The shifting and arbitrary defining terms. In faraway cities, around cabinet tables and university lecterns, social scientists and bureaucrats mused haplessly about the meaning of cultural origin, ethnicity, race, and peoplehood, and took part in discussions of eugenic theories that would create disasters in Europe.

My grandfather's landing document, the 1930 Calgary Folk Dance and Folk Song Festival, the forgotten Peretz School mandoliners: each reflects the shifting and unsure role of Jews in early Canadian imagination and public life. In some unquiet way all three point to what Canadians thought about Jews. In each case, it seems, they thought rather little, and if anything, their ideas were askew, based on confused notions and stereotypes that led up blind alleys. In the recent case of Ottawa's Holocaust monument, Jews were influential alongside non-Jewish public figures. But the embarrassing plaque, with its bland message leaving Jews unnamed, echoes earlier times when the relationship between Jews and the Canadian mainstream was a dance of mystery and misapprehension.

I have no photograph of my grandfather upon his arrival at Quebec. I do not have his Polish passport of the early thirties where his nationality was made clear. Of his travels across the country towards the coast I can only daydream. In Polish studio photos of the late 1920s he is a young man, bright-faced, at ease. Make of him what you will.

NOTES

1 William Faulkner, *Requiem for a Nun* (New York: Random House, 1968), 92.
2 Irving Abella and Harold Troper, *None Is Too Many: Canada and the Jews of Europe 1933–1948* (Toronto: Key Porter, 2000).
3 Louis Rosenberg, *Canada's Jews: A Social and Economic Study of Jews in Canada in the 1930s* [1939] (Montreal: McGill-Queen's University Press, 1993), 128.
4 *Third Great West Canadian Folk Dance Folk Song and Handicraft Festival. Calgary, March 19th to 22nd, 1930*, promotional pamphlet, 29.
5 Ibid., 17.
6 Ibid., 4.
7 Robert England, *The Colonization of Western Canada: A Study of Contemporary Land Settlement (1896–1934)* (London: P.S. King, 1936), 273–4.
8 *Third Great West*, 5, 14.
9 Brian S. Osborne, "Constructing the State, Managing the Corporation, Transforming the Individual: Photography, Immigration and the Canadian National Railways, 1925–30," in *Picturing Place: Photography and the Geographical Imagination*, ed. J.M. Schwartz and J.R. Ryan (London: I.B. Tauris, 2003), 162–91 at 176.
10 Ibid., 183–4.
11 Ibid., 185–6.
12 Ibid.
13 Ibid., 180.
14 "Some Types of the New-Comers," *The Canadian Courier*, 30 April 1910. 13.

13 Under Gentile Eyes: My Jewish Childhood in Hamilton, 1950–1967

JUDITH R. BASKIN

I was born in Hamilton, Ontario, in 1950, the eldest child of American parents newly arrived in Canada, and I lived there until I left for university in the United States in 1967.[1] I never returned to live in Hamilton or, indeed, in Canada. I married an American and our professional fortunes took us to the Pacific Northwest, to Eugene, Oregon. My formal education, personal encounters, and chance experiences after leaving Hamilton were undoubtedly significant factors in determining the paths I have followed as a university professor, administrator, and scholar, but the earlier influences of my Canadian Jewish childhood cannot be discounted. The sense of otherness I absorbed as a Jew in an overwhelmingly Christian city and as the child of Americans in a provincial and insular Jewish community shaped the choice of the subjects I studied – such as representations of gentiles in Jewish and Christian late ancient texts, Jews as a minority community in the Christian Middle Ages, and the roles and representations of Jewish women through the centuries – as well as the ways I approached them, for I have always been interested in depictions and performances of difference, whether of Jews under gentile eyes or of women within male-dominated Jewish societies.

In what follows, I outline the history of Hamilton's Jewish community and reflect on my experiences growing up in that city in the fifth and sixth decades of the twentieth century. I focus on the ramifications of being the daughter of a liberal rabbinical couple within a stratified Jewish community, the forms of Judaism that characterized our family and congregational lives, encounters with other Jews and with the gentile environment, and my growing consciousness of a larger world beyond Hamilton. While my experiences are my own, I believe they illuminate some of the contours of life in a relatively small Jewish enclave in a Canadian city in the second half of the twentieth century, a perspective that is often overlooked in discussions that focus on the large Jewish communities of Montreal and Toronto.

Hamilton and Its Jews

In the 1950s and 1960s, there were approximately three thousand Jews in Hamilton, 1 per cent of the population in a city that was dominated economically and culturally by a conservative Anglo-Saxon Protestant establishment.[2] A tiny assemblage, both as part of the city's larger demographics and among Canada's Jews as a whole, Hamilton's diverse Jews functioned not only as a distinct corporate unit but also in loosely designated religious and social groups within the larger whole.

Hamilton, a Great Lakes port and manufacturing city, is located on Lake Ontario, forty miles west of Toronto; it is an industrial centre that produces 60 per cent of Canada's steel. In 2020 the city encompassed an amalgamated metropolitan area of over 580,000 people. In recent decades, Hamilton's economic base has expanded beyond manufacturing, particularly in connection with the growth of McMaster University, which enrols more than 30,000 students, and its Michael G. DeGroote School of Medicine and Medical Centre, as well as other professional schools. The most recent government statistics indicate that 34 per cent of Hamilton's population self-identifies as Roman Catholic and 26 per cent as Protestant; Jews constitute .07 per cent, below Muslims (3.7 per cent), Buddhists (0.9 per cent), Sikhs (0.8 per cent), and Hindus (0.8 per cent).[3] At the beginning of the third decade of the twenty-first century, Hamilton is enjoying an economic and cultural renaissance, fuelled in part by new residents from the greater Toronto area who are attracted by less expensive housing, pleasant parks and conservation areas, a redeveloped harbour district, and a less congested and more manageable urban environment.

Although Hamilton's approximately 5,100 Jews constitute less than 1.5 per cent of Canada's Jewish population,[4] the Jewish presence in the city reaches back more than 160 years. City archives from 1853 identify thirteen Jewish families from German-speaking Europe who formed the Hebrew Benevolent Society Anshe Sholom Hamilton, soon renamed the Jewish Congregation Anshe Sholom of Hamilton, the city's first synagogue and the fourth to be founded in Canada. Anshe Sholom affiliated with the United States–based Union of American Hebrew Congregations in 1873, making it Canada's first Reform congregation.[5] In 1874 Anshe Sholom women formed the Deborah Ladies Aid Society, Canada's earliest Jewish women's service organization; minutes of meetings from its founding onwards survive. Until the mid-1890s they were written in German, as were early headstone inscriptions in the synagogue's cemetery.[6] Similarly, all sermons were delivered in German during the congregation's first twenty years.[7]

In 1883, recent immigrants from eastern Europe, uncomfortable with changes in traditional liturgical practices and rituals at Anshe Sholom, established the Beth Jacob Congregation, an Orthodox synagogue. Beth Jacob organized a Talmud Torah in 1901 and in 1908 a Ladies Aid Society was formed. (Beth Jacob changed its Orthodox orientation to Conservative in 1954.) An additional Orthodox synagogue was founded by newcomers from central Poland and Galicia in the early twentieth century, taking the name Adas Israel Anshe Poilen in 1914; its members formed a Loan Society in 1930, followed by a Ladies Auxiliary two years later.[8] All three of these congregations remain active today; Hamilton Hebrew Academy, a day school under the auspices of Adas Israel, was established in the 1960s. In the first half of the twentieth century Hamilton's Jews also founded a number of non-synagogue-affiliated organizations, including, among others, service organizations with Bundist and Zionist orientations,[9] benevolent societies, a lodge of B'nai B'rith, and chapters of the National Council of Jewish Women and Hadassah-WIZO. The Hamilton Jewish Federation now unites the educational, cultural, social service, and philanthropic undertakings of a number of these organizations,[10] although several continue to function independently.

In the period prior to the Second World War, Hamilton's Jews tended to reside in the east end of the city. Many were independent merchants or providers of industrial materials (particularly steel, scrap metal, and auto parts). Hamilton also had an active garment industry in which Jews were both factory owners and workers.[11] Few Hamilton Jews of that era attended university, although the Jewish community certainly included physicians, lawyers, educators, and other professionals. As much of the Jewish population moved into western areas of the city in the 1950s, the three major congregations followed as well. The Jewish Community Centre, however, chose to remain in the east end of Hamilton, the traditional area of first settlement, a decision that ultimately led to its demise as a communal institution by the end of the twentieth century. University education had become the norm for Hamilton's Jewish high school graduates by the mid-1960s, with most attending institutions elsewhere. The larger number did not return to Hamilton; many settled in Toronto, with some moving to Montreal, Vancouver, or the United States. This pattern, which continues into the twenty-first century, has been consistently offset by the arrival of Jewish newcomers attracted to the city by its occupational opportunities, its propinquity to Toronto, affordable housing, and the availability of a Jewish infrastructure offering synagogue choices and a Jewish day school.[12]

Growing Up in the Rabbi's Family

My family differed from most of Hamilton's Jewish families in those years because my parents, Rabbi Bernard Baskin (b. 1920) and Marjorie Shatz Baskin (1927–2005), born and educated in the United States, were not Canadian citizens during my childhood and did not choose to become Canadians until almost twenty years after their 1949 arrival in Hamilton. In addition, our lack of kinship ties locally or to other Jews in Canada set us apart, as did my parents' forward-looking political, civic, and social attitudes and my father's position as rabbi of Temple Anshe Sholom. They brought their diverse experiences as American Jews and their engagement with cultural and political currents both in and beyond the Jewish world to their new home. This outsider status in relation to Canadian Jewry in general, and the Hamilton community in particular, allowed them to move beyond a customary and perhaps expected Jewish reticence and enhance the Temple's communal and public role significantly. My father established the centrality of public affairs and larger social, literary, and artistic concerns within the synagogue's sermonic and programmatic discourse, and he consistently modelled a strong congregational commitment to interfaith dialogue.

The yeshiva-educated son of a Brooklyn Orthodox rabbi who had been ordained in Vilna, my father, Bernard, was a 1947 graduate of the Jewish Institute of Religion in New York City.[13] My mother, Marjorie, a native of Denver, Colorado, descended on her mother's side from German Jews who were affiliated with classical Reform Judaism. Her father, born in Colfax, Iowa, died as a young man; he was the son of an eastern European radical, the author of a utopian tome entitled *The Temple of Reason*. My parents met in Denver, where my father served as a visiting rabbi during the last years of the Second World War. They came to Hamilton in 1949, little thinking they would remain there for the next half-century and beyond. My father served Temple Anshe Sholom for forty years, an indication of the mutual satisfaction and esteem which existed between rabbi and congregation. However, a rabbinical family, even after such long residence, is rarely a true part of the community in which it lives. In the end, the rabbi is always an employee, and the rabbi and the rabbi's dependents cannot help but be wary of intimacy with congregants. A public figure and personality to those he or she serves, a rabbi is rarely perceived to be a person who is like other people. My childhood friends were always awed when my father appeared in our home setting; tongue-tied and abashed, they were astonished by his levity and jokes. And, certainly, the rabbi's children carry a great burden of expectations about how a clergyman's family should act, expectations that, at the least, can have a decidedly negative impact on a teenager's social life.

Jewish identity was not a source of confusion in my childhood but rather our family's defining characteristic: we were representative Jews, in a gentile, Canadian industrial city in which Jews were a distinct minority. My parents took their responsibilities as representative Jews extremely seriously. The Temple, like many Reform synagogues of that era, would welcome members of local Protestant churches to Friday evening worship. I vividly remember my father speaking to such groups in the sanctuary following the service, explaining Jewish symbols and practices, and answering the questions of the mostly female visitors. He was a frequent speaker at local organizations of all kinds, public school graduations, and at churches of many denominations throughout the decades of his rabbinate. My father continued well into his nineties to write articles for the *Hamilton Spectator* on Jewish observances and issues of Jewish concern. At the same time, for many years he also reviewed books and contributed opinion pieces to that newspaper on general topics of all kinds, gathering a following of admiring readers from the larger community. We all relished following his example by modelling and instructing others in Jewish practice.

My mother, like many *rebbitzens* of her era, was deeply involved in synagogue life; she served as the unpaid principal of the religious school for a number of years and participated actively in the Deborah Sisterhood. However, she resented the restraints of her role as a rabbi's wife and particularly disliked the constant scrutiny of others. She wisely insisted from the beginning that she and my father purchase their own home. While throughout her life she faithfully attended Friday night services, *b'nei mitzvot*, weddings, funerals, and other public events at which my father officiated or was a speaker, she also began to fashion her own professional life in the 1960s. A math major in college who had aspired to attend medical school, my mother began to work part time at McMaster University in various science departments, and ultimately took on a series of increasingly responsible full-time positions at the University Medical School and Hospital, eventually becoming director of public relations until she retired in the early 1990s.

The small Hamilton Jewish community that my parents first encountered in 1949 had little history of civic engagement and was insular by choice. My father reported that when he first arrived in Hamilton the Jewish community feared any public visibility, perhaps not surprising in those immediate post-Holocaust years. He recalled that few Jews had social or institutional contacts with Protestants and no Jews held public office of any kind.[14] My parents, by contrast, soon became involved in a number of civic activities and agencies far beyond the purview of the Jewish community. The Children's Aid Society, the Social Planning Council, the Hamilton Symphony, the Hamilton Art Gallery, and the Hamilton Public Library were among the organizations on whose boards my parents served, often in leadership roles. My father was named to the Board of Governors of McMaster University; he received an honorary degree, in addition to numerous other distinctions. Ultimately, he and my mother became Canadian citizens, a decision motivated in great part by their desire to continue and enhance their community service activities and opportunities. My mother was an elected official on the Wentworth County Board of Education for almost two decades; in the late 1970s she ran, unsuccessfully, for the provincial legislature as a candidate of the New Democratic Party.

My father was admired by his congregants because he performed his rabbinic functions well, represented the Jewish community with élan, and became widely known as a fine speaker and public intellectual. My mother was a different matter, at least outside the Temple membership. So strange did this Colorado-born, outspoken activist appear to the Hamilton Jewish community that rumours apparently spread about the unlikelihood of her Jewish origins. I remember a girl from another synagogue confronting me on the playground: she said her family was convinced that my mother must be a convert to Judaism. Certainly, the constraints of Hamilton's small and in many ways narrow Jewish community chafed on my mother and ultimately propelled her into paid employment and organizational involvements beyond the Temple and Jewish Hamilton as a whole.

I was always conscious of being the child of people who were highly visible and civically active, and I was particularly aware of being the rabbi's daughter. Often, I was called upon in school to explain the Jewish point of view on a topic, or simply expected to be able to talk about whatever issue my father was currently speaking or writing about publicly, be it euthanasia or existentialism. Mediating this tension between the demands and the appeals of the Jewish and the secular defined my family's life; my articulate and attractive parents passed quite well among gentiles, but the consciousness of being a Jew in a Christian world was always with us. And, certainly, the boundaries were always there. My most significant conflicts with my parents during my teenage years had to do with transgressing these borders: attending a Friday night basketball game or being seen downtown on a Friday evening were problematic, not only as personal Sabbath violations but because of the talk such actions by the Rabbi's daughter might generate. When I dated a non-Jewish young man from a neighbouring town during my senior year of high school, the pressure was even higher. When I was not permitted to invite him to the dance celebrating Confirmation and completion of religious school, since this would constitute a public confirmation of the relationship, I accepted the realities of a complicated situation.

My own career as Jewish apologist began early. In kindergarten, I was exposed to Protestant hymns and I was particularly taken with "Jesus Loves Me" and "He Sees the Little Sparrow Fall." Similarly, the nativity scene made a great impression, and I soon produced my own rendition and asked that it be hung on the kitchen wall with other examples of my work. My parents felt compelled to explain the differences between Judaism and Christianity, with an emphasis on Christianity's Jewish origins. I marched to school the next morning, filled with empowering knowledge and elated that Jesus now, in some way, also belonged to me. Mysteriously, there was no teacher in the classroom; seizing the opportunity I stood up on a chair, demanded silence, and announced to the astonished class of five- and six-year-olds that Jesus was Jewish. Just then the principal walked in with a substitute teacher. The confusing mixture of shame and triumph that I felt then has stayed with me for years; I did not tell my parents about it for well over a decade. Much later I learned that the principal had related it to others and that it had been reported to my parents, who found it very amusing. For me, however, that moment was and is extremely complicated, merging as it did the consciousness of personal otherness and a conflicting need to belong to the majority group. At the same time, it combined a wish to inform others of important facts, and the embarrassment of public exposure in front of authority figures. A year or two later, my younger brother informed his kindergarten teacher that the first human being was not Adam but X-man (this was in 1957). Given my brother's status as Rabbi Baskin's son, the teacher gave this view some credence and actually telephoned my father to get more information on this new version of creation.

Jewishness at Home and at Temple

My parents kept a form of observant Reform Judaism for their household and congregation that was based on family practice, synagogue worship, Jewish education, and social involvement and community activism. Jewish rituals within the family were based around the Sabbath and the festivals. The central event of our weekly domestic observance was Friday night dinner, rendered special by the rituals of candle lighting, *kiddush* (blessing over the Sabbath wine), and the blessing over the traditional Sabbath loaves. This meal was served in the formal dining room, at a table set with the best china and silverware. However, Shabbat dinner was not a leisurely repast since my parents had to be at Temple in good time for the 8:15 service, the synagogue's main Sabbath worship event. Children were not particularly encouraged to attend, since decorum was much valued. My father was known for his stated opinion that crying children in the sanctuary were like New Year's resolutions: they should be carried out. I did go to services sometimes during my elementary school years, lured by the lavish *oneg Shabbat* following the service, convened by the Temple Sisterhood.

The Deborah Sisterhood of Temple Anshe Sholom, like most such twentieth-century institutionally linked women's organizations,[15] was devoted to the domestic management of the synagogue and providing financial support for religious school and youth activities through various fundraising activities, as well as providing substantive programs for its members. Equally important, Sisterhood provided an opportunity for female fellowship and leadership, both locally and on the regional and national North American levels. Its activities included a day-long bazaar each December at which used clothing and household objects were sold to the general community. I often helped my mother at her booth, where she sold UNICEF "Season's Greetings" cards, a statement of philanthropic connection to the larger world and an affirmation that Christmas was not the only December holiday celebrated by Hamilton's residents. The Sisterhood particularly prized culinary skills, and these were on display at the Friday night *oneg* (reception) following the worship service and at other synagogue events. In addition to desserts produced by a local bakery with recipes provided by Sisterhood members, women brought in their own specialties, especially when they or their friends were hosting the *oneg* in honour of special family events. My mother was famous for her cheesecake, made with cottage cheese and topped with cherry or blueberry pie filling; she baked one each Friday to bring to Temple that evening.

These were not the only models of female accomplishment. On the Shabbat evenings when I attended services it was especially exciting for me to leave the social hall as the *oneg* crowd began to wane and ascend to the lounge adjacent to the choir loft where my mother, having performed her duties as *rebbetzin*, would talk with her friends. This inner circle and its conversations seemed to me exciting and full of wit. I felt that these were unconventional and intelligent people who read books and had ideas and who were engaged in valuable undertakings. My mother, who had strong convictions and forthrightly stated them, was always at the centre of what was going on. Domestically accomplished, she tacitly taught that women could also participate in public discourse and be heard.

My family's Judaism was Reform, although a type of Reform Judaism that was tempered by Canada's more conservative Jewish ritual practice. I was astonished in those years when I heard disparaging remarks about Reform Judaism from Jews of other traditions. Visitors from Montreal, a large and traditionally oriented Jewish community where Reform Judaism had made few inroads, tended to be particularly uninformed and negative in their understanding of Reform practice; many were uninhibited in expressing their views when they attended family members' life cycle events at Anshe Sholom. And prejudices were not only on one side; my mother, from a family of German Reform Jews, had absolutely no patience for Orthodox ritual observance; she delighted in denouncing what she saw as the hypocrisies and compromises of members of the traditional community. Thus, I grew up with little knowledge of or exposure to other models of Jewish life, whether traditionally observant Judaism or eastern European *yiddishkeit*.

Our Jewish world was the world of the Temple and its members, around 90 families when my parents arrived in Hamilton in 1949, and 350 by 1967. Religious school at the Temple began with kindergarten and went through Confirmation, the initiation to adulthood ceremony that German Reform Judaism had created for both girls and boys in place of bar mitzvah. Confirmation took place when students were sixteen, in conjunction with the late spring festival of Shavuot; in my year, made up of young people born at the height of the baby boom, there were fifteen confirmands. The religious school curriculum emphasized holiday and ritual observances, as well as mastery of liturgy, with Bible stories in the lower grades and Jewish history and ethics in the upper; art and music were also components of the educational program. Most of the songs we sang were in English. Special services for children took place during the High Holydays, and other major events of the school year included participating in the construction of a *sukkah* at the Temple; a Simhat Torah service at which kindergarten entrants to the Temple religious school were consecrated and received tiny Torah scrolls, while all children in attendance exited the building with a bag of candy; a Hanukah concert; a Purim carnival; a mock Passover *seder*; and religious school Closing Exercises at which diplomas were given and prizes awarded. Classes took place Sunday morning, and were a family event, since my mother was school principal for many years. My brother, sister, and I, like the other children, dressed up in our best clothes and party shoes for religious school; we had special "good" coats for synagogue wear. It was a family tradition to go out for lunch, often with another family, on the way home. Classes for young people of *b'nei mitzvah* age and older, met on Saturday mornings and included attendance at Sabbath morning services when *b'nei mitzvot* were scheduled.

Hebrew school for bar and bat mitzvah preparation was a separate enterprise that took place after public school twice a week, beginning in sixth grade. Not all of our classmates from religious school attended Hebrew school; most of the girls my age, for whose families bat mitzvah was still a foreign concept, were not present. Hebrew instruction was focused on facility in reading Hebrew and a simple introduction to modern Hebrew grammar and vocabulary. Our Hebrew school teachers, had we paid any attention to them beyond their classroom roles, could have taught us much more about the larger Jewish world. The elegant and reserved woman who taught the more advanced classes was Orthodox. She focused on improving our reading skills and never shared anything about her own life or practice. It is clear to me now, as well, that the hapless and accented pedagogue, who ran the Hebrew school for a few years, must have been a Holocaust survivor, but this subject, too, was never addressed.

Growing Up in the Jewish Community

Young people's Jewish social groupings in Hamilton, pretty much through high school, were determined by synagogue affiliation. Although I was acquainted with classmates who went to Congregation Beth Jacob, the Conservative synagogue, they were never among my or my siblings' close friends. My impression now is that there were unspoken class differences, however minimal, and self-definitions between those who belonged to the Temple and the congregants of Beth Jacob. In our admittedly biased view, Beth Jacob was the synagogue of wealthier business people who were overly concerned with fancy clothes and big cars while forward-looking professionals, intellectuals, and individualists chose the Temple. This is surely too simplistic, but it's how I perceived the communal divisions at the time. In fact, most of the people in the Hamilton Jewish community with whom I came into contact were solidly middle-class in their standards of living and aspirations. Certainly, there were less prosperous Jews in Hamilton, particularly those who had remained in primary areas of Jewish settlement, including some Holocaust survivors, but I did not know them, since my purview was almost wholly limited to the city's west end, where I lived, and by my synagogue affiliation. The reality that choice of residence and institutional connections depended on social and economic factors, was, of course, quite beyond my understanding at that time.

There was little interaction with young people from Beth Jacob outside of school, but when it happened – if, for example, a couple dated across synagogue lines – there was a consciousness of a culture clash and a traversing of boundaries. I never attended a bar mitzvah at Beth Jacob, and I had no notion of what Conservative Jewish worship was like. I do remember a group bat mitzvah I went to at Beth Jacob around 1964 at which girls read various parts of the evening service. It made me feel superior and proud to belong to a synagogue where girls were able "really" to become bat mitzvah and read from the Torah, and I imagine I was openly disdainful of Beth Jacob's restricted religious options for girls. Ironically enough, Anshe Sholom also imposed limitations on girls. While bat mitzvah ceremonies were introduced at the Temple around 1961, they could take place only on Friday evenings. And girls, for reasons that were never articulated, were not allowed to give speeches as the bar mitzvah boys did, although all other aspects of their participation in the service were the same, including reading a brief section from the Torah scroll. Immersed in the system as we were, however, neither I nor anyone else ever thought to question these strictures.

As for the Orthodox community in Hamilton, I was barely aware of it. There was a boy from a traditional family in my grade nine class for a while, but before we knew it he was sent off to an Orthodox high school in Toronto. No doubt others experienced the borderlines among Hamilton's Jews differently, since personal and family connections often cut across synagogue affiliations. It was not uncommon, in fact, for people to belong to more than one synagogue for business or social reasons. However, we had no family nearby, nor any close friends in other synagogues. While I know my father maintained cordial relations with his fellow rabbis, there were virtually no social interactions on the family level. We children never ate a Sabbath or festival meal in a traditional household. I did not see men pray with *tallit* and *tefillin* until I was on an El Al plane on my way to spend my junior year in Israel in 1969. The Reform movement in those years did not educate its young people about the differences in ritual and practice among the denominations of North American Judaism. The shock of my first confrontations with more traditionally observant Jews and the confusions they engendered about what constituted Jewish authenticity were profound and enduring.

The one neutral meeting ground for young people from all sectors of the Hamilton community was the Jewish Community Centre and especially its summer day camp, Camp Kadimah. The campers, as well as the teenagers who served as counsellors and counsellors-in-training, came from the various synagogues and from those few unaffiliated families who had remained in the old east end neighbourhood. Although there were occasional efforts to form B'nai B'rith and Young Judea groups, which could have bridged denominational boundaries, the dominant youth groups were those organized through the synagogues. These were affiliated with NFTY, the National Federation of Temple Youth, or USY, United Synagogue Youth. For many of us from the Temple, the weekend and summer conclaves in our NFTY region, which stretched from Toronto to Cleveland, Ohio, provided a welcome larger pool of friends and broadened our knowledge of Jewish options and teenage life in general beyond the confines of our small Canadian community.

Growing Up among Non-Jews

The province of Ontario supported and continues to support two school systems. The Separate School Board oversaw a Catholic educational system; public schools in those days were Protestant in orientation. This arrangement was enshrined in the 1867 Confederation of Canada, which brought together predominantly Protestant "Western Canada" (Ontario) and predominantly Catholic "Eastern Canada" (Quebec), together with the maritime provinces of Nova Scotia and New Brunswick, and included a provision permitting provincial support of denominational (in this case, Catholic) schools.[16] Most Roman Catholics sent their children to Catholic schools, so there was little social mixing between Catholic and non-Catholic children. Thus, the students in Hamilton's public schools at that time were mainly Protestants, with a small sprinkling of Jews in the few schools serving neighbourhoods where Jews lived. Students were required each year to identify their religion on forms that were filled out in class; Jewish children were told to enter the word "Hebrew." Daily recitation of the Lord's Prayer, followed by Bible reading, and religious education from a Protestant perspective were features of the school curriculum; in middle school, ministers from local Protestant churches visited once a week to offer religious education. We learned hymns and Christmas carols, and heard stories from both the Hebrew Bible and the New Testament; holiday concerts included choral readings of the nativity narrative from the King James version of the Gospel of Luke. Chanting "And there were in the same country, shepherds, abiding in the fields, watching over their flock by night" with my classmates did not seem incongruous in the cold Canadian winter as we imagined the shivering and snowbound shepherds and the celestial vision they were granted. In middle school the speech teacher undertook a choral reading for Easter based on one of the New Testament passion narratives. As in Grace Paley's short story, "The Loudest Voice," a Jewish boy with a precociously deep bass was chosen as narrator. This proved to be a little too much for the Jewish community; I gather that my father spoke to the teacher and the project was quietly dropped. In retrospect, I appreciate the educational value of the Christian hymns and New Testament texts to which I was exposed, but such instruction in school time was inappropriate and made me uncomfortable. My mother was an active member of the Ethical Education Association, which fought to remove mandatory prayer and religious education from the Ontario public schools. I applaud my parents and other like-minded people who worked to remove the religious component from the curriculum.

In our classrooms, students stood when answering questions and addressed male teachers as "Sir." Throughout middle school, we marched the halls in "gym order," organized by height; first the girls and then the boys. Needless to say, we looked somewhat ragged by the end of May. Neatness was much valued and memorization was the key to success; on high school exams incorrect spelling and punctuation could reduce the final grade up to 10 per cent. Grading was punitive, and the rare few who achieved averages above 80 per cent constituted the honour roll. It was a narrow and unimaginative educational philosophy, but one in which I did well. High school instruction in English literature and grammar, history, geography, and foreign languages was particularly strong, and I have had many occasions since to be grateful for the excellent preparation I received in these areas. The investment in four years of French, three years of Latin, and one of German paid significant dividends in graduate school. I had non-Jewish friends at school with whom I ate lunch for four years; I travelled home almost every day, from elementary school through high school, with one of them – my major academic rival, also named Judy – a Chinese Canadian girl, from one of perhaps five families of Chinese heritage in Hamilton at that time. Especially as we got older, socialization tended to be limited to our circle of Jewish kids from the Temple and a few fellow travellers – often gentiles who themselves were marginalized in one way or another by the larger Protestant culture, whether through ethnicity or family circumstances of one kind or another. This compartmentalized social segregation, although sometimes breached, was tacitly enforced by both the Jewish community and the Protestant Christian majority.

Growing Up in a Larger World

The Holocaust was simply not discussed during these years in any formalized educational or institutional ways. My mother gave me a copy of the *Diary of Anne Frank* when I was eleven or twelve and I came across a few books in the public library, most notably the memoir *All but My*

Life by Gerda Weissman Klein, which gave me some of the bare details. There were survivors and their children among us, of course. These individuals included not only survivors of the Nazi camps, but Jews who had escaped from German-speaking Europe before 1939, either by coming directly to Canada or as *Kindertransport* children who lived out the war in the United Kingdom and arrived in Canada as adults. A close family friend and her sister were concealed in a French convent; another congregant had been hidden in the Netherlands. Many of those who had immigrated to Canada as adults spoke accented English and had a strong aura of otherness; their previous lives were tacitly acknowledged but almost never discussed in any public way. The deeply reserved parent of one of my closest friends had been a *Kindertransport* child, but I simply thought of her as British. Only as adults did my friend and I acknowledge and discuss her mother's history. Some of Hamilton's survivors kept a distance from the Jewish community, or at least did so for some time. I vividly remember two brothers who appeared suddenly in religious school in the early 1960s for a year or two. They had an anglicized last name and had apparently only recently been told by their apparently English parents that they were Jews. These boys lived in a neighbourhood with few if any other Jews and did not attend the schools where most Jewish children were enrolled. It is hard to imagine that their exposure to Judaism and fellow Jews was anything but jarring and short-lived.

Conclusion

After high school, most of my Jewish peers left Hamilton for university elsewhere, mainly in Toronto, and only a few returned to Hamilton, often to work in a family business of one kind or another. For me, and for the larger number of those with whom I grew up, Hamilton was a pleasant and safe place in which to be children, to receive a quality public education, and to construct a Jewish identity through synagogue religious schools and Jewish communal activities. In many cases, close connections were forged in those years that persist more than half a century later. Although most of us live elsewhere now, we remember our Hamilton origins and many of us keep track of each other to an extent that surprises others from larger Jewish communities.

When I look back on growing up in Hamilton, I think of myself and most of the people I knew, and still know, less as Hamiltonians and more as Jews from Hamilton. My husband, on the contrary, who grew up in Brooklyn and Queens in communities were Jews were in the majority, says he is a New Yorker. For me, the formative reality was living as part of the only non-Christian minority in an Ontario city that was dominated by a conservative white Anglo-Saxon Protestant culture whose major anxieties were directed at Roman Catholics, themselves a segregated and inner-directed, although far larger, entity. While antisemitism in various forms was well engrained in the history and attitudes of many sectors of the city, its forms were generally genteel. By the late 1960s Jews still were not members of tacitly restricted clubs and friendship circles, but the playground slur was only occasional. On the whole, Hamilton's Jewish presence was too small to be perceived as a threat to the status quo; rather, Jews were a benignly regarded and economically valued sub-group.

Jews built and continue to build comfortable, connected, and Jewishly meaningful lives in Hamilton, but only a few have put down roots that have lasted beyond a generation or two. From the earliest days of this Jewish community, people have come and gone as economic and professional opportunities have dictated; in recent years, young people have increasingly been lured by the siren call of nearby Toronto. Given this sense of Hamilton as simultaneously home and home-for-the-time-being, I wonder if my experiences there might portend the future of other Canadian Jews outside of Canada's few major urban centres. Is a city like Hamilton a place that significant numbers of Jews will call home for the long term or is it, as so many other places have been, a waystation, pleasant and nurturing in its way, in the larger *durée* of Jewish history?

NOTES

1 Some of the autobiographical material in this essay appears in an expanded form in Judith R. Baskin, "The Scholar as Daughter: Growing Up in a Rabbinic Family," *Shofar: An Interdisciplinary Journal of Jewish Studies* 16, no. 4 (1998): 28–39.

2 Regarding unique elements in the Jewish experience in Canada, see Michael Brown, "The Beginnings of Reform Judaism in Canada," *Jewish Social Studies* 34, no. 4 (October 1972): 322–42. He writes, "Not the least of these has been contact with a conservative and often anti-Semitic Catholicism and a similar Protestantism" (322). While Catholicism played a major role in the history of the Jews in Quebec, in Ontario the power was overwhelmingly in the Protestant sector.

3 National Household Survey (NHS) Profile, 2011, https://statcan.gc.ca.

4 William Shaffir, "Hamilton," *Encyclopedia Judaica*, 2nd ed. (Detroit: Macmillan Reference USA, Thomson Gale, 2007).

5 On the congregation's founders and its early days, see Brown, "Beginnings of Reform Judaism," 326–7.
6 These records, along with other Anshe Sholom archival material, are housed in the American Jewish Archives at Hebrew Union College-Jewish Institute of Religion in Cincinnati, OH.
7 Brown, "Beginnings of Reform Judaism," 326.
8 Shaffir, "Hamilton."
9 Gerald Tulchinsky, *Canada's Jews: A People's Journey* (Toronto: University of Toronto Press, 2008), 165, 171, 254.
10 Shaffir, "Hamilton."
11 Tulchinsky, *Canada's Jews*, 146, 153, 155, 243.
12 Shaffir, "Hamilton."
13 Founded by Rabbi Stephen Wise in 1922, the inter-denominational Jewish Institute of Religion (JIR) generally advanced the precepts of Reform Judaism while promulgating a strongly pro-Zionist point of view, in opposition to the stance of Hebrew Union College (HUC) at that time. JIR ultimately merged with HUC in 1950.
14 Interview with Rabbi Bernard Baskin, 20 October 2017.
15 On the role of sisterhoods in Reform Judaism, see Pamela S. Nadell and Rita J. Simon, "Ladies of the Sisterhood: Women in the American Reform Synagogue, 1900–1930," in *Active Voices: Women in Jewish Culture*, ed. Maurie Sacks (Urbana and Chicago: University of Illinois Press, 1995), 63–75; and Pamela S. Nadell, "National Federation of Temple Sisterhoods," *Jewish Women: A Comprehensive Historical Encyclopedia*, Jewish Women's Archive, 20 March 2009, https://jwa.org/encyclopedia/article/National-Federation-of-Temple-Sisterhoods, who writes that "NFTS nationally and in its individual affiliates locally allowed Jewish women a venue for the creation of a female Reform Jewish culture."
16 Frank Peters, "Religion and Schools in Canada," *Journal of Catholic Education* 1, no. 3 (1998), 275–94, explains that "Section 93 of the Constitution Act of 1867 (known prior to 1982 as the British North America Act) established three principles on education. These were: the right of each provincial government to make laws regarding education within its territory; a guarantee to Protestants and Roman Catholics that 1867 legal rights regarding denominational schools would be constitutionally protected by provincial governments; and, the right of provincial governments to pass legislation supporting religious schools, thus furthering denominational education" (276).

14 Montreal and Canada through a Wider Lens: Confessions of a Canadian-American European Jewish Historian

LOIS C. DUBIN

Introduction

"No Better Home for the Jews ... than Canada?" When David Koffman invited me to participate in a symposium at York University, I expressed nervous surprise about the title. I understood that he wanted an arresting title, but this one struck me frankly as *hutzpadik* (nervy) and perhaps too provocative. *Let me be clear at the outset: of course I recognize that Canada has been a good home for the Jews.* Still, might not excessive or absolute assertions of well-being tempt the gods – even when tempered with a perhaps cautious Canadian question mark? As Jewish history has shown more than once, such assertions are no guarantees of long-lasting well-being. Yet, as historian of modern Jewry David Sorkin has written, "Virtually every modern diaspora Jewish community that has experienced extended periods of privileges or rights, accompanied by tranquility and prosperity, has asserted its exceptional status in one form or another, often by intoning quasi-messianic or messianic language or claiming to be the 'New Jerusalem.'"[1] So, why should Canada be an exception to the celebratory temptation? Though David Koffman certainly understood my misgivings, he urged me to put them aside, think beyond the title, and draw upon my upbringing as a Canadian Jew, my long experience as a graduate student and professor in the United States, and, not least, my scholarly expertise as a historian of modern European Jewry. So I decided to forget about the comparative of "better" edging into superlatives of "best" or exceptional, and rather to think about what strikes me as distinctive about Canadian Jewry.[2]

It was in the crucible of Montreal and Quebec, from the 1950s through mid-1970s, that my Canadian and Jewish identities were forged. I began to share my thoughts about that publicly in 2011, when I spoke at the Yeshiva University Museum symposium "Growing Up Jewish in Montreal" convened by Jacob Wisse, himself also a native Montrealer;[3] two of the participants there, Jack Kugelmass and Allan Nadler, were contributors to the conference that initiated this book too. Indeed, my vantage point on all matters Canadian has been that of a proud member of the card-carrying Montreal Jewish Diaspora. Many Montrealers, especially those who live elsewhere, maintain a nostalgic pride in their unique city and its strong Jewish community, which was for a long time the dominant and demographic centre of Canadian Jewish life, housing approximately half of all Canadian Jews. For a Montreal Jew, thinking about Canada as a home meant simultaneous awareness of the local Jewish community, the Protestant English-speaking sector of Montreal, the Catholic majority of Montreal and Quebec, as well as the entire country of Canada – and all of them embedded in the larger North American continent, which means of course the United States.

Like many a Canadian native who became a US resident and dual national, I often ruminate about the similarities and differences between my two countries. Indeed, the United States as reference point is simply unavoidable for most Canadians, and Jews and scholars of Canadian Jewry are no exceptions. The large colossus to the south is virtually always the elephant in the room, the dominant term in the binary equation, and the norm for comparison. As Jonathan Sarna, historian of American Jewry, wrote some forty years ago, "Historians of Canadian Jewry too often assume that the Jewish experience in the United States can serve as a model for understanding Canadian Jewish history."[4] Since then, fortunately, members of the Association for Canadian Jewish Studies / Association d'études juives canadiennes have done much to bring forth the specifics and uniqueness of Canadian Jewry, including the publication *Canadian Jewish Studies / Études juives canadiennes* starting in 1993. And yet, the numbers and energy of the neighbour to the south are hard to avoid. (And, though "American" would ideally refer to the entire Americas, I like others often use "American" to refer to the United States since there is no adjective United States-ian!)

Many default to the assumption or question: Is it merely the case that what happens first in the United States then happens later in Canada, perhaps on a smaller scale and on a different timeline, perhaps a generation or two later? Is *later* immigration from Europe the sole or main source of the differences between Canadian and American patterns of behaviour? Immigrants and their descendants make up a greater proportion of Canadian than American Jewry. The mass migration to Canada in 1900–20 brought more traditional and nationalist Jews than the mass migration to the United States in 1880–1900,[5] while the loosening of restrictions after the Second World War brought a larger percentage of Holocaust survivors to Canada relative to the existing Jewish population. By 1990 it was estimated that Holocaust survivors and their descendants comprised about 30–40 per cent of Canadian Jews but only 8 per cent of American Jews.[6] Will longer residence in Canada after immigration lead inevitably to higher, more American-type, rates of assimilation and intermarriage?[7]

Although the ties binding the Jews of Canada and the United States are close and tight, and the comparison of the two Jewries is inevitable, I maintain that the Canada–US binary lens is not sufficient. Canadian Jewry should not be seen merely as a smaller or paler reflection of American Jewry, or as a younger sibling playing catch-up. Years ago, Sarna proposed that comparisons go in both directions: that scholars of American Jewry ought to consider Canadian Jewry as a point of reference and comparison as much as Canadian scholars have tended to consider the United States. If issues such as revolutionary vs evolutionary political traditions, church–state separation, leadership, geographical and occupational distribution, sub-ethnic composition, and education be examined, then American Jewish historians might see the value of Canadian Jewish history and vice versa, and a genuinely comparative "North American Jewish history" might emerge to everyone's mutual benefit.[8] This would be promising indeed. Still, I contend that even if Sarna's comparative challenge were taken up seriously, it would not suffice for helping us to take the measure of Canadian Jewry. We have to go beyond North America. For, as I shall discuss below, there are other comparative perspectives that can prove valid and fruitful for studying Canadian Jews: the Atlantic world, Europe, and Latin America are all, I submit, "good to think with" (to borrow the words of anthropologist Claude Lévi-Strauss).[9]

When I was a young graduate student studying Jewish history and thought at Harvard in the late 1970s, fresh from McGill and one year in Israel, I was surprised to discover a shared outlook with a graduate student fresh from Turkey. From our respective Turkish and Canadian Jewish vantage points, Aron Rodrigue[10] and I found ourselves in agreement: somehow, European Jewish history seemed closer, more familiar and understandable to us, and less foreign than American Jewish history! No doubt the individualism, voluntarism, and apparently self-confident sense of belonging of American Jews did not resonate with either of us. Yet, I paused then and I still pause now: Was this sense of greater proximity to Europe than the United States not a little bizarre for a Canadian, a North American? I now explore this puzzling perspective by addressing two questions: (1) Why did European Jewish history seem relatively familiar to me? (2) What has European Jewish history – my scholarly specialization – allowed me to see when I reflect back on Canadian Jewish history?

Montreal

I say Canadian, but of course, I am speaking from my own experience as a Jew from Montreal, Quebec, a most distinct place. The city has displayed in its own unique way the "binationalism" of Canada, the successive *modi vivendi* developed between the French and English colonial settlers since the mid-eighteenth century; these two groups fashioned themselves as "Canada's founding peoples" after the British conquest of New France and after the "incomplete" conquest of Indigenous peoples by both French and English.[11] As is well known, the Catholic French formed a majority in Montreal and Quebec, while being a minority in Canada and North America overall, and the Protestant English, though well-entrenched and economically dominant, were a demographic minority in Quebec, while belonging to the vast English-speaking majority elsewhere in the country and on the continent. Montreal's social space was dominated by these "two solitudes," in the iconic title of Hugh McLennan's 1945 novel.[12] The British North America Act of 1867 and subsequent legislation guaranteed the English and French the right to retain their own identities, with their respective Protestant and Catholic schools as important cornerstones. Thus, in Quebec and some other parts of Canada, there was no American-model separation of church and state or non-denominational public school system, but rather state-sponsored and -supported confessional school systems.

It is often said, and with reason, that Montreal is the most European city in North America. Though often depicted as a city of duality, of *two* solitudes, it has in fact been a city of multiplicity – home to several First Nations, as well as many waves of immigrants (initially European, later also Asian, Caribbean, and North African), forming communities of diverse ethnicities, religions, and languages. Immigrants often lived along the long north-south artery Saint Laurent Boulevard in the middle spaces between the eastern primarily French part and the western primarily English part. For decades, "the Main" has been home to densely populated immigrant neighbourhoods, at different times Jews, Chinese, Italians, Portuguese, Greek, and others.[13] No surprise, a now-chic gourmet emporium on the Main, founded in 1959, goes by the name "La Vieille Europe." As stated above, with the relaxation in the late 1940s and early 1950s of the stringent immigration restrictions of the 1930s–40s, postwar Montreal – and Canada more generally – came to house a Jewish community with a greater proportion of European immigrants than other North American Jewish communities.[14]

Jews, like the other immigrant groups, were affected by the fraught struggles and changing relations between the two dominant groups. In Montreal, immigrant communities tended to remain cohesive not only because of the usual social dynamics of first-generation migration but also because of the texture of the city itself in which language, religion, and ethnicity loomed so large. For a long time, the French and English solitudes kept a distance from each other and from others, hardly welcoming newcomers in their respective midsts. In 1884, a recently arrived eastern European Jew to Montreal noted the ethnic, linguistic, and religious diversity of the city's population, including English speakers, French speakers, Irish Scots, Catholics, Protestants, and Indians, opining that "each and every group hates the others thoroughly" and that the Jews felt themselves to be objects of "hatred and contempt."[15] Hatred and contempt hardly characterized attitudes towards Montreal Jews throughout the next century, but antisemitism, of both Anglo and French varieties, did arise in certain periods. At the least, exclusion and prejudice on the parts of the two dominant groups helped strengthen the tight-knit bonds of immigrant communities. For a long time, the French and English in Montreal hardly constituted a "beckoning bourgeoisie" vis-à-vis Jews, such that the "Jews became a kind of third solitude within the Canadian mosaic, and certainly within Montreal."[16] The Jewish "solitude" was generally identified with the Protestant English-speaking minority of Quebec (an identification not changed even with the later immigration of francophone North African Jews). Both Anglo and Jewish minorities lived alongside the French Catholic majority, which itself had a well-honed sense of its own minority status within Canada overall.

Long past the stage of first-generation migration, Montreal Jews tended to cluster in their own very dense Jewish neighbourhoods and practised a large degree of social segregation. Jews maintained a high level of Hebrew and Yiddish, and Jewish identity was expressed and buttressed by many strong communal institutions. These ranged from political and defence organizations, such as the national Canadian Jewish Congress, to a panoply of local religious and cultural institutions, among them synagogues, Hebrew and Yiddish schools of every religious and nationalist stripe, summer camps, Zionist movements, the Jewish Public Library, and Dora Wasserman Yiddish Theatre, as well as hospitals and social welfare associations. A sense of the incomparably rich ideological range of Jewish schools is provided by Ruth Wisse in her recent memoirs, as well as by Allan Nadler, who proudly remembers the Jewish day-school hockey league![17]

The state system of confessional schools had a dual effect upon Jewish education: on the one hand, Jews waged a civil rights struggle in the early twentieth century to be allowed to study in the Protestant schools (the Catholic system being an absolute non-starter for them), while Jewish teachers and seats on the Protestant School Board of Greater Montreal came only much later; on the other hand, Jewish day schools eventually benefited from government support and funding, with the result that the percentage of Jewish children attending Jewish day schools is higher in Montreal than anywhere else in North America.[18]

However, given Jewish residential segregation, the Jewish children in even Protestant schools often went through their days surrounded by a large Jewish peer group. I, for one, living in the heavily Jewish neighbourhood of Côte-St-Luc, attended Wagar High School, a Protestant high school with a student population of more than 90 per cent Jews. As a child, seeing Catholic churches on street corners virtually everywhere in the city, the imposing St Joseph's Oratory on the western side of Mount Royal, and the illuminated cross atop the mountain and city at night, I knew that Christianity was established and dominant.[19] And throughout my years in Protestant elementary schools, every morning I saluted the flag (first the British Red Ensign and later the Canadian Maple Leaf), I pledged allegiance first to the Empire and later to the Commonwealth, I implored God to Save the Queen, and I sang the Protestant hymn "Jesus Loves Me, This I Know." Every morning, I participated in these ritual dramas, feeling full well that I was Canadian, though not Protestant. My Jewish identity was reinforced every time I sang "Jesus Loves Me" just as, albeit differently, it was reinforced when I chanted prayers in synagogue and afternoon Hebrew school and sang "Hatikvah" in a Young Judean Zionist summer camp.

What I read years later by observers of Canadian Jewry rang true to me. As sociologist Morton Weinfeld has put it, Jews in Montreal have considered their city to have a "unique ambience," simultaneously "cosmopolitan" and "intensively Jewish"; their residential segregation, long-time isolation from Québecois life, and position as a classic middleman minority were "more European than North American."[20] Some have described Montreal Jews as "tribal" and almost "ghetto-like"; or to express it more analytically, they attempted to define their "own Jewish confessional sphere within Québec society" and produced an "institutionally complete" ethnic polity.[21] I would put it this way: the sense of Jewish peoplehood was palpable. External as well as intrinsically Jewish factors led to the demographic density, the strong communal institutions and rich texture of Jewish life encompassing both religious traditionalism and determined secularism, and much in between, and the proudly rooted, almost natural, collective identity of Montreal Jews. Historian Gershon Hundert, a native of Toronto and long-time professor of Jewish Studies at McGill, sees a taken-for-granted, positive, self-affirming Jewish identity as an ongoing characteristic and legacy of Polish-Lithuanian Jews. Though both Montreal and Toronto Jews have been called tribal, it is Hundert's view that "Montreal Jews seem to have a more comfortable, more confident sense of Jewish identity," perhaps their place in the social landscape as a "third solitude" leading to greater self-confidence.[22] In a hierarchical, relatively conservative country, whose politics were characterized by evolutionary rather than abrupt change, Montreal Jews were also traditionalists in many respects: not beckoned overmuch to join a larger society, Jews nurtured their own religious and communal worlds.

By now, it should not be surprising why European Jewish history seemed somewhat familiar to me, a Montreal Jew who came of age in the 1960s and early '70s, during the momentous Quiet Revolution that radically transformed Quebec and made traditional Catholic Canadiens or French Canadians into secularizing and nationalist Québécois. Language, ethnicity, religion, education, collective identity, minorities within and alongside other minorities confronting a majority, a rising nationalist movement, relations between nations and states, independence or federalism – these were the preoccupations of public discourse and daily life. The duality or multiplicity of the city, whether construed as solitudes or mosaic; the preoccupation with issues of collective identity, especially language, memory, and survival (embodied in the motto *Je me souviens*); the increasingly nationalist register of both defensive and self-assertive Québécois strivings; the dominance of the Catholic Church and the ongoing yet incomplete struggles for secularization (so richly discussed in Genevieve Zubrzycki's *Beheading the Saint*);[23] the absence of a non-denominational, non-confessional public school system, so central to the US Jewish experience; the palpable sense of the Jews as a cohesive minority – both limited by the outside world and self-segregating – all this stuff seemed to be collectivist and European, and decidedly unlike the United States.

European Resonances

In the course of my graduate studies at Harvard, I chose to write my doctoral dissertation on the Jews of Trieste, the beautiful northeastern Italian Adriatic port city that served as the great port and hub of international commerce for the Habsburg Monarchy (later the Austro-Hungarian Empire) from the eighteenth century until the First World War. The result was my book *The Port Jews of Habsburg Trieste: Absolutist Politics and Enlightenment Culture*, as well as many subsequent articles.[24] I often cited many good reasons for my choice that pertained to eighteenth-century political and cultural European Jewish history: e.g., its appropriateness for studying Jewish movements for cultural and civic engagement with the surrounding European world (often called Jewish enlightenment, or *haskalah*, and emancipation in Jewish historiography), as well as the intrinsic fascination of a place that was both central European and Mediterranean. It took several years before I became aware of something more fundamental and visceral in the draw of Trieste upon me. Perhaps I felt "comfortable" or attracted to this port city and commercial hub precisely because of its heterogeneity: populated from the eighteenth century by diverse ethnic-national groups, namely, Jews, Greek and Serbian Orthodox, Protestants, and Armenians in the midst of a Catholic majority, Trieste was a distinctively cosmopolitan or multinational city; however, from the late nineteenth century, it became riven with linguistic and nationalist conflicts between Italians, Germans, and Slovenians as the Habsburg Monarchy strove unsuccessfully to create a supra-nationalist federalist identity. This confluence of diverse groups and languages and religions – living at times in separate formal communities, at times co-operating, at times in conflict – seemed like something I could wrap my head around, something I could grasp, something familiar.

I am not the only one to detect some similarities. Sherry Simon of Concordia University, scholar of French studies and translation theory, linked Montreal and Trieste in her fascinating book *Cities in Translation: Intersections of Language and Memory*. Long intrigued by cultural divides, bilingualism, and border crossing through translation, Simon had already reflected seriously upon Montreal itself in her book *Translating Montreal: Episodes in the Life of a Divided City*, in which she looked at English, French, and Yiddish alongside one another in the city's early history.[25] And Lothar Baier, German author and translator who made his home in Montreal, had drawn parallels between Montreal and east-central Europe, particularly Galicia, because of their multilingualism: "... c'est ainsi qu'à Montréal le passé est-européen entre en contact avec le présent nord-américain, dans la mesure où réapparaît outre-Atlantique un peu de cette coexistence des langues caractéristique de l'Europe de l'Est et aujourd'hui disparue."[26] Eventually, Simon broadened her purview to compare Montreal to Trieste, Barcelona, and Calcutta, three other "linguistically divided or dual cities." Simon analyses language relations, conflict, and creative interaction in this particularly complex type of dual-language city in which two historically rooted language communities feel entitled and make claims. Simon's work is rich and nuanced, as she takes account not only of historical and nationalist functions of languages in colonial settings, but also of English today as a global language – a factor that adds a new dimension to language usage and multilingualism in twenty-first-century Montreal (and elsewhere). She now calls Montreal a "translational city" because of its "cosmopolitan hybridity" and constant interplay of languages.[27]

However, long before reading Simon's book, I had been struck by resonances of my Montreal, Quebec, and Canadian experiences with my historical studies of the Habsburg Monarchy. I had often joked about parallels between the state-building and secularizing reforms of the Quiet Revolution in Quebec, begun by Liberal Premier Jean Lesage in 1960, and the centralizing "revolution from above" of Emperor Joseph II in the 1780s.[28] Both have been credited with radically altering inherited Old Regime institutions and patterns of behaviour. Then, at the 2001 annual conference of the Association for Jewish Studies, I had a eureka moment when I heard historian Marsha Rozenblit present her thesis of the "tripartite identity" of early twentieth-century Habsburg Jews: they were, she explained, politically Habsburg; culturally and linguistically German; and ethnically Jewish.[29] Though Jews sometimes aligned themselves with one side in a nationalist conflict between two competing nationalities, they were mostly proud Habsburg loyalists who staunchly maintained dynastic and federalist allegiances that went beyond nationalism. Rozenblit asserted that because of their multicultural and multinational polity, Habsburg Jews were freer than French or German Jews to affirm their Jewish ethnic identity.

Voila! I realized that I, too, like many an Ashkenazic Montreal Jew, had a tripartite identity, for I considered myself politically Canadian and federalist, linguistically English, and ethnically Jewish! The Habsburg example helped me understand something I had long felt but had trouble formulating: that contrary to the claim of most Quebec nationalists that all language choices were political, my having being raised in English and my using it had not been an inherently political decision at all, but rather a cultural and pragmatic choice. (When the father of the Triestine writer Italo Svevo told him that every decent businessman needed to know four languages at least superficially, that was hardly a political statement either.) Like many a Jew in east-central Europe, in the Habsburg Monarchy, and in Montreal, my identities and my languages were multiple: my mother tongue was English, I learned French rather well, and with a strong sense of ethnic-religious collective identity, I studied and spoke Hebrew too (as many other Jews in Montreal spoke Yiddish); further, as a scholar, I went on to learn other languages, notably Italian and German. I knew that languages have many functions, and they are not always expressions of a singular ethnic, nationalist, or political identity.

Let me repeat: when I gravitated in my professional work toward Trieste and the Habsburg Monarchy, I had no conscious awareness whatsoever that they had anything to do with my identity as a Montrealer and Canadian Jew. And yet, the parallels emerged. Not coincidentally, another Canadian Jew – my colleague at Smith, Justin Cammy, who is a scholar of Yiddish and eastern European Jewry – tells me that he thinks his background as a Jew from Ottawa and Montreal helped lead him to the study of Vilna.

Broader Horizons

I hope these excursions to Europe have shown that American Jewry need not be the only point of productive comparison for the study of Canadian Jewry. Situated between Britain/Europe and the United States and partaking of both, Canada melds British and European traditions with American aspects – in its broad history and in its Jewish history. Thus, we should ask: in what respects is Canadian Jewish history like British and European, in what respects like the United States, and finally, in what respects is Canadian Jewish history distinctive and unique?

Scholars of early modern European history will find some familiar themes in the early history of Canadian Jewish settlement. The first known Jew was in fact a hidden Jew, Esther Brandeau, who masqueraded as a male Catholic in New France of the 1730s because open Jewish life was forbidden. The first Jews to settle in British Canada after the conquest of 1760 were merchants and army purveyors.[30] Indeed, as Sarna has noted, Canadian Jews had their origins, like all Jewries of the Americas, in the dispersion of "port Jews" from western Europe in the seventeenth and eighteenth centuries. In the late 1990s, Sorkin and I defined port Jews as (primarily Sephardic) merchants engaged in international commerce who because of their commercial prowess were admitted to various locales in early modern western and central Europe on relatively favourable terms of residence and civil rights; they displayed a high degree of acculturation to their mercantile societies, and they often participated in the overseas expansion of their respective countries.[31] It would be worthwhile to compare the early port Jews of Canada with those elsewhere in the North American and Caribbean colonies of Holland and Britain, and eventually the independent United States.

In a sense, all these communities were "Atlantic port Jews," whether moving back and forth across that great oceanic and cultural basin, or remaining rooted on one side or the other, and Canadian Jewry, like the others, was an "Atlantic" Jewry. Sorkin has identified similar dynamics of the political struggles for civil and political rights, or "emancipation," among port Jews on both sides of the Atlantic.[32] Yet Jews in the British colonies of Canada gained some civil and political rights earlier than in other colonies and earlier than in Britain itself. For example, through the Emancipation Act that declared natural-born British Jews "entitled to the full rights and privileges of the other subjects of His Majesty," Jews in Lower Canada gained the right to hold public office without taking a Christian oath in 1832, while Jews in Britain could not do so until 1858.[33] Indeed, comparative study of the Dutch and British colonies shows that elsewhere Jews were granted privileges or rights in colonies before the home country.

In discerning a broadly similar civic and political pattern for Jews on both sides of the Atlantic, Sorkin challenges the hoary myth of US exceptionalism. In their book *Transnational Traditions*, Ava Kahn and Adam Mendelssohn have also called for treating US Jewry in broader comparative and transnational perspectives.[34] All Atlantic Jewries, including US Jewry, were in a certain sense trans-Atlantic and transnational. Unfortunately, while the book stresses that US Jewry will be understood better if seen within the broader anglophone diaspora, it pays attention to British Imperial possessions in the Caribbean, South Africa, and Australia, but hardly at all to Canada.

In fact, Canadian Jews ought to be included in all these larger categories: port Jews, Atlantic Jewries, British Imperial Jews, and the anglophone diaspora, and, not least, the Jewries of the Americas. Canadian Jewish history should be compared with the history of every Jewish settlement throughout the New World – not only in the United States, but indeed in the Caribbean and in Latin America, in the colonial and post-independence periods. There is much to be learned from comparing the mass migrations of eastern European Jews to Canada and Latin America in the late nineteenth and early twentieth centuries as well as in the post–Second World War period. Montreal, Toronto, Mexico City, Buenos Aires – all should be compared with one another, and not only with New York City.[35]

Let us fast forward. The State of Israel is known for its ingathering of Jewish exiles. However, complex Jewish ingathering from diverse locations also occurs elsewhere. The Ashkenazic Jews of Paris and Montreal have been joined in recent decades by many Sephardic and North African Jews. Montreal Jewry in fact partakes of both anglophone and francophone, Ashkenazic and Sephardic diasporas. Canadian Jews, and Montreal Jews in particular, certainly bear comparison with Jews in France and in Israel for the complexity of their "ingathering" of population. And as in France and Israel, Jews in Montreal and Toronto display an exceptionally wide range of religious and secular expression – from insular Hasidim to Jews who participate fully in Canadian culture and politics.

In conclusion, I return somewhat facetiously to the original question: Is there no better home for Jews than Canada? When I walk into Patisserie Hadar in Côte-St-Luc, a very Jewish suburb of Montreal, I agree! For both the "cosmopolitanism" and the "intensively Jewish" qualities are evident – in the infinite varieties of eggplant salad from Romanian to Moroccan to Yemenite, as well as the delicious baked goods that include bagels, rugelach, rye bread, and exquisite croissants! More seriously, let us not forget that historian Salo Baron wrote that Jews often fared better in multinational rather than mono-national or aspiring nation-states.[36] Historian Gerald Tulchinsky has suggested that the absence of a strong Canadian national identity may have helped strengthen Jewish communal identity and Zionism in Canada.[37] Reinforcing that view would be the argument that Canada long lacked a strong civil religion like that in the United States, primarily because of the French–English dualism and regionalism.[38] One could argue that the omnipresence of the national identity question in Quebec also contributed, albeit differently, to a strong and specific Jewish identity. Furthermore, when diversity and multiculturalism became de rigueur in Canada from the 1970s and '80s, there was public sanction for the assertion of Canadian Jewish ethnic identity. Perhaps as Habsburg Jews were able to affirm their Jewish ethnic identity in the multi-ethnic, multinational Austro-Hungarian Empire, so too did Canadian Jews find it easier to affirm their ethnic-religious identity in multicultural Canada than did Jews in the United States. Certainly, official Canadian policies of multiculturalism have helped Canadian Jewry flourish.[39]

Canadian Jews will still be compared, and rightfully so, to their US cousins, but I trust I have presented a convincing case for additional frames of reference. The contours and contexts for the study of Canadian Jewry should extend far beyond the immediate southern neighbour. Canada houses a vibrant and thriving Jewish community in a diverse society and mature democratic polity that honours the rule of law. The Canadian Jewish community has much to offer others – on its own distinctive terms, as well as in comparison with the Jewries of *all* the Americas, of Europe, and of the anglophone and francophone diasporas.

NOTES

1   David Sorkin, "Is American Jewry Exceptional? Comparing Jewish Emancipation in Europe and America," *American Jewish History* 96, no. 3 (September 2010): 175–200, at 200.

2 Readers may consult: Irving Abella, *A Coat of Many Colours: Two Centuries of Jewish Life in Canada* (Toronto: Lester & Orpen Dennys, 1990); Michael Brown, *Jew or Juif? Jews, French Canadians, and Anglo-Canadians, 1759–1914* (Philadelphia, New York, Jerusalem: Jewish Publication Society, 1986); Robert Brym, William Shaffir, and Morton Weinfeld, *The Jews in Canada* (Toronto: Oxford University Press, 1993); Ruth Klein and Frank Dimant, eds, *From Immigration to Integration: The Canadian Jewish Experience, A Millennium Edition* (Toronto: Institute for International Affairs B'nai Brith Canada, 2001); Gerald Tulchinsky, *Taking Root: The Origins of the Canadian Jewish Community* (Hanover and London: Brandeis University Press/ University Press of New England, 1993), *Branching Out: The Transformation of the Canadian Jewish Community* (Toronto: Stoddart, 1998), as well as *Canada's Jews: A People's Journey* (Toronto: University of Toronto Press, 2008); and Morton Weinfeld, *Like Everyone Else ... But Different: The Paradoxical Success of Canadian Jews* (Toronto: McClelland & Stewart, 2001).

3 "Growing Up Jewish in Montreal," Yeshiva University Museum program at the Center for Jewish History, New York, 1 May 2011, video available at https://youtu.be/rSzHPz7PkgM.

4 Jonathan Sarna, "Jewish Immigration to North America: The Canadian Experience (1870–1900)," *The Jewish Journal of Sociology* 18: 1 (1976): 31–42, at 31.

5 Weinfeld, *Like Everyone Else ... But Different*, p. 79.

6 Tulchinsky, *Canada's Jews*, pp. 422, 460.

7 In 2001, Harold M. Waller argued that Canadian Jewry has succeeded in carving out an independent *political* path among world Jewries, but that *sociologically* it has found it difficult to resist trends prevalent in the United States; Harold M. Waller, "A Community Transformed: The National Picture," in *From Immigration to Integration*, ed. Klein and Dimant, 149–64, at 162. On Canadian distinctiveness, see Brym, Shaffir, and Weinfeld, *The Jews in Canada*, 2–4, introduction, and 5–21, Gerald Tulchinsky, "The Contours of Canadian Jewish History"; and Weinfeld, *Like Everyone Else ... But Different*, 1–13, esp. 11.

8 Jonathan D. Sarna, "The Value of Canadian Jewish History to the American Jewish Historian and Vice Versa," *Canadian Jewish Historical Society Journal* 5, no. 1 (Spring 1981): 17–22, at 21. See Barry L. Stiefel and Hernan Tesler-Mabé, eds, *Neither in Dark Speeches nor in Similitudes: Reflections and Refractions between Canadian and American Jews* (Waterloo, ON: Wilfrid Laurier University Press, 2016).

9 Lévy-Strauss claimed that animals were "bonnes à penser" in *Le totémisme aujourd'hui* (Paris: PUF, 1962); the phrase has since gained widespread currency to indicate the value of particular categories and ways of thinking.

10 Rodrigue has since enjoyed a distinguished career as a scholar of Sephardic and Ottoman Jewries and professor at Indiana University Bloomington and Stanford University.

11 On Canada as a "binational, bireligious, bicultural, bilingual country"
from the mid-eighteenth century until well after the Second World War,
see Michael Brown, "From Binationalism to Multiculturalism to the Open
Society: The Impact on Canadian Jews," in *Changing Jewish Communities*,
Jerusalem Center for Public Affairs, no. 10 (16 July 2006), http://jcpa
.org/article/from-binationalism-to-multiculturalism-to-the-open-society
-the-impact-on-canadian-jews/. On Canada's "incomplete" conquests, see
Peter H. Russell, *Canada's Odyssey: A Country Based on Incomplete Conquests*
(Toronto: University of Toronto Press, 2017).

12 Hugh MacLennan, *Two Solitudes* (Toronto: Macmillan of Canada, 1945).

13 Pierre Anctil, *Saint-Laurent: Montréal's Main* (Silléry: Septentrion, 2002).

14 Tulchinsky, *Canada's Jews*, 422. On Canada's highly restrictive immigration
policies in the wartime period, see Irving Abella and Harold Troper, *None
Is Too Many: Canada and the Jews of Europe 1933–1948* (Toronto: Lester &
Orpen Dennys, 1983).

15 Yosef Eliyahu Bernstein, articles in *Ha-Melitz* 1884, now available as *The
Jews in Canada (in North America): An Eastern European View of the Montreal
Jewish Community in 1884*, trans. Ira Robinson (Montreal: Hungry I Books,
2004), 22–4. Yet Bernstein also noted that Jews were "equal in civil rights
with all the citizens of this land" and "enjoy[ed] the abundance of peace
and tranquility that exists in this country."

16 For "beckoning bourgeoisie," see Gershon David Hundert, *Jews in
Poland-Lithuania in the Eighteenth Century: A Genealogy of Modernity* (Berkeley: University of California Press, 2004), 4. On Jews as a "third solitude,"
see Morton Weinfeld, Introduction to Part 4: Intercommunal Relations,
in Brym, Shaffir and Weinfeld, *The Jews in Canada*, 168, and Pierre Anctil,
"Forging a Viable Partnership: The Montreal Jewish Community vis-à-
vis the Québec State," in *Québec: State and Society*, 2nd ed., ed. Alain-G.
Gagnon (Scarborough, ON: Nelson Canada, 1993), 372–88.

17 On Yiddish, see Rebecca Margolis, *Jewish Roots, Canadian Soil: Yiddish Culture in Montreal, 1905–1945* (Montreal and Kingston: McGill-Queen's University Press, 2011); on Jewish organizations and institutions in Montreal
(and elsewhere), see Weinfeld, *Like Everyone Else … But Different*, 161–252.
For engaging memoirs of Montreal Jewish day schools, see Ruth R. Wisse,
"Freedom; or, How a Family of Survivors Found Its Place in Jewish Montreal," *Mosaic*, 18 June 2018, https://mosaicmagazine.com, and Allan
Nadler, "Montreal, A Love Story," *Jewish Ideas Daily*, 28 June 2011 (*JID* has
been relaunched as *Mosaic*).

18 On Quebec Jews' civil rights struggle for public education through the
Protestant school boards, see Tulchinsky, *Canada's Jews*, 283–301, and David
Fraser, *Honorary Protestants: The Jewish School Question in Montreal, 1867–
1997* (Toronto: Osgoode Society for Canadian Legal History / University

of Toronto Press, 2015). On later provincial funding for Jewish day schools in Quebec and elsewhere, see Tulchinsky, *Canada's Jews*, 429–30.

19 Pierre Anctil, *Tur Malka. Flâneries sur les cîmes de l'histoire juive montréalaise* (Silléry: Septentrion, 1997). See the keen sense of place in A.M. Klein's 1940s poems "Montreal" ("And you above the city, scintillant, / Mount Royal, are my spirit's mother / Almative, poitrinate!"); "Lookout: Mount Royal"; "The Mountain" ("Who knows it only by the famous cross which bleeds / into the fifty miles of night its light / knows a night-scene"; and "Winter Night: Mount Royal," in A.M. Klein, *Complete Poems*, ed. Zailig Pollock (Toronto: University of Toronto Press, 1990), vol. 2: *Original Poems, 1937–1955 and Poetry Translations*, respectively 622–3, 686–7, 689–90, and 698–9.

20 Morton Weinfeld, "The Jews of Quebec: An Overview," in Brym, Shaffir, and Weinfeld, *The Jews in Canada*, 171–192, at 172, 185.

21 Weinfeld, *Like Everyone Else ... But Different*, 83, on tribal (for the record, he calls Toronto Jews tribal too), and 173, on institutional completeness, employing the term of sociologist Raymond Breton; Weinfeld, "The Jews of Quebec," 185, on ghetto-like; Anctil, "Forging a Viable Partnership," 373, on the Jewish confessional sphere.

22 Hundert, quoted in Weinfeld, *Like Everyone Else ... But Different*, 87.

23 Geneviève Zubrzycki, *Beheading the Saint: Nationalism, Religion, and Secularism in Quebec* (Chicago: University of Chicago Press, 2016).

24 Lois C. Dubin, *The Port Jews of Habsburg Trieste: Absolutist Culture and Enlightenment Culture* (Stanford, CA: Stanford University Press, 1999); "The Jews of Trieste: Between *Mitteleuropa* and *Mittelmeer*, 1719–1939," in *Bele Antiche Stòrie: Writing, Borders, and the Instability of Identity – Trieste, 1719–2007*, ed. Charles Klopp (New York: Bordighera, 2008), pp. 69–90; and "Diversity on the Frontiers in the 18th Century: Why Trieste? Then and Now," in Miriam Davide and Pietro Ioly-Zorattini, eds, *Gli Ebrei nella storia del Friuli-Venezia Giulia. Una vicenda di lunga durata* (Florence: Giuntina, 2016), 193–204. See also Tullia Catalan, *La comunità ebraica di Trieste (1781–1914): Politica, società e cultura* (Trieste: Lint, 2000).

25 Sherry Simon, *Translating Montreal: Episodes in the Life of a Divided City* (Montreal and Kingston: McGill-Queen's University Press, 2006), and *Cities in Translation: Intersections of Language and Memory* (London and New York: Routledge, 2012). See also Daniel A. Bell and Avner de-Shalit, "Montreal: The City of Language(s)," in *The Spirit of Cities: Why the Identity of a City Matters in a Global Age* (Princeton, NJ: Princeton University Press, 2011), 56–77.

26 Lothar Baier, *À la croisée des langues: Du métissage culturel d'est en ouest*, trans. Peter Krauss and Marie-Hélène Desort (Arles: Actes Sud/Leméac, 1997), 15.

27 Sherry Simon, "Against Translation: Quebec and the Charter of Values," in *Modern Horizons*, June 2014 issue: "Translation and Transcendence / La traduction et la transcendence," http://modernhorizonsjournal.ca/wp-content/uploads//Issues/201406/201406_Simon.pdf.

28 See, for example, the biography by Derek Beales, *Joseph II* (Cambridge: Cambridge University Press, vol. 1, 1987, and vol. 2, 2009), and H.M. Scott, ed, *Enlightened Absolutism: Reform and Reformers in Later Eighteenth-Century Europe* (Ann Arbor: University of Michigan Press, 1990).

29 See Marsha L. Rozenblit, "The Dilemma of National Identity: The Jews of Habsburg Austria in World War I," http://web.ceu.hu/jewishstudies/yb03/14rozenblit.pdf; and fuller exposition in *Reconstructing a National Identity: The Jews of Habsburg Austria during World War I* (New York: Oxford University Press, 2001).

30 Tulchinsky, *Taking Root*, 8–21, and Sheldon J. Godfrey and Judith C. Godfrey, *Search Out the Land: The Jews and the Growth of Equality in British Colonial America, 1740–1867* (Montreal and Kingston: McGill-Queen's University Press, 1995), 35–36 on Brandeau, and 73–126 on the first Jewish settlers in the British colonies of Nova Scotia and Quebec.

31 After I coined the term "port Jews," David Sorkin wrote his seminal article "The Port Jew: Notes toward a Social Type," *Journal of Jewish Studies* 50, no. 1 (1999): 87–97, and I discussed it further in Lois C. Dubin, "Researching Port Jews and Port Jewries: Trieste and Beyond," *Jewish Culture and History* 4, no. 2 (2001) [special issue: Port Jews]: 47–58, and "'Wings on their feet ... and wings on their head': Reflections on the Study of Port Jews," *Jewish Culture and History* 7, nos. 1–2 (2004) [special issue: *Jews and Port Cities*]: 14–30. See Lois C. Dubin, "Port Jews Revisited: Commerce and Culture in the Age of European Expansion," in *The Cambridge History of Judaism*, vol. 7: *The Early Modern World, 1500–1815*, ed. Jonathan Karp and Adam Sutcliffe (Cambridge: Cambridge University Press, 2018), 550–75. On Atlantic port Jews, see *Jewish History* 20 (2006), special issue "Port Jews in the Atlantic World: Dubin introduction," 117–27, and Jonathan Sarna, "Port Jews in the Atlantic: Further Thoughts," 213–19.

32 Sorkin, "Is American Jewry Exceptional?"

33 See "Emancipation Act (1832), Assembly of Lower Canada," in *The Jew in the Modern World: A Documentary History*, 3rd ed., ed. Paul Mendes-Flohr and Jehuda Reinharz (New York: Oxford University Press, 2010), 172; and Godfrey and Godfrey, *Search Out the Land*, 171–89 and 199–204. On fascinating earlier eighteenth-century developments, see also Godfrey and Godfrey, 69, 93, 100–1, 136. For example, it was unprecedented in Britain or its colonies when in 1768 John Franks was sworn into office taking his oath upon "the true faith of a Jew," after his appointment by commission as overseer for chimneys for the town of Quebec. On p. 69, they assert:

"The granting of civil and political rights to Jews in the land later known as Canada came much earlier than in England and, contrary to popular belief, often earlier than in the future United States of America." Though Jews were earlier granted equality for holding civil offices, they were then excluded from civil offices in Lower Canada from 1791 to 1831; hence the need for the 1832 Emancipation Act.

34 Ava F. Kahn and Adam Mendelssohn, eds, *Transnational Traditions: New Perspectives on American Jewish History* (Detroit: Wayne State University Press, 2014).

35 See, for example, Judith Elkin Laikin, *The Jews of Latin America*, 3rd rev. ed. (New York: Lynn Rienner, 2014); Haim Avni, *Argentina and the Jews* (Tuscaloosa: University of Alabama Press, 2002); and Ilan Stavans, *Return to Centro Histórico: A Mexican Jew Looks for His Roots* (New Brunswick, NJ: Rutgers University Press, 2012).

36 Salo W. Baron, *A Social and Religious History of the Jews*, 1st ed., 3 vols (New York: Columbia University Press, 1937), vol. 2: 39, and 2nd rev. and expanded ed., 18 vols (New York: Columbia University Press, and Philadelphia: Jewish Publication Society, 1952–1983), vol. 11: 199.

37 Tulchinsky, "Contours of Canadian Jewish History," 5–21, at 15.

38 Andrew E. Kim, "The Absence of Pan-Canadian Civil Religion: Plurality, Duality, and Conflict in Symbols of Canadian Culture," *Sociology of Religion* 54, no. 3 (1993): 257–75. I wonder whether scholars would still agree today that Canada lacks a civil religion.

39 Weinfeld, *Like Everyone Else ... But Different*, 7–8; Michael Brown, "From Binationalism to Multiculturalism to the Open Society," and "Canadian Jews and Multiculturalism: Myths and Realities," *Jewish Political Studies Review* 19, nos. 3–4 (Fall 2007): 57–75 (also available at Jerusalem Center for Public Affairs, 14 November 2007, http://jcpa.org/article/canadian -jews-and-multiculturalism-myths-and-realities/.)

15 Forgetting and Forging: My Canadian Experience as a Moroccan Jew

YOLANDE COHEN

Like most teenagers, I dreamed of getting free from all the hurdles and family obligations. It was in the 1960s and I was then living in Meknes, Morocco, a city where I felt I had no place. Immersed at school and with my friends in the mainly English music and film subculture, I longed to live elsewhere, maybe in America. My American fantasy seemed unreal: too far, too complicated. But I still had a strong desire to escape a tight and stifling atmosphere. I did not entirely belong to the Jewish community because I was not part of the *Mellah*, as I was living in the French *ville-nouvelle* and went to French schools; and I could not take part in the French colonial culture, since I was an *Israélite marocaine*, even though I spoke French *sans accent*. Nor, as a Jew, did I belong to the Muslim Moroccan majority. Like many other Moroccans, I spoke enough *darija* Arabic but not classical Arabic, even though I took four years of Arabic classes in the French lycée I attended. Truly, I spoke Judeo-arabic, the language of my grandmother. And even though I had friends in each sector of this outpost of the French colonial empire, where the Alaouite had once constructed theirs, I felt estranged from all of them. Growing up in Meknes as a Jewish girl, I was caught in the maelstrom of the last decade of the French colony and the explosion of Moroccan independence. So, when I finished high school, after a year of accrued tensions with my family and at the high school, I decided to go to France to study at the university. I am still amazed that I was able to "convince" my parents of such a project.

How could an eighteen-year-old girl leave her family and hometown in the 1960s? I figured that I could finally be free from my family and from the community tensions that were overwhelming our daily lives. Those tensions became volatile with the Arab-Israeli wars and the exile of most of our Jewish neighbours and friends in the 1960s and 1970s. For the minority of Jews who stayed in Morocco then, the relation to

Israel was complex: a dream for the promised land as well as a land overtaken by wars. We received little news from my father's family – his four brothers and three sisters and their many young children – who moved to Israel in September 1948. But my newlywed parents, who had already moved to Marseille to join them, knew that the war was raging and were reluctant to follow them. Instead, they came back to Meknes and raised their four children there. Still, we could not talk in public about Israel, since the Israeli-Palestinian wars had direct consequences on us living in Arab-Muslim lands. My own memories of Israel were contradictory: both present and absent. It was constantly there but had to be silenced. This feeling, it turned out, would be enduring, even in my life in Canada.

As soon as I could travel alone, at eighteen I made my first visit to Paris and then to Israel. Even though I was not engaged in Zionist activities, I was drawn by the kibbutz life and all the socialist rhetoric I heard about it. I wanted to check with many of my friends in high school who had been ardent Zionists and had made *Alyah* in 1967. I stayed at a kibbutz in the Galilee, and even enrolled as a student at the Hebrew university in political science. But very quickly, after a few months of *Oulpan*, I had to leave. I was unable to make Israel my own country and went back to Paris to study. This does not mean I didn't have the strongest ties to Israel. How could it be differently when half of my family lived there? Yet, I felt that it was not for me.

A baby boomer, educated from grade one in the French schools, I thought of myself as mainly French. I did not really share my friends' idealism, since, unlike them, I was not a Zionist. I thought I belonged in Paris. In fact I did not think I had any other choice, even though other friends went on to study in Casablanca or Rabat, which had public and tuition-free universities, or in Israel, if they were Zionists; but most of my peers at the French lycée went to France. For the brightest students of either nationality and for all the French, France's universities seemed to be the only "choice." For some Jewish girls who had family in France, it was also one of the best options. Eager to give me a good education but unable to stop me, my parents accepted my decision to leave. I promised to stay with family in Paris, but quickly I found another place to live my student life.

In Paris it did not take long to discover that I was not French, but a Jewish girl of Moroccan nationality. Alongside all the other migrants seeking to get their official papers, I spent many hours at the Préfecture de Police in Paris, year after year, to renew my papers. Nothing was more concrete than this bureaucratic experience to understand the colonial logic: it was a litmus test of its contradictions. How could it be that I had to ask for a visa to stay in Paris, when I was raised with the idea that France was my only *patrie*? Feeling rather than knowing the effects of the colonization on the colonized, I thought this was utterly unfair. I thought maybe I should tell them that I was *almost* French, and clear up the situation by seeking French naturalization. Twice I went through the naturalization process, filed naturalization forms, thinking that this would correct what I thought was just a mistake, a misunderstanding, a "malentendu," as Camus put it. After all, the French in Morocco taught me how to speak and behave like a French girl; they certainly succeeded, and I felt like one of them! I kept wondering why my applications were rejected. Not long ago, years after the fact but with the emotions linked to this blunt rejection still vivid, I went to the archives to check the "reasons" given by the French officials for rejecting my naturalization applications. They turned out to be pretty obvious: I was a student, my parents were still living in Morocco and not in France, and I had no regular income. Like most Moroccans, I did not have special access to French citizenship. This fuelled my anger even more: against the French government, against the French colonial power, against the capitalist order.

May '68 in Paris

I had joined the student movement that was booming in 1968. By then, the events of May-June 1968 were still unfolding in the universities. I joined a leftist group, which changed my life altogether. I finally found a place where I could belong: a cosmopolitan and internationalist movement was the ideal way to convey my anger and transform it into political activism. It also provided the ideal space where I could forget who I was and forge a new identity as an active citizen of the world. As a history student, I started thinking that I might one day want to teach and use my skills to make a living and become a professional historian. If studying in Paris presented me with some administrative problems, it was nothing compared to finding a job in the profession I wanted.

Not being a French citizen, I could not prepare the *concours d'agrégation*, the key that opened the doors of teaching in the high school or university system in France. I sought the advice of my thesis supervisor, who was a communist and later became the head of the Ligue des droits de l'Homme. All she said was that a Moroccan Jewish girl like me could not pretend she could get a job as a teacher because such positions were reserved for nationals; even her own son could not get one! (And he was much better credentialed than I was!) My hard-won degrees could not translate into a career. It took me some time to realize the implications of this situation, and I almost dropped out from the university as I was finishing my dissertation, working all the while at minimum wage on the side. It was clear that I was not going to find a job in Paris, other than the odd ones that a cousin could provide in his business. And even though I was very active in the Trotskyist and feminist movements there, which really were filling my life, I could not envision staying there once I got my citizenship rejected.

At that point, my parents and siblings had finally decided, after much thought, to move from Meknes to Montreal. It was 1974. It crushed me to see that they were finally quitting our hometown, where almost none of our family and friends remained. But their decision was made. They would join my mother's family, already established in Montreal. I visited them the following summer, and – surprisingly – very much liked Montreal and the Laurentians, where my cousins and their friends had a chalet.

Moving to Montreal

Even though Quebec was not at all in my plans, the fact that my parents had moved there, and that I did not see any interesting future for me in Paris, led me to make the move a couple of years after them. It was pretty easy to get the visa as an immigrant in Canada compared with the hurdles I went through in France. As it happens, I got my doctorate degree, found a job at UQAM, and have been teaching contemporary French history ever since. I remained attached to my friends in Paris and keep going back often. I go back to Morocco, too, as well as Israel, where I have a large family and a strong emotional attachment. Even though I still bear the stigma of an immigrant, traumatized by my family's quick departure from Morocco and by the hardship of multiple migrations, Montreal became the place where I found myself: I got married, raised two beautiful children, and pursued the career I dreamed of.

For me, there is no better place to be than Montreal! I became a Québécois and a Canadian, with a Moroccan Jewish origin. In a way, the possibility of keeping a multiplicity of belongings is perhaps the greatest factor that makes Canada a hospitable place for immigrants.

How does this personal narrative fit within the wider story of Moroccan Jewish post-colonial migration? While there are as many narratives as there are immigrants, my personal trajectory fits well within the evidence-based history of Moroccan Jewish migration in Quebec and, more broadly, in Canada. Overall, this group has fared quite well economically, and has been successful in settling in Canada, compared with other groups who arrived at the same time, such as the Haitians or the Chileans. Two main factors account for this success. On the one hand, the new immigrants were quite young and educated. On the other, their integration was facilitated by a vast mobilization of Montreal's Jewish institutions and their professional social workers.

The essential role played by JIAS, the Canadian Jewish Congress, and the main Canadian and American organizations in lobbying the governments (both in Canada and in Morocco), selecting and helping them migrate from Morocco and settle in Canada, cannot be underestimated. Their actions not only were crucial to help open the Canadian borders to non-Europeans, but they also helped find jobs and housing for new migrants and afforded them opportunities to socialize, initially inside the mainly Ashkenazi community, first in Montreal and then in Toronto. Maybe the feeling of being too much indebted to the established community led some of them to worry about how they could give it back. A fierce people with strong community traditions, Moroccan Jews resented the humiliating position they were in. Many of them who told our research team[1] their story of migration had "forgotten" the help given to them by JIAS: they did not remember the migration process as being a hard one, nor did they recall being helped to arrive in Montreal. Forgetting the hardship of immigration is one sure way to hide or deny the trauma of leaving one's country. The problem is that it becomes complicated to relate to your own story and to make sense of it. In my view, this is what happened with the changes that followed in their/our own representation.

Stories of Moroccan Jews in Canada: Becoming Sephardi Jews

For the last thirty-five years I have been doing fieldwork in a community I belong to, alternating between sharing its fate (my personal emotions) and keeping a necessary distance (the scholar's gaze). I'd like to outline some of the complicated accommodations that have been going on since I arrived in Canada.

I found that most of this population had clung to its long-held tradition of maintaining its own community organizations. In Morocco, it was meant to preserve its identity, as a Jewish minority; in Quebec it was a way of preserving its Moroccan Jewishness. We can see this influence in two very important institutions Moroccan Jews created as soon as they arrived: their own synagogues and schools. Even if most of these migrants were secular Jews, the few young men, with some women, who founded the Association Francophone des Juifs Nord-Africains, which became the Communauté Sépharade du Québec (CSQ), wanted to establish themselves as an autonomous group, but not a religious one. Their model was the Conseil des Communautés Israélites du Maroc, which functioned as a federation of local communities, electing a board approved by the king. The rabbis, although relatively autonomous, were nominated by the community, and the nomination of the head rabbi was also to be approved by the king. The rabbis chosen to compose the judiciary (Tribunal rabbinique) for all civil questions are officials paid by the Ministry of Justice. It is interesting to note that in a monarchy, where state and religion are not separated, all matters of religion are clearly delineated to fit the status of each religious group.

We could see that this model was brought to Quebec by those who built the structure of the CSQ, only this model does not quite fit within the Montreal Jewish Community. So when they decided to bring a rabbi from Morocco (Rabbi Sabbah) to perform what they thought could be the Sephardi Chief Rabbi, they were opposed by the Vaad (the Montreal Rabbinate) and faced the difficult task of delineating its field of competence within the CSQ. It did not take long to see the arrangement fail, mostly due to in-fighting but also to the different organization of the Jewish communities in Quebec. So instead of having one chief rabbi, Moroccan Jews had several rabbis who officiate at the many synagogues they founded in Montreal and Toronto. If in Canada the state is secular, unlike in Morocco, Judaism can be practised without any established authority, with the result that there is a plural market for "Moroccan Judaism" here that the immigrants themselves never knew back home. It was therefore not very difficult for Moroccan Jews to continue to practise their religious rituals the way they wanted. The large number of synagogues and religious centres devoted to Sephardi or Jewish Moroccan cults and traditions in Montreal and Toronto attest to that.

As far as the schools were concerned, the strong influence of the Alliance Israélite Universelle, established in Morocco with its mixed school system, is obvious. The creation of the École Maimonide in Montreal by the CSQ as early as 1969 clearly indicates Moroccan Jews' will to assert their presence in separate institutions. In Toronto, they did not create such schools but integrated in the predominantly anglophone school system, whether Jewish or otherwise. But they created their own cultural centres (such as the Kehillah Centre for instance) to transmit their Jewish Moroccan traditions and rituals, as well as Hebrew lessons and religious education.

As most of the new Moroccan Jewish immigrants spoke French at a time when French was becoming Quebec's predominant language, it was quite clear that this meant that Moroccan Jews diverged from Jewish immigrant patterns of integrating in the mainly anglophone group. Their determination to keep French as their main language and to establish themselves in the French culture became their main asset in a time when Quebec was asserting the predominance of French in its laws (Bill 101, for example). The arrival of this group of immigrants gave birth to a separate entity based on a renewed Sephardic identity. It is difficult to know exactly how the decision to change the name of their Association des Juifs Nord-Africains came about, but the consensus fell on the term "Sephardic" Jews, rather than "Arab," "Oriental" (which would be the translation of Mizrahi), "North African," or "Maghrebi." Some members who came from formerly Spanish Morocco (Tanger, Melilla) found that Sephardic would be the appropriate name for them, since it meant retaining their old traditions from Spain. Some others wanted to gather the other Jews who were already present in Montreal – such as the Egyptians, the Iraqis, and others – under their umbrella.

The Spanish and Portuguese Synagogue, which attracted many Moroccan Jews on their arrival, was founded by Sephardic families 250 years ago. This particular combination of people and the overall landscape of the Jewish community in Montreal led some to identify with an ancient Sephardic world. For the anglophone leadership, which was very much aligned with Israel and cared much about its pro-Israel support, it was also an acceptable compromise. After many years of tensions and recriminations, exiles and departures to Toronto or elsewhere, it became obvious to all that a francophone segment of the Montreal Jewish community could be an asset in Quebec. It is striking to note that while French Canadians were renewing their own identity as Québécois, Jews of Moroccan origins became Sephardi as well as Québécois.

After many years of difficult debates to get some public recognition for Moroccan Jews as a community, the question of asserting its own different identity ceased to be important after 11 September 2001. The harsh reality of a growing antisemitism, fuelled both by the populist and extreme right and by an expanding Islamist radicalism, changed their perception and the ways in which they could relate to the greater Jewish community. Religious radicalism, and Islamophobia in particular, and the pre-eminence of religion in the public sphere are now at the centre of the political realm. If in Canada the multicultural position has always encouraged the expression of individual and community (religious) identity, it is not so in Quebec, where a strong movement in favour of integral secularism (laicité) is prevalent. It was finally time for the Sephardi community to join with the rest of the Jewish community in reasserting their identity as Jews.

Commemoration of Canadian History: Jews as Settlers and Immigrants

Numerous celebrations marked the 150th anniversary of the foundation of the Canadian federation. The many groups composing the Canadian mosaic had different, often contradictory, views of why and how Canadians should remember this moment in particular, since many people could claim different dates to celebrate. For the First Nations, it was at best a non-event, since they were the founding nations, well before anybody claimed their lands. For others, including many in Quebec who resented the federation as an imposition of a colonial power on their own sovereign nation, there was nothing worth celebrating. If anything, this moment meant the subjection of a proud people (the Québécois) to what they perceived as a foreign power (the Anglo-Protestant Canadians).

For us Jews, who as a religious minority have long lived in the margins, if not excluded or discriminated against, we can seize this moment to think about our past and present relations to this history. I like to think that, as a member of the Spanish and Portuguese Synagogue, I am now connected to an ancient migration. Jewish migration and settlement in New France have made the Jewish contribution to Canadian history important and ancient. We are celebrating the 250th anniversary of the Spanish and Portuguese Synagogue, the second synagogue on the continent that was established by English settlers of Sephardi origins in Montreal. Those pioneers kept the name of their countries of origin, even though they were the descendants of the survivors of the 1492 Catholic Inquisition, which chased them from Spain and Portugal. The Hart and Joseph families named their congregation Shearith Israel, the Remnants of Israel now scattered in Canadian soil. Their contribution is hardly known, but mostly their ancient presence has contributed to the making of Canadian history.

The mention of Jewish officers and merchants in the British contingent arriving in Quebec in 1763 signals their participation to the colonial enterprise. This small Jewish group of Sephardi settlers who built the first institutions of the Montreal Jewish Community was part of the anglophone elite of Montreal. Rapidly overwhelmed by the arrival of large waves of Jewish immigration from the central European ghettos in the late nineteenth and early twentieth centuries, the Montreal Jewish community was transformed into a plurality of ethnic groups who spoke both Yiddish and English. The rapid integration of this small Sephardic group in the Anglo-Protestant elite was quickly forgotten with the arrival of an important contingent of eastern European Jews. The

Sephardi elite narrative of Canadian Jewish history receded behind a new narrative focused on Ashkenazi non-elites. The backbone of this new Canadian Jewish narrative has it that Jewish migrants, expelled and fleeing their old countries' antisemitism, built thriving communities and experienced first-hand, as ethnic groups, the pluralism of Canadian polity. Not only has the Sephardic content of this history disappeared but its settler's aspect has been replaced by a migrant one. So even if (Sephardi) Jews have settled in Canada for over 250 years, Jews' settlement in Canada became synonymous with twentieth-century Ashkenazi migrations.

As a relatively new migrant myself, I was happy to dig into this history to find those ancient Sephardic traces in Montreal, which make me part of an ongoing history, albeit very distant and different from my own. But I also keep on drawing comparisons between here and there, Montreal and Meknes my home town in Morocco, and between Paris, the city where I studied and got engaged with adult life, and Montreal, the city where I now live and work. I am happy to celebrate with my family Jewish holidays at the Spanish Synagogue. It gives me a sense of purpose to set my foot where other Sephardi Jews have been. For me, and perhaps for others like me, migrating to Canada was a dream come true. Here, I feel that I can renew my attachments to a larger Sephardi diaspora, rooted in a very ancient history and now dispersed all over the world.

A Sephardi Jewish Diaspora of the Modern Times, with Israel as Its Centre

Does this mean that there is a global Sephardi Jewry with a more or less unique way to see oneself, whether we live in Paris, Tel-Aviv, or Montreal? There are many ways to be part of a Jewish diaspora today as there are as many ways to be Sephardi. Living today in Montreal, Canada seems to me even better than my dream of going to the United States. If the attraction of the United States has been extraordinary for my generation in the 1960s and '70s, not too many Moroccan Jews made it directly there. Instead we came to Canada largely because of the organized migration led by JIAS.

I too share an attachment to religion, Israel, and the Holocaust, which are considered to be the three main pillars that define today's North American Jewry. My emotional attraction, one associated with expressing my identity, is a feeling of being different. When I was a child, I was taught that being Jewish meant having a strong family/community attachment, representing our alliance with God, and respecting some if not all the rituals, which in effect were differentiating us from everybody else around us. Did it mean I was religious? Not really. I considered myself a Jew in an Arab world, in which religion defined everyone's identities. My relation to the Holocaust and Israel are part of what we are today as Jews, forever part of my identity. And I am quite aware that being a Jew and a Canadian citizen are all compatible with these ties to another country and other emotional attachments.

A plural society allows for such diverse loyalties. Canada is such a place.

NOTES

I want to thank the anonymous reviewers and the editors for their work to improve this text, written in July 2018. I am also grateful for the support of an SSHRC grant to be able to work on this large project on the migrations of Moroccan Jew.

1 Yolande Cohen, dir., *Les sépharades du Québec: trajectoires de juifs Nord-Africains* (Montreal: Delbusso Éditeur, 2017); Yolande Cohen, Martin Messika, and Sara Cohen-Fournier, "Memories of Departures: Stories of Jews from Muslim Lands in Montreal," in *Beyond Testimony and Trauma: Oral History in the Aftermath of Mass Violence*, ed. Steven High (Vancouver: University of British Columbia Press, 2015), 311–31; Yolande Cohen, "The Migrations of Moroccan Jews to Montreal: Memory, (Oral) History and His-torical Narrative," in *Sites of Jewish Memory: Jews in and from Islamic Lands in Modern Times*, ed. Glenda Abramson (Oxford: Routledge, 2014), 120–45.

16 Nothing Is Forever: Remembering the Centennial

JACK KUGELMASS

Escape to New York

A sense of journey underlies an academic career. For those in the humanities that journey is often propelled by a sense of unease or lack of fit in one's place of origin. Hence, the passion for other languages and cultures or the act of immersing oneself in another era. This is certainly so for an anthropologist or for a would-be one. Coming of age in the turbulent 1960s, if there was anything I did not want to be it was who or what any upwardly mobile Canadian Jewish parents thought a son should become – a doctor. I had long been fascinated by archaeology, or, at least by what I thought archaeology was, much to my parents' distress. Then, after I started college, cultural anthropology seemed to have all the romance and intellectual excitement that academic archaeology lacked. Although it would be some years before I would begin to use a narrative approach in my own writing, the tenor of this piece is characteristic of anthropology's shift away from positivism to a humanistic, critical, and sometimes self-reflective endeavour. It's an approach in keeping with the kind of graduate training I would pursue at the New School for Social Research. So, after completing a BA in anthropology at McGill I escaped from what seemed to be a stultifying future in what then felt like a sad city and moved to the great metropolis to the south. Ironically, in the 1970s, New York City, too, was a very sad city. Mainstay sectors of the economy such as light manufacture were in decline, the city's subway cars were old, rickety, and covered with graffiti, and the city's crime rate was high with frequent shocking news reports of seemingly random murders. Vast sections of the city's housing stock were crumbling and, in some areas, burning. (Interestingly, it was in one of those areas where I would find a creative voice as a writer and photographer.) Unless you were living in the right areas and could avoid the blight, the nastiness, the sweltering heat, or the unreliability of public transit, New York wasn't a very pleasant place. But it had its allures, especially its museums and cultural institutions. And its beautiful buildings and thoroughfares with endless brownstone neighbourhoods undergoing gentrification. In short, despite its many problems, New York City felt more European than American. As a Jew, I felt there was so much to attract. There were still the many traces of mass Jewish migration to the United States in the small and grand turn-of-the-century synagogues, late nineteenth-century storefronts, and faux signs meant to evoke Yiddish or Hebrew. And there were still functioning Jewish bakeries and restaurants. The Lower East Side had the charm and aura of an accessible Old Country. Not that those elements were entirely absent up north. But in New York City it was on a much grander scale and seemed to have a living and, until quite recently, sustainable link to the past. Back then, who would have imagined the Lower East Side gentrified? Another attraction were the Yiddish institutions – the YIVO, the Atran Foundation, the Bund Archives, and even the Yiddish *Forverts* whose high-rise headquarters dominated the Lower East Side and out of which came a daily still sold at many Manhattan newspaper kiosks. And there were the traces, too, of the migration of refugees from Hitler's Germany – the so-called Fourth Reich of Washington Heights and the refugee scholars who once populated the graduate faculty of the New School for Social Research. Formerly known as the University in Exile, even in the 1970s its roster of distinguished scholars included more than a few Old World luminaries.

Truthfully, New York City was only slightly farther from home than Toronto, where many of my cousins and classmates eventually migrated. But Montreal and New York City were worlds apart. And the difference wasn't just about size or the distinctive origins of Montreal's Jewish population, nor even about the city's unique urban culture and architecture. It lay in the different mentality of the countries in which each is situated. For reasons that are well known, that gulf remains every bit as wide today as then, when the United States was deeply embroiled in a fruitless war in Southeast Asia, domestically pitting so-called hawks against doves.

The Centennial

At seventeen, some four or five years before moving south, I was given an opportunity to travel west within Canada. In those days the country was infused by a new nationalism stimulated initially through government prodding yet quite unexpectedly transmogrified into a vast popular movement to mark 1967, the centennial of Confederation. I was particularly receptive to the mantra of bilingualism and biculturalism and felt deep in my heart that Canada was different from the United States for reasons that were as much cultural as social and political. The Centennial celebrations included a year-long blowout of events: some ridiculous, others less so. These included the minting of a new coin, the awarding of centennial medals, and the naming of Centennial babies for those born on 1 July. But other efforts at celebration had far less gravitas: one Ottawa resident established a museum for his collection of ten thousand bottles. A dry-cleaner organized a "Fly a Clean Flag" program, offering to clean Canadian or Centennial flags without charge.[1]

Nor were all the whimsical projects ephemeral. St Paul, Alberta constructed a flying saucer landing pad that included a forty-foot concrete wall on which was displayed a map of Canada so that alien visitors would know where they were. The landing platform would eventually serve as the entrance to the town's recreation grounds, a speakers' podium, and dance floor.[2] A thirty-mile bathtub race across the Straight of Georgia to Vancouver was apparently repeated even after the Centennial.[3]

Heritage was also suddenly in vogue, or as Pierre Berton put it, in 1967 "Canadians began to realize they had a past – not the drab, date-oriented past of the school texts but a vibrant and exciting history."[4] And so the Centennial included historical re-enactments. Perhaps the most ambitious of these was a cross-country canoe pageant – the entire event as well as the canoe itself a symbol of Canada's romantic past – involving one hundred participants.[5] The route took the paddlers from the headwaters of the North Saskatchewan all the way to Montreal – some 3,283 miles. Portages had to be done using only the technology of the voyageurs, that is, canoes and gear were hand carried. It lasted 104 days and in true Canadian spirit its organizers took pride in the fact that all one hundred participants made it to Montreal. As with so many other events that took place that year, Canadians were busily exploring their own land and acknowledging their history often by recreating it.[6]

There were also any number of projects that were intended to endure – musical commissions, documentary films, literary works, a spectacular photo book commissioned by the National Film Board, new buildings such as Ottawa's National Arts Centre, plus a few very ambitious and remarkably successful projects: an exhibition on Canadian history that crisscrossed the country on a train, and Expo 67, the Montreal world's fair that ran for six months.

As Helen Davies points out in her study of the Canadian Centennial celebrations, these events were planned within a broader context in which the need to celebrate Canada's achievements and to proclaim national unity as a bulwark against an underlying current of social unrest. She cites the oppositional youth culture of the '60s, the feminist movement, the demands for human rights for Aboriginal people, and the growth of Quebec nationalism.[7] I'm not sure I'd give equal weight to all, but it's fair to say that by the '60s the consensus culture of the postwar era was crashing. And for a bifurcated society like Canada whose key social and demographic divides are largely mapped onto the country's geography, this was particularly problematic. The Centennial celebrations, therefore, were intended to be "more than just a birthday party ... [but] a political statement about what it meant to be Canadian."[8] They were intended to unify.

Among the lesser known of the ephemeral events intended to have a particularly enduring impact was a program set up by the Centennial Youth Travel Commission of sending groups of two dozen high school seniors equally divided between males and females to different parts of the country for a one-week sojourn in a host community. These same students would also receive a group from a different part of Canada. The idea of using travel to unite a country that lacks the kind of mobility that has helped counteract the regionalism of Canada's neighbour to the south was an interesting idea and it's too bad, that aside from press clippings sporadically preserved at Library and Archives Canada, we know nothing about its achievements or failures. Although a documentary on the program was included in the annual budget of the Centennial planners in 1964, I have found no trace of it. But film or no film, this much information I could find: the program began in 1964 and was expected to peak in 1967 the year in which 4,000 students would participate in 170 travelling groups.[9] By the fall of 1967 some 528 groups had been launched. They included 1,056 adult escorts and 12,728 travellers.[10] Of course, it was expected that this sort of contact across Canada's divides would lead to greater understanding. It's an assumption that needs some interrogation, which I will do shortly.

Citing the merits of the travel program, one newspaper editorial indicated that organizers had begun to understand the need to continue the program since "there is nothing like travel and contact with people in other parts of this vast country to widen the horizons of understanding."[11] Reading between the lines one sees two things: first, that Canada's multiplicity, its so-called ethnic mosaic had been distilled into a fundamental binary opposition; second, the great linguistic divide between francophones and anglophones was, in most parts of Canada,

Figure 16.1 Centennial Youth Travel Poster (courtesy of Library and Archives Canada) © Government of Canada. Reproduced with the permission of Library and Archives Canada (2020).
Source: Library and Archives Canada/Paul Hellyer fonds/MG32 B 33 94, file number 21

bridgeable only in the most superficial manner. One Saskatchewan town played host to a group from Rouyn, a town in northwestern Quebec. The local newspaper described how residents "have hit their dictionaries and French-language phrase books to meet them [the Quebec students] halfway." Halfway? I doubt that any of them had such phrase books let alone something as formidable as a French-English dictionary. Moreover, bilingualism and biculturalism for Saskatchewanians, as the article noted, was an academic exercise: as one local mused, "Differences don't bother us out here. We have our own melting pot, and French by no means is the only alternative to English. Les Quebecois are welcome."[12] The article concluded, "Knowledge among people of good heart can spark a lasting feeling of brotherhood and understanding and sincere accord. The youth exchange scheme should be expanded."[13]

Winkler, Manitoba

If truth be told, my own experience as a Youth Traveller was somewhat different. But let me begin at the beginning. How I found out about the initiative I no longer remember, but I assume that flyers and applications were mailed to schools and then posted. I seem to have been the only one from my high school who applied. Not that I could expect to travel with a familiar face since the groups were intentionally mixed, and aside from me and a girl who attended an English Catholic school, my cohort was entirely francophone. I had hoped to visit British Columbia, which is probably why I applied to go in the first place. No such luck. The travel program wanted to bring urbanites to rural Canada and French speakers to English Canada and the reverse. We were going to Manitoba. Winkler, Manitoba, to be more precise. Winkler! – a Mennonite farming community very close to the American border. The town is apparently an agricultural redistributive centre for southern Manitoba so it's large enough to house a small museum today. But if it ever had a newspaper I found no trace of it.

Like all the Centennial Youth travel tours heading in either direction that crossed through Ottawa, we toured the capital and saw an American blues concert of Sonny Terry and Brownie McGhee at the recently completed National Arts Centre. Some 1,300 miles of track later, we disembarked in Winnipeg and were given a tour of St Boniface by a young Métis woman. And it was in the St Boniface Cathedral that I was baptized – a prank rather than a ceremony – when Michel, who had become my closest buddy on the trip, *shpritzed* me with holy water.

One way to understand these trips is that they were a kind of "Birthright" *avant la lettre*. But these were much less scripted than the Jewish Birthright trips to Israel, much less intended to evoke an emotional response other than to admire the neo-gothic majesty of Parliament or to recognize the vastness of one's native land and the friendliness of local residents. Indeed, one rather lame effort at scripting was the inclusion of the songbook *Young Canada Sings* in the souvenirs each traveller received prior to embarkation. As the director of public relations for the Centennial Commission notes, the '67 perennials were campfire songs rather than patriotic panegyrics and no effort was made to insert ob-scure Canadian folk songs.[14] But it was assumed that each group would have at least one guitar-playing participant, so one imagined the trains barrelling across the prairies with their occupants singing "This Land Is Your Land." Here was nation-building on a micro scale, inscribing into the minds of young citizens something they would long remember.[15] (Actually we did sing as we rolled through the prairies. However, it wasn't anything patriotic but rather a ribald French drinking song, "Chevaliers de la table ronde." But scripted or no, the very composition of the group as ethnically and linguistically mixed, meant it would be ten days of intense cross-cultural encounters along divides of language, religions, and ethnicities. And because I was there, ultimately it would include the very place of the Jew in between and across those divides. Indeed, if these Canadians shared one thing in common, it was that they were all Christian of one sort or another. I was not, baptism aside.

Whatever the feelings and inner thoughts of my francophone fellow travellers, I never experienced anything negative from them. But re-garding Jewishness, southern Manitoba proved a bit of a shocker. To begin with, we were hosted for a lunch sponsored by the town's only Jew, who owned the local hardware store. The food was ham sand-wiches. HAM! He also knew no Hebrew, so an initial greeting with *shalom* rather than *shulem aleykhem* proved to be the very opposite of an ice breaker. I'm not sure that the Yiddish greeting would have faired better. Another shocker came when all of us – guests and hosts – had been paired into couples. A local high school girl who became my host-ess for the day divulged that the moment I stepped off the bus from Winnipeg, her mother pointed at me and said, "He's a Jew." And there were some odd displays among a few of the town's youth but probably more in regard to insignia and tattoos than actual politics, which, thank God, they kept to themselves. By their attire I assumed that they were not NDPers. They did invite me and a few others to a get-together for beer in a ramshackle home on the outskirts of town. At any rate, if they were neo-Nazis or some such thing, they were well behaved and even polite. At least nobody threatened me.

By contrast with these other encounters, my host family was, una-bashedly, philosemitic. The trip was shortly after the Six Day War, and they were wildly pro-Israel, an extension apparently of their hatred for the Soviet bloc. I recall the father's outrage over the fact that decades after the war, Berlin was still divided. (At that time, I felt differently on the matter, though I kept that thought to myself.) The father's outrage and virulent anti-communism may be why I had my doubts about the family's philosemitism. Indeed, I'll relate shortly one chilling anecdote that long stuck in my mind, and I raise this because in reviewing the files on the Centennial Youth travel it was expressly stated that the purpose of the program was to bring Canadians together in order for young people to experience the nation's diversity and thereby bridge its gaps. Judging from the files, "primary gaps" were understood then as francophone vs. anglophone and urban vs. rural. There was no consideration given to matters of ethnicity or race.

Canada does have a large First Nations population. Although some attempts were made to include a few in the travel program, in 1964 only one out of the 128 youth groups originated in the Northwest Territories, while for 1965, out of 180 proposed groups, two were expected to come from the north.[16] Whether or not these groups were Indigenous I could not tell. But I have my doubts. I should also add that there is a historically important Black community in the Maritimes and I do not know whether visits to that community were on the itinerary. I found nothing in the files to suggest they were. But, to the credit of the organizers, the Métis community of Winnipeg was part of our itinerary. Still, the Métis are integral to Canadian history as traditionally formulated – a living legacy so to speak of the French explorers. But addressing matters of ethnicity and race or economic disparities was not on the table because, at least in 1967, the national agenda was not about *diversity* as we have since come to think of it. It was about bilingualism and biculturalism and how to unify a country of two distinct nations.

My Country

Some of the local high schools had produced a play as a Centennial project. It celebrated the French explorer Pierre Gaultier de Varennes et de la Verendrye. He was born in Trois-Rivières in 1685, joined the French army in 1704, where he participated in the wars with the British, and returned to New France in 1712. In 1726 he joined a fur trading venture near Lake Superior, where he came to believe that a fuller exploration of Lake Winnipeg and "the great western river" would reveal the route to the Pacific Ocean. He convinced the governor in Quebec that the west could enrich New France while a French presence would be a counterweight to the British domination of Hudson Bay. La Verendrye left Montreal in 1731 with a party that included three of his sons but with no financing. After three years he had sent back a quantity of furs. Having reached Lake Winnipeg, but not having discovered any sign of the Pacific, La Verendrye saw his reputation in Quebec suffer. A year later, La Verendrye set out for the west determined to make good on his original objective. He reached the mouth of the Assiniboine River and the site of what would become Winnipeg, entered North Dakota, and then returned to Montreal. When he returned to the west once again he busied himself planning forts in the areas already "discovered" and sent his sons onward. They eventually reached the foot of the Rocky Mountains. In 1743 La Verendrye returned to Quebec, but received no official recognition for his or his sons' discoveries. Some years later shortly before his death he received the Croix de Saint Louis for his service and was awarded the management of a few western posts. After their father's death, the sons received nothing for his or their own accomplishments.[17] A tragic narrative. But for Manitobans a heroic founding story.

My Country's History

One evening we were treated to an outdoor performance of a play. Much to my astonishment, the script introduced a Shylockian figure into the early history of New France – a man to whom the explorers turned in order to finance their expeditions, and, base Jew that he was, he refused them the money they needed to make Canada great. In the end the funds were secured, I don't remember how, but to add an element of bizarre misrepresentation, upon finalizing the agreement the explorers celebrated with a toast using a jug of Mogen David wine! I didn't think this was an intentionally parodic element, but probably what passed for wine in rural southern Manitoba. The next morning my host family asked what I thought of the play. I was diplomatic – after all, I was a guest – and suggested that it needed some improvement. In what way? A little more knowledge of early Canadian history would help. But as I already knew, Canadians, especially Anglo-Canadians, know practically nothing about Canadian history.

Ignorance is a vacuum that demands to be filled. So why not invoke the imaginary Jew here? Perhaps the Shylockian character appeared because where would the story be without an obstacle, without some sort of villainy? Unfortunately, without the full text of the play (which seems to be lost), I'm only guessing at the meaning of this element. If the search for financing took place in France, La Verendrye *might* have encountered a Jewish moneylender, but Jews were not the only ones from whom one might secure a loan at that time. And if the search took place in New France the person he turned to could not have been a Jew since there were no Jews in Quebec until after the British conquest in 1759. Moreover, my recollection of the performance is that the Jew played an ancillary role, more a bit of colour than key to the narrative. So let me take a stab at the possible meaning of the Jew in the play. The explorers' partially thwarted wish was to leave civilization, penetrate the interior, and claim nature's bountifulness for the homeland, either France or Quebec. The attempt is interrupted by a low form of life (the Edenic snake?) – a being, the Jew that is, whose place of órigin is neither of the Occident nor of the Orient (except by heritage) and whose anomalousness is a categorical transgression that society perceives as a danger to the moral order. The eternal stranger, the Jew's interests are distinct from those of the nation. The Jew's interests are monetary, the well-being and preservation of self and family, while the national project is presented here as selfless and noble: to open and take possession of the land.[18] There is no mention in the play of stealing anything from Native peoples.

What I would give to rediscover how this conflict was resolved![19] But what is apparent in this play is that the then current Canadian zeitgeist of bilingualism and biculturalism is addressed here by appropriating La Verendrye as a native son. That receptiveness of Anglo-Canadians to their francophone compatriots is commendable. But how did the Jew get into this story since there were no Jews in New France at the time?[20] It's easier than one would think. A 2007 survey of young Canadians revealed that less than half knew who the first prime minister was while only a quarter knew the date of Confederation![21] So why be surprised by the liberties taken in narrating history in the Winkler play by people who knew nothing at all about the presence or absence of Jews in early French Canada? For Americans, it's common knowledge, I think, or at least it is among Jews, that a man named Hayyim Salomon helped finance the American Revolution. Perhaps less well known even among Jews is that apparently the only competent member of the Confederacy's cabinet was a Jew. It's probably not really fair to berate the absence of knowledge of the Jew within Canadian history by the population of a small town in southern Manitoba without finding a small rural population within the United States to compare it with. Indeed, if the recent resurgence of white supremacist marchers is indicative, and as Sacha Baron Cohen demonstrates in some of his outrageous skits, there's a cross-section of the American population who would have considered the political, indeed, historical, inconsistencies of Winkler's centennial play as Gospel truth.[22] Still, what struck me wasn't just the possibly unintended antisemitism but the ignorance of Canadian history. At the same time, it was irksome to think that an Anglo-Canadian affirmation of New France's history as part of all Canadians' patrimony required the exclusion of a less labile outsider. If this trip was, indeed, a Canadian Birthright *avant la lettre*, it was hard for me after watching the play to feel a part of it, to feel at home in this country of mine. Ironically, as this play invokes the past in order to assert Canada's glorious future, some 1,500 miles to the east of Winkler, two Jews were instrumental in the remarkable success of the crown jewel of the Centennial celebration. A little more about that shortly.

One final note regarding Winkler. After returning to Montreal, I was sitting with my mother in the family living room on a Friday late afternoon waiting for my father to return from work when the doorbell rang. Standing outside were two respectably dressed men. One was younger and the other middle aged. They said they were there to convey greetings from Winkler, so we let the men in. They sat down, and as we began to talk it became clear that the two were missionaries and were visiting at the suggestion of the family I had stayed with. They offered us some pamphlets and a Bible, which we did not accept, and they politely left when we asked them to. The interior of our house was robustly Jewish – menorah for *shabes* candles, various Jewish *tchotchkes* including souvenirs from Israel, and an oil painting of an imagined service from a medieval Spanish synagogue that my parents had bought on a trip to Spain, watercolours from Tsefat that my older brother had purchased on a trip to Israel, and an image of a Hasid at the Western Wall and a small figurine of a fiddler on a roof comfortably stationed on the piano. Much of it was tourist art, for sure, but it was essential decor for a prosperous North American Jewish home. Surely, these were clues enough to even these hapless missionaries that they were barking up the wrong tree. *Goyishe kep!* The fact that they had entered the house through a ruse felt not just like a betrayal, but even a violation. It was proof that the midwest outpost of the real Canada preferred its country without real Jews. So much for peace, love, and understanding. And it does make me wonder whether the Shylockian figure in the play was less the result of invoking a stock trope at the expense of historical veracity than a deeply rooted religious belief. This Birthright tour had exposed something that it really wasn't supposed to. It certainly made me feel rather unwelcome in this supposed homeland of mine.

Hosting Others

Also on a negative note but with nothing to do with Manitoba was the fact that my group hosted students from British Columbia. My guest was what we call progressive, which even then meant decidedly anti-Israel. Conversations between us did not go well. There were no agreements to agree to disagree, and with no gaps bridged, silence reigned. We forget sometimes how volatile 1967 was and how much anti-Israel sentiment had emerged within the Left especially on university campuses. Funny to think about it, because in theory there were no settlements yet, and if I'm not mistaken, Palestinians were less the rallying cause of the day than were the progressive pretences of Nasser and his supporters in the Soviet bloc. For "progressives," Israel's swift victory had upset the apple cart.

Finally, let me try to recall some of the memorable things that happened on the train trip to and from Manitoba. I do not recall how proficient most of the francophones were in English, though for sure some were not. We spoke to one another in French and I was, to my shame now, particularly pleased by how demure the other anglophone student was because I could act as the principal go-between during the trip. Indeed, that role became even more pronounced once we met up with our host community in Winkler. Who better than the Jew to interpret goyim for other goyim?

I was not the only member of my group who spoke both languages. Truth be told, my buddy Michel had native or near-native fluency in both English and French. I envied him that. And I also envied his and his classmates' apparent promiscuity. Montreal Jews of the 1960s had been bred not to enjoy life but to save themselves for success in the professions. Michel and I remained friends for a year or two after the trip. Though not frequently, we did visit each other at home. Michel's mother was a schoolteacher. I don't recall meeting his father. I laugh when I think of his mother feeding Michel's young siblings when I arrived at their home one evening and she admonished her children that they were to listen carefully to how I spoke so that they, too, would speak proper French!

In the mid-1960s language instruction at least in my high school made the shift from an international to a Parisian French. This was thanks to the recent immigration of Moroccan Jews, some of whom became employed as French teachers in anglophone schools. I had become like the colonial subjects Moroccan Jews were – determined to achieve distinction by mastering the linguistic nuances of the metropole. I should add that already in grade school my parents were adamant that I learn French and learn it well. Probably because they were also committed to a Yiddish education for their children, they did not have me pursue the route followed by one friend whose Romanian parents enrolled her in a French collège. It's too bad, really, because by high school Yiddish education was an after-school disaster. Still, having studied Yiddish, Polish. and Hebrew after leaving Montreal, and despite so many years of minimal contact with French, the language, especially as it's still spoken by some segments of the Quebec population, feels to me like *mameloshn* (Yiddish, lit. mother tongue) and my current facility has atrophied. The truth is that if you know the economic sociology of Montreal Jews at the time, it was really *tateloshn* (father tongue), since fluency in French enabled our fathers to engage in trade. The mothers I knew mostly stayed home, and unless they worked full time in family stores, they were generally less comfortable with the local vernacular.

The Best Place for a Jew?

So, has there ever been a better home for Jews than Canada? Growing up in Montreal especially in the 1960s, I, like many others, would have answered at the time no. In the 1960s we had Expo, possibly the best World's Fair ever. And its success had much to do with two Jews in particular. First, it was a retired Jewish army officer who instituted the "critical path" that enabled the completion of the planning. Almost miraculously, the exposition was delivered on time despite scepticism that Montreal could achieve it, since it was built on a dramatically curtailed time frame after Moscow suddenly reneged on its commitment to host.[23] Second, it was an Israeli immigrant and graduate of McGill's School of Architecture whose doctoral dissertation became Expo's most enduring installation – Habitat – and probably the most important modern building ever designed in Canada. It's still a stunning tribute to brutalism. By the time Expo was over, Moshe Safdie had become "the most talked-about architect in the world."[24] Of course, not everything in which Montreal Jews took pride had a Jewish connection: the hockey team was legendary, and there was a beautiful new subway that became a model for systems elsewhere including Mexico City and Washington, DC. There was an impressive new performing arts centre that continues to act as an anchor for new arts-related buildings including music, dance, and cinema and new apartment buildings for those who want to live near them. Just above Central Station the city sported a striking new skyscraper. The work of I.M. Pei, its design took a cue from the most iconic symbol of the city, the cross on top of Mount Royal. Not a Jewish symbol to be sure, but not of much concern to local Jews, whose own imprint on the city was through food. By the time the cross had lost its symbolic gravitas among Catholic Montrealers, bagels and smoked meat were vying for pre-eminence with poutine. Unlike Pei, Mies Van der Rohe ignored local icons when he put his imprint on the western edge of downtown with the elegant Westmount Square. And Old Montreal adjacent to the port, which had been spared from earlier plans for demolition, had begun its revival as a tourist destination and soon-to-be-popular up-scale residential quarter, and gave the city a distinctly European ambience. The city had a large number of universities including at least two of international stature. And the country had a new prime minister who was sexier in his own way and certainly smarter than anyone else's leader. And he was one of our own – a Montrealer. In Lenny Bruce's famous parsing of Jewish and goyish, Trudeau was Jewish. He ran in a Jewish riding. And my aunt was his campaign manager.

Still, the undercurrents of discontent were there, and with violence already erupting, a pall was cast on Montreal's lustre and perhaps on the very future of Canada. In the 1970s when doomsayers thought Canada might not survive, what seemed to hold it together was Canadians' fear of losing their health insurance and being absorbed by the United States. Today, many Americans I talk to marvel at their neighbour to the north. They admire Canadian cities, with their low crime, vibrant downtowns, and mass transit. And they envy Canadians for their affordable universities, stable retirement plans, single-payer health insurance, and a respectable leader who at the very least does not make the country ashamed. As the caption for a comical ad showing an extremely handsome Justin Trudeau reads: "Hey girl, I'll cover your preexisting condition." It's as if America had a pre-existing condition that Canada alone knows how to mend.

Is Canada the best place for a Jew to live? Maybe, or at least arguably, yes. But it's had more than a few rough spots, as the essays in Alan Davies's edited volume or Ira Robinson's book make clear.[25] And truly shameful ones at that, as Irving Abella and Harold Troper reveal in their deeply disturbing indictment of Canada's lack of response to the plight of European Jewry before, during, and even after the Second World War.[26] But, that was a long time ago. Moreover, Canada's reluctance to accept refugees stemmed not only stem from antisemitism. It also had to do with the economic sluggishness of the 1930s and the fear that new immigrants would compete with older Canadians for jobs. The postwar political realignment and the belief that immigration would spur economic development created a climate in favour of immigration. The prosperity that ensued and the need for more workers and consumers made Canada all the more open to increased immigration, though initially with preferential consideration of the "right" people in terms of ethnic and national background and with the "right" skills, that is labourers. The more the economy expanded, the larger the number of immigrants allowed into the country. The more insignificant

Jews were proportional to the non-Jews, the less of a problem Jewish immigration became.[27]

As long as Canada remains prosperous and not run by a moron, it might very well claim to be the best place for a Jew to live. But Australia would probably make the same claim were it not on fire and probably doomed unless we find a solution to global warming. Jewish residents of the UK used to feel that way until neoliberal mismanagement started threatening to run the economy off the cliff. And for a very long time France did as well, though continuing economic doldrums plus an underclass of unemployed Arab youth seem to have made the country feel less and less a place in which Jews want to live. Germany once was as well, and were it not for the taint of its terrible modern history might be able to make that claim legitimately. Though here too, some, perhaps many of its Muslim immigrants have not yet learned that as new Germans they, too, must now assume responsibility for the Holocaust just as North American Jews must for the murder of the Indigenous people of the New World and for US slavery. And Babylon and Morocco were once good places for Jews to live. We forget that Baghdad was once a very Jewish city. And Jews certainly left their mark on Istanbul. For a couple of centuries Poland was a pretty good place for Jews. And Spain and Portugal before that. And both of the latter two had a better climate and much better wines than Canada. Medieval Hebrew poetry celebrates them. And if I'm not mistaken, ancient Rome was not such a bad place for a Jew once he or she was manumitted.

My point is that good places for Jews have a lot to do with robust economies, with stable governments, and a consensus in which difference is at least tolerated and immigrants welcomed because they're good for business. All are labile, as the histories of the multiple examples above make clear.

As my own recollection of a southern Manitoba Centennial play suggests, given the peculiar place of the Jew in Western thought – whether as Judas or as Shylock – there exists a readily accessible reservoir of suspicion towards this eternal outsider that can be called upon to support distorted and often conspiratorial histories. Fortunately, in Canada those drawing from that reservoir have largely been a lunatic fringe. Without the panic that accompanies declining classes because of waning industries, persistent economic crises, and the declining value of housing and currency, all of which provide the fuel for rabble rousers, conspiracy theories will remain no more than that. So, what can I say? Enjoy the good times while they last. Nothing is forever. But right now is certainly Canada's time, as it is for Canada's Jews.

NOTES

1 Helen Davies, *The Politics of Participation: A Study of Canada's Centennial Celebration* (Winnipeg: University of Manitoba, 1999), 182–3.
2 Pierre Berton, *1967: The Last Good Year* (Toronto: Doubleday Canada, 1997), 43.
3 Ibid., 44.
4 Ibid., 40.
5 Ibid., 49
6 Ibid., 48
7 Davies, *The Politics of Participation*, 19.
8 Ibid., 25.
9 *Guelph Mercury* (Ontario), 26 July 1966.
10 Peter H. Aykroyd, *The Anniversary Compulsion: Canada's Centennial Celebrations: A Model Mega-Anniversary*. (Toronto: Dundurn Press, 1992), 146.
11 *Guelph Mercury*, 26 July 1966.
12 *Swift Current Sun* (Saskatchewan), 12 April 1966.
13 Ibid.
14 Aykroyd, *The Anniversary Compulsion*, 145.
15 Ibid.
16 Memorandum to Board of Directors. Youth Travel Exchange Program, Part I – Federal-Provincial Youth Travel, Budget, Appendix B (BD 65-56).
17 "The Explorers," *Virtual Museum of New France*. Canadian Museum of History.
18 For a discussion of the different symbolic repertoires of centennial and bicentennial celebrations in Australia and the United States as well as the different emphasis on political and geographic themes, see Lyn Spillman, *Nation and Commemoration: Creating National Identities in the United States and Australia* (Cambridge: Cambridge University Press, 1997), 125–6.
19 I should note that relying entirely on memory for this essay is problematic, and I am curious to know what else is in the play that I didn't make note of back then. So, I did try to track down a copy of the script. There is a historical society in Winkler and even a museum. But so far no trace of the play. If there is or was a local newspaper, the Library and Archives of Canada could find no trace of one.
20 Richard Menkis, "Antisemitism and Anti-Judaism in Pre-Confederation Canada," in *Antisemitism in Canada: History and Interpretation*, ed. Alan Davies (Waterloo, ON: Wilfrid Laurier University Press, 1992), 12–13. For a more extensive consideration of this issue see Pierre Anctil's *Histoire des juifs du Québec* (Montreal: Boréal, 217), 19–38.
21 Caroline Alphonso, "Canadians Don't Know Their History, Study Shows," *Globe and Mail*, 9 November, 2007.

22 See the discussion of the indifference to an antisemitic *Borat* skit performed in a Tucson bar in Neil Strauss, "Sacha Baron Cohen: The Man behind the Mustache," *Rolling Stone*, 30 November 2006, and from the same film his conversation with a group of frat boys on the power of minorities including Jews.

23 Berton, *1967*, 266.

24 Ibid., 299.

25 Davies, ed., *Antisemitism in Canada*; Ira Robinson, *A History of Antisemitism in Canada* (Waterloo, ON: Wilfred Laurier University Press, 2015).

26 Irving Abella and Harold Troper, *None Is Too Many: Canada and the Jews of Europe 1933–1948* (New York: Random House, 1982), 282.

27 Ibid., esp. 238–78.

17 *In der heym in kanade*: A Survey on Yiddish Today

Introduction

Yiddish has served as a portable homeland for centuries and continues to do so in changing ways in contemporary Canada. A language forged out of the Jewish diaspora experience, Yiddish formed an integral part of a thousand-year-old European civilization. Today, a century after the period of mass Yiddish-speaking immigration from eastern Europe and some seventy years after the Holocaust marked the obliteration of that Yiddish heartland, the language continues to offer an emotional, cultural, intellectual, and spiritual home to a diverse group of Jewish – and some non-Jewish – Canadians. Yiddish offers a key to a history and heritage, to family, to the losses of the Holocaust, to values of social justice, to literature and music, to religious tradition, and to comfort. This sense of Yiddish as home is enduring and multifaceted. In this chapter I explore the place of Yiddish in Canada today based on the results of a recent survey I conducted as part of my larger research project titled "Cultural Transmission after Catastrophe: Yiddish in Canada after the Holocaust."[1]

During the last century, Yiddish has been transformed from the daily spoken language of a vast majority of the Canadian Jewish population to a language increasingly expressing connection with heritage, memory, and ethnicity. Yiddish as mother tongue of Canadian Jews (first language learned) declined from a high of 96 per cent in 1931 to about 3 per cent in 2016, according to census statistics, due to the attrition of its daily speakers and lack of intergenerational transmission. Within the Canadian mainstream, Yiddish is most often encountered in individual words such as *shmooze* (to chat) or *kibitz* (to joke around) or as lyrics to klezmer music. The language now functions as a key to an immigrant or pre-Holocaust past, a facet of Jewish identity or other forms of personal identity, or as a tool for creativity or research, but is spoken by a very few. Outside of insular Hassidic enclaves in the Montreal and Toronto areas, where the language is spoken across generations in deliberate continuity with a traditional Jewish collective past and to form a deliberate barrier from the mainstream, Yiddish is increasingly *invoked* rather than spoken, employed as punctuation or accessed in translation rather than used for communication. Rhetoric associated with Yiddish as "dead," "dying," or as undergoing "revival" abounds in both scholarly and popular realms. And yet, as my recent Canada-wide survey indicates, the connections of Canadians to the language remain strong and compelling, diverse, in flux, and oftentimes surprising.

Today, engagement with Yiddish within Canada's mainstream – Jewish and non-Jewish – is always voluntary. As a language historically maligned by outsiders, Yiddish formed a flashpoint for the ideological battles emerging from Jewish Enlightenment (Haskalah/Haskole) of the nineteenth century, which incited activists to fight for the recognition of Yiddish as a language of modern life and cultural production.[2] As the shared Jewish vernacular for a majority of European Jewry, Yiddish came to form the basis for a large-scale and resilient Jewish cultural life in Europe and its immigrant hubs worldwide that spanned the ideological spectrum from Orthodox to secular and radically left-wing. A vast majority of the six million victims of the Holocaust were Yiddish speakers. Decimated by the Holocaust, the hegemony of Ivrit (modern Hebrew) as part of the founding of the state of Israel, severe repression in the Soviet Union, and linguistic acculturation worldwide, modern Yiddish culture moved to the margins of Jewish life.

Only in the Hassidic world, where engagement with Yiddish increasingly serves as a community boundary marker from the mainstream, has the vernacular use of Yiddish increased. Here scholars frame Hassidic Yiddish as a "one-way barrier" to the secular world as well as a manifestation of positive values,[3] or as a marker of a distinctive Hassidic ethnicity that embodies the community's cultural values.[4] Estimates place the number of Yiddish speakers worldwide between 500,000 and one million, virtually all of them Hassidim. Given that the Hassidic population doubles each generation due to high birthrates and retention, the global number of Yiddish speakers is certain to expand. Canada's census indicates a marked increase in the number of people claiming Yiddish as the language most often spoken at home between 2006 to 2016 from 3,130 to 7,080, from 1 per cent to closer to 2 per cent of the Canadian Jewish population.[5] We can assume that this rising population comprises Hassidim, by far the fastest growing demographic in today's Jewish population.

Ivrit (Hebrew) has largely assumed the role of Jewish ethnic language in Canada, in particular within Jewish day and afternoon schools. Within traditional eastern European Jewish civilization, Hebrew and Yiddish co-existed in a system of diglossia (internal bilingualism), with Hebrew as the language of prayer and sacred text and Yiddish the language of communication. With the decline of Yiddish as vernacular, Hebrew maintained and expanded its role as the global Jewish language. Today, Hebrew serves as language of Jewish prayer and sacred text, and the communicative language of the state of Israel and an Israeli culture that has been disseminated worldwide. Hebrew functions as an international Jewish language and Yiddish is associated with one Jewish ethnic group, predominantly linked to the Ashkenazi experience. With subsequent waves of Jewish immigration from non-Yiddish-speaking countries such as Morocco and Algeria, Yiddish ceased to serve as the lingua franca of Canadian Jewry. According to Leo Davids's article "Hebrew and Yiddish in Canada: A Linguistic Transition Completed," Yiddish has ceded its place to Hebrew as the Jewish ethnic language.[6] On the most recent 2016 Canadian census, some 75,000 people declared themselves to have knowledge of Hebrew, including some 20,000 who declared the language as mother tongue (Israelis and their families living in the country), compared with 21,000 people declaring knowledge of Yiddish and some 13,000 with Yiddish mother tongue.[7] This Yiddish mother tongue group is increasingly composed of Hassidim, who enact the model of traditional Ashkenazi diglossia. Knowledge of Hebrew and Yiddish is by no means mutually exclusive and the two languages were taught side by side in networks of Jewish day schools across Canada for decades ranging from Communist to Labour Zionist to traditional. However, with demographic changes and the accompanying decline in a collective rationale for teaching or otherwise promoting the language, Yiddish has largely vanished from the mainstream of Jewish life as a communicative language. One younger respondent in my survey identified a division of labour between Yiddish and Hebrew: "I was raised with Yiddish music and expressions, along with Hebrew music and language."

In the mainstream, Yiddish forms a "usable past" for descendants of a vanished European Jewish civilization, adherents of leftist ideologies, those who seek an alternative to Israeli or religious culture, or those who are compelled by the challenge to the dominant, heteronormative world view offered by the non-hegemonic and marginal culture of Yiddish (also known as queer Yiddishkeit). Popularly referred to as *"mame loshn"* (mother tongue or mother's language), Yiddish continues to evoke positive feelings or values for many. One can posit that those descendants of Yiddish eastern European civilization who remained committed to the language are acting in continuity with their family heritage. One can also identify those who engage with the language – Jewish and non-Jewish – as countercultural, resisting dominant linguistic and cultural trends in Jewish life. Unlike other heritage, ethnic, or second languages, there is no Yiddish homeland to travel to, welcome immigrants from, or benefit from culturally. Yiddish yields no economic or political advantages. Even the once-existing sense of an international Jewish collective with Yiddish as its shared denominator has faded. In sum, why would anyone engage with Yiddish today? Is it simply a memorial to a lost past or a form of nostalgia? Does Yiddish have a future in Canada outside of the Hassidic world?

As a scholar of Yiddish Canada, I have documented the shift in the language from a dominant vernacular during the period of mass Jewish immigration through today with a focus on the shifting cultural expressions of the language: literature, education, theatre, and, most recently, film. After the period of rich Yiddish cultural productivity in Canada before 1950, the trajectory has been one of decline. However, as someone who has devoted two decades to studying and often working with the language's various promoters – writers, teachers, actors, theatre and film producers – and as an instructor of Yiddish in university and community settings, I am fascinated by the enduring engagement of Canadian Jews with the language and the ways in which it continues to change and evolve. It appears unlikely that mainstream Canadian Jewry as a whole will ever return to speaking Yiddish with any fluency or raise their children in the language; it is also unlikely that Canadian Jews will cease to seek out connections with the language in innovative and dynamic ways, in particular given the advent of new technologies to facilitate outreach and dissemination. For example, the web sitcom *YidLife Crisis* (2014–2020, ongoing) – created by, and featuring, two Montrealers conversing in Yiddish about contemporary life – went viral via the web-sharing platform of YouTube and became a site for hundreds of thousands of viewers to hear Yiddish dialogue that was translated into Yiddish from an original English script and offered with subtitles. Producing creative projects in Yiddish no longer requires fluency in Yiddish, nor does expressing a sense of personal identity connected with the language. The language no longer needs to be passed down through the generations: it can be learned in a university or community classroom, or in an interactive online course. Yiddish can be encountered in music within a growing klezmer "revival" scene established in the 1970s one of whose hallmarks is the pairing of instrumental music rooted in Jewish tradition with Yiddish lyrics.[8] These innovations will continue to mould and alter the course of Yiddish in Canada as well as globally. Through it all, Yiddish remains resilient and flexible.

The Survey

Here I present the findings of my Yiddish survey and investigate what they suggest in terms of the present and future of the language in its Canadian context. Launched in September of 2017 with a national campaign targeting individuals involved with Yiddish through existing cultural organizations as well as social media, the SurveyMonkey online questionnaire consisted of ten questions that took an average of five minutes to complete. An invitation to complete the survey was emailed to contacts I had within the Canadian Yiddish world – language instructors in university programs and community settings, performers, and cultural organizations – as well as two assistants who are well connected in the Yiddish world based in Toronto and Vancouver.[9] The survey was also posted on social media sites, including Facebook and Twitter. Respondents further circulated the survey itself. It snowballed; I received almost five hundred responses from individuals ranging from leading figures in the world of Yiddish performance and seasoned translators to relative newcomers to Yiddish. My interest here is not as a social scientist but rather as a researcher of the cultural evolution of Yiddish Canada. Rather than attempt to provide an exhaustive quantitative analysis, I offer a qualitative analysis where I identify and analyse some of trends I observed in the survey data regarding Yiddish in Canada today.

Through the short format and inclusive questions, I hoped to elicit a wide sample of responses from people who self-identified as engaging with Yiddish. My intended audience was anyone who selected to take a few minutes to share their connections to the language; it did not assume any fluency in speaking, reading, or writing, nor did it assume a Yiddish heritage or Jewish background. Given the format of an online survey in an unquestionably secular context, I did not expect – or receive – responses from the Hassidic community, where my research has instead focused on in-person interviews with questions that assume fluency in the language. Rather, I reached out to a broad swath of the Canadian Yiddish world to get a sense of who was engaging with the language, and how they were doing so, within the mainstream. As such, I tried to construct questions that might reflect this diversity. I anticipated – and received – relatively high numbers of responses from respondents who identified as secular Jews who have historically aligned Jewishness with culture and history rather than religious observance or practice; this group draws on values of social justice such as those associated with the left-wing labour movement of the Yiddish immigrant period as well as its traditions of literature and song. In keeping with the amorphous concept of Yiddishkeit/Yiddishkayt, the Yiddish terms for "Jewishness" and the positive values it embodies, I received responses from across the religious spectrum, from traditionally observant to "Just Jewish/ethnically Jewish," as well as non-Jewish.

Given the demographics of Yiddish use today within mainstream Canada, the survey focused more on the users' engagement with Yiddish than on the language itself. Respondents indicated that they access Yiddish in a variety of contexts that do not require sustained fluency in the language. As to the reasons when, where, or why they speak or engage with Yiddish, respondents provided varied responses to the open-ended questions that drew on their personal histories, hybrid identities, or interests. This stands in sharp contrast to my findings within the Hassidic communities, where the same interview question received fairly consistent responses: "I speak Yiddish with my family, friends and community and do so most of the time. I learned it at home and speak it with my children/grandchildren."[10] The question, "Why do you speak Yiddish?" was more often than not met with mild shock or amusement and a simple, "Because it is my language" by Hassidic respondents, who were far more interested in offering their ideas on topics such as how the language itself has changed in terms of influences from English. The survey results confirmed what I had previously guessed: those who choose to engage with Yiddish today outside of the Hassidic world do so in a deliberate and eclectic manner. The language is far from "dead" or "dying"; rather, it is adapting itself to new contexts within an amorphous and diverse community of people who choose to engage with it and do so in individualized and fluid ways. Here I present some of the questions from the survey followed by an analysis of the responses.

Question: Please state your name, year and place of birth, and where you were raised.

This question elicited a wide variety of responses that point to the diversity of those engaging with Yiddish in Canada today. Of the total 485 responses, 89 did not provide a date of birth. For the remainder, I was not surprised to find the largest demographic of responses (204) from those born between 1943 and 1962 ("baby boomers"), a cohort that includes the children of the last generation of European-born Yiddish speakers born during and after the Holocaust. Their parents would have theoretically spoken Yiddish with or around their children, involved them in Yiddish cultural activity, sent them to schools where Yiddish was taught, and imbued them with a love for the language. If they were raised within the dense Jewish immigrant neighbourhoods such as Montreal's Mile End district, they might have experienced an immersive Yiddish environment where the language was spoken in various contexts: at home, on the street, in school, and at cultural activities. As bilinguals, one would expect their connections with Yiddish to be deep-rooted and abiding. Further, as potentially recent retirees, this cohort might have new time and energy to devote to Yiddish cultural activity.

The next largest group, born before 1942 (100), includes European-born native Yiddish speakers or the children of an earlier generation of Yiddish speakers from the mass eastern European Jewish immigration that took place from 1900 to 1920. This demographic would have experienced Yiddish mass culture first-hand in Europe or following immigration to Canada. The number of survey respondents was limited by the shrinking of this cohort due to natural aging as well as potentially less familiarity with technology such as online surveys compared with the younger group.

I expected the number of respondents to diminish rapidly under the age of 50 and indeed, they did. Here, the relative number of younger people involved with Yiddish is reduced by the fact that most of these younger respondents would have come to Yiddish in ways other than intergenerational transmission: they might be grandchildren of European-born Yiddish speakers, have studied the language, or embraced Yiddish performance. They would have had to deliberately seek out Yiddish as an interest. What I found is that the cohorts born between 1963 and 1982 ("Generation X") and 1983–1997 ("Millennials") – which comprised 50 and 41 respondents respectively – did, in fact, engage with Yiddish more via performance than as a spoken language. I received a single response from a respondent born after 1998.

Indeed, raising children in Yiddish outside of the Hassidic world today is challenging and undertaken by a tiny minority for various ideological reasons. Ingrid Piller's study "Private Language Planning: The Best of Both Worlds?" discusses childhood bilingualism where parents decide to raise their children to speak a second language that is not widely spoken. Her findings that this minority phenomenon is largely the purview of "elite bilinguals" – "middle-class international couples, expatriates, academics who raise their children in a non-native language, etc."[11] – applies to Yiddish if one extends the concept of "elite" to include those most ardently and ideologically committed to the continuity of Yiddish as a living, spoken language. My own research indicates that the rare cases of non-Hassidic Canadian families raising Yiddish-speaking children tends to occur in households where there is a second non-official language spoken. For example, one Ottawa family that I interviewed operates in Yiddish (a native language of the husband, the son of a Yiddish activist raised in both Yiddish and Italian) and Cantonese (a native language of the wife), with English as the shared home language. Raising children in Yiddish requires a basic ease of fluency that most non-Hassidic parents today lack. Those who have taken Yiddish courses will likely still lack the distinct vocabulary of childhood; even in Hassidic communities where children are raised in Yiddish, women have had to evolve a particular idiom in which to do so.[12] The challenges of raising Yiddish-speaking children in the mainstream are compounded by a lack of playmates and childcare facilities as well as a dearth of resources such as toys, games, books, or audiovisual materials. The exception is Yiddish children's songs, which exist in abundance, but even these have not been widely recorded.

For young adults seeking to engage with the language, myriad organizational websites encourage interactive online exploration of the Yiddish past and present. For example, *The Yiddish Daily Forward* is an online newspaper whose website allows readers to mouse over words to learn their English meaning as well as offers a selection of short, subtitled videos; the Yiddish Book Center offers free access to an almost entirely digitized Yiddish literature (some 11,000 titles) as well as hundreds of audio files in Yiddish. These sites, combined with immersive and online educational programs to promote Yiddish, foster and bolster enduring interest in Yiddish among future generations.[13]

These survey data may also suggest a trend around stage of life: perhaps interest in Yiddish increases with age, in particular around retirement? Anecdotally, I can attest to having taught Yiddish in adult education contexts for over twenty years and always having an enthusiastic cohort of 55–75-year-old learners in the class. If Yiddish is connected to genealogical investigation or a search for ethnic roots, a degree of ongoing popular interest may be abiding, in particular in connection with the expansion of heritage tourism trips to eastern Europe.

In terms of geographic origin and current location, the responses indicated over sixty locations around the globe. Given the long-standing history of Yiddish immigration and enduring cultural activity in Canada's urban centres of Montreal, Toronto, Winnipeg, and Vancouver, I expected – and received – responses primarily from those areas. Due to its particular importance as a focal point for national Yiddish cultural activity, reception of the largest group of Holocaust survivors and home to a majority of Hassidim, Montreal was particularly well represented. I received 112 responses from Montreal, 95 from Toronto, 40 from Winnipeg and 14 from Vancouver. I also expected to find respondents originating from pre- or immediately post-Holocaust Europe who arrived in Canada as Yiddish speakers; this expectation was also borne out: 14 indicated origins from Poland, 12 from Russia, and another dozen from Uzbekistan, Ukraine, and other eastern European locations. The 20 respondents from Germany (all of them born before 1962) included individuals whose families had survived the Holocaust and found themselves in German displaced-persons camps as well as a few of non-Jewish German origin who had gravitated towards Yiddish. The remainder of the respondents came from Israel (10), New York (9), smaller cities across Canada (Ottawa, Calgary, etc.), as well as individual responses from Latin America, South Africa, and New Zealand.

These responses underline the global character of Canada's Yiddish community as well as its concentration in urban hubs with strong infrastructure to support Yiddish cultural activities. While the structure of organizations to promote Yiddish – in particular a once vibrant educational network for youth – has dwindled across Canada, the main hubs offer diverse opportunities to engage with Yiddish. To mention just a few organizations active during the time of the survey: the city of Montreal boasts the award-winning Dora Wasserman Yiddish Theatre (founded 1958), Yiddish courses and activities at Jewish Public Library (founded 1914); and Klezkanada, an organization that promotes Yiddish culture through music and performance (founded 1996); Toronto is home to an active Friends of Yiddish group that sponsors programming (founded 1984) and the Ashkenaz Festival (founded 1995) that showcases Yiddish performance; Vancouver's Peretz Institute for Secular Jewish Culture (founded 1945) offers Yiddish cultural activities and classes.

Question: List any areas of your present involvement with Yiddish.

I speak Yiddish;
I read in Yiddish for pleasure (works of literature, newspapers);
I write in Yiddish (literature, memoirs, etc.);
I do research in Yiddish;
I translate from Yiddish into another language;
I translate from another language into Yiddish;

I listen to Yiddish music;
I sing Yiddish music;
I perform Yiddish theatre;
I study Yiddish in a group setting;
I participate in a Yiddish reading or conversation group;
I go to Yiddish events such as lectures, plays, or concerts;
I teach Yiddish;
Other

I structured this question to anticipate very diverse forms of engagement with Yiddish beyond speaking the language based on my current research on Yiddish transmission in Canada as well as my own informal experiences in the Yiddish world as a speaker, educator, and participant. I anticipated intersecting access points for Yiddish: through music and performance, language courses, reading texts, or engaging in conversation groups. I also assumed to find respondents who speak no Yiddish at all and are still very engaged with the language in other ways.

This question as a whole is informed by several intersecting socio-linguistic theories on how Yiddish functions today. The concept of "postvernacular Yiddish," as scholar Jeffrey Shandler expresses it, suggests a mode where "the symbolic level of meaning is always privileged over its primary level: the very fact that something is said (or written or sung) in Yiddish is at least as meaningful as the meaning of the words being uttered – if not more so."[14] In contrast to "vernacular Yiddish," where the language is widely used by a diverse group of speakers for a host of purposes – daily communication, literature, performance, and so on – in the "postvernacular" mode, Yiddish functions as a symbolic capacity, found in fragmented form rather than in whole, communicative language. In fact, Shandler suggests:

> Contrary to established definitions of its legitimacy as the equal of other languages, *Yiddish in the postvernacular mode is not necessarily thought of, or even valued, as a separate, complete language.* Its partial, restricted use, including frequent atomization into a limited inventory of individual idioms and words (and even fragments of words), suggests that Yiddish is esteemed for its difference from, rather than its similarity to, other languages. This notion can be understood as enriching rather than impoverishing Yiddish culture by opening up its linguistic boundaries, thereby enabling a variety of engagements with the language other than conventional fluency ... Indeed, as the value of Yiddish as a whole language declines, the esteem of its fragments increases.[15]

A recent example of "postvernacular Yiddish" is the 2017 performance of a Yiddish version of Canada's national anthem performed in honour of the country's 150th birthday. The brainchild of Hindy Nosek-Abelson, a Toronto-based translator of Yiddish poetry and song, the anthem was performed by 150 multigenerational and multicultural choristers for television and widely disseminated via Zoomer Media and promoted via social media.[16] Here Yiddish functioned as a means to bring diverse people together rather than as a means of communication. Tsvi Sadan's 2011 study "Yiddish on the Internet" suggests that Yiddish has entered a new socio-linguistic stage as a "cyber-vernacular," where the advent of the internet allows Yiddish speakers to form virtual speech communities in cyberspace with a potential return to the vernacular mode in a virtual setting.[17] His theory that Yiddish speakers in far-flung geographic locations could meet in cyberspace has not yet been borne out, but with the rapid advent of virtual reality (VR) technology, which includes virtual meeting places for language practice, a virtual Yiddishland might yet be possible. Netta Avineri's study "Yiddish Endangerment as Phenomenological Reality and Discursive Strategy: Crossing into the Past and Crossing out the Present" introduces the concept of "nostalgia socialization" to suggest that Yiddish can form a core component of secular Jewish group identity without being learned or spoken at all; within this "metalinguistic community," discourse takes place *about* (and not *in*) the language, with an emphasis on the notion of Yiddish as endangered.[18] My own study on new media technologies and Yiddish, notably in the areas of social media and film, suggests a further theoretical model for contemporary Yiddish transmission: the "transvernacular," or "communicative Yiddish constructed through translation," for example in the production of Yiddish dialogue for a movie or play.[19] As a researcher, I am interested in the extent to which "postvernacularity," and the increasingly symbolic significance of the language to those who engage with it, relates to the post-Holocaust Yiddish culture produced by Canadian Jews. How has Yiddish culture in Canada moved into the realm of secondary, symbolic level of meaning? What are the implications of this mode for Yiddish cultural transmission?

The survey results confirmed my expectations of diverse points of engagement with Yiddish in Canada today. Of the 485 respondents, 308 indicated that they speak Yiddish, with a majority across all age categories except for those born from 1963 to 1982, where the total was just slightly less than half. The youngest age category, with one respondent, amounted to 100 per cent. This raises some complex questions: what does "speak Yiddish" mean: Fluent ability to communicate? Passive knowledge? Conversational skills derived from a Yiddish course or group? Ability to read or translate a text? The same issue exists with respect to the statistics on language use gathered by the Canadian Census and other agencies: there is no impartial test to determine who is the speaker of a language. Noteworthy for the purposes of this survey is the fact that respondents identified as speakers of Yiddish. This indicates that, in fact, a vast majority are not relating to Yiddish in a strictly "postvernacular" manner but as a vernacular language that they speak.

At the same time, the data point to a multi-pronged commitment to Yiddish, in particular among the demographic born in 1962 or before, which comprise a majority of those who declared themselves Yiddish speakers. With Yiddish as a lesser-spoken, heritage language, one finds high participation in passive activities such as listening to music or attending events such as concerts, lectures, or plays: 321 and 273 respondents respectively. These modes of engagement are accessible in that they do not necessarily require knowledge of Yiddish. However, rather than being predominantly passive, a majority of the respondents actively engaged with Yiddish by singing, reading, or translating as well as attending groups to read or speak in the language.

Music represented the largest area of engagement, with 222 respondents reported singing in Yiddish on a regular basis. Yiddish song has historically played a core role in modern Yiddish culture, with the singing of different repertoires representing a collective activity in all walks of life and across the ideological spectrum: schools, summer camps and youth groups, political gatherings, cultural events, and so on. Yiddish song represents continuity as well as innovation. For some, Yiddish song represents the element of Yiddish that remains most deeply emblazoned from childhood. For others, Yiddish music offers a site of new creativity as Canadian artists have spearheaded projects that feature new interpretations of Yiddish song and involve diverse groups of artists. For example, Henri Oppenheim's album *Tur Malka: New Songs of Yiddish Montreal* (2016) sets the poetry of Canadian Yiddish immigrant writers to new melodies performed by renowned Montreal vocalist Karen Young.[20] Perhaps most famously, eclectic Montreal-based artist Josh "Socalled" Dolgin collaboratively blends Yiddish lyrics with hip hop in his albums *Hiphopkhasene* (2003), *The Socalled Seder* (2005), and *Ghettoblaster* (2007) and has most recently created an original Yiddish musical, *Isaac Babel's Tales from Odessa* (2017).[21] Yiddish musical creativity is supported by an infrastructure of established Canadian organizations – notably Ashkenaz and KlezKanada – as well as international networks that promote concerts, immersive retreats, workshops, and other learning opportunities. Yiddish music has become tremendously diverse in terms of genres and performers, with hybrid forms combining klezmer, jazz, heavy metal, hip hop, rap, rock, and folk produced worldwide by performers with or without Jewish lineage. This vast musical repertoire is widely available for consumption on video-sharing sites such as YouTube as well as in accessible events such as Montreal's popular Klezmer Brunch series that integrates a culinary and musical experience for a wide audience.[22] Not surprisingly, the youngest survey respondent indicated that (s)he speaks Yiddish, listens to Yiddish music, and sings it, which suggests an abiding interest among youth.

Yiddish literature remains a compelling point of engagement for Canadians, according to the survey results. A total of 113 respondents indicated that they read Yiddish literature for pleasure and 48 reported that they write literature in Yiddish; 103 participate in a Yiddish reading or conversation group. This participation in Yiddish literary life is perhaps not surprising, given the seminal role that literary production has played in modern Yiddish culture. Within an eastern European Jewish civilization based on the collective study of sacred text, writers of modern Yiddish literature moved to the fore of Jewish life within the process of secularization of the nineteenth and early twentieth centuries. The *klassiker* (Classic Yiddish Writers) Sholem Aleichem (Shalom Rabinovitz; 1859–1916), Mendele (Mendele Moykher-Sforim, born Sholem Yankev Rabinovotch, 1835–1917), and I.L. Peretz (1852–1915) wrote in both Yiddish and Hebrew, but it was the former in which they reached mass audiences rather than Hebrew, which was at that time a language of a small intelligentsia. Within an explosion of modern Jewish cultural production, thousands of major and minor writers in centres worldwide published in newspapers, journals, and books for wide readerships. As I discuss in my book *Jewish Roots, Canadian Soil: Yiddish Culture in Montreal, 1905–45*, Canada formed the site of multiple daily newspapers and literary journals that published hundreds of Yiddish writers across the country – J.I. Segal, Ida Maze, Chava Rosenfarb, Rokhl Korn, and others – as well as diverse literary organizations.[23] Today, most of this literature is digitized and available open access. New and vastly expanded dictionaries in the *Comprehensive Yiddish-English Dictionary* (2013) and the *Comprehensive English-Yiddish Dictionary* (2016),[24] including online platforms,[25] help facilitate the process of both reading and writing.

The decline of Yiddish as a spoken language has been accompanied by a rise in translation activity. As I suggest in my study "Yiddish Translation in Canada: A Litmus Test for Continuity," translation into and out of Yiddish has played an important role in the history of modern Yiddish literature.[26] The survey respondents indicated their active involvement, with 73 translating out of Yiddish and 36 translating into Yiddish. Until the 1920s, a mass Yiddish readership was introduced to world literature – ranging from European belles-lettres to works of Eastern philosophy – through translation into the language. In the interwar period, a group of writers published Yiddish translations of Canadian and world literature and sacred Hebrew text for a wide readership. Translation into Yiddish today is most often associated with rendering dialogue into Yiddish for theatre productions and other performance projects. In Canada, the Dora Wasserman Yiddish Theatre has commissioned numerous translations of world theatre for its productions, most famously Michel Tremblay's Québécois classic, *Les belles soeurs*. Translation out of Yiddish represents an area of growth, with Yiddish literature most often accessed via translation into other languages. Canadian translators have produced a growing body of anthologies and dedicated volumes of Yiddish poetry, prose, and other genres into English and French. Among Canada's most prolific translators are Pierre Anctil and Chantal Ringuet (Yiddish to French), and Vivian Felsen, Shirley Kumove, Rhea Trebegov, and Goldie Morgentaler (Yiddish to English), to mention just a few. New ventures in crowd-sourcing Yiddish translation such as the "Yiddish Translation Hub" of the Ontario Jewish Archives may serve to promote wider activity.[27] Two final areas of expanding activity in Yiddish are research and education, which point to the increasing prominence of Yiddish in scholarship. Of the survey respondents, 36 engage in research using Yiddish sources and 26 teach Yiddish.

Question: The Yiddish speakers in my family are ... (please choose all that apply)

No one
Me
My spouse or significant other
My parents
My grandparents
My siblings
My children
My grandchildren

For this question, I expected relatively limited choices, with perhaps one or two selections. My research has indicated that Yiddish has not been transmitted intergenerationally in a consistent way after the first immigrant generation within the mainstream Jewish community. With English as the dominant language of economic life and public school education in Canada, Yiddish-speaking immigrants as a group rapidly acculturated linguistically and encouraged their children to embrace English, often opting not to transmit the language at all. The pattern is one of linguistic rupture rather than continuity for the survey respondents. Yiddish-speaking immigrants who arrived in Canada after the Holocaust in the survey's oldest cohort spoke Yiddish with their spouses, siblings, or parents as well as friends and the wider community; their children's first language was Yiddish. The Canadian-raised children – the "Baby Boomer" generation – then attended English-speaking public school and became bilingual, speaking Yiddish at home and English in all other contexts. This second generation raised its own children in English, perhaps turning to Yiddish as a secret language they used among themselves when they did not want the child to understand them. The third generation – "Generation X" and "Millennials" – grew up with a smattering of Yiddish phrases, words, and songs but without the ability to conduct a conversation. They may have engaged with Yiddish in a symbolic capacity or sought to learn the language. These trends were exacerbated by stigmas against maintaining ethnic languages that permeated the Jewish community during the initial period of Yiddish immigration in the late 1940s and early 1950s. By the time Canada embraced policies of official multiculturalism in the 1980s that might have encouraged deliberate retention of Yiddish as a second or third language, the final significant period of immigration of Yiddish speakers in the postwar period had long since passed. Yiddish-speaking immigrants to Canada created milieus to transmit and perpetuate culture in the language. These included school systems where the language was taught, theatres for actors and audiences to engage with Yiddish, community organizations such as libraries, a network of literary associations, publishing projects, and youth-driven initiatives to encourage young people to speak Yiddish (notably Yugntruf [Youth for Yiddish], formed in the 1960s). Ultimately, however, these did not stem the tide of linguistic attrition of Yiddish as a daily spoken language outside of the Hassidic world. Today, it remains very rare to find three generations of Yiddish speakers within the same family. The songs are passed down, but the whole, spoken language is not.

According to scholars of ethnic language retention, this pattern of a bilingual second generation and minority of speakers in the third generation is common among Canadian immigrant groups more broadly. Statistics Canada analyst René Houle identifies factors behind ethnic language retention such as marriage within the group, ongoing immigration to replenish the population of speakers, and abiding connections with the homeland.[28] For Yiddish, the homeland was destroyed in the Holocaust and the last sizable wave of Yiddish-speaking immigrants arrived in its wake. Today, only the Hassidic enclaves – established in New York, Montreal, Paris, London, and Jerusalem – experience a transnational Yiddish-speaking community. For the Canadian mainstream, there is no Yiddish-speaking homeland to return to or to replenish the population of speakers. Further, Yiddish offers limited popular culture to appeal to the mainstream in terms of television programs, movies, or other media that might encourage Yiddish use. While such products are produced for a mass market within the Hassidic world, their religious orientation and ideology as well as the particular variant of Hassidic Yiddish (with its own spelling system and prominence of religious terminology) render them less accessible or appealing to the mainstream.

Contrary to my expectations, the survey responses point to multi-generational and multi-pronged networks of Yiddish speakers, in particular among the cohort born before 1962. In the 1943–62 group, respondents who spoke Yiddish indicated that they did so with multiple family members across the generations: parents, spouses, and siblings. About a sixth of this group (20 out of 115) said that they regularly spoke with their children, although only 2 said that they spoke with their grandchildren. The younger respondents tended to list older relatives as Yiddish speakers, including both parents and grandparents. For the survey question "I expect that my grandchildren will be Yiddish speakers: True; False; Maybe," I expected – and received – an overwhelming response of "false" here, in contrast to posing the same question to Hassidim in my interviews, where all respondents answered "true." A majority of survey respondents who spoke Yiddish stated that they acquired their Yiddish from their homes/families or school as children, but also worked independently to improve it. Many had attended university or other Yiddish language classes, engaged in independent study and read Yiddish texts, or were involved in some form of Yiddish performance. This indicates that for many of the respondents, Yiddish represents a commitment to which they devote both time and energy.

**Question: Please answer one or both: I speak Yiddish because ...
I am involved with Yiddish because ...**

This open-ended question yielded multiple responses that underline the deep meaning that Yiddish holds for those who engage with it today. These are presented here organized into two broad categories:

connections to family and the past, and connections to the arts and professional activity.[29]

Connection to family and the past formed the most common response. Respondents across the various age cohorts wrote of honouring, remembering, and identifying with family ancestry – often in an emotional way – regardless of whether or not the respondent was a Yiddish speaker. Many of the responses expressed the important place Yiddish holds in their hearts and souls. For example, a respondent from the 1983–97 cohort wrote, "I am involved with Yiddish because I identify with its surrounding culture and its emotional significance occupies a deep space in my heart. I also do it to honour my late grandparents and learn about their earlier life." Another from the 1963–82 cohort stated, "I am involved with Yiddish because it speaks to my heart, my *neshomeh* [soul] and it connects me to my grandparents and the world they came from." A respondent from the 1943–62 cohort stated, "Yiddish touches my heart and connects me to my ancestors." Respondents wrote of Yiddish reminding them of parents or grandparents and feeling like the language was their first language, even if it was not. They expressed a sense of responsibility to upholding their Yiddish heritage and the cultural and political legacies associated with it. For some, the language also represented a way of being Jewish, as one respondent born 1963–82 stated: "It connects me to my Yiddish-speaking ancestors and grandparents (who passed before I began learning Yiddish). As a secular Jew and Atheist, Yiddish language and culture are also the primary way I interact with my Jewish heritage and practice Jewishness in my daily life." Respondents who had heard Yiddish as children expressed strong sentiments of comfort and home, as a respondent from the 1943–62 cohort stated poetically: "I nestle into the sounds of Yiddish, sounds from my childhood." Being "Yiddishly involved" expressed bonds with family members who had loved the language and passed away. For many, Yiddish existed in "echoes" or in the words of children's vocabulary and offered a link to their own childhood years. Some sought out Yiddish activities in the wider community when there were no family members left to speak to them and, as one respondent stated, "it got lonely" (cohort born before 1942). Respondents also expressed the concept of Yiddish as a "secret language" that they spoke with siblings when they did not want others to understand.

More broadly, many respondents spoke of Yiddish as part of a wider Jewish collective past that must be preserved. As one respondent stated (no age given), "[Yiddish] is a big part of who I originally am. It created my 'original instructions.' I continue to make an effort because I don't want to throw our *yerushe* [heritage] in the garbage. And I think the marginalization of Yiddish in the Jewish community is the result of trauma and bringing it back will heal us all." Another respondent, born between 1963 and 1982, referred to Yiddish as "an expressive language and connects me to my Eastern European Jewish roots." Respondents cited a sense of responsibility to learn more about Yiddish, despite it having been uprooted: "If my grandparents hadn't been forced out of Europe, there's a good chance we'd still be living in Yiddish today. The arrival of European Jews on North American soil – or any other soil – does not erase that thousand-year history. Yiddish is the story of how the Jews got to the present moment; isn't it worth exploring that story?" (cohort born 1983–97). Respondents spoke of wanting to learn Yiddish for emotional reasons: "I speak Yiddish, or rather am trying to learn Yiddish, because it makes me laugh and brings me joy. It is close to my heart – and rooted in my Jewish heritage" (cohort born 1943–62). Others spoke of existential reasons, as one respondent born 1942 or earlier expressed: "I am involved with Yiddish because, more than *mama loshn*, it is what, in its use to define politically and culturally the Jewish state of being, influenced how I made my life, and with whom I made my life. And, I think more can be wrung out of the past and used to build a future for the idea of Yiddishkayt." Respondents referred to the obligation to keep Yiddish alive across the age cohorts: "[Yiddish] means the world to me. Hitler murdered six million Jews, a huge proportion of which spoke Yiddish. It is my duty to do what I can to ensure that Yiddish, the language of the Jewish people, does not die with my generation" (cohort born 1943–62); "I love the Yiddish Language and dread the thought of it becoming obsolete" (cohort born 1942 or before). The younger cohorts offered similar ideas: "I speak Yiddish because if I don't who will? I am involved with Yiddish because 'where there is no leader, be a leader'" (cohort born 1983–97); "It is a big part of my family heritage, and we need to make sure that this aspect of Jewish culture does not die off" (cohort born 1998 or after).

Yiddish held a strong emotional connection for the survey's respondents. Among the cohort born before 1962, Yiddish was commonly cited as mother tongue or a language learned early in life. Many mentioned having spoken only Yiddish at home and having only learned English in school. Some had ceased to speak Yiddish once they entered kindergarten while others had maintained the language throughout their lives. As one respondent born before 1942 stated, "It is my first language and sometimes what I want to express can only be done in Yiddish." These respondents expressed a deep emotional connection to the language as well as the broader culture. Some intended to learn to speak it again. A love for or fascination with the language, its sound or expressiveness was expressed by many respondents across the age groups. Respondents expressed a "love" for Yiddish and often presented it as uniquely expressive and untranslatable: "I speak Yiddish because it allows me to express myself like no other language does!" (cohort born 1983–97); "Because I love the language and I feel that it is able to express the many feelings and thoughts that I cannot do in English" (cohort born 1963–82); "I am involved with Yiddish because it is my favourite language – expressive, subversive, hilarious" (cohort born 1963–82); "It's a beautiful language with wonderful expressions and insights which are lost in translation" (cohort born 1943–62); "I LOVE to speak and hear Yiddish … it makes my heart happy to hear it and the colourful way in which everything is described in Yiddish" (cohort born 1943–62); "I love Yiddish, the colourful expressions that cannot be translated and the 'soul' of the language" (cohort born 1943–62); "I love the richness, the humour and the wonderful idiomatic language. I also love sharing stories and expressions with friends" (cohort born 1942 or before); "I speak Yiddish because I love the language and the treasury of expressions it contains" (cohort born 1942 or before).

The second main category of involvement with Yiddish – arts and professional activity – exists in four main areas: music, theatre, research, and professional activity. Several respondents revealed that klezmer music marked a point of entry into Yiddish for them as musicians: "Since we are playing in a klezmer ensemble, the songs should be sung in Yiddish. There's so much interesting repertoire" (cohort born 1983–97). The responses indicate that klezmer music can lead to some language acquisition: "I was initially drawn into it through the klezmer world but I'm at the point where I have a passive vocabulary of a few hundred words" (cohort born 1963–82). The Yiddish theatre, notably the Dora Wasserman Yiddish Theatre (DWYT), offers an intergenerational connection to Yiddish: for example, one respondent stated, "I have always felt a deep connection with Yiddish language and culture. I grew up with the DWYT, watching my mother on the stage. I became involved with the theatre as a child as well. We sang Yiddish songs at home, around holidays and otherwise. My entire Jewish identity is bound up with Yiddish culture" (cohort born 1963–82). The theatre can also offer a point of entry for those with no previous Yiddish background: "I am involved with Yiddish because the DWYT is the best community theatre group around. As a non-Yiddish speaker, non-Jewish person I still want to be a part of it and getting to learn a new language and culture is great" (no age given).

While, as indicated earlier, over 30 respondents indicated that they researched in Yiddish and over 100 indicated that they translated out of or into Yiddish, these areas of activity did not feature prominently in the open-ended questions. One respondent from the 1943–62 cohort stated, "I'm involved with Yiddish because it's the language of my ancestors. Also, I translate and teach Yiddish literature because I want my students to learn that Yiddish literature is world literature and has much to offer today's multicultural readers." A few respondents stated that they spoke Yiddish to interact with clients in professional settings such as Meals on Wheels deliveries. However, research, teaching, translation, and professional uses did not appear as reasons per se as to why the respondents engaged with Yiddish. Rather, these reasons were far more centred on broader meanings behind the language and culture. This points to a postvernacular underpinning of Yiddish in Canada today: those who engage with Yiddish do so for a host of reasons that have far less to do with the practical uses of the language than with its emotional or symbolic value.

These open-ended questions indicate commonalities and differences among the age cohorts. The older cohort appears to relate to Yiddish as a known entity, spoken and familiar, and linked to memories of family and home. Respondents speak of love of the language, family and emotional ties, and its particular characteristics such as expressiveness. The younger cohort seems to relate to Yiddish more as a construct that represents values or ideas – Yiddish honours family members of the past and embodies a specific heritage. This group also relates to Yiddish as a component of musical or theatrical performance and points to the importance of community organizations such as Montreal's Dora Wasserman Yiddish Theatre. Both models of engagement with Yiddish offer avenues for present and future growth of the language as it remains a positive part of people's consciousness. Revealingly, none of the respondents stated that they disliked Yiddish, connected it with negative values or experiences, or felt coerced to speak it, which bodes well for the future. A language can evoke the best version of oneself, and its usage can express the person that one wishes to be, ideologically and creatively.

Concluding Remarks

As a researcher who has been involved with Yiddish for much of my life, I am optimistic about the continued place of Yiddish in Canadian life outside of the Hassidic world. Yiddish continues to offer a home on multiple and fluid levels: it offers a link to family, lineage, heritage, or tradition, and it does so in highly adaptable ways. On a personal note, I first learned Yiddish in Montreal's system of leftist-Zionist Jewish day schools in Montreal (Jewish People's and Peretz Schools and Bialik) in the 1980s during a time when many of my teachers were native speakers, some of them Holocaust survivors, who were able to imbue the language with emotional significance, even if we students did not fully understand why we were learning the language in a classroom. Most of my fellow students had Yiddish-speaking grandparents and we heard Yiddish widely spoken by older people at the local Jewish delicatessens and the Jewish Public Library. I did not have to seek out Yiddish until after I left high school, when I realized that my exposure to Yiddish had been unusual for someone of my age. It was then that I opted to study Yiddish further at the undergraduate and graduate levels, ending up in a doctoral program in Yiddish Studies at Columbia University with a cohort of dedicated New York–based Yiddishists of all ages. As a scholar and someone involved with Yiddish, I became deeply interested in the changing place of Yiddish, in particular within a Canadian context, where the language had once been Montreal's third most-spoken language and the lingua franca of generations of immigrants who built a resilient and wide-reaching cultural life. My investment in the present and future of Yiddish is not unusual in the world of Yiddish academia, where a great many researchers are educated and trained within the networks of Yiddish institutions that are committed in its ongoing use. The results of this survey point to the abiding place of Yiddish, both among the descendants of those Yiddish-speaking newcomers and the wider mainstream. Yiddish offers a diffuse, malleable, linguistically rooted home on multiple levels: it is a link to a noble past and a better future, a historical underdog that embodies values of social justice, an alternative way of expressing Jewishness, and a key to rich repositories of literature, music, and theatre. Yiddish can offer an idealized site for self-definition in a home that is absolutely fluid and inherently inclusive. And it appears to be a home that will remain as part of Canada's Jewish mainstream and beyond.

NOTES

1 This research was supported by the Social Sciences and Humanities Research Council of Canada (SSHRC) in an Insight Grant for the study.
2 The scholarly literature on these developments is extensive beginning in the 1980s. See Sandor L. Gilman's *Jewish Self-Hatred: Anti-Semitism and the Hidden Language of the Jews* (Baltimore: Johns Hopkins University Press,

1986); Emanuel Goldsmith, *Modern Yiddish Culture: The Story of the Yiddish Language Movement* (New York: Shapolsky Books, 1987); Benjamin Harshav, *The Meaning of Yiddish* (Berkeley: University of California Press, 1990).

3 Miriam Isaacs, "Haredi, 'haymish' and 'frim': Yiddish Vitality and Language Choice in a Transnational Multilingual Community," *International Journal of the Sociology of Language* 138 (1999): 9–30.

4 Tatjana Soldat-Jaffe, "Yiddish without Yiddishism: Tacit Language Planning among Haredi Jews," *Journal of Jewish Identities* 3, no. 2 (2010): 1–24.

5 Census Profile, 2016 Census, https://www12.statcan.gc.ca/census-recensement/2016/dp-pd/prof/details/Page.cfm?Lang=E&Geo1=PR&Code1=01&Geo2=&Code2=&Data=Count&SearchText=Canada&SearchType=Begins&SearchPR=01&B1=All&GeoLevel=PR&GeoCode=01.

6 Leo Davids, "Hebrew and Yiddish in Canada: A Linguistic Transition Completed," *Journal of Canadian Jewish Studies* 18–19 (2011): 39–76.

7 Census Profile, 2016 Census.

8 See Abigail Wood, *And We're All Brothers: Singing in Yiddish in Contemporary North America* (London: Routledge, 2016).

9 My thanks to Vivian Felsen and Celia Brauer.

10 My thanks to Steven Lapidus.

11 Ingrid Piller, "Private Language Planning: The Best of Both Worlds?" *Estudios de Sociolingüística* 2, no. 1 (2001), 62.

12 Ayala Fader, *Mitzvah Girls: Bringing Up the Next Generation of Hasidic Jews in Brookyln.* (Princeton, NJ: Princeton University Press, 2009).

13 *The Yiddish Daily Forward/Forverts*, http://Yiddish.forward.com; Yiddish Book Center, https://www.Yiddishbookcenter.org/.

14 Jeffrey Shandler, *Adventures in Yiddishland: Postvernacular Language and Culture* (Berkeley: University of California Press, 2006), 22.

15 Ibid., 194; italics in the original.

16 "The Making of Yiddish O Canada," Zoomer TV, 29 June 2017, http://www.visiontv.ca/shows/Yiddish-o-canada/.

17 Tsvi Sadan, "Yiddish on the Internet," *Language & Communication* 31 (2011): 99–106.

18 Netta Avineri, "Yiddish Endangerment as Phenomenological Reality and Discursive Strategy: Crossing into the Past and Crossing out the Present," *Language and Communication* 38 (2014): 18–32.

19 "New Yiddish Film and the Transvernacular," *Geveb: A Journal of Yiddish Studies*, December 2016, https://ingeveb.org/articles/new-Yiddish-film-and-the-transvernacular.

20 *Magillah: The Music of Henri Oppenheim*, http://www.eng.magillah.com/tur-malka1.html.

21 *Socalled*, https://www.socalledmusic.com.
22 *Klezmer Brunch*, https://www.facebook.com/events/457826584685595/.
23 Rebecca Margolis, *Jewish Roots, Canadian Soil: Yiddish Culture in Montreal, 1905–45* (Montreal and Kingston: McGill-Queen's University Press, 2011).
24 Solon Beinfeld and Harry Bochner, eds, *Comprehensive Yiddish-English Dictionary* (Bloomington: Indiana University Press. 2013); Gitl Schaechter-Viswanath, Paul E. Glasser, and Chava Lapin, eds, *Comprehensive English-Yiddish Dictionary (based on the Lexical Research of Mordkhe Schaechter) / Arumnemik English-Yidish Verterbukh (bazirt Af Di Leksishe Zamlungen Fun Mortkhe Shekhter)* (Bloomington: Indiana University Press, 2016).
25 *Yiddish Dictionary Online*, http://www.Yiddishdictionaryonline.com/.
26 Rebecca Margolis, "Yiddish Translation in Canada: A Litmus Test for Continuity," *TTR (Traduction Terminologie Rédaction)* 19, no. 2 (2006): 149–89.
27 *Yiddish Translation Hub*, Ontario Jewish Archives, http://www.ontario jewisharchives.org/Programs/Yiddish-Translation-Hub.
28 René Houle, "Recent Evolution of Immigrant-Language Transmission in Canada," *Canadian Social Trends*, no. 92 (2011): 3–12.
29 I thank my research assistant William Felepchuk for his contributions to this analysis.

18 Which Canada Are We Talking About? An English-Language Polemic about French in Canadian Jewish History

PIERRE ANCTIL

When I was first invited to the conference upon which this volume is in part built, I initially replied that I had no input to offer specifically because the main question was addressed for the most part to Jews. What could a *goy* convey from a personal and emotional point of view in front of a group discussing the extent to which Jews feel at home in Canadian history and society? As should be evident to even researchers unfamiliar with the discipline, non-Jews do not tend to approach the subject along these evaluative lines and usually refrain from passing judgment from a community-oriented point of reference. In my case, I generally argue in my work that Canadian Jewish history is an invaluable tool to understand the general movement of Canadian history as a larger whole; I study the treatments that British Canadians and French Canadians offered to minorities at different periods in time. A good understanding of Montreal Jewish history is also crucial in reconstructing the city's past in the twentieth century, notably in the economic sphere, in the area of social militancy, and with regards to human rights activism. Montreal Jews have also made important contributions, in many languages, in the realm of literature and the arts, through various forms of creativity broadly defined. In a sense, the lens through which the *goyim* tend to examine Canadian Jewish history is from the specific to the universal, in the hope of shedding light on long-term evolutions that affect all citizens and project new values into the future. The effort in my case is to bring elements of Jewish culture and Jewish identity into the larger narrative of Québécois or Canadian history, solidifying and challenging already existing notions of pluralism, diversity, and religious complexity.

Upon second thought and through the insistence of the organizer of the symposium, I began to see a different side to this question. Not abandoning entirely the distinction based on personal upbringing, community affiliation, and ethnicity, when approaching Canadian Jewish history, I decided to dwell mostly for my presentation on the distinction between research produced in the English and French languages. Curiously, in a sense, the divide in our field between Canada's two official languages reproduces rather closely – with notable exceptions – the difference between Jewish and non-Jewish interpretations of Canadian Jewish history. Most of the scholars and graduate students who approach this history from the angle of the French language do not belong to the Jewish community and cannot claim to have a Jewish heritage by birth.[1] In research produced in English, the opposite is generally true. This separation, which is largely the product of circumstances and did not appear by design, is perhaps somewhat easier to deal with than issues having to do directly with ethnicity. After all, almost nobody would claim that being Jewish is a prerequisite to engaging academically in Jewish history or culture, even if in Canada the vast majority of significant careers in this field rest on solid personal Jewish backgrounds. Essentialist considerations, most scholars would agree, do not lead to great advances in knowledge; quite the opposite. With language, the discussion might be somewhat more pertinent, and perhaps we should dare engage in that direction within the broader context of Canadian university life, and Jewish studies within it.

My remarks in this respect should be conceived as a gesture of goodwill and as an attempt at mutual understanding, not as a pique to criticize virulently a field of study that is much in need of new start in this respect. I am personally very attached and committed to the field, and would certainly refrain from any pronouncements likely to hurt some of my colleagues. I am nonetheless convinced that francophone and anglophone researchers interested in Canadian Jewish history have not really learned to work together, or have often failed to take advantage of the advances achieved in the recent years by their counterparts across the linguistic divide. This dichotomy has produced a split that is close to becoming unbridgeable, unless serious efforts are devoted to reducing the distance between the two camps. As usual in a Canadian context, the estrangement is more severe on the side of those using the dominant language for their work and publications, namely English, and somewhat less intense among those, usually French speakers, who can read both official languages fluently. What could be more Canadian than such a statement, perhaps even more Canadian than strictly Jewish Canadian? The consequence of this mutual alienation has been the emergence in the recent years of two separate domains in the study of Canadian Jewish history, each with its own set of variables and perceptions. Communication between these academic entities has been minimal, if not non-existent, with the result that we are wasting precious energy and are failing to come to terms with pressing issues altogether.

It has come to a point where a serious disconnect has manifested itself between francophone and anglophone practitioners of Canadian Jewish history on several key issues, precisely because we are not examining archival material the same way or at least not reading the historical narrative from the same point of reference. Perhaps even this much is lost to most observers. In other social sciences, this dichotomy would be taken as an occasion to press forward into unchartered territory, in a common effort to decipher the not-so-distant past. In our field we have mostly missed the occasion to stand up to a serious challenge. This increasing isolation of research done in the English language from its francophone equivalent has produced a dissonance that is very embarrassing to contemplate and difficult to justify outside our immediate domain, if it is perceived at all. In certain cases we have come to diametrically opposed interpretations of Canadian Jewish history, without realizing it or without being willing to face the actual significance of these glaring inconsistencies and contradictions. Data used in French-language publications for years has in many cases been absent from discussions taking place in the other official language – often for lack of linguistic competence – if it is not ignored altogether because of a professed indifference to other cultural approaches. Likewise, the prolonged absence of contact with specialists in the field of Jewish studies has hindered francophone efforts to grasp more fully and conclusively the consequences of structural antisemitism in Catholic teaching before the Vatican council and in certain French Canadian nationalist movements. Most troubling is the fact that much of the French-language historical sources available to Canadian Jewish historians have not been seriously consulted or analysed due to lack of linguistic skills.

This disaffection is nowhere more visible and more embarrassing to contemplate than in the study of the relations of Jews historically to French Canada. Students are often prompt in my Canadian Jewish studies graduate classes at the University of Ottawa to point to the irreconcilable differences of interpretation between English- and French-language monographs published in the last few years on the subject. Many times I have read dismay on their faces upon discovering that different authors point in clearly opposite directions, do not cite each other, or do not refer in their conclusions to all the data available. Such discrepancies do not speak very highly of our field or its level of professionalism. In fact, it points to a silo mentality where individual trajectories are the norm, an approach that tends to leave out of the picture the broader critical discussions that usually underpin solid academic advances. My graduate students find that well-known English-language books in the field that propose to analyse French Canada's reaction to the great eastern European migration of the early twentieth century do not contain French-language sources or discuss key elements broached by their francophone equivalents.[2] In some cases, the methodological weaknesses and omissions are so overwhelming on the part of certain authors that I have had to strike them from my course syllabi. Sometimes I feel I am unable to offer the students reading material that is deeply flawed about French Canada or based entirely on secondary sources, not to mention unsubstantiated opinions rife with prejudice.

One of the most famous occurrences of blatant historical distortion found in the English-language Canadian Jewish historiography is the often-cited assertion, by Stuart E. Rosenberg, that Adrien Arcand was a member of the Duplessis government. This statement is from his two-volume monograph entitled *The Jewish Community in Canada* and has been reproduced in countless other books since. Every semester, a few of my undergraduate students in the "History of the Jews in Canada" class refer in their final essays to this one sentence from Rosenberg's study: "Adrian [*sic*] Arcand was actually the Minister of Labour in the Union national [*sic*] government of Maurice Duplessis in 1935,"[3] this despite the recent publication of two excellent French-language biographies on the Canadian fascist leader.[4] Not only is everything factually wrong in this citation from Rosenberg, but this is about all the author has to say about the subject of antisemitism in Quebec during the interwar period in any organized manner. This is only one of many delirious quotes culled from a long list of misinterpretations published over the years in English on the subject.

The least that can be said about the relations of the francophone Catholic population to the Montreal Jewish community is that it deserves more serious and professionally motivated attention on the part of historians. The presence and influence of French Canada is a crucial component of Canadian Jewish history up to the present, and the subject cannot not be taken lightly, as has all too often been the case. Until the 1960s, a plurality of Canadian Jews lived in Montreal, in the heart of French-speaking Canada and in a city with an overwhelmingly Catholic majority. This strategically situated rapport between the two groups counts as one of the key elements of Canadian Jewish history, as can be surmised by even a cursory examination of the historiography, notably books like *None Is Too Many, Canada's Jews,* and *A History of Antisemitism in Canada.*[5] To this day, the difficulty remains that there is no clear path to approaching the subject, and that two groups of researchers – each in a different official language – work in relative isolation from each other on this issue, producing vastly different interpretations of the same phenomenon. In recent years, francophone historians have absorbed a better understanding of the Jewish contribution to the development of Montreal, and serious input on the subject has begun to appear in French-language journals and publications. Some of the better-known authors have even learned Jewish languages to achieve more fluency in the field and to be able to consult Jewish community archives. The result of these efforts is that Jewish history is now perceived by many French-speaking researchers as a basic component of Montreal and Québécois history. In the fall of 2017 alone, three important French-language monographs have appeared with substantial Jewish historical content: *Histoire du Mile-End* by Yves Desjardins, *Dictionnaire historique du Plateau Mont-Royal* by a group of historians and *Histoire des Juifs du Québec* by myself.[6] In the fall of 2019 a collective book appeared edited by Ira Robinson and myself on the Hassidim in Montreal, entitled *Les Juifs hassidiques de Montréal*, detailing the history, sociology, social networks, and economic structures of these communities.[7] None of this existed ten years ago.

There remains one area in particular where researchers fundamentally disagree concerning the impact of French Canada on Canadian Jewry, and this difference of interpretation runs along a linguistic fault line. Outside of issues dealing specifically with Judaism as a system of religious belief, the single largest debate in Canadian Jewish history has been over the prevalence, significance, and long-term consequences of francophone antisemitism. The public controversy has raged without much interruption since the publication of *None Is Too Many* in 1982. By comparison, hostility to Jews on the part of Anglo-Protestant Canadians – a much-documented fact in Canadian Jewish history – has elicited little attention outside of academic circles. Yet much of the work done in the English language on Québécois antisemitism was done without serious knowledge of French-language sources or even of the French language itself, not to mention the importance of examining the underlying belief system and doctrinal apparatus of the Catholic church in the modern era. In many cases, conclusions were reached by examining only secondary sources in English and by reading observations supplied by historical witnesses who stood at a distance from francophone society. The main task confronting Canadian Jewish history, if it is to achieve a measure of intellectual legitimacy, is to try to reconcile these two conflicting narratives or at least to acknowledge their respective forces and weaknesses. Failure to do so, as has been the prevalent trend up till now, will perpetuate a disastrous situation that can only bring discredit to the field academically.

Among the more pressing issues to re-examine in this respect are three misappropriations commonly found in Canadian Jewish history concerning the long-term influence of French Canada since the signing of the 1867 British North America Act. Reading authors who have approached the subject of Québécois antisemitism in the English language, one often finds the notion that francophones were unanimous in their condemnation of Judaism and in their detestation of Jews, particularly in the thirties.[8] According to many who have dwelled on the issue at length, French Canada is afflicted at all levels by an ingrained, deep, and permanent suspicion of Jewish realities, a trend clearly noticeable among the clerical elites. French Canadian society is also seen in this vein as a highly powerful and organized entity able to seriously harm Jewish interests at the federal level and in the central administration of the country. Finally, there is almost universal agreement in this school of thought that francophone antisemitism is more vicious and threatening than its anglophone counterpart in the Protestant tradition. Ironically, there is something in these unsubstantiated and often undocumented suppositions that mirrors the myth of the almighty and powerful Jews prevalent historically in some segments of French Canada. More than anything else though, univocal and poorly nuanced notions such as these reveal a tendency on the part of certain authors to ignore important French-language documentation found in the historical record, or to neglect serious methodological principles common to all research in the social sciences.

In this respect, one issue in particular has attracted a great deal of attention in the recent years: the role played by the French-language press historically in the spread of antisemitism in French Canada, particularly by the Montreal daily *Le Devoir*. On this subject specifically, there is a great deal of disagreement. Opinions range from a blanket condemnation of *Le Devoir* as a source of universal antisemitic sentiment among the political elite of Quebec, to a view that Bourassa's paper was instrumental all by itself in blocking the immigration of Jewish refugees to Canada at the time of the 1938 Evian Conference. The fundamental problem here methodologically is that very few researchers have actually read the historical sequence published in *Le Devoir* and that many come to specific conclusions without having broadly consulted the available evidence. In any field, this would be a serious breach of the scientific consensus regarding the importance of collecting as much data as possible to substantiate a prevailing hypothesis. Throughout my career as a historian, I have felt personally challenged by this bias in Canadian Jewish history regarding Quebec's francophone press and resolved to come to terms with it, particularly in the case of *Le Devoir*. An occasion presented itself to obtain better and more conclusive data when the newspaper celebrated in 2010 its one hundredth anniversary. In this context, I proposed to les Éditions du Septentrion, with the help of historian Michel Lévesque, the preparation of an anthology containing the most significant editorials published in *Le Devoir* from its inception to the Quiet Revolution, thus covering approximately fifty years in the daily's history.[9]

While running in detail through every editorial published in *Le Devoir* from January 1910 to February 1947 for the specific purpose of better understanding the editorial positions taken by the paper in general, I set aside all those that mentioned Jews or Judaism, even tangentially. This was still a partial examination of the content of *Le Devoir* touching on our subject, but at least the exercise covered almost four decades and examined the newspaper's most significant political statements, those offered on page one, day in day out. Overall, my analysis revealed the existence of 209 editorials devoted entirely or in part to a Jewish theme during the thirty-seven-year span. Statistically, and considering that about 11,000 editorials were published in *Le Devoir* during this period, this amounted to roughly 2 per cent of the total. Of these two hundred editorials, about half expressed outright hostility to Jewish persons, often members of the federal or provincial parliaments, or to forms of Jewish identity found in Canada at the time. All together, during this time span, which covered both world wars and the Great Depression, there were about forty full-blown editorials devoted to Jewish immigration in Canada or to Jewish issues, manifestly written with the intent of strongly opposing Jewish intentions.[10] Quite clearly, antisemitism did not consume the attention of *Le Devoir*, although it was part of the paper's ideological frame of reference. Once again, in my historical analysis of the *Le Devoir* editorials, I was confronted with the situation that upon closer examination conceptions developed in the English-language historiography with different methods – or no method at all – diverged radically with my findings and those of other francophones in recent years.

How should we react as scholars to such disconcerting differences of interpretation concerning a key element of Canadian Jewish history? Visceral hostility to Jews remains one of the most compelling historical phenomena that motivate academics to dwell on the long-term evolution of Jewish communities within the country and in the world. This is especially true at times of crisis, when other Jewish populations in

Europe faced intense discrimination or when immigration to Canada
was a matter of life and death for many individuals expelled from their
country of birth. Severe economic downturns, as experienced during
the thirties, and the rise of fascist ideologies were also circumstances
that fostered a densification of racist attitudes across the Canadian political spectrum. War and the threat of invasion, real or imagined, had
the same effect on Anglo-Canadians, creating forms of hysteria and
collective panic that had truly negative repercussions on racialized minorities, including Jews. Historians of Canadian Jewry agree on these
general parameters, but do not seem able to grasp fully the *complexity*
and diversity of mainstream Canadian society under such duress, especially its different linguistic, regional, and religious components. The
difficulty here is that French Canada in particular possessed markedly
different historical points of reference at the time from Anglo-British
Canada. It also absorbed in large part the events unfolding just before
and during the Second World War as a victimized minority, particularly regarding the issue of conscription for overseas service. Likewise, because of the demographic forces at play since the signing of
Confederation, francophone Canadians did not perceive international
immigration and large movements of population across the oceans as
positively as English Canada, regardless of the debate concerning specifically the admission of Jews within that context. For the most part,
immigrants tended to join forces with the anglophone majority, even
in Montreal, and this demographic trend was perceived as a cause for
alarm in a group that represented in 1931 about 30 per cent of the total
Canadian population.

Jewish Canadian studies, as the name of the field implies, refers to
a broader category and is in part subsumed under the vast domain of
Canadian studies. It will not do for practitioners of Canadian Jewish
history to neglect the full implication of this larger field in terms of
academic accountability. Debates surrounding the examination of Canadian society – and there are many – inevitably affect Jewish Canadian
studies and challenge us to come to terms in our specific approaches
with bilingualism, regional nationalism, and cultural pluralism in all
its forms. We are past the point when it was sufficient to consider examining only the historical rapport of the Jewish community or communities to the Canadian state and its Anglo-Saxon elite, for the most
part ignoring other facets of Canadian reality or just glossing over them
superficially. Jews in this country interacted constantly with Canadians of origins other than British anglophone and, depending on where
they resided and how they earned their livelihood, encountered a great
deal of cultural and religious diversity at every turn. Adaptations were

made historically by local Jewish populations to varying circumstances, and languages other than English were learned and used frequently, particularly in areas where recent European immigrants formed large pockets of population or in cities and regions where the French language was dominant. There is even an argument to be made about studying the rapport that Jews developed with the First Nations at various moments in Canadian history, an issue that certainly cannot be considered marginal today.

I am too attached to the field to want only to distribute blame and find fault with the monographs published in the last forty years or so. Canadian Jewish studies is still an emerging domain, and, like all relatively young academic pursuits, it bears the limitations imposed upon it by its origins, namely the fact that it was at the beginning mostly the purview of community activists wishing to preserve the Canadian Jewish past for the benefits of younger generations of Jews. This is a position that is perfectly tenable in view of perpetuating a strong Canadian Jewish identity and maintaining vibrant forms of Judaism in the country. It is not tenable, however, within the confines of the current academic world where non-Jews are an increasing proportion of the scholars reflecting on Canadian Jewish history. If the field is to have long-lasting significance in Canadian scholarship, it needs to connect to broader themes and detach itself from community-building issues relevant in the Jewish sphere only. It may also have to abandon discursive strategies designed to condemn past injustices and to posthumously defend victims of older forms of antisemitism. Skills required of Canadianists in general, and the expectation that all minorities should be acknowledged in the academic domain, apply to scholars of Canadian Jewish studies as they do to other specialists of Canadian history. Barriers and obstacles that stood traditionally before Canadian Jewish history on university campuses are now dissolving rapidly. This too should convince us to start defining the field differently.

One solution to the current impasse might be to begin working together across linguistic and cultural divides more efficiently. We are beyond arguing, or at least should be, that there is a definitive political purpose to writing Canadian Jewish history. Likewise, our audience is no longer mostly Jewish and community oriented. Should we not in this context share knowledge and data more broadly, confronting different perspectives as they emerge on the academic scene? Welcoming divergent interpretations and varying degrees of disagreement on a common issue would strengthen the field, not to mention animate debate and discussion. We tend to favour consensual thinking, dogmatic reaffirmations, and already agreed-upon positions, to the detriment of innovation and boldness of approach. Perhaps one of the pitfalls of Canadian Jewish studies has been the tendency to define the field too narrowly, almost as if only what is strictly Jewish should be of interest to researchers and readers. Sadly, authors and academics who for various reasons are converging onto this unique crossroads are not necessarily heard or read unless they adopt the classic position of the Jewish ethno-historian. As it is, mainstream Canadianists may have other objectives when they approach Jewish history, which is to study how the majority has been affected by issues of say, minority rights, religious diversity, or immigration regulation. Acceptance, full participation, and tolerance of differences are crucial components of democratic life and require the attention of academics, who may turn to the treatment metred to Jews historically to try to measure progress achieved by Canadian society over long periods. Likewise, the prevalence of prejudice, discrimination, and marginalization are legitimate objects of study for all Canadianists, regardless of origins or religious persuasion.

Perhaps we have not insisted enough on the constant interweaving of Canadian Jewish and mainstream Canadian histories, as if there existed an airtight separation between the two narratives. Certainly, we can identify a social or communal space where Jewish issues are primarily borne and where they find a specific resonance. Nevertheless, notions and perceptions that first emerged in Jewish contexts, or were absorbed mainly at the beginning by Jewish historical actors in specific Jewish time frames, can easily cross into ethnically neutral terrain and reach very broad Canadian audiences. When correctly identified and explained, these initially more pointed Jewish contributions will stimulate new interest in the field of Jewish Canadian studies from researchers further afield. I have already alluded in my *Histoire des Juifs du Québec* to many such instances of "concealed" and "undisclosed" Jewish input into francophone Québécois society, beginning with the transfer of the organizational skills and world view of eastern European Jews active in the industrial unions to French Canadian workers entering that work force. Eventually, forms of specifically radical political militancy did penetrate beyond strictly Jewish quarters and did effect change in other strata of Montreal society, transforming accepted ideas of workers' behaviour and passive acquiescence to capitalist exploitation. That most of the initial impetus for this metamorphosis of the French Canadian working class came from Jewish activists, such as Lea Roback, Fred Rose, and Bernard Shane, certainly merits more than a passing comment.

Similarly, the impact of Jewish artists, writers, and social activists has been profound on Canadian society, both English- and French-speaking citizens, not to mention individuals who actually held elected positions in various governments. There are many aspects of this narrative that have not been explored sufficiently or with a broader approach in mind. In this respect, some Jewish contributions proved to be of great importance and have left lasting legacies in many domains not necessarily associated directly with Judaism or presented as such. The example of Henry Morgentaler immediately comes to mind, who tirelessly fought for the right of women to abortion and challenged accepted views in court and in the public arena. Many times Morgentaler alluded in interviews to the suffering imposed on him and his family by Nazism during the Holocaust, circumstances that prompted him to resist forcefully injustice and unequal treatment of individuals along ethnic, gender, or national lines. At the same time, opponents of political liberalism and of free access to abortion clinics publicly attacked Morgentaler as a Jew and a survivor of death camps. Such forms of intense involvement in favour of a human rights culture in Canada have indeed transformed our society and the situation of women generally. One can certainly debate whether Morgentaler truly expressed his Judaic origins while addressing concerns of social justice and feminist liberation, but there can be little doubt that he belongs to a long line of Jewish activists who throughout the twentieth century left a deep mark on our society.

The same argument could be made of many entrepreneurs and businesspersons who singlehandedly transformed our habits as consumers, even in places as private as the family kitchen. There are countless examples across the country of Jewish real estate investors who made it their life pursuit to build entire residential neighbourhoods for average Canadians. Likewise, many Jewish industrialists and large-scale retailers fed and clothed large segments of the Canadian population for many decades, sometimes under commercial names that clearly revealed their Jewish origins. In the end, some of these merchants and promoters were so successful that they permanently modified the social and cultural behaviour of the general population, introducing types of food or methods of marketing that were entirely new. A case in point is Sam Steinberg, who was the first in the thirties to exploit the concept of the large self-serve supermarket in the Montreal region and developed over the years what became the largest grocery store chain in Quebec. In its heyday in the 1980s, the Steinberg Company owned and operated a series of shopping centres and commercial banners that profoundly altered traditional business models in the province and contributed to the rise of an entirely new suburban environment. In the process, the lives of most Québécois were seriously modified and their perception of food preparation forever altered. Yet few researchers have given serious attention to this angle or paid attention to the transformative quality of Jewish contributions.

Perhaps Canadian Jewish history, as I argued forcefully on another occasion, is too oriented towards chronicling the obstacles that Jews encountered on their way to becoming full and equal citizens of this country.[11] Most of the energies in the field have been spent documenting antisemitism at crucial periods in Canadian history and reflecting on what prompted segments of the population and mainstream churches to ignore the plight of European refugees at times of political crisis. Such forms of discrimination were real and truly harmful, reflecting poorly on the humanitarian impulse manifested at the time by Canadians of all religious persuasions. Most researchers would argue today that these negative circumstances must be better known and factored into the teaching of Canadian history at all levels of society. Nonetheless, other elements in the unfolding of Canadian Jewish history point in different directions and should also be taken into consideration. Oftentimes, Jews found room to manoeuvre in the midst of otherwise mounting difficulties and contributed to key advances in society by their creativity and openness of mind. The field of Jewish Canadian studies, I would argue, should gain tremendously from producing a more balanced approach to the complex issue of the constantly fluctuating rapport that Jews entertained with their non-Jewish environment, in both official languages. This expanded sensitivity to a very complex interaction would no doubt contribute significantly to enriching our at times embattled domain of study and to attracting new cohorts of creative students. After all, the question remains, as this volume suggests, was Canada a place where a broader Jewish contribution was possible, and if so, under what conditions and with which tangible results? If so, our task is to retrace the history of this input in the widest possible sense and take into consideration the full cultural and religious diversity of Canadian society.

NOTES

1 There are notable exceptions. Yolande Cohen published in 2017 an important book on Quebec Sephardim under the title *Les Sépharades du Québec, parcours d'exils nord-africains* (Montreal: Del Busso Éditeur, 2017) and David Ben-Soussan edited *Anthologie des écrivains sépharades du Québec* (Montreal: Éditions du Marais) in 2010. In 2007, Jean-Claude Lasry, Joseph J. Levy, and Yolande Cohen edited a collective volume entitled *Identités sépharades et modernité* (Quebec: Presses de l'Université Laval, 2007).

2 "Deux poids, deux mesures: les responsabilités respectives du Canada de langue anglaise et de langue française dans la crise des réfugiés allemands," in a special issue of *Canadian Jewish Studies / Études juives canadiennes*, entitled "Au-delà de None Is Too Many / None Is Too Many and

Beyond" 24 (2016): 16–37. The article also appeared in an English translation: "A Double Standard: The Respective Responsibilities of English- and French-Language Canada in the German Refugee Crisis," Special insert in *Canadian Jewish Studies / Études juives canadiennes* 26 (2018). An example of this trend is found in L. Ruth Klein, ed., *Nazi Germany, Canadian Responses: Confronting Anti-Semitism in the Shadow of the War* (Montreal and Kingston: McGill-Queen's University Press, 2012).

3 Stuart Rosenberg, *The Jewish Community of Canada*, vol. 1 (Toronto: McClelland and Stewart, 1970), 194.

4 Jean-François Nadeau, *Adrien Arcand, führer canadien* (Montreal: Lux Éditeur, 2010), and Hugues Théoret, *Les chemises bleues: Adrien Arcand, journaliste antisémite canadien-français* (Quebec: Éditions du Septentrion, 2012).

5 Irving Abella and Harold Troper, *None Is Too Many: Canada and the Jews of Europe, 1933–1948* (Toronto: University of Toronto Press, 2012 [1983]); Gerald Tulchinsky, *Canada's Jews: A People's Journey* (Toronto: University of Toronto Press, 2007); and Ira Robinson, *A History of Antisemitism in Canada* (Waterloo, ON: Wilfrid Laurier University Press, 2015).

6 Yves Desjardins, *Histoire du Mile End* (Quebec: Éditions du Septentrion, 2017); Jean-Claude Robert et al., *Dictionnaire historique du Plateau Mont-Royal* (Montreal: Éditions Écosociété, 2017); and Pierre Anctil, *Histoire des Juifs du Québec* (Montreal: Éditions du Boréal, 2017).

7 Pierre Anctil and Ira Robinson, eds., *Les Juifs hassidiques de Montréal* (Montreal: Presses de l'Université de Montréal, 2019).

8 Other influential authors in this school of thought include Lita-Rose Betcherman, Alan Mendelson, Martin Robin, and David Rome.

9 Pierre Anctil, *"Fais ce que dois": 60 éditoriaux pour comprendre Le Devoir sous Henri Bourassa, 1910–1932* (Sillery: Éditions du Septentrion, 2010), translated by Tonu Onu as *"Do What You Must": Selected Editorials from* Le Devoir *under Henri Bourassa, 1910–1932* (Toronto: Publications of the Champlain Society, 2016); *"Soyons nos maîtres": 60 éditoriaux pour comprendre* Le Devoir *sous Georges Pelletier, 1932–1947* (Sillery: Éditions du Septentrion, 2013); and Michel Lévesque, *"À la hache et au scalpel": 70 éditoriaux pour comprendre* Le Devoir *sous Gérard Filion, 1947–1963* (Sillery: Éditions du Septentrion, 2010.

10 Anctil Pierre. *"À chacun ses Juifs": 60 éditoriaux pour comprendre la position du Devoir à l'égard des Juifs, 1910–1947* (Sillery: Éditions du Septentrion, 2014), translated by Tonu Onu under the title *A Reluctant Welcome for Jewish People: Voices in* Le Devoir's *Editorials 1910–1947* (Ottawa: University of Ottawa Press, 2019).

11 Pierre Anctil, "'Nit ahin oun nit aher': Yiddish Scholarship in Canada," *Canadian Jewish Studies / Études juives au Canada* 21 (2013 [2014]): 69–90, in a special issue entitled "Oyfn Veg: Essays in Honour of Gerald Tulchinsky / Mélanges en l'honneur de Gerald Tulchinsky."

Thin Canadian Culture, Thick Jewish Life

DAVID WEINFELD

I celebrated my first Canadian Thanksgiving at age nineteen, in Cambridge, Massachusetts. The Harvard Canadian Club invited me, and all other Canadian students, to eat turkey and stuffing on a Monday in October. Some of the other club members were surprised I had never celebrated Canadian Thanksgiving before, considering I was born and raised in Montreal. But I had a simple answer. "I'm Jewish," I replied. "Canadian Jews don't celebrate Canadian Thanksgiving."

There are, no doubt, exceptions to this rule, but for the most part, it holds. And of course, this isn't a uniquely Jewish phenomenon. First Nations Canadians, Québécois, non-white Canadians, non-Christian Canadians, and many descendants of recent immigrants do not usually partake in the holiday. It seems only those Stephen Harper would call "old stock" Canadians – i.e., anglophones of Christian heritage (Protestant or Catholic) – indulged in this borrowed tradition.

This stands in contrast to the United States, where almost everyone, regardless of religion or ethnicity, celebrates American Thanksgiving. Thinking about this difference led me to realize something I liked about Canadian culture: it was thin enough to allow me to think of myself as Jewish first, Canadian second. Where Jewish culture feels thick, durable, and substantive, Canadian culture feels shallow, flimsy, and unformed. Yet that is Canadian culture's greatest strength. By having a thin culture, Canada allows other cultures to feel at home.[1]

Canadian Prime Minister Justin Trudeau seems to agree, at least with the assessment of Canadian culture. "Countries with a strong national identity – linguistic, religious, or cultural, are finding it a challenge to effectively integrate people from different backgrounds. In France, there is still a typical citizen and an atypical citizen. Canada doesn't have that dynamic," the PM said in a 2015 interview. "There is no core identity, no mainstream in Canada. There are shared values – openness, respect, compassion, willingness to work hard, to be there for each other, to search for equality and justice. Those qualities are what make us the first post-national state."[2]

This postscript will examine the Canadian Jewish experience of this post-national state, relying on both personal anecdotes and scholarly analyses, while weaving in material from the previous chapters of this book. Though idiosyncratic, I believe my experiences reflect a broader truth, that Canada's thin culture has allowed Canadian Jewry to flourish, while at the same time bringing them closer to their co-religionists in the United States.

My argument leads me to two somewhat contradictory conclusions. First, because Canadian Jews are so Jewish, they are more similar to American Jews than they are to Canadian gentiles. Second, despite this similarity, Canadian Jews have been able to forge a uniquely Canadian Jewish culture that distinguishes them from their American counterparts. As an addendum, because so much of Canadian Jewish culture is rooted in nostalgia, especially for the Montreal Ashkenazi community, it is unclear how much staying power it has. That unique community, largely shaped by linguistic and religious boundaries, allowed for an augmented Jewishness, supplemented by a very particular form of Canadian consciousness.

This was my reality growing up in Montreal's west end Anglo-Jewish bubble.[3] All my friends were Jewish, and all were anglophone Ashkenazim apart from a handful of francophone Sephardim (with whom I conversed in English). At my public English-language CEGEP, Dawson College, I met some anglophone gentiles, and a couple of women we called "Francophone Emily" and "Francophone Jen" to distinguish them from Anglos in our program.[4] But my world remained English, and my social circle was remarkably narrow.

Funnily enough, Harvard provided me not only with my first Canadian Thanksgiving, but also my first real conversation with a Québécois peer. One weekend I took the Greyhound bus from Boston to Montreal. I recognized a classmate, a francophone from Longueuil, and we sat next to each other for the six-hour ride, talking most of the time. I had never before had that lengthy a conversation with a francophone Quebecker, and it was eye-opening. He was somewhat supportive of the Quebec separatist movement, and in discussing it I realized his views resembled Zionism. I never became a separatist, but from that moment on, I understood my own Zionism better and became more sympathetic to Québécois nationalism.

Beyond that realization, another exchange stands out in my memory. I mentioned the Harvard Canadian Club and asked him if he joined. He said he had, but just to be nice. I then asked him if he felt that he, as a Québécois, felt any connection to someone from Vancouver or Toronto. He said no.

His response made me think about my own Canadian and Jewish identities, and how much thicker the latter was than the former. It became clear to me that I had more in common with a Jew from New Jersey than a non-Jew from Toronto. This is even more true for Orthodox Jews, *haredi* or modern, whose daily lives are governed by *halakha*, a bond far stronger than any national border. But even in my case, as a semi-observant Reconstructionist, my mores and mannerisms, my interests and experiences, tied me to other Jews more than they did to non-Jewish Canadians. And the ties were strongest with Jews in the United States.

Before continuing, it is worth examining the notion of a national Canadian culture. The benevolent thinness of Canadian culture is most apparent in Toronto, Canada's largest, most prosperous city, now home to over 200,000 Jews. As Harold Troper notes in chapter 9, prior to the Second World War, Toronto had a sleepy, stiff, white Anglo-Protestant culture, captured by the bland label "Toronto the Good." Today, Toronto is a giant, multicultural metropolis. What is most Canadian about Toronto is its multiculturalism. Torontonians from around the globe are bound together by the city's ethos of tolerance and celebration of diversity. Aside from multiculturalism, Toronto has only a weak unifying culture, which combined with Canada's motto from the British North America Act of 1867, "peace, order, and good government," allows different groups to thrive on their own. Including Jews.[5]

To be sure, not all of Canada has such a thin culture, and many areas have regional and local cultures that are both thick in their own right and distinct from the rest of Canada. Quebec, the Maritimes, Newfoundland, and the Prairies have unique, thick cultures all their own, distinct from anywhere else in Canada, with particular languages, accents, cuisines, political preferences, religious persuasions, and musical traditions. By contrast, Vancouver is at least as much a progressive west coast city as it is a Canadian one, more connected culturally to the United States' Pacific Northwest than it is to conservative Alberta.[6]

Is there anything like a Canadian national culture? When I was growing up in the 1980s and 1990s, hockey, socialized medicine, and the CBC (Canadian Broadcasting Corporation) were the three social or cultural entities most Canadians associated with Canada. Hockey still feels Canadian but has become much more international. Universal healthcare distinguishes Canada from the United States, but not from the rest of the developed world. The government-run CBC is modelled after the

United Kingdom's BBC. The difficulty to define Canadian culture is indicative of its relative thinness, especially compared with ethnic and religious states around the globe, but even with multicultural ones like the United States and Australia.

How has this thin Canadian culture affected Canadian Jews? Like most Canadians, Canadian Jews are hockey fans, benefit from single-payer health insurance, and watch the CBC.[7] But the thin Canadian culture has minimal impact on who they are as Jews. In their day-to-day lives, in their behaviour, marital patterns, educational and occupational outcomes, and of course, religious observance, they have much more in common with American Jews than they do with gentile Canadians. That is a good thing for Canadian Jews who are invested in Jewish continuity.

Despite these commonalities between the two communities, their differing histories and demographics have led to some noticeable differences today. Due to its population size, America looms much larger than Canada in the transnational Jewish imagination. As Hasia Diner points out in chapter 2, Canadian rabbis are trained there, and rabbinical organizations are based there. Canadian garment workers joined American unions headed in New York. Perhaps this dependent relationship explains the relatively weak Jewish cultural affinity for Canada. Jews have maximal political loyalty to Canada, but culturally, the United States looms larger, and more for Jews than for other immigrants. While Portuguese in Canada can look back to Portugal, Canadian Jews rarely have fond memories of Poland. They look to Israel and the United States, the former a manifestation of religion or politics (or both), the latter for culture and sensibility.

Age and language also led to differences. The American Jewish community is older and larger. Due to earlier and greater Jewish immigration from German-speaking lands, Reform Judaism gained a strong foothold in the United States in the nineteenth century, one that continues to this day. The Reform presence in Canada is much weaker. In the United States, Jews have a unique, complicated relationship with the country's largest non-white minority, African Americans. As David Koffman shows in this volume, Canadian Jews' complicated relationship with Indigenous peoples in Canada is equally unique.[8]

Canada has a disproportionately large number of Holocaust survivors and recent Jewish immigrants in general as compared to America, where Ellis Island and the Lower East Side at the turn of the century are the more foundational immigration experiences.[9] Because of the French presence in Quebec, a third of Jews in Montreal are now Sephardic and francophone, rendering the Montreal Jewish community different from any Jewish community in the United States, where anglophone Ashkenazim are the overwhelming majority.

Because of these differences, by nearly every measure, Canadian Jews are more "Jewish" than their American counterparts. They are more religiously observant, more Jewishly knowledgeable, more likely to give (and give more) to Jewish charities, and more engaged with Israel. These differences are important, as are the data on economic performance, integration, comfort, and antisemitism that Morton Weinfeld mentions in the lead chapter of this book, where he argues that Canada may very well be the best place for Jews in the Diaspora, if not the world.[10]

A paradox to the success of Canadian Jewry is the extent to which they are ignored by scholars of Judaic studies. Certainly size has mattered here. The United States was the destination of choice for the vast majority of Jews immigrating from Europe in the nineteenth and twentieth centuries. As Hasia Diner notes early on in this volume, this has shaped the historiography. Scholars of Canadian Jewish history typically look to the United States for perspective and context.[11] Scholars of American Jewry, meanwhile, are free to ignore Canada – and so they have.

The archives are a different story, demonstrating the strong historical links between Canadian and American Jews. One ironically rich place to research Canadian Jewish history is in American sources. Collections concerning American Jewish labour organizations, political movements, youth groups, religious denominations, and even the American Jewish Yearbook all include Canadian material. For example, between 1901 and 1920, the Federation of American Zionists (FAZ), today known as the Zionist Organization of America (ZOA), published a monthly journal out of New York called *The Maccabaean.* One function of the magazine was to report on Zionist activity around the globe, including Canada. Lo and behold, the February 1903 issue reported on the Zionist societies of Montreal, including a statement by the secretary of the city's Agudos Zion, my distant cousin Henry Weinfield.[12]

The FAZ typically lumped Canadian Zionist organizations in with their larger American counterparts. Despite the differences between the Canadian and American Jewish communities, the Canadian Zionist societies had more in common with the American ones than they did with European ones, for reasons of proximity and the shared structure of North American society and government. The transnational dimension of Jewish history suggests that bonds of religion and culture stretched across the border, in some cases creating stronger ties among Jews across political boundaries than the ties of citizenship between Jews and gentiles in particular countries.[13]

These strong transnational bonds of religion and culture are for many
Jews and other minorities a positive by-product of the thin nature of Canadian culture. These connections facilitate the diversity that makes so
many Canadians proud, and that made Prime Minister Pierre Trudeau
declare in 1971 that "multiculturalism" would be an official policy of
the Canadian government. As Jeffrey Veidlinger shows in chapter 3,
the road to Trudeau's declaration was a complicated one, with Jews
and Ukrainians playing outsized roles. Nonetheless it succeeded in establishing a sort of conventional wisdom for patriotic Canadians: while
the United States is a melting pot that pushes assimilation, Canada is
an ethnic mosaic that embraces diversity and allows for multiculturalism.[14] This dichotomy is thought to originate after the Second World
War, but it is in fact much older, and rooted in Quebec.

The term "melting pot" as a metaphor for diversity became popular as the title of a 1908 play about immigration to the United States.
Written by British Jew Israel Zangwill, *The Melting Pot* tells the story
of a Russian Jewish immigrant to New York, David Quixano, who falls
in love with a Russian Christian immigrant, Vera Revendal. A hokey
Americanized take on Romeo and Juliet, it was hugely popular with
the assimilationist crowd, including sitting president Teddy Roosevelt,
who attended the opening night performance in Washington, DC.
Some Jews, however, felt its implicit endorsement of intermarriage
foretold the end of the Jewish people. As the details of the play faded
from memory, the metaphor stuck, remaining one of America's most
enduring symbols.

This was not the first use of that metaphor. Perhaps the earliest use
of the term "melting pot" as a metaphor for American diversity occurred in an 1889 article in the *New York Times* titled "Canada's Home
Trouble," covering the conflict between English Protestants and French
Catholics in the recently constituted country. Considering the potential
US annexation of Canada, the article noted that "French Canadians had
a misgiving that if they too were cast into the American melting pot
they would yield to that mysterious force which blends all foreign elements into one homogeneous mass."[15]

Meanwhile, the *Times* editors feared the sturdiness of French Catholic
identity, especially given its distinct language, schools, and religious
institutions, leading the *Times* to reprint an earlier editorial at the conclusion of the article about the annexation of Canada and especially
of Quebec. "Nothing could be more preposterous, at a time when it is
evident that the chief danger of this country is the unrestricted flow
of immigration that a proposition to add to the Union an alien State
the citizens of which will offer the same stubborn resistance to being

Americanized that they hitherto offered to being anglicized."[16] In this racialized, anti-Catholic screed, Québécois were portrayed as a thoroughly alien other, totally unassimilable in anglophone Canada and the American melting pot. Even in 1889, observers witnessed the "two solitudes" of English and French Canada in Quebec.[17]

The divide has produced an interesting history. Yolande Cohen's experience as a Moroccan Jew immigrating to Montreal demonstrates how some Jews have successfully navigated these tensions (chapter 15). She celebrates the "multiplicity of belonging" as "one of the factors that makes Canada now a hospitable place for immigrants." On the other hand, Montreal has long been defined by conflict between anglophone Protestants and francophone Catholics. This tension created a space for Jews to become more Jewish than Canadian, or English or French, a "third solitude" identity that persists long after the aforementioned religious conflict faded into the linguistic one it is today. In this third solitude, Canadian Jews could be both similar to and different from their American counterparts.

A recent volume, *Neither in Dark Speeches nor in Similitudes: Reflections and Refractions between Canadian and American Jews*, reinforces the notion of thin Canadian culture facilitating Jewish ties across the Canada–US border. The book's articles invoke the concept of "borderlands" when discussing the relations between Canadian and American Jews. The idea of borderlands has developed to understand spaces that are connected, usually physically, always intellectually and culturally, in ways that transcend national or political boundaries. Rigidly defined borders are modern inventions that change as a result of wars and treaties. Studying those regions requires thinking beyond the nation.

The lands that connect the United States with Mexico are perhaps the most commonly cited example of borderlands, but the term is equally applicable to the American border with Canada. While much scholarship involving Canada and the United States is rightly comparative, the premise of a borderlands argument is that the Canadian and American Jewish communities share such a profound link that it can distort our understanding of the communities by dividing them into distinct national, political, or territorial units.[18]

The best articles in the book exemplify the transnational link between Canadian and American Jewry. One explores the collaboration between nineteenth-century Sephardic rabbis in New York and Montreal on a Jewish calendar.[19] Another looks at the mid-twentieth-century relationship between a synagogue in Quebec City and the Orthodox seminary of Yeshiva University.[20] These connections underscore the close relationship between the two communities.

Though there are clear differences between the communities that are worth exploring, there are also very practical reasons the borderlands argument resonates. Canadian and American Jews are bound not only by religion but also (mostly) by language, culture, and relative proximity. Yiddish and English facilitated communication. Zionist publications in the United States like *The Maccabaean* paid attention to their Canadian counterparts, and often attended the same conventions. Secular Jewish institutions like B'nai Brith transcended the Canada–US border.

These bonds were especially strong in the realm of religion. Rabbis, even Canadian-born ones, have long been and are still trained in the United States. Their institutional ties are American. Judith R. Baskin's upbringing in Hamilton was unique in that her father was a rabbi and both her parents were American (chapter 13). And yet the uniqueness of her Hamilton childhood, as compared with the upbringing of other Hamiltonians, reflects a broader pattern of strong ties between Canadian Jews and those in the United States.

Because of its much smaller size, the Canadian Jewish community has always been the junior partner in this relationship, yet the Canada–US border is porous, and especially so for Canadian Jews. For me, and for many of my Montreal Jewish peers, the United States was a vastly more important frame of reference than the rest of Canada. Many of us vacationed in Florida over the winter. We had visited Manhattan, and were just as likely to have relatives in Westchester or Long Island as in Toronto or Vancouver. Some of us went to summer camp in northern Quebec or Ontario, but others in Maine or upstate New York. When we watched *Seinfeld*, we saw ourselves.

Nonetheless, Richard Menkis's examination of exhibits on Canadian Jewish history concludes with a plea that we should consider: "*there should be a museum of the Canadian Jewish experience*" (chapter 11). He is right. Yet this raises the question: what would be the content of this museum? One can imagine exhibits on Jewish involvement in many aspects of Canadian life, from the fur trade to labour unions, from food to the arts, to municipal, provincial, and federal politics. There would be displays on Yiddish culture, on antisemitism, on Moroccan Jewish immigration to Montreal, and many other topics.

Not all of these things are exclusively Canadian. Some are probably not distinctly Jewish. But together, they tell a uniquely Canadian Jewish story, one that lives in memory. In the Canadian Jewish conscience, Montreal occupies a special place. As Kalman Weiser notes, from before the First World War until mid-century, many Jewish observers regarded "the Vilna on the Saint Lawrence" as a major centre of secular Yiddishkeit.[21] The collective memory of that bygone era still resonates.

In that narrative, Montreal was the locus of Canadian Jewry. Today more than twice as many Jews live in Toronto. Ira Robinson's examination of the effect of the 1976 election of the Parti Québécois on the Montreal Jewish community is thus largely a story of decline (chapter 10). But it is also a story of nostalgia. This nostalgia grips anglophone Jewish Montrealers to this day, not only for Ashkenazi foods like bagels and smoked meat, but also for the places of their past, even long after they have departed for Toronto, elsewhere in Canada, or the United States.

My Montreal connection to the Plateau neighbourhoods of Mordecai Richler was one of twenty-minute drives to the iconic Schwartz's delicatessen. My parents were both born in Montreal after the war, the children of Holocaust survivors, and grew up far from Boulevard St Laurent.[22] My family has its own kind of Montreal Ashkenazi nostalgia, distinct from the Richler version, though the latter is often portrayed as ubiquitously Jewish Montreal as the Lower East Side is Jewish New York.[23]

The Yiddish-language web series *Yidlife Crisis*, the brainchild of Montrealers Eli Batalion and Jamie Elman, offers a more up-to-date take on this nostalgia. The show provides a modern setting that hearkens back to an earlier time, as described by Rebecca Margolis in chapter 17, when Canada and especially Montreal was considered a heartland of secular Yiddish culture, particularly in the interwar period.[24]

Filmed and set in contemporary Montreal, *Yidlife Crisis* follows Leizer (Batalion) and Chaimie (Elman), fictionalized Yiddish-speaking versions of themselves, as they kibitz and nosh around the city. It feeds off Montreal nostalgia, almost literally, as the first three episodes feature, respectively, poutine (French fries, cheese curds, gravy), smoked meat deli sandwiches, and Montreal-style bagels. While poutine is something my parents' generation never seems to have embraced, smoked meat and bagels are Ashkenazi foods familiar to Montrealers of all ages.

After the credits roll on the second episode, however, an image appears of a building being demolished, along with the words, "In loving memory of the Southern Quarter of the Cavendish Mall (1973–2010)" along with the Hebrew prayer, *"L'Shana Haba'ah B'Yerushalayim"* (Next Year in Jerusalem).[25] The Cavendish Mall, known locally as "The Shmall" and a fixture for Côte-St-Luc and other west-end Jews for decades, was being reduced and reconfigured. Over the years The Shmall has housed a kosher butcher, Israeli restaurant, movie theatre, numerous hairdressers, and stores of every stripe where Jews of all ages congregated and shopped. It was certainly a heart, if perhaps not the heart, of the Montreal Jewish community. And even if we mocked it, many of us were sad to see it diminish in size.

By making The Shmall a site of Montreal Jewish nostalgia, Batalion and Elman shifted the communal locus forward in time, away from the hustle and bustle of Mordecai Richler's Plateau, and even the post-Holocaust Snowdon Deli era, to the blandly suburban Côte-St-Luc. Despite Côte-St-Luc's seeming suburban sterility, this Jewish nexus proved more inclusive of Sephardim than old Jewish Montreal, located in proximity of three(!) Jewish day schools: Bialik (non-denominational, Yiddishist/Zionist), Hebrew Academy (Orthodox), and École Maimonides (French-language and majority Sephardic). The Shmall was frequented by Jews ranging from secular to Haredi, Ashkenazi and Sephardic, anglophone and francophone. A recent CBC report noted: "the Cavendish Mall was a sanctuary for Holocaust survivors."[26] Perhaps every diaspora Jewish population centre has its version of The Shmall, but few had the same ethnic and linguistic diversity, except for the winter weeks or months, when much of the population of The Shmall transplanted itself to the Boca Raton Town Center.

Beyond Côte-St-Luc, food provides another window to the uniqueness of the Montreal Jewish community. Take the aforementioned bagels and smoked meat. In the United States, there is one city truly known for its bagels: New York. All across America and the world, there are shops advertising New York bagels. In Canada, the bagel mecca is Montreal. All across Canada, and even some places in the United States, there are shops selling Montreal bagels. As anyone who has tasted the two kinds of bagels knows, they are radically different foods. They share some ingredients and are similarly shaped, but the Montreal bagel is thinner and sweeter and better; it's most commonly served with sesame or poppy seeds and never plain. It's a whole different delicacy. With regards to bagels, Montreal is like every other North American Jewish community, but different.

A similar dynamic unfolds when comparing delicatessen meat. New York is the originator of deli in the United States.[27] There are great delis in LA and Michigan and elsewhere, but they are all patterned after the New York deli. They all serve pastrami or corned beef, with deli mustard, or as part of a Reuben sandwich. Montreal delis, from Schwartz's to Snowdon Deli, do not serve any of the above. They serve "smoked meat," a Montreal hybrid of pastrami and corn beef. And they do so with yellow mustard, and never in a Reuben (I had no idea what a Reuben was until I moved to the United States).[28]

While you cannot find New York–style delis or bagels in Montreal, you can find Montreal-style bagels and deli in New York, thanks to the efforts of Montreal native, restaurateur, and self-taught chef Noah Bernamoff, who founded Mile End Deli in Brooklyn.

This reality, and the differences in these foods, are not trivial. They suggest that there is a concerted effort to distinguish Montreal Ashkenazi cuisine within the gastronomic borderlands of North American Jewish food. Of course, regional culinary differences exist in the North American Jewish world, as demonstrated by Marcie Cohen-Ferris's book *Matzoh Ball Gumbo* on Southern Jewish cooking.[29] But that two of most significant foods in the North American Ashkenazi repertoire seem to have only two styles: New York or Montreal, suggests a powerful uniqueness that has extended, to a degree, to the entire Canadian Jewish community.

Does this Montreal Jewish uniqueness, with its lingering residue in Toronto and everywhere else in Canada that Jews live, indicate that Canada is the best place for Jews to live in all the diaspora? Certainly the thickness of Jewish culture in Canada contrasts with both a thinner American Jewish culture, as well as a thinner generic Canadian culture. But is thicker better? I would say yes, but the question is subjective. Certainly, Canada is a wonderful place for Jews to live today. But I doubt it can compare to the places of Canadian Jewish memory and nostalgia, which live forever in individuals, only to be forged anew with each generation.

NOTES

1 For more on Canada's lack of an easily definable culture, see Douglas Todd, "Is Canada a Blank Slate, with No Culture?," *Vancouver Sun*, 14 March 2015, and Douglas Todd, "What Canadian Culture? Part II," *Vancouver Sun*, 19 March 2015. For a dissenting view, see Philip Carl Salzman, "Yes, Canada Does Have a Culture," *Inside Policy: The Magazine of the MacDonald-Laurier Institute*, 13 February 2017.

2 Guy Lawson, "Trudeau's Canada, Again," *New York Times Magazine*, 8 December 2015.

3 My experiences resembled those of Jonathan Kay, as documented in his recent memoir article, "Guilty Memories from an Anglo Jewish Childhood," *The Walrus*, 15 December 2016. Though Jewishness played a role in Kay's experiences, it was not as pronounced, because he attended Selwyn House, an elite private school, and thus had more regular interactions with gentiles when growing up.

4 CEGEP stands for Collège d'enseignement général et professional (College for General and Vocational Instruction). Students in Quebec are in primary school K–6, high school (secondary school) 7–11, and then typically do two years of a pre-university program before entering university for three

years to complete a bachelor's degree. Dawson College, located in lower Westmount near downtown Montreal, is the largest English-language CE-GEP in the province.

5 The Jewish future in Toronto is strong but shows some signs of weakening. Though the Jewish population of Toronto has been growing slowly over the last several decades, the number of students in Jewish day schools there has been declining. This in contrast to London, where affordability has made Jewish day school a more attractive option. See Schnoor, "Jewish Education in Canada and the United Kingdom: A Comparative Perspective" (chapter 5 in this volume).

6 My analysis in this chapter focuses on the Jews of Montreal and Toronto, by far the largest communities and the ones I know best. For a different Jewish experience, see Norman Ravvin's speculations on his grandfather's immigration from Poland to Saskatchewan, "Pictures of New Canadians: An Immigration Story for Our Time" (chapter 12 in this volume), or Jack Kugelmass's memories of the 1967 Canadian Centennial in Manitoba (chapter 16 in this volume).

7 For the connection between Canadian Jews and hockey, see Elan Dresher, Norbert Hornstein, and Lipa Roth, "The Montrealer Seder," in *The Big Book of Jewish Humor*, ed. William Novak and Moshe Waldoks (New York: Harper and Row, 1981), 114–16.

8 See David S. Koffman, "The Unsettling of Canadian Jewish History: Toward a Tangled History of Jewish–Indigenous Encounters" (chapter 6 in this volume).

9 According to some estimates, nearly 40 per cent of current US citizens can trace at least one ancestor to Ellis Island (see www.history.com/topics/ellis-island for more information). For American Jews, that number must be significantly higher. While settling in the Lower East Side of Manhattan was not a ubiquitous American Jewish experience, it was by far the most likely destination for eastern European Jewish immigrants to the United States in the late nineteenth and early twentieth centuries. For more reflections on "Canada as Point of Arrival" from Holocaust survivors, see Mia Spiro's analysis of some of their memoirs in chapter 7 this volume.

10 Full disclosure: Morton Weinfeld is my father. For more comparative data between Canadian and American Jews, see Morton Weinfeld, Randall Schnoor, and Michelle Shames, *Like Everyone Else but Different: The Paradoxical Success of Canadian Jews*, 2nd ed. (Montreal and Kingston: McGill-Queen's University Press, 2018).

11 One important exception was the late historian of Canadian Jewry Gerald Tulchinsky (1933–2017), who endeavoured to write Canadian Jewish history that stood on its own. See Gerald Tulchinsky, *Canada's Jews: A People's Journey* (Toronto: University of Toronto Press, 2008).

12 Unknown author, "The Montreal Societies," *The Maccabaean*, February 1903, 122–3.

13 This was not always the case; some Jews held equal or greater loyalty to the countries they lived in. For examples of this national loyalty, see Derek J. Penslar, *Jews and the Military: A History* (Princeton, NJ: Princeton University Press, 2013).

14 For a dissenting view, see Jeffrey G. Reitz and Raymond Breton, *The Illusion of Difference: Realities of Ethnicity in Canada and the United States* (Toronto: C.D. Howe Institute, 1994).

15 Unsigned article, "Canada's Home Trouble," *New York Times*, 2 September 1889, 5.

16 Ibid.

17 As Pierre Anctil notes in the preceding chapter, more research needs to be done using French-language sources, which might further illuminate how Jews fit within Quebec's linguistic divide, especially in the early twentieth century.

18 Barry L. Stiefel and Hernan Tesler-Mabé, eds, *Neither in Dark Speeches nor in Similitudes: Reflections and Refractions between Canadian and American Jews* (Waterloo, ON: Wilfrid Laurier University Press, 2016). An earlier book, edited by Moses Rischin, *The Jews of North America* (Detroit: Wayne State University Press, 1987), contained articles about either the United States or Canada, and was not really comparative or transnational.

19 Zev Eleff, "They Who Control Time: The Orthodox Alliance of Abraham De Sola and Jacques Judah Lyons and the Nineteenth-Century Jewish Calendar," in *Neither in Dark Speeches nor in Similitudes*, eds. Stiefel and Tesler-Mabé, 95–110.

20 Ira Robinson, "Finding a Rabbi for Quebec City: The Interplay between an American Yeshiva and a Canadian Congregation," in *Neither in Dark Speeches nor in Similitudes*, ed. Stiefel and Tesler-Mabé, 111–28.

21 Kalman Weiser, "Vilna on the St Lawrence" (chapter 4 in this volume). Weiser also cites the following relevant sources: David G. Roskies, "A Hebrew-Yiddish Utopia in Montreal," in *Hebrew in America. Perspectives and Prospects*, ed. Alan Mintz (Detroit: Wayne State University Press, 1993); Rebecca Margolis, *Jewish Roots, Canadian Soil: Yiddish Culture in Montreal, 1900–1945* (Montreal and Kingston: McGill-Queen;s University Press, 2011); Pierre Anctil, *Histoire des Juifs du Québec* (Montreal: Éditions du Boréal, 2017).

22 In this way, they resemble Bernice Eisenstein, who grew up a child of Holocaust survivors in Toronto, as examined in Ruth Panofsky's chapter 8 in this volume.

23 For an examination of the Lower East Side as the real and imagined American Jewish experience, see Hasia Diner's *Lower East Sides Memories: A Jewish Place in America* (Princeton, NJ: Princeton University Press, 2002).

24 See also Rebecca Margolis, *Jewish Roots, Canadian Soil*.

25 Webseries, "The Schmaltz," *Yidlife Crisis*, season 1, episode 2, written and performed by Eli Batalion and Jamie Elman, 25 September 2014, www. yidlifecrisis.com.

26 Joshua Levy, "Joshua Levy Remembers the Heyday of Côte-St-Luc's Cavendish Mall," *CBC News*, 23 June 2018, https://www.cbc.ca/news/ canada/montreal/joshua-levy-remembers-the-heyday-of-côte-saint-luc-s-cavendish-mall-1.4713461.

27 For a history of the deli, see Ted Merwin, *Pastrami on Rye: An Overstuffed History of the Jewish Deli* (New York: New York University Press, 2015); and the documentary film *Deli Man*, directed by Erik Greenberg Anjou, 2014. For a broader history of Jewish and immigrant food culture in the United States, see Hasia Diner, *Hungering for America: Italian, Irish, and Jewish Food-ways in the Age of Migration* (Cambridge, MA: Harvard University Press, 2003).

28 For more in-depth analysis of the distinctions between different styles of deli, see David Sax, *Save the Deli: In Search of Perfect Pastrami, Crusty Rye, and the Heart of Jewish Delicatessen* (New York: Mariner Books, 2010).

29 Marcie Cohen Ferris, *Matzoh Ball Gumbo: Culinary Tales of the Jewish South* (Chapel Hill: University of North Carolina Press, 2010).

Contributors

Pierre Anctil is a full professor in the Department of History of the University of Ottawa, where he teaches contemporary Canadian history. He has a PhD in social anthropology from the New School for Social Research in New York. His main fields of interest are the history of immigration in Quebec and in Canada, and Jewish culture in Montreal. He has also done work in the history of the French-language press in Canada, notably concerning the ideological evolution of *Le Devoir*.

Judith R. Baskin is Philip H. Knight Professor of Humanities Emerita at the University of Oregon. Her books include *Pharaoh's Counsellors: Job, Jethro, and Balaam in Rabbinic and Patristic Tradition* (1983) and *Midrashic Women: Formations of the Feminine in Rabbinic Literature* (2002), and the anthologies *Jewish Women in Historical Perspective* 2nd ed. (1998), *Women of the Word: Jewish Women and Jewish Writing* (1994), and *The Cambridge Guide to Jewish History, Religion, and Culture* (2010), co-edited with Kenneth Seeskin, a 2011 National Jewish Book Award winner. She also edited *The Cambridge Dictionary of Judaism and Jewish Culture* (2011).

Yolande Cohen is a professor in the Department of History at the Université du Québec à Montréal (UQAM). She is the author of numerous books including *Femmes philanthropes: Catholiques, juives et protestantes dans les organisations caritatives au Québec, 1880–1945* (Presses de l'Université de Montréal, 2010).

Hasia R. Diner is the Paul and Sylvia Steinberg Professor of American Jewish History at New York University. She is the author of a number of books including *Julius Rosenwald: Repairing the World* (New Haven, CT: Yale University Press, 2017) and *We Remember with Reverence and Love: American Jews and the Myth of Silence after the Holocaust, 1945–1962* (New York: New York University Press, 2009).

Lois C. Dubin is Professor of Religion at Smith College in Northampton, Massachusetts. She teaches Jewish history and thought, as well as courses on world religions; food, ritual and other aspects of lived religions; and women's religious politics. She publishes on Jews and Judaism in early modern Europe, focusing on themes of citizenship, religious adaptation, culture and commerce, and civil marriage and divorce; she also writes on contemporary feminist theology and spirituality. Her award-winning book *The Port Jews of Habsburg Trieste: Absolutist Politics and Enlightenment Culture* appeared also in Italian. She has held visiting appointments at Harvard, University of Michigan, EHESS-Paris, and University of Pennsylvania.

David S. Koffman is the J. Richard Shiff Chair for the Study of Canadian Jewry and an associate professor in the Department of History at York University. He is the author of *The Jews' Indian: Colonialism, Pluralism, and Belonging in America* (Rutgers University Press, 2019), and serves as the editor-in-chief of the journal *Canadian Jewish Studies / Études juives canadiennes*.

Jack Kugelmass is a professor of anthropology and the director of the Center for Jewish Studies at the University of Florida. He is a cultural anthropologist with a focus on the anthropology of Jewish life, especially in Poland and the United States.

Rebecca Margolis is Director and Pratt Foundation Chair of Jewish Civilisation at Monash University, Australia. Her studies of modern Yiddish cultural life, Canadian Jewish literature, and Jewish film have appeared in numerous scholarly journals and edited volumes. She is the author of *Jewish Roots, Canadian Soil: Yiddish Culture in Montreal, 1905–45* (2011) and *Yiddish lebt! Language Transmission in Canada* (forthcoming). Her current research on New Yiddish Cinema examines film and television produced in Yiddish in the twenty-first century.

Richard Menkis is a professor of history at University of British Columbia and the author of a number of articles and books, including *More Than Just Games: Canada and the 1936 Olympics* (University of Toronto Press, 2015: co-authored with Harold Troper).

Ruth Panofsky, FRSC, is professor of English at Ryerson University, where she specializes in Canadian literatures and cultures. She is editor of *The New Spice Box: Canadian Jewish Writing* (2017) and the award-winning *The Collected Poems of Miriam Waddington* (2014) and author of *The Force of Vocation: The Literary Career of Adele Wiseman* (2006).

Panofsky's new book of poems, *Radiant Shards: Hoda's North End Poems*, gives lyric voice to the protagonist of Wiseman's 1974 novel *Crackpot* and is forthcoming in 2020.

Norman Ravvin writes and teaches in Montreal. Recent publications include his fourth novel, *The Girl Who Stole Everything*, and the essay, "You Say You've OD'd on Leonard Cohen: Canadian Jewish Writing and the Mainstream," in *The Oxford Handbook of Canadian Literature*. Other works include *A House of Words: Jewish Writing, Identity, and Memory*; *Hidden Canada: An Intimate Travelogue*; and the story collection *Sex, Skyscrapers, and Standard Yiddish*. For thirteen years he directed Concordia University's Institute for Canadian Jewish Studies in the Department of Religions and Cultures. A native of Calgary, he is at work on a memoir of Jewish immigration to the Canadian west in the 1930s.

Ira Robinson is Professor of Judaic Studies in the Department of Religion of Concordia University. He has published a number of books and articles including *A History of Antisemitism in Canada* (Waterloo, ON: Wilfrid Laurier University Press, 2015).

Randal F. Schnoor, a sociologist, specializes in the qualitative study of contemporary Canadian Jewish life. He has been teaching Jewish studies for more than a decade at the Koschitzky Centre for Jewish Studies at York University. He has published sociological works on Jewish identity, Jewish day schools, Hasidic Jews, and gay Jews, among other contemporary topics. His 2008 book, co-authored with Alex Pomson, was entitled *Back to School: Jewish Day School in the Lives of Adult Jews* (Wayne State University Press). In 2018 Pomson and Schnoor published their sequel work *Jewish Family: Identity and Self-Formation at Home* (Indiana University Press).

Mia Spiro is Senior Lecturer in Modern Jewish Culture and Holocaust Studies at the School of Critical Studies, University of Glasgow. Her published work includes *Anti-Nazi Modernism: The Challenges of Resistance in 1930s Fiction. Series: Cultural expressions of World War II* (Northwestern University Press, 2013) as well as work on Virginia Woolf, Jewish representation in the interwar period, and the Jewish Golem myth in modern and contemporary film and literature.

Harold Troper is a professor at the Ontario Institute for Studies in Education, University of Toronto, and author or co-author of ten books. He is perhaps best known for *None Is Too Many: Canada and the Jews of Europe, 1933–1948*, chosen by the *Literary Review of Canada* as one of the one hundred most important Canadian books of all time. Troper's most recent books are *The Defining Decade: Identity, Politics and the Canadian Jewish Community in the 1960s* and *More Than Just Games: Canada and the Nazi Olympics*, co-authored with Richard Menkis of the University of British Columbia.

Jeffrey Veidlinger is Joseph Brodsky Collegiate Professor of History and Judaic Studies and Director of the Frankel Center for Judaic Studies at the University of Michigan. He is the author of the award-winning books *The Moscow State Yiddish Theater: Jewish Culture on the Soviet Stage* (2000), *Jewish Public Culture in the Late Russian Empire* (2009), and *In the Shadow of the Shtetl: Small-Town Jewish Life in Soviet Ukraine* (2013). He is the editor of *Going to the People: Jews and Ethnographic Impulse* (2016), and is currently writing a book on the pogroms of 1918–21.

David Weinfeld is a visiting assistant professor of religious studies and the Harry Lyons Professor of Judaic Studies at Virginia Commonwealth University in Richmond, Virginia. He earned his PhD in history and Hebrew and Judaic studies from New York University, with a focus on American Jewish history. Born and raised in Montreal, David wrote a monthly column for the *Canadian Jewish News* from 2017 to 2020.

Morton Weinfeld is a professor of sociology at McGill University, where he holds the chair in Canadian Ethnic Studies. He has taught a course on the sociology of Jews in North America at McGill since 1977, to an estimated 3,600 students. He has published extensively in the areas of Canadian Jewish studies, as well as on ethnic, racial, and multicultural issues in Canada. He has consulted widely with Canadian governmental and Jewish communal organizations. His most recent book, with Randal Schnoor and Michelle Shames, is *Like Everyone Else but Different: The Paradoxical Success of Canadian Jews*, 2nd ed. (McGill-Queen's University Press, 2018). His current area of research deals with alleged cases of suspect minorities and challenges of dual loyalties in Canada.

Kalman Weiser is the Silber Family Professor of Modern Jewish Studies at York University in Toronto. He is the author of *Jewish People, Yiddish Nation: Noah Prylucki and the Folkists in Poland* (University of Toronto Press, 2011), as well as co-editor of *Czernowitz at 100: The First Yiddish Language Conference in Historical Perspective* (Lexington Books, 2010), the second, expanded edition of Solomon Birnbaum's classic study *Yiddish: A Survey and a Grammar* (University of Toronto Press, 2015), and *Key Concepts in the Study of Antisemitism* (Palgrave, 2020).